News of the Earth

Homero Aridjis

Translated and edited by Betty Ferber

[M]

Mandel Vilar Press

This book is typeset in Adobe Garamond. The paper used in this book meets the minimum requirements of ANSI/NISO Z39.48-1992 (R1997). ∞

The editors of this book have, where possible, retained the style of the articles and other documents that originally appeared in English. Translated articles follow the guidelines of *The Chicago Manual of Style*, 16th edition.

Designed by Barbara Werden
Cover photo/illustration by Betty Ferber

Publisher's Cataloging-in-Publication Data

Names: Aridjis, Homero. | Ferber, Betty, translator, editor.
Title: News of the Earth / Homero Aridjis ; translated and edited by Betty Ferber.
Other Titles: Noticias de la Tierra. English
Description: Simsbury, Connecticut : Mandel Vilar Press, [2017] | Translation of: Noticias de la Tierra. México, D.F. : Debate, an imprint of Penguin Random House Grupo Editorial, 2012.
Identifiers: ISBN 9781942134091 | ISBN 9781942134107 (ebook)
Subjects: LCSH: Environmental protection. | Endangered species. | Ecology. | Mexico—Environmental conditions. | Latin America—Environmental conditions. | Aridjis, Homero—Political activity. | Grupo de los Cien. | Intellectuals—Political activity—Latin America. | LCGFT: Essays.
Classification: LCC PQ7297.A8365 A613 2017 (print) | LCC PQ7297.A8365 (ebook) | DDC 864—dc23

Printed in the United States of America
17 18 19 20 21 22 23 24 / 9 8 7 6 5 4 3 2 1 [fix numbers?]

Mandel Vilar Press
19 Oxford Court, Simsbury, Connecticut 06070
www.americasforconservation.org | www.mvpress.org

Preface xi
Acknowledgments xiii
Abbreviations xvii

The Birds 1

Part 1. Mexico City and the Group of 100 7
LOVE POEM IN MEXICO CITY

A Declaration by 100 Intellectuals and Artists Protesting Air Pollution in
    Mexico City 9
"The 100" Exhibit on Contamination Draws Favorable Response 10
No Reply from the Government to the Group of 100's Eight Proposals
    for Reducing Pollution 12
The Group of 100 Insists on Don't Drive Today 14
The Group of 100: Human Life Is in Danger in Mexico City 15
The Group of 100 Says This Year's Thermal Inversions Worse than in
    1987 17
The Group of 100 Calls the Federal District a Vale of Death 18
The United Nations Found Dangerous Microorganisms in Mexico City's
    Air 19
Mexico City's Viceroys: Ecology and Democracy 21
Blue Gas, Green Rhetoric 23
The Rains Came 25
Don't Breathe Today 27
Pollution and the Doubledecker Freeway 29
Sister Water 32
Breathing in Death 34
Mexico–Tenochtitlan–Federal District 36

Part 2. Grandeur and Misery of the Monarch Butterfly 43
TO A MONARCH BUTTERFLY

The Monarch Butterfly: Memory and Poetry 45
Forest Fires and Loggers Are Destroying the Monarch Butterfly
    Sanctuaries 50

Grandeur and Misery of the Monarch Butterfly   51

Deforestation Could Lead to Their Extinction Twenty Years from
    Now   55

Conspiracy against the Monarch   56

Twilight of the Monarchs   58

An Alliance against the Monarch   60

The Banality of Destruction   60

The Extent of the Logging   63

Censored Butterflies   66

The New Monarch Butterfly Reserve   69

Butterflies in the Storm   71

Should the Army Protect Monarchs?   73

Marked for Death   76

Gold for Monarchs   79

The Winter of the Monarch   82

Last Call for Monarchs   84

A Milkweed-Butterfly Recovery Alliance   87

40 Years Ago the World "Discovered" Mexico's Monarch Habitat; Today
    Its Survival Is at Stake   91

Endangered Monarch Butterflies Face Their Greatest Threat High in the
    Hills of Central Mexico   95

Dear Obama, Trudeau, and Peña Nieto: Act Now to Save the Monarch
    Butterfly   98

Part 3. Sea Turtles, a Torturous Road to Extinction   103
UNEXPLAINED PHENOMENA, 2

Of Sea Turtles: A Cautionary Tale   105

Mexico Proclaims Total Ban on Harvest of Turtles and Eggs   111

An End to Sea Turtles   114

Saving the Leatherback   115

SEMARNAT under a Carapace   118

Louisiana's No Friend to Sea Turtle   120

Part 4. And God Created the Great Whales   123
THE EYE OF THE WHALE

One Country against the World   125

The Silence of the Whales   128

Whale Meat Sushi   132
Whales in the Desert   135
Friends of Japan, Enemies of Whales?   136
Heritage and Democracy in Danger?   139
The Anatomy of a Victory: The Saving of San Ignacio Lagoon   140
Save Them, Eat Them   146
Bloody Seas   149
Savior of the Whales   150

Part 5. Our America   153
FRAY GASPAR DE CARVAJAL REMEMBERS THE AMAZON

A Latin American Ecological Alliance   155
Writers and Artists Ask Brazilian President José Sarney to Save the
    Amazon   159
Open Letter to President Sarney: The Fate of the Amazon   161
The Destruction of Amazonia   163
Syphilis, the Other Quincentennial   166
The Meeting of Two Natures   170
One Hundred Years of Indifference   173
The Demographic Reconquest   175
Dear Mr. President   178
Instead of Trump's Wall, Let's Build a Wall of Solar Panels   180
How a Solar Border Could Help Save the Planet   183

Part 6. Our Mexico   187
THE JAGUAR: *TEPEYOLLOTLI*, HEART OF THE MOUNTAINS

Montes Azules and the End of Lacandonia (Part 1)   189
Montes Azules and the End of Lacandonia (Part 2)   191
Montes Azules and the End of Lacandonia (Part 3)   193
Montes Azules and the End of Lacandonia (Part 4)   194
Montes Azules and the End of Lacandonia (Part 5)   196
Montes Azules and the End of Lacandonia (Part 6)   197
Talking about the Forest While the Forest Disappears   200
A Proposal to Save Forests   203
The Ravaging of Montes Azules   204
Fox versus the Usumacinta River   207
The Giant Cactus Must Stay in Mexico   211

The Collapse of the Nautical Ladder   212
The Rape of the Reef: The Threat to Baja's Underwater "Rain
    Forest"   216
Beyond the Legend   218
Where the Sky Is Born: Sian Ka'an, Quintana Roo   222

Part 7. The Indigenous Labyrinth   229
    FROM THE TEMPLE TOP MOCTEZUMA SHOWS CORTÉS
    HIS EMPIRE

Slaves and Guerrillas, Forests and Blood   231
The Indigenous Labyrinth   232
For the Indigenous Poor, All Roads Lead to Mexico City   238
Survival of Indigenous Cultures   240
Indian Is Beautiful   242
The Huichol versus the Miners   245

Part 8. Mexico in Flames   249
    THE JUNGLE AFLAME

Group of 100: Mexico in Flames   251
Where There's Fire, There's Smoke   253
Requiem for a Paradise   255

Part 9. Endangered Mexico   259
    IN VIOLENT TIMES

Nuclear Sleep Produces Monsters   261
Lead in Our Blood   264
Natural Sovereignty   266
Coatzacoalcos, the River of Death   269
The Case of the Tainted Milk   273
The Science Teacher and the Ecologists   275
The Children of Guanajuato   278
A Historic Legal Victory   280
Our Flood   281
The Seeds of Wrath   284
And the Birds Will Speak   287
Cuatro Ciénegas: Fox's Crime against Nature?   291
The Sun, the Moon, and Walmart   293

Migrants Ride a "Train of Death" to Get to America and We're Ignoring the Problem 296
Enough! Mexico Is Ready to Explode 300
Mexico's 1985 Earthquake Awoke a Social Earthquake That Is Still Roiling 305
A Letter to Donald Trump from Mexico: Don't Turn Our Dreams into Nightmares 309

Part 10. The Global War on Animals 315
GRAY WHALE

Defending Dolphins 317
Animal Rights 319
The Global War on Animals 321
The Absence of the Bees 328
Requiem for a Dolphin 331
A Jump Backwards 334

Part 11. The Earth Belongs to Everyone 339
THE DESIRE TO BE ONESELF

The Rights of Nature 341
A Letter to the Pope about the Blue Planet 342
The Morelia Symposium: Approaching the Year 2000: The Morelia Declaration 344
The Age of Ecology/The Earth Sun 347
Earth Rights and Human Rights 350
The Second Morelia Symposium: Approaching the Year 2000: Overpopulation 354
El Niño of the Century 356
The World's Thirst 359
The Fifth Sun, the Earth Speaks 362
Get Close to the Stars 365
Development and Sustainability: How Much, for Whom, until When? 367
Approaching the End of the Millennium 371

Appendixes 381

A. Signers of "A Declaration by 100 Intellectuals and Artists Protesting Air Pollution in Mexico City"   381

B. Signers of "A Milkweed-Butterfly Recovery Alliance"   382

C. Signers of "Dear Obama, Trudeau and Peña Nieto: Act Now to Save the Monarch Butterfly"   383

D. Signers of "Open Letter to President Sarney: The Fate of the Amazon"   385

E. Signers of "Writers and Artists Ask Mexico's President to Cancel Mining Concessions in the Sacred Territory of the Huichol People"   386

F. Signers of "The Morelia Symposium: Approaching the Year 2000: The Morelia Declaration"   387

G. Signers of "The Second Morelia Symposium: Approaching the Year 2000: Overpopulation"   387

News of the Earth can be read as a biography of my relationship with the natural world through my writings and my activism as founder in 1985 and president of the Grupo de los Cien (Group of 100). Featuring a wide-ranging and comprehensive selection from more than five hundred opinion articles I have published during the past thirty-three years, longer pieces in defense of nature and the environment, media coverage of the Group of 100's actions, and the group's most important campaign ads and statements, this book provides a chronicle of the group's principal battles and victories, evidence of the rise of environmental awareness in Mexico, and precise, detailed documentation of critical environmental events and threats to ecosystems and wildlife in my country since 1985, many with global implications. It is a primer for environmental activists. As an accurate historical record, it will be an invaluable resource for researchers. I am not a scientist, but I have always turned to scientists for information, advice, and support.

After thirty-three years of environmental advocacy—my commitment to the Earth is much older—I am impressed by the growth of environmental awareness in the world, the proliferation of large and small organizations dedicated to a variety of the causes, and the availability and prompt dissemination of information over Internet and social networks.

However, I am gravely alarmed by the unwillingness and lack of action on the part of governments and corporations to confront climate change, the looming extinction of countless animal and plant species, the expansion of massive dead zones in the oceans, the severe depletion of global fish stocks, the relentless destruction of tropical forests, and the addition of seventy-four million people to the planet's population every year.

TRANSLATOR'S NOTE: When necessary, some of the articles have been enriched with additional information, while others have been abridged to avoid repetition. Preliminary translations of several articles were done by Jeremy Greenwood.

Acknowledgments

W e would like to thank all the colleagues and nongovernmental organizations that have collaborated with us over the past thirty-three years. First of all, among the environmental community in Mexico, which has grown substantially since 1985, we must mention Fernando Césarman; Georgita Ruiz (sea turtles); Maria Elena Sánchez (Teyeliz); our pro bono lawyer, Rodrigo Jara; Dr. Jeffrey Wilkerson (Lacandon rain forest); Dr. Jesús Estudillo, founder of La Siberia tropical bird refuge; Miguel Álvarez del Toro, founder of ZooMAT in Tuxtla Gutiérrez; Dr. Arturo Gómez Pompa (tropical forests); Humberto Bravo of the Centro de Ciencias de la Atmósfera at the Universidad Nacional Autónoma de México; Jaime Maussan and his pioneering television program *60 Minutos*; Alfonso Ciprés Villarreal (Movimiento Ecologista Mexicano); Alejandro Calvillo, founder of Greenpeace Mexico in 1993; Miguel Alemán Velasco; Arturo y Lila Lomelí (Asociación Mexicana de Estudios para la Defensa del Consumidor); Manuel Fernández (Federación Conservacionista Mexicana); Pacto de Grupos Ecologistas; Gustavo Alanís (Centro Mexicano de Derecho Ambiental); Luis Manuel Guerra (Instituto Autónomo de Investigaciones Ecológicas); Las Madres Veracruzanas contra Laguna Verde Nuclear; Araceli Domínguez (Grupo Ecologista del Mayab); Fundación Ecológica de Guanajuato (the Silva reservoir); Luis Bustamante (Comité Nacional para la Defensa de los Chimalapas); Miguel Angel García (Maderas del Pueblo del Sureste); Juan Carlos Cantú (Defenders of Wildlife, Mexico); Humberto Fernández (Conservación Humana); Yolanda Alaniz (Conservación de Mamíferos Marinos); Laura Sarti, leatherback turtle expert; Valeria Souza (Cuatro Ciénegas); Guillermo Zamora (radioactive milk powder and the CONASUPO campaign); Elena Kahn (Guerreros Verdes); Ramón Ojeda Mestre (environmental law); Jorge González Torres, founder of the Ecologist Green Party of Mexico; Josele Varela (Ecoturismo Kuyima); Oscar Moctezuma (Naturalia); Rodrigo Medellín, bat conservationist; Dr. Pablo Jaramillo-López (monarch butterflies); Tiahoge Ruge (environmental communication); Elideth Fernández (Movimiento Consciencia; animal rights); and Daniel Estrada (Pure Earth/ Blacksmith Institute; lead-free pottery).

The advice, support, and active participation of scientists, activists, and nongovernmental organizations outside of Mexico have been invaluable, and we are especially grateful to Lincoln Brower (monarch butterflies); Serge Dedina and Wildcoast (gray whales, sea turtles, Baja California ecosystems); Dick Russell, author of *The Eye of the Whale*; Jack Woody, national sea turtle coordinator, U.S. Fish and Wildlife Service; J. Wallace Nichols (sea turtles); John Adams, Robert F. Kennedy Jr., Joel Reynolds, Jacob Scherr, Lynn M. Fischer, Sylvia Fallon, and Carolina Herrera at the Natural Resources Defense Council (NAFTA, San Ignacio Lagoon, forest fires, glyphosates, and Monsanto), which gave Homero Aridjis its Force for Nature Award; the International Fund for Animal Welfare (gray whales and San Ignacio Lagoon); Todd Steiner (Sea Turtle Restoration Project); GrupoTortuguero de las Californias; F. Sherwood Rowland, awardee of the Nobel Prize in Chemistry; Tom Hayden; Jewell James, Kurt Russo, and the Lummi Nation (Lacandon Project); Amory Lovins (Rocky Mountain Institute); and Sidney Holt, author of the international moratorium on commercial whaling that went into effect in 1986 and known as "the savior of great whales."

We also thank David R. Brower, Dave Phillips, Mark Berman, and Mark Palmer (Earth Island Institute); Herb Chao Gunther (Public Media Center); Christine Stevens (Animal Welfare Institute); Jonathon Porritt (Forum for the Future); the Whale and Dolphin Conservation Society; the Orion Society, which conferred its John Hay Award on Homero Aridjis; Craig Van Note (Monitor Consortium, CITES, and the International Whaling Commission); Sue Arnold (the California Gray Whale Coalition); Ben White, heroic defender of dolphins, whales, sea turtles, and forests; Steven Swartz, Stephen Reilly, and Bruce Mate (gray whales); John Twiss (former executive director, US Marine Mammal Commission); Dan Morast (International Wildlife Coalition); Geert Drieman (Greenpeace Nederland); Paul Watson (Sea Shepherd Conservation Society); Cetacean Society International; Jean-Michel Cousteau (Ocean Futures Society); Baja Discovery; and Lester Brown, founder of the Worldwatch Institute and the Earth Policy Institute.

We also wish to thank Chris Shaw, Dave Pentecost, and Ríos Mayas (dams on the Usumacinta River); the National Audubon Society (Silva Reservoir); Mikhail Gorbachev and Matt Petersen (Green Cross International and Global Green USA, which gave Betty Ferber and Homero Aridjis the Green Cross Millennium Award for International Environmental Leadership); Sylvia Earle and the Harte Research Institute for Gulf of Mexico Studies; the Humane Society of the United States; the Rainforest Action Network; Sierra Club; Fondation Brigitte Bardot; Petra Deimer (Gesellschaft zum Schutz der

Meeressäugetiere); Tethys Research Institute; Robin des Bois; the Environmental Investigation Agency; Nathan Gardels (*World Post/Huffington Post*); and Irene Vilar (Americas Latino Eco Festival).

We would like to thank the Rockefeller Foundation and Alberta Arthurs, the foundation's former director of arts and humanities, for the grant that enabled us to hold the Morelia Symposium: Approaching the Year 2000 in 1991 and 1994; we are also grateful for support given to the Group of 100 by the Marisla Foundation and the International Community Foundation; Sir James Goldsmith; Federico Mayor Zaragoza, former director-general of UNESCO; and Fort Hill Construction.

We wish to acknowledge the many Mexican and international writers, artists, and scientists who willingly cooperated with the Group of 100 by providing information, support, and advice or lending their names to campaigns. A letter written by philosopher and poet Ramón Xirau complaining about air pollution in Mexico City and published in *Unomásuno* in February 1985 inspired the birth of the Group of 100.

Without the interest and understanding shown by many members of the national and international media it would have been impossible to get news of our activities out to a broad audience. Carlos Payán, founder and former director of *La Jornada*, courageously published my articles criticizing the government, and Emilio Azcarraga Milmo, owner of mass media company Televisa until his death in 1997, showed loyal solidarity with our campaigns against whaling and in defense of the monarch butterfly and gave generous coverage to the 1991 and 1994 Morelia Symposium: Approaching the Year 2000. We also thank Ricardo Salinas Pliego and the Fundación Azteca for support given to our campaigns in defense of sea turtles.

AICM	Mexico City International Airport
AMLO	Andrés Manuel López Obrador
Banrural	National Rural Credit Bank
CAME	Environmental Commission of the Megalopolis
CDI	National Commission for the Development of Indigenous Peoples
CEC	Commission for Environmental Cooperation
CEMDA	Mexican Center for Environmental Law
CFE	Federal Electricity Commission
CIBIOGEM	Intersecretarial Commission on Biosafety of Genetically Modified Organisms
CINVESTAV	Center for Research and Advanced Studies of the National Polytechnic Institute
CIQRO	Quintana Roo Research Center
CISEN	Center for Investigation and National Security
CITES	Convention on International Trade in Endangered Species of Wild Fauna and Flora
CNC	National Peasant Confederation
CNDH	National Human Rights Commission
CNSNS	National Commission on Nuclear Safety and Safeguards
CONABIO	National Commission on Biodiversity
CONAGUA	National Water Commission
CONANP	National Commission for Protected Natural Areas
CONAPESCA	National Commission of Aquaculture and Fisheries
CONASUPO	National Public Subsistence Company
CRIACH	Council of Indigenous Representatives of the Chiapas Highlands
CUD	Unified Coordination of Earthquake Victims
DEA	US Drug Enforcement Agency
EIA	environmental impact assessment
EPA	Environmental Protection Agency
ERP	People's Revolutionary Army
ESSA	Exportadora de Sal, SA

EU	European Union
EZLN	Zapatista Army of National Liberation
FAO	Food and Agriculture Organization of the United Nations
FDN	National Democratic Front
FIDEHULE	Trust Fund for Rubber
FIRA	Trust Funds for Rural Development
FOBAPROA	Banking Fund for the Protection of Savings
FONATUR	National Trust Fund for Tourism Development
GATT	General Agreement on Tariffs and Trade
GEMA	Grupo Ecologista del Mayab
GMO	genetically modified organism
HA	Homero Aridjis
HVDC	high-voltage direct current
IAC	Inter-American Convention for the Protection and Conservation of Sea Turtles
IBAMA	Brazilian Institute of Environment and Renewable Natural Resources
IFAW	International Fund for Animal Welfare
IMECA	Metropolitan Air Quality Index
INAH	National Institute of Anthropology and History
INE	National Institute of Ecology
INEGI	National Institute of Statistics and Geography
INI	National Indigenous Institute
INPA	National Institute for Research in Amazonia, Brazil
INPE	National Institute for Space Research, Brazil
IUCN	International Union for Conservation of Nature
IWC	International Whaling Commission
LGEEPA	General Law on Ecological Equilibrium and Environmental Protection
LPG	liquefied petroleum gas
LSIESP	Laguna San Ignacio Ecosystem Science Program
MBBR	Monarch Butterfly Biosphere Reserve
MiQRoo	Maderas Industrializadas de Quintana Roo
MORENA	National Regeneration Movement
NAAEC	North American Agreement on Environmental Cooperation
NACEC	North American Commission for Environmental Cooperation
NAFTA	North American Free Trade Agreement

NAICM	New International Airport of Mexico City
NGO	nongovernmental organization
NRDC	Natural Resources Defense Council
OCEZ	Emiliano Zapata Peasant Organization
PAN	National Action Party
PANAL	New Alliance Party
Pemex	Petroleos Mexicanos (Mexico's state oil company)
ppm	parts per million
PPP	Plan Puebla-Panama
PRD	Party of the Democratic Revolution
PRI	Institutional Revolutionary Party
PROFEPA	Federal Attorney General's Office for Environmental Protection
PVEM	Ecologist Green Party of Mexico
Red MOCAF	Mexican Network of Peasant [Small-Scale] Forester Organizations
RENCTAS	National Network to Fight the Trafficking of Wild Animals (Brazil)
SAGARPA	Secretariat of Agriculture, Livestock, Rural Development, Fisheries, and Food
SARH	Secretariat of Agriculture and Water Resources
SCT	Secretariat of Communications and Transportation
SE	Secretariat of Economy
SEDENA	Secretariat of National Defense
SEDESOL	Secretariat of Social Development
SEDUE	Secretariat of Urban Development and Ecology
SEMARNAP	Secretariat of the Environment, Natural Resources, and Fisheries
SEMARNAT	Secretariat of the Environment and Natural Resources
SEMIP	Secretariat of Energy, Mines, and State Industry
SEPESCA	Secretariat of Fisheries
SEZ	Special Economic Zone
SG	Secretariat of the Interior
SIEPAC	Central American Electrical Interconnection System
SRA	Secretariat of Agrarian Reform
SRE	Secretariat of Foreign Affairs
STRP	Sea Turtle Restoration Project

SUMA	Secretariat of Urbanization and the Environment of Michoacán
UAM	Universidad Autónoma Metropolitana; Metropolitan Autonomous University
UNAM	Universidad Nacional Autónoma de México; National Autonomous University of Mexico
UNCTAD	United Nations Conference on Trade and Development
UNEP	United Nations Environment Program
UNESCO	United Nations Educational, Scientific and Cultural Organization
UNFCCC	United Nations Framework Convention on Climate Change
UNORCA	National Union of Autonomous Regional Farmers' Associations
USFWS	U.S. Fish and Wildlife Service
WHO	World Health Organization
WTO	World Trade Organization
WWF	World Wide Fund for Nature
WWF	World Wildlife Fund (official name for World Wide Fund for Nature in Canada and the US)

The Birds

In Contepec, the village where I was born, I was ten years old when I came home from playing soccer and saw a shotgun that a friend had lent my brother to go duck hunting propped against the wall. I tucked the gun under my arm and went to the backyard, where my parents were building a new kitchen. Shotgun in hand, I clambered up a pile of bricks and scanned the sky.

I pointed the gun at a flock of birds silhouetted against the blue, but when I pulled the trigger I aimed away. These free-flying birds reminded me of the caged birds my mother kept, whose singing woke me every morning, and I couldn't bring myself to kill them. I let the gun drop and the butt hit the bricks. A volley of shot pierced my belly and hand. My body was on fire.

My parents came running when they heard the news. They bundled me into Contepec's only taxi, and we drove to the nearest town. Luckily for me, the local doctor was out, probably on a drinking spree. Eight hours passed before we reached the city of Toluca. At the first hospital my father found, the doctor who was on call told him to take me home, as I was going to die, and there would be a lot of red tape getting my corpse out of Toluca. My father pleaded with him to operate.

I opened my eyes the next afternoon in a hospital room. My parents were staring down at me as if I had returned from the dead. During my recovery, I read *King Grisly Beard* by the Brothers Grimm and *Sandokan*, a pirate swashbuckler by Emilio Salgari that my father had bought in Toluca's only bookstore.

Nineteen days later it was a different Homero, one who had seen the face of death, who returned to Contepec. My childhood had been split in two. I spent all day reading and writing and playing chess instead of soccer, since sports were now forbidden to me. Perhaps because my father was Greek, my brother gave me *The Iliad* and *The Odyssey*.

Years later, while walking with my wife and daughters on Altamirano Hill, a peasant called out to me, "Homerito, I read your book and I liked it very much!"

"Which book?" I asked.

"*The Iliad*, Homerito, *The Iliad*; they made us read it in school. When are you going to write another book?"

"I'm already writing it."

"What's it called?"

"*The Odyssey*."

Contepec is a long way from any ocean or jungle and nearly ten thousand feet above sea level. I had never seen whales or dolphins, or tigers or lions, or scarlet macaws or sea turtles, but these animals soon filled my imagination and became part of my childhood mythology. My first lion was a colored illustration in a boring story. My elephant was a clay figurine I had won at a ring-toss game at the fair held every October in honor of Saint James.

But one day a sad old elephant, the star attraction of a traveling circus, came to Contepec. I did not know then that the fabulous elephant was being slaughtered in Africa for its tusks. I had no idea that wild animals were being killed for their skins, flesh, organs, and eggs, or for the mere sport of taking their lives, but I had already learned the lesson that on this Earth, in the sphere of the living, there is no greater luxury than life itself, for humans and for animals and for plants and for the birds that I had thought of killing on the day when I almost killed myself.

My accident led me to books and to writing; my near-death experience permeates my life and sensibility as a writer, and the birds sparked a passionate concern for the environment. I understood that somehow my own survival was connected to theirs.

Like so many other Mexicans, I left my hometown for the big city, in my case to study and to write poetry, but my dreams always took place in Contepec, my natural sanctuary.

While I was Mexico's ambassador to the Netherlands in the 1970s, the seeds of conflict between my personal convictions and my official duties were sown when I sent President José López Portillo letters we had received protesting the slaughter of sea turtles in Oaxaca. He replied angrily, asking me why I bothered him about turtles when there was important work to do, such as selling Mexico's oil, uranium, and natural gas.

A few years later I moved back to Mexico. One smoggy day in February 1985, a philosopher friend, Ramón Xirau, wrote to the *Unomásuno* newspaper complaining about the pollution. I knew no one would pay attention to one small voice, but I thought that if many of us denounced Mexico City's deadly air pollution, we stood a chance of being heard. I wrote the text, friends made phone calls, and on March 1 a declaration signed by one hundred prominent writers and artists came out in the Mexican and foreign press, stating that "this pollution is killing us all." The Group of 100 was born. Coming from Mexico, where writers are public figures whose opinions are respected, and where they are expected to play an active part in the country's affairs, championing human rights and the environment, advocating social justice, and fighting corruption, whether through literature or through their actions, I took both roads.

In the winter of 1987, as the city suffocated under a blanket of smog, in the Alameda Park downtown I gathered dead birds that had fallen victim to the poisoned air we were all breathing. We compelled the government to publish daily reports of air pollution levels and to remove lead from gasoline. Thanks to us, a program was started called "Hoy no circula": "Don't drive today." We stopped the filling in of a migratory bird sanctuary in Lake Texcoco to enlarge the international airport. And when we found out that a government company called CONASUPO had imported thousands of tons of powdered milk contaminated by fallout from the nuclear plant accident in Chernobyl, we prevented its distribution in Mexico.

Early in 1990, I published five newspaper articles in *La Jornada* about the slaughter of sea turtles in Mexico. These articles became the basis for an international campaign to halt the killing. In May 1990, President Carlos Salinas de Gortari announced a ban on the capture of sea turtles that swim in Mexican waters and nest on Mexican beaches and on trade in sea turtle products. My book *Searching for Archelon: Odyssey of the Seven Sea Turtles*, featuring a female leatherback turtle who leads six of her fellows on a journey through today's oceans in search of Archelon, ancestor of all sea turtles, has been called a *Lord of the Rings* of the seas.

Contepec nestles against Cerro Altamirano, which is home every winter to millions of monarch butterflies. Well before the Group of 100 was founded, and before 1975, when scientists "discovered" that the butterflies flew from as far away as Ontario to the oyamel fir forests in the states of Michoacán and Mexico, I had written in *The Child Poet* about the monarchs, who were part of the landscape of my childhood. After I moved away, I would return every year to climb the mountain, and during those visits I learned about logging and fires on Altamirano and at the other monarch sites. In April 1986, I convinced President Miguel de la Madrid to protect the monarch butterfly forests, including Cerro Altamirano. In 2008, as Mexico's ambassador to UNESCO, I was able to get the Monarch Butterfly Biosphere Reserve listed as a World Heritage Site. Now the monarch's survival depends to a certain extent on the drug traffickers who operate in the state of Michoacán. My novel *Butterfly Mountain* was inspired by my life in Contepec and my relationship with the monarchs.

In March 2000, five years after I denounced a plan by Mitsubishi and the Mexican government to build the world's largest solar saltworks in Baja California Sur, on the shores of San Ignacio Lagoon, a pristine breeding and calving haven for the gray whales that migrate down the Pacific Coast from Alaska, President Ernesto Zedillo canceled the project in the face of widespread international opposition spearheaded by the Group of 100, giving as his main reason that it would alter the landscape.

Since 1985 my articles in Mexican newspapers have given me a platform to voice my opinions, but my visibility has been a lightning rod as well as a shield, because politicians and businessmen who feel targeted often view environmental activism as a subversive activity. Over the years I've made many enemies, and I've received death threats for defending dolphins from tuna fishermen, denouncing loggers in Michoacán and Chiapas, and stopping dams from being built on the Usumacinta River that would have meant flooding up to five hundred square miles of the Lacandon rain forest and Mayan ruins and displacing indigenous communities. In 1997, midway through the long fight to save San Ignacio Lagoon, the threats made to me and my family were serious enough for me to accept full-time bodyguards, who shadowed us everywhere for a year. I will never know whether the government supplied the guards to protect me or to spy on me, as Cuauhtémoc Cárdenas hinted to us shortly after his election as mayor of Mexico City that year.

Perhaps because I learned about the fragility of life at an early age, the possibility of a man-made apocalypse has always haunted me. My first millenarian fantasy was the play *A Spectacle of the Year Two Thousand*, when a Divine Light appears in Mexico City's Chapultepec Park during the last instants of the year 1999. Next I wrote *The Last Adam*, a reversal of Genesis in which all Creation is destroyed in six days and the last man and woman join in a final coupling on Earth. Not long before his death, the Spanish filmmaker Luis Buñuel wrote to me that he was sorry he was too old to make a movie based on my book, saying: "That the apocalypse will be the work of man and not of God is, for me, an absolute certainty. Therein lies the difference between the apocalyptic delirium of Aridjis's *The Last Adam* and Saint John's mediocre apocalyptic descriptions. Obviously, man's imagination has been enriched over the centuries." The final installment of my apocalyptic trilogy is the play *The Grand Theatre at the End of the World*, a re-imagining, when the world no longer exists, of their favorite episodes of history by a group of actors who have survived a nuclear hecatomb.

I traveled back to the end of the first millennium in *The Lord of the Last Days: Visions of the Year 1000*, when the appearance of a blood-red comet was interpreted as heralding the end of days. My growing obsession with a Last Judgment finally resulted in a book-length reflection on the last one thousand years that I called *Apocalypse with Figures*, in homage to Albrecht Dürer's series of woodcuts.

Constant immersion in the grim reality of Mexico City inspired me to write *The Legend of the Suns*, a mythological-environmental thriller and mosaic of daily life in Mexico in the year 2027. According to Aztec legend, the era of the Fifth Sun, which is the present era, will end with earthquakes, and the *tzitzimime*, or monsters of twilight, will devour the remains of humankind and take over the world. The companion piece to *The Legend of the Suns* is *Who Do You Think About When You Make Love?* Both are set in Ciudad Moctezuma (a metaphor for Mexico City). When you live in a megalopolis like Mexico City-Tenochtitlan-Federal District, you know that myths can come true.

As leader of the Group of 100 I have often felt like Sisyphus, confronting the same environmental problems over and over again, or Cassandra, prophesying disaster, or Don Quijote, because we sometimes seem like madmen tilting at windmills. Although the plant and animal species we defend, or the rivers and forests, will never know we defended them, often at risk to our lives, "in dreams begins responsibility," as William Butler Yeats wrote, and for me there is nothing more tyrannical than a dream.

Mexico City and the Group of 100

LOVE POEM IN MEXICO CITY

In this valley, surrounded by mountains, there was a lake,
and in the middle of the lake a city
where an eagle tore a serpent apart
on this thorny plant in the ground.

One morning bearded men arrived on horseback
and tore down the temples to the gods,
the palaces, the walls, the cemeteries,
choking off the springs and the canals.

Over the ruins, the vanquished built
the victors' houses out of those same stones,
raised churches to their God and streets
down which the days poured out of memory.

Centuries after, the masses conquered it once more,
pressing up the hillsides and down into the gorges, channelling off the rivers and
    felling the trees,
and the city began to die of thirst.

One evening, along a thronging avenue, a woman came my way,
and all of one night and one day
we walked the nameless streets, the scarred neighbourhoods
of Mexico-Tenochtitlan-Federal District.

In and out of the packed people and jammed cars; through
markets, squares, hotels we came
to know our bodies, turned two bodies
into one.

Then, when she went away, the city was left, marooned in its own millions,
its dried-up lake, the smog-bound sky,
the unseeable mountains.

HOMERO ARIDJIS (*hereafter HA*) (*translated by George McWhirter*)

A Declaration by 100 Intellectuals and Artists
Protesting Air Pollution in Mexico City

The News, Mexico City, March 1, 1985*

The Mexican Ecology Movement has revealed that it has irrefutable data concerning the degree of pollution asphyxiating us: Mexico City, 97.5 percent; Naucalpan, 92 percent; Tlalnepantla, 93 percent. One hundred percent is the limit; when the limit is reached human existence itself is threatened.

Apart from the enormous preoccupation weighing on us which this threat causes, what astounds us most is the lack of action on the part of the authorities. We who live beneath this viscous mushroom that covers us day and night have the right to life. A life from which we may suffer irreversible damage ceases to be life. In Mexico, as in other parts of the world, this is the highest priority facing human life today. Because of this, we ask that the government forget about speeches and plans that are never carried out and instead take immediate action to defend and protect the inhabitants of this city from the slow death that corruption and negligence have condemned them to for years.

There's a lot of talk about the crisis, hunger, and unemployment as obstacles in the struggle against pollution. But there is always money for widening or narrowing sidewalks and painting dividing lines on the streets, for the congressional campaigns of candidates, and for people's forums on pollution—a pollution that is already known, consumed, breathed, and lived by all.

Doctors have unceasingly pointed out that lead and other components in gasoline provoke cerebral lesions when absorbed into the blood. Why not, as the first measure within the government's reach, have Pemex (Mexico's state oil company) take the lead out of gasoline, thus saving millions of people, especially our children, from irreversible damage?

The truth is that with or without the crisis, now, just as in the past, we live in the world's most polluted city and nothing is being done about it. Yet

---

*Homero Aridjis (HA) wrote and, in a few cases, cowrote, all the press releases in this book. The articles not written by HA are based on interviews with him. HA also wrote (sometimes with help from scientists) the open letters to presidents, etc.

thousands of trees are cut down in Chapultepec Park to build the Metro, and green areas are destroyed to build subdivisions. The three million vehicles and the 130,000 factories that daily spew out 11,000 tons of chemical wastes into the air continue to do so. The intercity and Route 100 buses still blacken the streets with their lethal fumes.

How long will we be able to survive this daily ration of lead, carbon dioxide, sulfur, cement dust, emissions from poor-quality gasoline, garbage, fecal dust, noise? And the eye, stomach, respiratory, and skin infections that result? This pollution kills close to 30,000 children, some 100,000 people, a year and it is killing us all. It alarms the entire world but not the authorities responsible.

It is said that Mexico City will be dead by the year 2000, if not before. With the city goes a good part of our history, from Tenochtitlan to the present. Our life does not carry a price, nor does our history. There is no crisis that justifies our sacrifice. We all have a right to live.

[For the list of 100 signers, see Appendix A.]

"The 100" Exhibit on Contamination Draws Favorable Response

Jacqueline Mosio, *The News*, Mexico City, April 21, 1985

The City of Mexico, now one of the largest and most polluted in the world, just may not die if the efforts of its defenders are heeded. Last Wednesday, concerned artists, writers, and citizens came to the Foro de Arte Contemporáneo in a massive expression of concern for this city.

Works of art by Rufino Tamayo, Arnold Belkin, Francisco Toledo, Pedro Coronel, Ana Pellicer, Gabriel Macotela, Francisco Icaza, and Felipe Ehrenberg, among others, barrage the viewer with visual testimony of the city's dire plight.

Writers Octavio Paz, Ramón Xirau, Miguel León Portilla, Victor Sandoval, and many more contributed letters, poems, and prose documenting their preoccupation.

Poet Homero Aridjis, one of the originators of the Declaration against

Contamination in Mexico City, marveled at the turnout and the feeling in the air. "Everyone senses it and is touched by it—this concern for the city and its people."

"There's a strong feeling among the participants that they are speaking for those who don't have a voice," said Aridjis.

"People have come from different parts of Mexico—Oaxaca, Morelia, Patzcuaro—to participate in this outpouring of protest against ecological destruction."

Aridjis pointed out that the exhibit was put together solely by the effort and cooperation of the participants. Neither the government nor any private institution is involved.

Archeologist Eduardo Matos Moctezuma, who supervised the excavation of the Great Temple in the city's center, said, "This artistic, poetic, and theatrical manifestation has a common denominator—protest. Protest against the disintegration of the city, against the process that is making it uninhabitable."

"I was responsible for the excavation of the temple, the old treasures, the gods. And I brought them into this? Maybe it would be better if I buried them all again. The gods will suffocate here."

We live in a city that is committing suicide, that is rotting, but it is its visionaries who are raising their voices, calling on the forces of the human spirit to come to the city's aid.

One of these visionaries is theater director Juan José Gurrola, creator of Ajax in Mixcoac, which featured the domineering representative of the higher forces that be in the person of Athena. She was accompanied by the faithful Odysseus, unmistakable with his safari helmet, life jacket, and proudly carried golf club.

Ajax, read by Gurrola, spoke of defying the Olympian bunch sitting on high. "We don't need them. Our gods are the real gods, the gods of the earth, of water, wind, corn."

"What we did wasn't a happening or a performance," said Gurrola. "I went back to older forms of theater. From Spanish theater I took verse and lofty language and brought it into counterpoint with Mexican dialog, especially chilango—urban Mexican—speech."

The character can be seen on any street corner talking to his chompiras— good buddies. His language at once conceals and reveals what's on his mind: "What are they called functionaries for, anyway? They don't really function, do they?"

At the end of the presentation appears an awesomely masked visitor from the underworld.

"With the appearance of the underworld god, I'm saying that we lack a sense of mystery, an aptitude for life, and the gods have come forth to tell us this. The discovery of the Great Temple, here in the very center of the city in the 20th century, is a kind of miracle that is telling us that if we are to survive we have to remember the old gods," said Gurrola.

"The song that we end with asks 'And so?' We are so unsure. Yet I am convinced that we haven't come to a dead end. We humans are the earth's antibodies. We will save the planet."

The exhibit will continue for six weeks at the Foro de Arte Contemporáneo, Calle del Oro 23.

No Reply from the Government to the Group of 100's Eight Proposals for Reducing Pollution

Brenda Arístides, *Unomásuno*, June 3, 1985

As part of its actions in the urgent fight against air pollution, during a lunch meeting on April 22 the Group of 100 presented a list of eight proposals to Carlos Salinas de Gortari, secretary of programming and budget; Guillermo Carrillo Arena, secretary of urban development and ecology; and the mayor of Mexico City, Ramón Aguirre Velázquez.

The proposals, outlined to us in a conversation by poet Homero Aridjis (one of the declaration's originators and founder of the group), and which have yet to receive a response, are as follows:

1. Remove lead from gasoline and sulfur from diesel fuel.
2. Install antipollution devices in the Route 100 municipal bus fleet and in trucks.
3. Tackle the problems of open-air garbage disposal and toxic waste, and promote recycling.
4. Control the indiscriminate use of private transportation in the city by

taking each car off the streets one day a week, according to its license plate number.

5. Move the most highly polluting industries, such as cement and paper factories, the refinery in Azcapotzalco, and others, out of the metropolitan area.

6. Restore green areas, especially Chapultepec Park, the Desierto de los Leones, and Cumbres del Ajusco National Parks and Xochimilco, in an orderly and continuous fashion and cancel the project to enlarge the Mexico City International Airport in the reclaimed area of Lake Texcoco, which would not only obliterate the remaining vestiges of the lacustrine zones that still survive in the basin but also increase the hazards associated with the airport, since the birds that have returned to the zone, thanks to the restoration work, could collide with planes. Going ahead with the airport extension would mean cancelation by the government of its own investment and work on the lake in favor of a different project, which doesn't make sense.

7. Change the laws for crimes against the environment, because current penalties for destroying a forest, a lake, or a river, for example, are minimal. "Let the polluter pay."

8. Respect the right of citizens to be informed about pollution levels in air, water, soil, and food in Mexico City so they can be aware of the need to take necessary precautions.

Homero Aridjis pointed out that they have also tried to get out information about the subject, to stimulate discussion not only among environmentalists but also among the country's citizens, so there will be public questioning about the pollution we are subjected to, not only in health problems, but also at social, moral, and financial levels. To this end they have made statements, given interviews to the press and television, and mounted a show at the Foro de Arte Contemporáneo that will move to the Universidad Autónoma Metropolitana (UAM) in July. A roundtable, Art, Pollution, and the Environment, was held, as well as a poetry recital on Radio Universidad, and a book about the show, which has been dubbed the World's First Ecocide Art Salon, is in the works. Walls will be painted, posters printed, and informative flyers distributed to reach as many people as possible.

"We want the government to do its job and the citizens to do their part in solving the city's problems and determining the country's future. The current economic crisis, as well as problems of overpopulation and environmental destruction, appear to have hit us without most people having anything to say about it. Nevertheless, we are all responsible, if not by our complicity then by our silence," Aridjis said.

"We never think about the Mexican children who live and die among garbage, the so-called garbage pickers, a real social and moral problem; or about how we are victims of visual and noise pollution. Just look at all the political propaganda fouling the city now. If the money spent on that were to go instead to one concrete action against pollution, it would be much better for the country. The ads are pointless eyesores that will become garbage after the elections—let's hope there's at least some plan to recycle them," Aridjis concludes with a smile.

The Group of 100 Insists on Don't Drive Today

REDUCING VEHICULAR TRAFFIC THIS WINTER
IS URGENT—GROUP OF 100

La Jornada, December 3, 1986

Faced with the environmental pollution emergency in Mexico City and persistent thermal inversions, a reduction of vehicular traffic during December and January is urgent, Homero Aridjis, president of the Group of 100, declared yesterday.

He said the group's proposal to decrease the number of cars on the city's streets by 20 percent each day according to license plate numbers is still in force. Pointing out that cars are responsible for 80 percent of the city's air pollution, he stressed that pollution could not be reduced without limiting traffic and relocating industries.

"Pollution won't disappear by magic," he said, and "immediate measures must be taken in light of the high ozone levels that have been reached."

As for the eight measures the group proposed to the government a year ago, he lamented that to date, after last January's frequent thermal inversions, "we don't see anything being done to control the problem."

He explained that the proposal to reduce the number of cars in circulation entails keeping 20 percent of the two and a half million cars in Mexico City off the streets one day a week.

"There's an urgent need for action. People can't just be left to their fate," he added.

Aridjis also recommended setting up emissions checkpoints at highway exits to monitor trucks and buses coming into the capital. Officials could fine vehicles whose emissions are above permissible levels and keep them out of the city.

Finally, he criticized the government's suggestion to carry out a survey about staggering office hours in the city. "There's no time for surveys. Measures to control air pollution can't wait."

The Group of 100: Human Life Is in Danger in Mexico City

URGENT: MOVE 271 INDUSTRIES OUT OF THE CITY AND REDUCE TRAFFIC

Luis García Rojas, *Unomásuno*, February 19, 1987

The Group of 100 warned that human life is in danger in Mexico City, as the recent death of birds from air pollution shows, and any substantial reduction in environmental pollution depends on the departure of 271 highly polluting industries from the Valley of Mexico and reduction of vehicle traffic by 20 percent every day.

During a ceremony in which President Miguel de la Madrid swore in the Mexico City Chronicle Council, the borough president of Azcapotzalco, Fernando Garcilita Castillo, explained that 25 percent of the borough's 35 square kilometers (14 square miles) is occupied by 2,300 industries, of which "a minimal percentage are polluting," and he specifically referred to Azcapotzalco's 18th of March oil refinery, from which "many" underground pipelines cross the borough, alleging "nonstop maintenance and preventive actions to ensure the greatest possible safety in protecting and operating the refinery." He repeated Pemex (Mexico's state oil company) officials' explanation that there is no money "in the short term" for relocating the refinery. He said Azcapotzalco is overcrowded and there's nowhere for businesses to expand, so many are moving elsewhere in the Valley of Mexico or to the Bajío area [the "lowlands" in north central Mexico].

Homero Aridjis, president and founder of the Group of 100, stated, "We sent the birds that died downtown in February 1986 for lab tests, and the results showed they died from lead poisoning. The dead birds found this year are the same migratory species, and they must be tested for air, water, or food poisoning, all serious and worrisome. Animal—and human—life is at risk in Mexico City."

He also demanded that industries be removed from the Valley of Mexico, especially the 271 industries that contribute most to air pollution, such as foundries, tire manufacturers, asbestos producers, and chemical companies, "beginning with, and above all, the Azcapotzalco refinery."

By the year 2000 there won't be any more residents, only eight million cars, Aridjis predicted, emphasizing that the vastness of the city's problems stems from decades of environmental deterioration and lack of attention to environmental problems.

As for the Secretariat of Urban Development and Ecology's (SEDUE's) report about the bird deaths, Aridjis said, "What happened should not be played down or blown up. Sensationalist groups may be exaggerating, but the official line shouldn't be to minimize it. I'm for hearing the truth, and yes, SEDUE is minimizing the problem."

UPDATE: On March 18, 1991, after two weeks of record-breaking air pollution, President Carlos Salinas de Gortari announced the immediate closing of the 58-year-old Azcapotzalco refinery, reducing pollution in Mexico City and removing a potential source of catastrophe from the metropolitan area. Sixteen years later, Pemex handed over 55 hectares (136 acres), and a cleanup and bioremediation program began on the site. In November 2010 President Felipe Calderón inaugurated the Parque del Bicentenario as part of the bicentennial celebrations of Mexico's independence from Spain.

The Group of 100 Says This Year's Thermal Inversions Worse than in 1987

Group of 100 press release, *La Jornada*, November 21, 1988

Temperature inversions during the past 10 days have been much more severe than last year's worst days, December 10 and 22, 1987, and have exceeded 1985 levels, Homero Aridjis, president of the Group of 100, revealed, after comparing information from the Air Monitoring Network for those years.

In a press release, the group pointed to an increase in sulfur dioxide, carbon monoxide, and ozone and found that "during the past 10 days emissions were higher than in December 1987."

The highest pollution levels were recorded in Pedregal and Plateros, "although there was no official notification to residents of severe pollution in their areas, and the Secretariat of Urban Development and Ecology (SEDUE) only released information about ozone levels, which, according to the World Health Organization, should not exceed 0.10 parts per million (ppm)."

The group also noted that SEDUE undersecretary Sergio Reyes Luján "admitted last week that the ozone limit is exceeded more than 300 days a year, so we wonder how much pollution it will take for officials to do something about it."

The Group of 100 quoted information released last week by National Pediatric Institute doctors which revealed that during the past three years conjunctivitis, chronic catarrh, and respiratory illnesses—including asthma, rhinitis, and sinusitis—have increased by 40 percent, and that 80 percent of 60 children examined each day have asthma. Student absenteeism due to respiratory ailments has surged, the group notes.

Measures must be taken during the winter months to prevent risks to health, especially by reducing vehicle traffic by 20 percent with a "compulsory 'Don't drive today' program."

The Group of 100 Calls the Federal District
a Vale of Death

Angélica Lovera Hidalgo, *El Financiero*, February 22, 1989

The Group of 100 has called Mexico City a valley of death, noting that pollution levels rise daily, unchecked by government programs and polls. Despite alarmingly high levels this month, the Secretariat of Urban Development and Ecology (SEDUE) has yet to implement its contingency plan, and SEDUE's readings do not reflect reality.

"Once people start to die en masse, the pointless speeches and polls will stop," the group said.

If policies continue along these lines, Mexico is heading for "the greatest disaster of the century," the environmentalists warned. The government's prescriptions for car owners to tune their engines are "aspirins." The activists called for drastic measures, urging SEDUE to evict 1,000 polluting industries from the Valley of Mexico or to make industrial pollution filters compulsory.

Public transportation must be increased dramatically to reduce the emissions of 2,800,000 vehicles, and Pemex (Mexico's state oil company) has to improve its gasoline.

The group warned that SEDUE's measurements are unreliable: "Many IMECAS [Mexican Air Quality Index, with 100 IMECAs being the maximum allowable standard] only reflect readings taken during a few hours in a particular area, or weight the averages with zeros to lower the levels made public."

"Quite a few monitoring stations have been out of order for months or are not measuring pollutants correctly; suspended particles are not measured in the majority of stations."

At Plateros, on Wednesday, February 15, at 3:00 p.m., 0.250 parts per million of ozone were reached, and the level remained above tolerable limits until 16:00 p.m. According to the Mexican norm, an adult cannot be exposed to above 0.11 ppm for more than an hour, and only once a year. A reading of 0.389 ppm was registered at the UAM Iztapalapa station on Wednesday, Feburary 8, where 0.251 ppm had already been reached at 2:00 a.m.

Carbon monoxide "black days" have been frequent. The Mexican norm is an average of 13 ppm during eight hours. At the Lagunilla station, from 7:00 p.m. on December 28 through 1:00 p.m. on December 29, readings held at 49 ppm; for 18 hours the population was subjected to 400 percent more carbon monoxide than the permitted norm.

The United Nations Found Dangerous Microorganisms in Mexico City's Air

BONUSES AT EMBASSIES AND FOREIGN COMPANIES—
ARIDJIS

Nidia Marín, *Excélsior*, April 20, 1989

Homero Aridjis revealed findings in a confidential report issued by the United Nations Environment Program that studies carried out in the metropolitan area found pathogenic microorganisms such as Staphylococcus aureus, Streptococcus, Diplococcus, Micrococcus, Enterobacter, Escherichia coli, Clostridium perfringens, Salmonella, Shigella, and amoebas in the air.

The United Nations study found that the incidence of respiratory illness in children and the elderly has increased significantly, due to elevated emissions of sulfur dioxide and suspended particulate matter.

According to information obtained by the Group of 100, every day air pollution in the Valley of Mexico is breaking its own records, and neither the Secretariat of Urban Development and Ecology (SEDUE) nor Mexico City officials "are doing anything about it."

Its chaotic urban growth, millions of vehicles, and thousands of polluting industries have earned Mexico "its sad renown as the most polluted city in the world." Soil and water pollution have reached new levels, and a major tragedy will occur if the government waits for a killer smog to hit before taking action, Aridjis warned.

He said that during the past winter sulfur dioxide levels of 0.35 parts per million were reached for seven hours in the Northwest (the Mexican norm is

0.13 ppm for 24 hours; the World Health Organization's norm is 0.04 ppm for one hour's exposure). Carboxyhemoglobin was detected in the blood of 2,500 persons exposed to elevated concentrations of carbon monoxide.

A level of 22.5 micrograms of lead per 100 milliliters of blood (22.5 mcg/100 ml) was found in Mexico City residents, nearly four times higher than levels in Tokyo (6 mcg/100 ml) and more than double levels found in Baltimore, Stockholm, and Lima (less than 10 mcg/100 ml).

Aridjis added that embassies and foreign companies in Mexico City take measures to protect their personnel. Some recommend not having a baby while here or leaving young children in their home country (high lead levels were detected recently in the blood of two babies of staff at the German embassy). Being posted to Mexico City is considered high risk for foreign diplomats, whose stays are limited. Hardship bonuses are paid to diplomats at the Japanese, Swiss, Canadian, British, German, New Zealand, Danish, Swedish, and American embassies. German diplomats stationed in Mexico are credited with two years of service towards retirement for each year spent here and undergo regular compulsory medical examinations.

The British embassy rents a house in Cuernavaca for employees' use; Japanese diplomats are given extra vacation time, including three paid five-day trips to Acapulco each year and 60 days in Japan for 18 months spent in Mexico.

Swiss and Dutch diplomats enjoy additional vacation days and periodic trips home. The French get an extra week of vacation, the usual 24 months of service are reduced to 20 in Mexico, and personnel are examined medically before and after their stay in Mexico. The Danish ambassador can send embassy personnel outside affected areas if air pollution becomes severe. Australian diplomats receive two extra weeks of vacation, three trips per year by car to Acapulco, two trips to Florida, and a reduction in posting to Mexico to two years.

The Swedish embassy pays its personnel for a flight to Acapulco (or similar place), including hotel, once a year. The US embassy has a health-care unit on the premises and intends to put into practice various actions, such as empowering the ambassador to reduce personnel to the essential number in the event of an environmental emergency or a prolonged thermal inversion, recommending periodic trips outside the city to be subsidized by the US government, and immediately beginning an independent study of health risks posed by Mexico City's air pollution to assess the level of risk and which persons are most likely to be affected.

Aridjis stated that air pollution in the Valley of Mexico is already a worldwide disgrace, and we can't wait until the city becomes the scene of one of the century's greatest environmental disasters for officials to take honest and efficient action.

"Even being optimistic, as a recent study carried out by the US embassy in Mexico says, if strict measures against pollution in the metropolitan area were undertaken right now, air quality could be stabilized and slight improvements might be noted within 10 years, that is to say, by the year 2000."

Mexico City's Viceroys: Ecology and Democracy

HA, *La Jornada*, March 19, 1990

In the Federal District, whose mayor is appointed by the president and whose 16 borough heads are chosen by the mayor, the ecocidal biography of these officials could well become part of a universal anthology of infamy. Their arterial thoroughfares and deforestation of green areas are scars that have permanently disfigured the city.

There has been notable environmental progress during the past few years in cities and countries where the electoral process is democratic. The people have elected or turned out of office politicians and functionaries according to their behavior toward the environment; in referendums they have closed down nuclear power plants; they have succeeded in protecting forests, lakes, and rivers; and they have achieved legislation controlling the production and use of pesticides and polluting industries and vehicles.

This is chiefly due to the increase in environmental measures that governments of many nations have taken and the formulation of environmental policies that represent the interests of their citizens and are in keeping with the times. When a politician is elected on a platform promising a better quality of life, he owes his job to the electorate, and not to the president who appointed him. As for Mexico City, it's not a question of which mayor or borough head has done or is doing a good or bad job, but that the entire electoral process is stacked against the public.

Over the past few months we have had lessons in political democracy from countries on the left (in Eastern Europe) and the right (in Latin

America), but in Mexico all the government is willing to give is *perestroika* without *glasnost*, congresspeople sporting Rolexes, a lawless Securitate, and fiscal terrorism that targets the middle class and intellectuals. As we approach the twenty-first century and the third millennium, the country has yet to emerge from PRI-history. PRI-history, as Jorge Luis Borges said about his mother when she neared 100 years of age, threatens to be immortal.

Inhabitants of Madrid, Washington, DC, and Paris, and of many other capitals, including those of Mexican states, can elect their officials, but not we who live in the world's largest and most congested metropolis on the planet. Its administrators have no time for democracy, gripped by a frenzy of building and busy concocting self-serving projects (some good, others not) for Xochimilco, Santa Fe, Polanco, the Ajusco, the historic center, the National Auditorium, the Convention Center, or the Villa Centroamericana, now being built in a protected ecological area to house participants in the 1990 Central American and Caribbean Games. These projects are usually made public only after work has begun, showing how much city officials take the citizenry into account.

Every day trees are cut down in the Valley of Mexico: on the Ajusco mountains, in Los Remedios National Park, or in the Desierto de los Leones, where the Secretariat of Communications and Transport is turning the forest into a genuine desert. Our bureaucrats are about to allow Protecol, SA, a subsidiary of Waste Management Inc., to erect Latin America's largest toxic waste disposal plant in the dry lake bed of Lake Texcoco, turning it into Latin America's largest toxic waste dump and guaranteeing the continued operation here of the most highly polluting industries. Even the Mexico City Festival, organized by Socicultur with a multimillion-peso budget and a deluge of publicity—more publicity than quality—is staged with almost no input from artists and writers living in the metropolitan area.

This city has no need of big projects; it already has big problems. It needs attention to such simple things as water and air quality. It needs to reduce the pollution that is making us sick every hour of every day. It needs to respect the physiognomy and nomenclature of its neighborhoods and streets. It needs democracy so its inhabitants can decide their own future. We're all paying for the pillaging of Mexico City by the few.

And so while money is squandered on unpopular megaprojects, property taxes and water bills rise to further strangle a population already overwhelmed by a ten-year-long crisis. Voters have no say about the viceroys of Mexico

City charging them the same taxes that are charged in the countries that loan us money. Perhaps our salaries will go up by magic so we can pay.

The first *virrey* arrived in the year 1535. The Council of the Indies, fully formed by then, had understood that, to give support to the authority of the Royal Audiencia and to superimpose itself over the rights that those who had conquered the land believed they had, and the claims of the Church, which had assumed the absolute legal capacity of the conquered family, the presence of the monarch himself in the Colony was necessary, embodied in a viceregent, in a *virrey*. . . . The virrey was the king; his mission was to keep control of the land, that is to say, to preserve at all costs the domination of the sovereign in New Spain.

Justo Sierra's words about the arrival of Don Antonio de Mendoza to Mexico could well help to explain the present situation in Mexico City, adding that, after more than 450 years, the virrey is still here; the inhabitants of this ravaged valley still cannot elect their leaders.

Blue Gas, Green Rhetoric

HA, *La Jornada*, June 4, 1990

Every day at noon a faintly bluish toxic gas drifts over the Valley of Mexico: it's the photochemical oxidant known as ozone, formed by the reaction of sunlight on air containing hydrocarbons and nitrogen oxides.

Every day at noon the inhabitants of Mexico City are subjected to elevated doses of this oxidant, which inflames the respiratory system, damages the lungs, irritates the eyes, and harms vegetation. Studies of chromosomal changes in tissues appear to show that ozone is a mutagenic agent that may cause cancer. No degree of exposure to ozone, no matter how small, is free of impacts on human health.

The maximum Mexican norm for permissible ozone levels is 0.11 parts per million one hour a year, but every day during the months of April and

May we have had from four to nine continuous hours of high ozone levels, occasionally twice and three times the maximum allowable.

Looking at three different parts of the city, we see the elevated ozone levels we've experienced during May: In Pedregal (an upper-middle-class residential neighborhood in the south of the city), on Thursday, May 17, a reading of 0.31 ppm was registered at 1:00 p.m., and ozone levels remained above the maximum norm for seven hours. In the same area, last Wednesday, May 30, a reading of 0.30 ppm was registered at noon, and it continued above the norm for five hours. In all, from May 5 to 30, ozone levels in Pedregal were above the maximum permissible norm for 100 hours, which, as I said, should not exceed 0.11 ppm one hour a year. And ozone was not the only pollutant in the area: on Thursday, May 24, at 10:00 a.m., a level of 0.24 ppm of nitrogen oxides was registered, when the maximum norm is 0.21 ppm one hour per year.

In the Merced (a working-class neighborhood downtown, near the National Palace and City Hall), that same Thursday, May 17, a level of 0.27 ppm of ozone was registered at 11:00 a.m., and it remained above the maximum norm for nine hours. On Tuesday, May 29, also at 11:00 a.m., ozone reached 0.25 ppm and remained above the norm for six hours. Don't forget Friday, April 27, when the Merced monitoring station registered 0.32 ppm, with nine hours above the maximum. In sum, from May 5 through 30, the Secretariat of Urban Development and Ecology's (SEDUE's) norm was exceeded during 91 hours. Between Sunday, May 20, and Tuesday, May 22, residents of the Merced endured 39 hours of nitrogen oxide levels above the permitted norm; for 14 hours readings were above 0.30 ppm, reaching a high of 0.44 ppm on Sunday, May 20, at 6:00 p.m., with nine consecutive hours above 0.30 ppm.

At the Plateros station, on May 17, an ozone level of 0.32 ppm was registered at 1:00 p.m., with six hours above the norm, which was also exceeded on May 30, with 0.30 ppm at noon. In all, the residents of the Plateros neighborhood experienced 101 hours of ozone concentrations above the recommended norm of one hour per year.

We are subjected to elevated ozone levels, but no official seems concerned about the health of more than 20 million human beings living in this polluted valley. As far as I know, neither on May 17 nor on any other day was there a public alert, and no environmental emergency was declared; on the contrary, industries and automobiles continued to pollute as usual, and the city went on giving license plates to every jalopy in sight, bent on filling the streets with decrepit cars to sabotage its own Don't Drive Today program.

The data show elevated ozone levels during 25 days in May in Pedregal, Merced, and Plateros (which doesn't mean other parts of the city haven't enjoyed their own fatal cocktail of air and water pollution). That's why I say that pollution is the most equally distributed thing in Mexico City.

Green rhetoric consists in believing that pollution is a communication problem that can be solved with slogans, jingles, triumphalist newspaper ads, and official acts without taking the necessary measures to really protect the environment and human health. Green rhetoric is just another kind of noise pollution.

UPDATE: In 1992 the World Health Organization identified Mexico City as the most polluted city in the world.

The Rains Came

HA, *El País*, June 23, 1994

The rains came to the Valley of Mexico. You can hear Gabriele D'Annunzio's poem "The Rain in the Pinewood" playing on windows and roofs and remember E. E. Cummings's "nobody, not even the rain, has such small hands." And ask yourself, like the author of Proverbs, "Does the rain have a father?" or "Who gathered the drops of dew?"

The rains came to this city that everything pollutes: cars, factories, people, poverty, violence.

The rains came to streets fouled by political propaganda, ugly and unimaginative. How far removed from art are our presidential candidates, both the major and the minor ones, and their choruses of intellectual frogs.

Plastic campaign posters dangle from lamp posts and spindly trees, and you don't feel like voting for anyone. Pedestrians overwhelmed by noise and pollution walk meekly beneath them. As the Tibetan Saraha wrote in his *Treasury of Songs*, "The whole world is tormented by words / And no one can do anything without words / But only when one is free from words / Can one really understand words."

The rains came to the mountains encircling the Valley of Mexico, and they found shanty towns and fewer trees. That pernicious moral pollution called corruption has climbed to their summits, brandishing permits and chain saws. The president of the National Chamber of Forest Industries recently declared that "annual deforestation in Mexico amounts to 500,000 hectares [1,235,527 acres], not the 200,000 [494,211 acres] claimed by the Secretariat of Agriculture and Water Resources."

The rains came to Mexico City, and markets are brimming with fruits and vegetables, reminding us there are fields and orchards in our country. Fruits and vegetables cost more than in the United States because we live under the North American Free Trade Agreement. If the Mazatec *curandera* María Sabina, who knew how to swim in the sacred, were still alive, she, like so many indigenous women in the country, would not be able to buy them. The rains came to this city of scarce book stores, with such a limited and unchanging selection that the books seem permanently glued to the shelves and tables. Elections are coming, so few people are reading; there's a world championship soccer tournament, so few people are reading; there's television every day of the year, so few people are reading.

The rains came, and searching for poetic images as lingering drops slide down the windows of my room, I recall rains in my own work, in Contepec beneath an archway, gangsters dueling in a drizzle, and the poem with "the ancestral music of the rain / its ancient footfall, its dissolving voice." And I remember the moment on September 15 in *Noche de independencia* (Independence eve) when a pair of lovers do the *danzón* under an umbrella in the Zócalo. Everyone has their own rain, just as everyone has their own first love and builds their own death living out their life.

The rains came, and when it stops raining the black storm clouds hovering over Mexico will not disappear: there's Chiapas; there are the assassinations of Cardinal Posadas and presidential candidate Luis Donaldo Colosio; there are the kidnappings of big businessmen and small shopkeepers; there's daily violence, and all unresolved.

The rains came, and in this smoggy and traffic-choked valley how distant and foreign the poet Ryokan's haiku about himself sounds: "On rainy days / melancholy invades / Ryokan the monk."

Don't Breathe Today

HA, *Reforma*, January 28, 1996

The maximum permitted pollution levels in the Valley of Mexico are exceeded nearly every day of the year, and nearly every day the Environmental Contingency Plan could be set in motion. With winter pollution upon us, officials are announcing desperate, repetitive, cosmetic, useless emergency plans, trumpeting programs such as "21 Measures," "100 Needed Actions," or "Integral Program to Combat Air Pollution" (PICCA). They crow about funding for these programs from the World Bank and national coffers, but governments come and go, the money vanishes, pollution is still here, and people get sick.

Although the admissible limit for ozone exposure is 0.11 parts per million (100 IMECAs) no more than one hour per year, from five to seven hours every day readings rise above that level, sometimes to double or triple the permissible amount. That adds up to 1,500 to 2,000 hours a year. The Secretariat of Health points out that ozone increases symptoms of mucous membrane irritation and labored breathing and that the entire population is at risk, although children, the elderly, the sick, and smokers are the most vulnerable. Studies carried out in California have shown that ozone damages lung tissue and reduces life expectancy. Any exposure to ozone, no matter how brief, can affect health.

In November 1994, the Metropolitan Commission for the Prevention and Control of Air Pollution recognized that "suspended particulate matter is the second most serious air quality problem in the metropolitan area." Judging by the extremely high levels reached in the northeast of the city, no progress has been made towards solving this problem, which has instead gotten worse. The Secretariat of Health has identified a correlation between PM 10 (particles 10 micrometers in diameter or smaller for which no hourly norms exist, only norms for 24 hours) and mortality rates. Studies in the United States show that the causes of death most related to PM 10 and total suspended particles are chronic pulmonary emphysema, cardiovascular disease, and lung cancer. What became of the agreement between Pemex, the Mexican Petroleum Institute, and the Los Alamos National Laboratory, whose second phase was supposed to carry out a detailed analysis of particulate matter in Mexico City's air, which we swallow every day? Are there preliminary results to evaluate the magnitude of the problem, or will it be like the first phase (to which Pemex and the US Department of Energy purportedly gave five million dollars each), for which there are no results to date? Rodolfo Lacy, director of ecology for the city government, had announced that after the study "they would develop a visibility index for Mexico City similar to the existing index in Denver, which would measure light [sic] and the levels would be reported daily." Where is it? And what about the program to recover vapors at filling stations? Since June 1994, credit number 3543-ME for 17.4 million dollars has been open at the World Bank, and more than 60 million pesos in gasoline taxes have been collected from drivers, so why haven't funds been handed over to the 360 gas stations in the metropolitan area? We need to know how this money was employed or why it hasn't been used yet.

The outlook is deplorable, and everything seems to point to an approaching large-scale environmental disaster: population growth and destruction of green spaces in the Valley of Mexico are incessant; Pemex pollutes with the fuels it produces; the Federal Electricity Commission lacks equipment to control nitrogen oxide emissions at its thermoelectric plants; pollution from vehicle traffic is out of control; police (some armed with machine guns and wearing bulletproof vests) are busy helping people park their cars in streets where parking is forbidden, turning Mexico City into the world's largest open air parking lot; and the mayor, who has no environmental policy nor public transport program, plans to build freeways (second stories over the Periférico, the Viaducto, and Avenida Chapultepec) to encourage more private car use, increase pollution, and further destroy the urban fabric. Additionally, factory owners, alleging multimillion-peso losses while the Environmental Contingency Plan is in force, are pressuring officials to remove 500 companies from the Phase 1 list of industries required to curtail activities during an emergency. While it's true that monitoring of the manufacturing sector is vitiated by corruption and generations of inept functionaries, and that the list includes nonexistent companies and several with very few employees, such an exemption can't be taken lightly, especially when elevated levels of PM 10, total suspended particulates, and nitrogen oxides are registered daily.

To make matters worse, officials in charge of the environment in Mexico City's government and the Secretariat of the Environment, Natural Resources, and Fisheries (SEMARNAP) have publicly shown they are confused and incompetent. On Friday, January 18, Julia Carabias, secretary of SEMARNAP, warned, "We can't have clean air until 20 years from now." This means that today's children will be in their 20s, with damage already done, before they can hope to breathe decent air. That's four governments away. The elderly won't see it. As things stand, the next program they will launch is "Don't Breathe Today."

UPDATE: Current levels of overall air pollution and risk to the population are still reported on the homegrown IMECA (Metropolitan Air Quality Index), rather than in micrograms per cubic meter ($\mu g/m3$), making it difficult for most people to compare levels here with those elsewhere, or with World Health Organization air quality guidelines. The Secretariat of the Environment and Natural Resources (SEMARNAT) is only focusing on vehicular emissions in the metropolitan area. Regulations limiting industrial particulate emissions and emissions of organic compounds are urgently needed.

Pollution and the Doubledecker Freeway

HA, *Reforma*, January 6, 2002

Now that autumn with its multiple thermal inversions in the Valley of Mexico is past, and the postholidays air pollution climb, when a significant percentage of the population will suffer from respiratory and eye problems, lies ahead, we wonder what happened to independent reports about emissions in the Valley of Mexico and who can guarantee that the current information is reliable? How many of the Automatic Air Monitoring Network's stations are working, and why are some pollutants measured and others not? What about the environmental contingencies these last two years? Or did pollution disappear magically because Andrés Manuel López Obrador (AMLO) is now mayor of one of the world's most polluted cities? What should the city government and the Secretariat of Health be doing about PM 10 and PM 2.5 suspended particles that make their way into our bodies through the respiratory tract and are extremely harmful? And why is the media only spreading official bulletins about air pollution without verifying them or comparing them to data from independent sources? *Reforma* reports that every day 54 tons of PM 10 particles are produced in Mexico City. Carlos Santos-Burgoa, an environmental epidemiologist, stated, "Not having an environmental contingency is like not having an economic contingency; that's fine, but it doesn't mean the country is developing or that people's health is protected." Although López Obrador's government is giving a political twist to information about the environment, the dirty air we're breathing is here, sick people are in the streets, children's futures are endangered, and thousands of industries and more than 3.5 million vehicles are still there.

A recent study done at the University of California in Los Angeles showed that pregnant women living in areas with high levels of ozone and carbon monoxide have three times greater chance than other women of giving birth to babies with serious heart problems. A study carried out over 20 months found that smog levels in Mexico City were well over air quality standards in the United States, and that 63 percent of city-dwelling children examined had pulmonary hyperinflation. Last month Santos-Burgoa stated that in 2001, a total of 1,584 people, including 845 children, died of respiratory and cardiovascular ailments due to exposure to elevated ozone levels, despite the fact that city officials have claimed significant results in air quality improvement in the metropolitan area.

To make matters worse, López Obrador announced that construction of 8 miles on the Viaducto (viaduct) and 11.8 miles on the Periférico (beltway) freeways of a 98.4-feet-wide second story will begin this April at a cost of 1,500 million pesos for the first 3.7 miles. This is the wrong way to go, as it is universally acknowledged that building more roads only attracts more cars and leads to more traffic, a phenomenon known as induced demand. Instead of the second story, money should be poured into public transport and campaigns carried out to persuade people to use their cars less, to limit and regulate valet parking—a business for making money out of public thoroughfares—and illegal parking on busy streets, which only enriches policemen and borough heads. Make it harder for people to drive.

Ever since the Group of 100 was founded in 1985, we have called for high-quality, punctual, nonpolluting buses that would have dedicated lanes and be attractive to all sectors of the population. Another solution is to expand the Metro network. In the United States a number of double-deck freeways have been torn down, replaced by widening the lower level or building tunnels. Upper decks pose a risk during earthquakes, such as the October

17, 1989, Loma Prieta quake in northern California, in which 41 people were crushed to death when the double-deck Cypress Viaduct in Oakland collapsed. No politician can ignore the seismic hazards of Mexico's capital.

Before AMLO decides on his own, he has to explain the project in detail and present its environmental impact assessment, because the impacts will be considerable. Experts in the field, environmental groups, and the general public must have access to the project and the study, and both should be made freely available on the Internet, with opportunities for public comment. The entire process must be open, democratic, and legal, and the final decision should reflect citizens' opinions and interests. Two previous mayors, both from the PRI, toyed with the idea of building second stories but had to withdraw their proposals in the face of widespread opposition.

Once the entire project and its impacts become public knowledge, I hope it will be obvious that building second stories over the Periférico and the Viaducto would be a huge and unforgivable step towards the destruction of our city. AMLO has already named the engineer in charge, David Serur Edid, and set the date for starting work, but there is no consensus among citizens. Other questions need answering: Where will entrances and exits be located? Will ramps be built? How will exit streets be widened? How many houses will be torn down? How many people will have to live with the second story right outside their windows, breathing in foul air? The project is like a body with two hearts feeding a single system of veins and arteries, leading to an inevitable breakdown.

If construction of a new airport on the Lake Texcoco lakebed goes forward, years of traffic chaos lie ahead, accompanied by nightmarish urban sprawl, rendering life in the city unbearable. And we thought the days of totalitarian decision-making about the capital's future were over.

UPDATE: There are now 5.3 million cars in the metropolitan area, 58.83 kilometers (36.5 miles) of second-story toll freeways, 226.5 kilometers (140.7 miles) of Metro, and 6,565 bicycles at 452 bike stations. Six Metrobus routes cover 125 kilometers (77.7 miles) in dedicated lanes. [Information provided by the city government.]

Sister Water

HA, *Reforma*, March 12, 2006

Mexico City will soon be drowning in a sea of words. During the next 10 days the activities taking place around the Fourth World Water Forum include a water fair, a world water expo, a ministerial conference, a forum held by the Federal District government, the International Forum in Defense of Water, meetings of children and of indigenous and religious groups, cultural events, and protest marches, such as one to be held in Acapulco by opponents fighting construction of La Parota Dam and the massive march in defense of water scheduled for March 16, inauguration day of the Fourth World Water Forum, which will begin at the Angel of Independence and wind up at Centro Banamex, the forum's venue.

The solution to the Valley of Mexico's water problems has been known for decades. Rainwater must be harvested, not only by storage in a network of small reservoirs but also by capture at homes and large buildings for channeling into the aquifer instead of going down the drain into the sewer system, from where it is vomited up in the annual flooding that scourges low-lying Iztapalapa and even hilly Lomas de Chapultepec. Wastewater must be treated and recycled (less than 15 percent is treated), and more than 35 percent of available water is lost from leaks throughout the distribution system, which have to be fixed. It's insane that storm water and sewage go straight into the deep drainage system—a misguided engineering feat—to make its way into the Tula River and then be spewed into the Gulf of Mexico. The metropolitan areas's 22 million residents hog the water pumped with difficulty and at great expense from hundreds of miles away, leaving other parts of the country parched with thirst, while overexploitation of the aquifers under the city has led to significant subsidence in many areas.

Quantity and quality are the water problems in the rest of the country: shortages for supplying cities, towns, and villages; a growing demand for agricultural use; pollution of rivers and lakes; and galloping deforestation. Today's great debate is over privatization of water resources. Bottled water drunk in Mexico is a business for a handful of companies such as FEMSA, bottler for Coca-Cola, where President Vicente Fox rose from driving a delivery truck to lead its operations in Mexico and Latin America and where Cristóbal Jaime

Jáquez, general director of the National Water Commission (CONAGUA) and copresident of the forum's organizing committee, had also headed the company. According to Pablo Cabañas Díaz (*Forum*, March 2006), 27 concessions have been granted to water and soft drinks bottlers during the Fox administration, 19 to extract groundwater and eight to dump its waste back in. Cabañas writes, "Every year these concessions extract 5,131,011,131 gallons of water, the equivalent of 27,713,013,590 cans of Coke. Or, if one cubic meter of water (264 gallons) is equal to 1,056 quarts, and a human being usually needs to drink about 3.2 quarts of water a day, the water concessioned to these companies is the equivalent of 8.6 million years of one person's daily water consumption."

Big money is made in the water business from the extraction, supply, and treatment of the so-called blue gold. Opponents of privatization are at the boiling point over the possibility that the right to drinking water could be sold at an inflated price for juicy profits. Supporters of increased private participation argue that businesses will be more efficient, invest more capital in cutting-edge technology, and allow slimming down of the state.

While some are drawing water to their own mill and others have just one oar in the water, given the impossibility of getting water from a stone we should remember the words of Saint Francis in "The Canticle of the Creatures": "All praise be yours, my Lord, through Sister Water, so useful, humble, precious and pure."

UPDATE: After a May 2017 investigation in Mexico, a UN rapporteur on human rights to safe drinking water and sanitation found that a significant number of people have "extremely limited or non-existent" access to these services. The Human Rights Commission of the Federal District states that 70 percent of the population receives water for less than twelve hours a day. Climate change will exacerbate the shortage. Due to subsidence, the Grand Canal deep drainage system is working at 30 percent of its capacity.

Breathing in Death

HA, *Reforma*, January 13, 2008

It's official: high levels of carbon dioxide in the air increase human mortality. Although it seems obvious, it was only in December 2007 that an American scientist made plain the direct relationship between carbon dioxide, respiratory illness, and death. The study carried out by Mark Jacobson, a professor at Stanford University, shows that the air pollution resulting from each increase of 1 degree Celsius caused by carbon dioxide would lead to 1,000 additional deaths each year and many more cases of respiratory illness and asthma. He suggests that, worldwide, each year this greenhouse gas may cause at least 20,000 air-pollution-related deaths for each increase of 1 degree Celsius. According to Jacobson, "The study is the first specifically to isolate carbon dioxide's effect from that of other global-warming agents and to find quantitatively that chemical and meteorological changes due to carbon dioxide itself increase mortality due to increased ozone, particles, and carcinogens in the air." At the same time, ozone and suspended particles cause cardiovascular and respiratory ailments, emphysema, and asthma. The computer model of the atmosphere developed by Jacobson for the study is considered the most complete in the world.

The study is being made public shortly after the US Environmental Protection Agency denied the attempt by 17 states, including California, where six out of ten US cities with the worst air quality are located, to set their own emissions limits for carbon dioxide, on the grounds that no reliable information exists about the impacts of this gas on public health. Jacobson foresees an increase in deaths related to carbon dioxide in his state if special measures are not taken.

During the winter of 1985–86 there were repeated thermal inversions in the Valley of Mexico (people thought thermal inversion was the name of an illness), and the Group of 100 accused the Secretariat of Urban Development and Ecology (SEDUE) of hiding the measurements of pollutants made by air quality monitoring stations. In response to our pressure, on January 23, 1986, for the first time ever, pollution levels were made public, although only partially and expressed by means of a sui generis norm baptized the Metropolitan Air Quality Index (IMECA). The southwestern part of the

Federal District had the highest ozone reading that day, at 189 IMECAs. The undersecretary said the pollution "isn't serious"; the Secretariat of Health went on alert but did nothing. One day in December 1987, ozone downtown reached 0.365 parts per million. Eighteen years ago I published "Blue Gas, Green Rhetoric," an article based on the information I was secretly able to get for monitoring station readings.

Taking into account implementation of environmental contingencies programs, vehicle turnover (although there are still many old cars on the streets), and the compulsory vehicle emissions testing program, the catastrophic levels of past decades have gone down, but without a doubt the health of the Valley of Mexico's inhabitants is still in jeopardy from pollution caused by burning fossil fuels. In 1985 close to three million vehicles were in circulation; now there are more than four million. Unless circulation of private cars is drastically reduced and public transport options increased, negative impacts will continue to grow. The Federal District's Secretariat of the Environment has acknowledged that on 220 days in 2007, air quality was bad, a rise from 214 bad air days in 2006, and has issued warnings about the increase in suspended particles, for the smallest and most harmful of which (PM 2.5) there is no norm.

In the near future, perhaps 20 years from now, Mexico's oil fields may well dry up. If we're lucky, the twenty-first century will be a century of renewable energy, above all solar. Investment and technical advances are still needed, as manufacturing and transporting solar photovoltaic cells for domestic use can produce more heavy metal and greenhouse gas emissions than their use avoids. Wind power must also be developed with much greater care to minimize bird mortality, since the winds that turn the turbines blow through the main migratory bird flyways. If mandatory greenhouse gas emission limits could be agreed upon globally—experts speak of reducing carbon dioxide emissions 80 percent by 2020—finding alternatives to fossil fuels that would be healthier for the Earth and its flora and fauna would become an imperative rather than a postponable fantasy. And only then will we stop breathing in death.

UPDATE: The World Health Organization reported that the air in Mexico City has an annual average of 20 µg/m3 of PM 2.5 particles. That's 100 percent more than the WHO safe level. According to the Environmental Commission of the Megalopolis (CAME), in 2016 breathing Mexico City's air was equivalent to smoking 40 cigarettes each day on the 212 days when air quality was bad.

Mexico-Tenochtitlan-Federal District

HA, inaugural J. H. Tans Lecture, University of Limburg,
Maastricht, the Netherlands, 1991

WATER

In the Aztec calendar year 2 House, AD 1325, the ancient Mexicas, or
Aztecas, guided by their god Huitzilopochtli ("Blue Hummingbird on the
Left"), reached the Valley of Mexico. In a place where there were still marshes
and reed beds, they saw an eagle perched on a red-fruited prickly pear cactus
devouring a snake, a sign that their pilgrimage had come to an end. The
priests took possession of the place by a ritual immersion in the water on an
island lying between two lagoons, one of salt water, the other of fresh water.
There, as Fernando Alvarado Tezozomoc wrote in 1609, they passed the first
eight years fishing with nets in the lagoon and making use of the lacustrine
system in the region.

Mexico Tenochtitlan ("The Place of the Prickly Pear"), Albrecht Dürer's
Ideal City, had canals and streets of water and an economy based on water.
With its theocratic architecture (its doors faced the four directions of space
and its walls enclosed sacred sanctuaries) and its ritual calendar (governed by
human sacrifices), it was almost totally laid waste by Hernán Cortés. The
surveyor Alonso García Bravo drew up the plan of the Spanish city, and many
thousands of Indians labored day and night carrying beams, tezontle volcanic
rock, and limestone on their shoulders, receiving no wages. The stones from
the Main Temple served as building material for the new city. On the plan
squares and streets were laid out, with two plots given to each conquistador
and one to each settler. The Mexicas were confined to the outskirts of the
traza, or city center, with their wattle-and-daub *jacales* and thatched roofs,
their reed huts and adobe houses, and with the *chinampas* (floating garden
plots), the lagoons, the collective farmlands (*calpullis*), the orchards, and the
markets. Years later, in his description of Mexico in 1554, Francisco Cervantes
de Salazar wrote about the noxious miasmas from the lagoon, about the
watercourse that ran along Tacuba Street, about the aqueduct that supplied
water to the city, and about the springs in Chapultepec.

This is all pertinent, because I fear that should the city die one day it will be of thirst, because there is no river or well able to furnish enough water day and night to more than 20 million people. The Federal District and the surrounding municipalities literally drink up two rivers (the Lerma and the Cutzamala) and more than 800 wells (some say 1,300). Aboveground or encapsulated rivers carry rainwater and wastewater away from the city, especially the Grand Canal, which flows into the Tula River basin, the largest expanse on the planet watered with sewage.

The most populous metropolis in the world swallows up nearly 16,000 gallons of water per second, and 323 miles of wide-diameter pipelines relay water to collection points from where 7,456 miles of the secondary network of distribution pipelines bring it to users. In 1985 an estimated 475,509,694,245 gallons were being extracted per year, but only 211,337,641,887 gallons were being recharged into the aquifer; 57 percent of the water went for domestic use, 14 percent to industry, 11 percent for public services, and 3 percent to businesses; and 15 percent was lost to leakage in the distribution network. Many pipelines suffered damage during the September 1985 earthquakes, above all in the historic center, and are contaminated by solid waste.

Every day we who live in the metropolitan area read in the news about whole neighborhoods without water, sometimes for weeks, sometimes chronically; every day our fear is greater that in the not too distant future the entire city will be gripped by an enormous water crisis.

AIR

Air pollution is the most fairly distributed commodity in Mexico City. Our dawn is sullied by carbon dioxide, nitrogen oxides, and suspended particles; our midday is shrouded in a bluish gas called ozone; our nightfall is heavy with carbon monoxide and lead. Schoolchildren and athletes don't know what's the best—or worst—time of day for doing physical exercise; women wonder which is the least polluted season of the year for giving birth. Every season of the year has its own scourge: autumn and winter specialize in thermal inversions, trapping pollution as warm air settles over cooler air; suspended particles abound in the spring; and in the summer, during the rainy season, acid rain falls. Each season has its particular ailments, but topping all throughout the year in morbidity and mortality are respiratory illnesses.

Air pollution has been so severe during the past six years that the government has often activated the Environmental Contingency Plan that requires industries to reduce their activities by 30 percent until the alert is lifted. The most recent occasions were in December 1990 and March 1991. Additionally, to protect schoolchildren's health, school hours and the academic calendar have been changed. But these measures have only amounted to circling around the smog without attacking its sources: three million vehicles and 35,000 industries in the Valley of Mexico. However, as of March 18 the government has taken the first concrete steps to reduce this pollution, which has become an enormous health problem, by closing the government-owned oil refinery in Azcapotzalco and dozens of factories in the Valley of Mexico.

The Valley of Mexico reached by the wandering Aztecs—that was the amazement of the conquistadors and was admired by a host of travelers, painters, and poets—was the most transparent region of the air (celebrated by Alexander von Humboldt and Alfonso Reyes). Now, solely to justify our nostalgia, from time to time we get a glimpse of a blue sky.

EARTH

Mexico City has been conquered twice, first by the Spaniards and then by the multitudes. The second conquest is turning out to be more lasting, and more devastating, than the first, because much of the environmental deterioration the Valley of Mexico is undergoing is the product of the population explosion.

In 1524, when the Spaniards laid out the new city on the ruins of ancient Tenochtitlan, one of the most totally obliterated cities of modern times was not only destroyed physically but also religiously. There were 30,000 inhabitants on one square mile. By 1705 it had grown to 105,000 inhabitants and 2.55 square miles. In 1800 there were 137,000 inhabitants in 4.15 square miles. A century later the population barely reached 541,000 inhabitants and 10.5 square miles. By 1930 both numbers had more than doubled, to 1.230 million and 33.2 square miles, growing 10 years later to 1.76 million, and 45.4 square miles. In 1953 it was at 3.480 million inhabitants and 93 square miles; in 1960, 5.186 million and 139 square miles; in 1970, 8.797 million and 218 square miles; and in 1980, 14.5 million and 386 square miles. Nobody knows exactly how many of us there are in the Federal District and the surrounding urban areas, for the hills, ravines, plains, rivers, and forests of the adjacent states have now become new cities, clustering around the heart and brain of the country, which is Mexico City. It's a city that's not a state, but a country. A city whose residents can't elect their mayor or borough chiefs. A city whose historic center is sinking because it's built on layers of clay, and its aquifer is being depleted by merciless pumping of groundwater. During the past 100 years, the city has sunk from 23 to 29.5 feet (the subsidence varies), and it continues to do so by as much as a foot and a half per year.

The metropolitan area's millions each day produce 8,000 tons of garbage, which are trucked to dumps that began as mountainous holes but have now become mountains of trash visible from afar. Their names are already part of a mythology of fetidness and putrefaction: Santa Fe, whose ravines are no longer passable for trucks; Santa Cruz Meyehualco, where once pigs being fattened for sale foraged in the rubbish, closed down in 1983, two years after it erupted in flames and burned for five days; the Bordo de Xochiaca (also known as the Bordo Poniente), built on the dry lakebed of Lake Texcoco; and Santa Catarina, which replaced Santa Cruz Meyehualco in 1984 as the stronghold of Rafael Gutiérrez Moreno, the Garbage Czar, the *cacique* who controlled the lives and earnings of thousands of garbage pickers (*pepenadores*) who lived around the dump, taking in up to 70,000 dollars a day, busing 3,500 scavengers to holiday in Acapulco once a year, exercising *droit du seigneur* with the pickers' women, "marrying" at least 38 times, begetting more than 100 children (he was aiming for 180), and ending his days in March 1987 when one of the wives had him shot.

Amidst the congestion that has burst beyond the limits of urban sprawl, the encomiums lavished on Mexico City by Bernal Díaz de Castillo, who likened its beauty to Rome's or Constantinople's, or by Alexander von Humboldt, who wrote: "Mexico is undoubtedly one of the finest cities ever built by Europeans in either hemisphere," seem unreal; nevertheless, the city works, and millions are supplied with food and services, more or less. We are left with Alfonso Reyes's reproach to his fellow Mexicans in his "Palinodia del polvo" (Dissolution of dust): "Is this the most transparent region of the air? What have you done, then, with my lofty metaphysical valley? Why does it lose its luster, why does it turn yellow? Eddies of earth scurry over it like will-o'-the-wisps. . . . Oh, drainers of lakes, loggers of forests! Truncators of lungs, shatterers of magic mirrors! . . . Planet doomed to desert."

FIRE

It's not unusual to read in the papers about rivers on fire: rivers that burn, laden with flammable waste discharged into them by the petrochemical industries in Xalostoc, Santa Clara Coatitla, Tulpetlac, and Ecatepec, the most polluted spots in the metropolitan area. The industrial waste catches fire when struck by the sun's rays or flows in liquid flames during the night.

In a spectacle worthy of Dante's *Inferno*, several times a year a sewage ditch ignites spontaneously, and the fire spreads through the sewer system in the Valley of Mexico. Rivers elsewhere in the country, including the Lerma and the Coatzacoalcos, have also caught fire.

Residents of this region, where companies dealing in liquefied petroleum gas, foundries, petrochemical plants, and a thermoelectric power plant have become established, watch the sewage burn up, since firefighters are unable to extinguish the flames.

However, not only rivers burn in the Valley of Mexico. So far this year (1991) there have been more than 5,000 fires in the country, of which 98 percent were intentional. Thanks to the hand of man, nearly 193 square miles have been lost to forest fires, very many on the slopes of the Popocatépetl, Iztaccíhuatl, and Ajusco volcanoes.

Wildlife has died in the fires. While they destroy already damaged and irreplaceable ecosystems, loggers and arsonists are endangering the fauna native to these habitats. The animals have nowhere else to go, thanks to pollution, habitat destruction, hunting, and pesticide use.

Temperatures have risen, and the rivers and forests of the Valley of Mexico burn, our contribution in pollution and flames to the global greenhouse effect.

A LITERARY ENDING

Mexico–Tenochtitlan–Federal District, city, state, or country, has been known to its inhabitants by these names. History has walked its streets on water and solid ground; Moctezuma, Cuauhtémoc, Hernán Cortés, Bernal Díaz del Castillo, the Anonymous Conquistador, Pedro de Gante, Bernardino de Sahagún, Francisco Cervantes de Salazar, Francisco Hernández, Sor Juana Inés de la Cruz, the Marquise of Calderón de la Barca, Maximilian and Carlota, Benito Juárez, Joaquín García Icazbalceta, José María Velasco, José Guadalupe Posada, Diego Rivera, and Frida Kahlo have all passed through it. Its streets have lost their original appearance and names; its rivers have disappeared, imprisoned in concrete or turned into open-air sewers; its neighborhoods have been gutted to give passage to smog and noise or have been flattened by earthquakes. Few cities have endured the destructions that have been perpetrated against Mexico City over the centuries by conquistadors and rulers, who have never stopped plundering it.

Mexico–Tenochtitlan–Federal District, a living organism spilling over its boundaries and devouring itself. Uncontrollable, insatiable, an amoeba gobbling up ravines and hills, villages and forests, razing trees and drinking up rivers. Its incessant evacuations travel for many miles to reach Tula, where the mythological Toltec stone giants are witness to its defecation.

Founded by the Aztecs in water, its trees and rivers now dead, drained dry and gutted, sunken, the city will die of thirst. And if the city dies, we die with it, and a good part of our history, collective and individual, because the city has been the heart and brain of a centralized country in all its myths and rituals. Its decay will be the decay of our own bodies, of our spirit, and of our history.

And once we're dead, once we're corpses, upon remembering this Coatlicue of a city—with its 20 million sacrificed and sacrificing offspring—we will say nostalgically, "This city, in its terrible beauty, poisoned our water, air, and earth, burnt up our lives, but we love it so much that we wouldn't want to live anywhere else but in the lethal space it offered us."

UPDATE: The French company Veolia has signed a thirty-year contract with the city government to build and operate a "thermo-valorization" plant for burning 4,500 tons of each day's 13,000 metric tons of urban solid waste to power the Mexico City Metro. Critics call thermo-valorization a euphemism for incineration, and warn of possible emissions of highly toxic dioxins and furans. Veolia currently sells water to residents in three of the city's 16 boroughs.

2

Grandeur and Misery of the Monarch Butterfly

TO A MONARCH BUTTERFLY

You who go through the day
like a wingèd tiger
burning as you fly
tell me what supernatural life
is painted on your wings
so that after this life
I may see you in my night

HA (*translated by George McWhirter*)

The Monarch Butterfly: Memory and Poetry

HA, talk given during the PEN International–UNESCO Symposium of Writers and Scientists, "The Earth in the Year 2000," Mexico City, January 2000

The town of Contepec, in eastern Michoacán, is surrounded by hills. The highest is Cerro Altamirano, and every year the monarch butterfly, *Danaus plexippus*, arrives from Canada and the United States to the Plain of the Mule at its summit. Drawn to the microclimate of the oyamel fir-pine (*Abies religiosa*) forests in central Mexico, the monarch's ancestors are believed to have existed half a million years ago.

When the sun shines in the clear, bright days of winter, millions of butterflies, layered like tarnished gold on the trunks and branches of the oyamel trees, burst out of their heavy clusters. As the day warms, their flight above and among the trees becomes more frenetic, peaking at noontime when the sky comes alive with a flapping of tigerish wings that rustle like a breeze of dry leaves in the deep silence of the woods. As night falls, the butterflies roost on the trees, disappearing into the perfect camouflage of darkness. As spring nears, a sea of butterflies swoops down the slopes of Altamirano and past Painter's Glen in search of water, turning the streets of Contepec into aerial rivers. Toward the end of March, the colony heads north, only to return, different and yet the same, the following November.

An Indian legend has tried to connect the arrival of the butterflies to the return of the souls of the dead on November 1–2, the Day of the Dead, linking the insect's presence to the ceremonial rites that pay homage to man's ghostly passage on Earth. Coincidentally, the ancient Greeks used the same word, *psyche*, for butterfly and soul. I think this legend was concocted to answer reporters' questions about the existence of Nahuatl, Mazahua, or Tarascan stories mentioning the monarchs.

I was born in Contepec, and every year the butterflies would fly into our garden. From my house I could see Cerro Altamirano, like a bird with outspread wings always about to take flight, but always there. At its summit, the Plain of the Mule kept the secret of the butterflies and the ladybugs, hundreds of thousands of ladybugs.

We who were used to seeing the million-strong colonies of monarchs arrive each fall had no idea the butterflies came from Canada and the northern United States in a migration of several thousand miles, flying at an average speed of nine miles per hour, covering between 50 and 100 miles a day, and that each butterfly was the great-grandchild of a butterfly that had flown away the previous spring. It was only in 1975, following decades of research by Canadians Norah and Fred Urquhart and Americans Lincoln Brower and William Calvert, that Kenneth and Cathy Brugger happened upon one of the colonies in Mexico and solved the mystery of where the monarchs overwinter.

When I began to write poetry, I would take long walks on Altamirano Hill, home to owls and hummingbirds, coyotes and rattlesnakes, gopher snakes and skunks, and so the hill became the landscape and the substrate of my memories.

At seventeen, I went to Mexico City, supposedly to study journalism, but really to write poetry. In 1966, my wife, Betty, and I embarked on a voyage through the United States and Europe that lasted 14 years, but every year I returned to Contepec during the winter months and climbed to the butterfly sanctuary with my wife and daughters. Peasants told me about logging and fires during my absence. Each year more oyamels were felled in the Plain of the Mule, and fewer butterflies came. The natural beauty that had inspired my writings was ravaged, and the images that had nourished my childhood were destroyed. The possibility that Contepec could become a wasteland ringed by bare hills, like so many other towns in Mexico, made me desperate, and the lack of respect for the forest shamed me as a human being. We revere man-made masterpieces in museums, but we blindly destroy the masterpieces of Nature as if they belong to us and we have the right to decide on the survival of a species that has been on Earth since time immemorial.

I understood that for people living in the region it was hard to think about saving butterflies and trees when they had their own urgent needs to satisfy. I also knew that professional loggers were doing more harm than local residents who cut down trees. Once the trees were gone, the people were as poor as ever, but now their surroundings were ruined. The loggers who were breaking the chains of life were committing a social and moral crime by destroying the forest, polluting the water, and eroding the soil—all in the name of economic progress. But what kind of economic progress cripples ecosystems and makes the land barren and unlivable?

I dreamed about Altamirano becoming a national park, although I knew a decree was no guarantee of survival for the butterfly sanctuaries when even the forests on the Popocatépetl and Iztaccíhautl volcanoes were being cut down. All over Mexico scarcely a mountain or a jungle has escaped the axe and the chain saw, from the Lacandon rain forest to the old-growth forests in Chihuahua, from the Chimalapas cloud forests to the moist and dry forests of Veracruz and the tropical and pine-oak forests of Michoacán.

In April 1986, a year after the Group of 100 first spoke out demanding an end to the environmental degradation of the Valley of Mexico, I convinced the government to give the butterfly overwintering sites official protection. During a visit to a thermoelectic plant with Manuel Camacho Solís, then secretary of urban development and ecology, I persuaded him to press President Miguel de la Madrid to take action on my request. The news was announced by Camacho on Children's Day, April 30, as a gift to Mexico's children. Weeks later, I was summoned to a meeting, and I learned that only the core—and not the buffer zone—of each sanctuary would be fully protected, and obviously not the entire hills. Worst of all, Altamirano was being left out because a conservationist at the meeting didn't know about the Plain of the Mule. I succeeded in getting my hill included in the presidential decree published on October 9, 1986, designating Sierra Chincua, Sierra El Campanario, Cerro Chivatí-Huacal, Cerro Pelón, and Cerro Altamirano as protected areas for the migration, hibernation, and reproduction of the monarch butterfly as part of the Monarch Butterfly Special Biosphere Reserve covering 16,110 hectares [39,809 acres]. The core zones, 4,491 hectares [11,100 acres], were meant to provide the indispensable habitat necessary to ensure "the continuance of the migratory phenomenon . . . and the gene bank of the various species that live there." A "total and permanent ban on logging and use of the vegetation and wildlife" was decreed. The buffer zones, 11,620 hectares [28,714 acres], were to "protect the core zone from outside impact, and productive economic activities were allowed, within environmental norms."

However, the felling of trees and the setting of fires continued, even after the official decree. In the winter of 1989, after a fire and unchecked cutting of oyamels on Altamirano, the butterflies came but did not stay. They avoid cleared areas, so I felt sure that the delicate balance between climate and habitat had been upset, that the spirit of place had departed, and that the butterflies would never come back to Contepec. Near the other sanctuaries, the only sound heard at dawn was the buzz of chain saws, and the only industry that seemed to flourish in the state of Michoacán was lumbering. Smoke-belching trucks piled high with logs hogged the roads.

In the unusually cold winter of 1992, a massive butterfly die-off took place, and up to 70 percent of some colonies perished. The ground was carpeted with dead monarchs, their wings broken and abdomens frozen. We blamed this alarming mortality rate on excessive deforestation. As the eminent monarch butterfly expert Lincoln Brower said, "The oyamel forest, which shields the monarch butterflies from severely inclement weather, had become a blanket full of holes."

At a meeting of scientists and environmentalists convened by the government at Avándaro, in the State of Mexico, in February 1993, we drew up recommendations for conserving the oyamel fir forest, including redrawing the boundaries of the reserve to include more territory and encompass the colonies discovered since 1986. No logging permits should be given for any area where monarchs had established colonies, whether within or outside the core zones. Alternative means for local residents to earn a living should be developed, and until a management plan is approved, there should be a moratorium on building new roads. In closing, we predicted the possible collapse of the overwintering phenomenon in Mexico within 15 years if cutting of trees in the reserve was not stopped. The recommendations were given to the president of Mexico and the pertinent cabinet members. There was no response.

Five months later, however, new permits were issued by the Secretariat of Agriculture and Water Resources [SARH] for logging in the buffer zones of the sanctuaries protected under the 1986 decree. That same month, when I toured the region by helicopter with government officials, my conversations with the peasants who earn their livelihood by chopping down the trees left me with two overwhelming impressions: that they are wretchedly poor, and that they have a prodigious number of children. In the Asoleadero *ejido* [cooperative], family size ranged from 8 to 15 children. The head of the Rosario ejido boasted that he had fathered 45 children. When I asked the men how they supported their families, they replied, "By chopping down trees." And when I asked them how their children and grandchildren would survive, they answered, "By chopping down trees." And when I asked them what would happen when there were no more trees, they said, "We'll go to Mexico City or to the United States."

In the aftermath of 1997's severe drought, lack of water forced the butterflies to leave Contepec almost immediately after their arrival. In the 1998–99 season, the monarchs returned to Altamirano Hill, forming two colonies in the crater at its summit, over 3,000 meters [10,000 feet] above sea level.

On a visit to the Plain of the Mule with the mayor of Contepec, among the stumps and wood chips of freshly cut trees we saw thousands of crushed butterflies littering the forest floor. Later, I learned that the *ejidatario* charged with guarding the forest was selling wood to potters in a neighboring town. In 1999–2000, soon after the Day of the Dead and the arrival of monarchs, 17 truckloads of illegally logged wood from the reserve on its way to sawmills were confiscated. It was widely believed that local officials, some responsible for overseeing the reserve, were in cahoots with the loggers. The butterflies came to Altamirano but did not stay, and the cutting went on, with burros dragging logs to the brick makers at the foot of the hill. Since then, monarchs have been scarce in Contepec, and on the Plain of the Mule the oyamel forest is thinner every year.

Each year brings new problems, more logging, more fires. The monarch population is shrinking, but the human population in the region is burgeoning. The government lacks the political will, or the ability, to protect the sanctuaries. Now that the Secretariat of the Environment, Natural Resources, and Fisheries [SEMARNAT] has announced plans to expand the limits of the reserve, we are afraid that legal and illegal loggers are hurrying to cut down trees.

During negotiations for the North American Free Trade Agreement in the early 1990s, I suggested the monarch butterfly as the ideal symbol for a partnership between the United States, Mexico, and Canada, elevating environmental protection to as high a priority as business and trade. Preventing the monarch butterfly migratory phenomenon from disappearing in the coming decades is up to these countries.

In a world where tigers and orangutans may become extinct, where rhinoceroses are slaughtered for their horns and elephants for their tusks, where crocodiles are crushed by bulldozers, where thousands of birds and monkeys are captured and sold illegally every year, where nameless organisms disappear en masse, perhaps a hill and a butterfly are not that important. But if we can save the monarch butterfly and Altamirano Hill, the landscape of our childhood and the backdrop for our dreams, from the depredation of our fellow men, perhaps other human beings can save their hill and their butterfly, and all of us together can protect Earth from the biological holocaust that threatens it. Because, after all, is not the long journey of this butterfly through earthly time and space as fragile and fantastic as the journey of the Earth itself through the firmament?

Forest Fires and Loggers Are Destroying the Monarch Butterfly Sanctuaries

Group of 100 press release, *La Jornada*, March 28, 1989

As though there had never been a decree, with the complacency and complicity of Michoacán and State of Mexico officials, the Secretariat of Agriculture and Water Resources (SARH) and Secretariat of Agrarian Reform (SRA), abetted by the indifference of the Secretariat of Urban Development and Ecology (SEDUE), criminal fires and illegal logging (to which officials turn a blind eye) are decimating the forests where the butterfly overwinters.

Every day 40 to 50 woodcutters use trucks and 70 mules to haul big trees from Cerro Altamirano, bringing down the young 8- to 10-meter (26-33 foot) pine and oyamel trees at night. The loggers say it's all dead wood, since they had already hacked at the trees to expose them to the elements and to disease. On the Plain of the Mule, where the butterflies roost, there are clearings and mature 30- to 35-meter (98 to 115 foot) oyamels lying on the ground, awaiting the chain saw. Contepec residents say that armed men from the State of Mexico side of Altamirano are logging on the Michoacán side, which is guarded by an unarmed local man. Uncontrolled hunting is also a problem, and a few days ago a fire on the hill did as much damage as a blaze in March 1983.

Earlier this month several fires were set in the mountains around Tlalpujahua by loggers who were then allowed to gather the dead wood as a prize for their feats. Near Chincua fires in 10 to 12 hectares (25–30 acres) of forest were put out.

Industrias Resistol (an adhesives manufacturer that uses cellulose) is logging in El Rosario, Protimbos (a state-run company charged with protecting the forest) in Valle de Bravo, Celulósicos de Chihuahua in Epitacio Huerta (razing Cerro Frío, where in one year a nine-year allotment of trees was cut down). *Ejidatarios* and pseudo-ejidatarios are felling trees in these sites and on Chivatí-Huacal, Cerro Pelón, and Altamirano. The political situation in Michoacán emboldens the loggers, and local authorities are helpless to defend the sanctuaries, which, without protection, will disappear.

Neither companies nor loggers plant new trees, and logging intensifies once the butterflies have flown north. We urge that the following measures be taken as soon as possible to avoid deforestation of the mountains in and around the reserve:

1. A new decree is needed to protect the entirety of the forests where the monarch overwinters, and not just the areas where colonies are formed, because the SARH uses this as a pretext to grant permits for logging in the so-called zone of influence near the sanctuaries, whose boundaries are not defined.
2. Forest rangers should be armed and empowered to arrest or defend themselves against loggers and arsonists who pose a threat to the forest cover in the reserve.
3. Loggers and arsonists, whether government employees or not, companies, and local bosses profiting from cover-ups by the SARH or the SRA must be prosecuted.
4. Scientists from Mexico, the United States, and Canada should be allowed to carry out research all year round in the reserve, enabling them to constantly monitor the integrity of the sanctuaries.

Grandeur and Misery of the Monarch Butterfly

HA, *La Jornada*, February 17, 1993

The monarch butterfly is surviving despite deforestation and harm done to the planet. Millions still reach the sanctuaries, but logging in the oyamel forests is a severe threat. There's good news and bad.

Three new sanctuaries have been located in the state of Michoacán: in Lomas de Aparicio, on the border beween Michoacán and the State of Mexico; on Cerro Grande near Ciudad Hidalgo; and at El Cedral near Tlalpujahua. However, forests at Piedra Herrada, Las Palomas, and Cerro Picacho, where colonies have formed, were not included in the 1986 presidential decree.

On February 7, *ejidatarios* and communal landholders from Los Oyameles, in the village of Crescencio Morales, in the city of Zitácuaro,

Michoacán, asked the president of Mexico to take action to preserve the monarch butterfly sanctuary on their land on Cerro Boludo. They say that other monarch sites accessible by road have suffered, as "loggers and local people can rapidly destroy the forest, causing the monarchs to move elsewhere." They claim that the butterflies have remained in Lomas de Aparicio "thanks to us, because we have taken care of the forest." Illegal logging worries them, because they fear the few remaining springs will dry up. They want studies to be done so that the Lomas de Aparicio site can be decreed a federally protected area. The worst threat is posed by Zitácuaro's mayor, who wants to carve out a road for loggers to bring trees down from the sanctuary. Ejidatarios and communal landowners have warned, "First they'll have to ride over us."

The Cerro Grande overwintering site, which is not protected, is being logged posthaste by former Ciudad Hidalgo congressman Roberto Molina Loza and Sabino Padilla, former mayor of Ciudad Hidalgo, who together bought the site. People are clamoring for its immediate protection. The question is, if a former congressman and a former mayor can buy a sanctuary to log it, why is the government opposed to environmentalists and conservationists buying the sanctuaries to protect them?

After touring the region, we gleaned the following information from government officials and local residents: the buffer zones in nearly all the sanctuaries are being devastated by logging permitted by the Secretariat of Agriculture and Water Resources (SARH). The monarch colonies continually move from the core to the buffer zones. Logging permits for these areas must be canceled now. Yale University forestry expert Laura Snook warns, "The extraction rate is greater than the growth rate, so it is not sustainable." According to Miguel Ángel Musálem, silviculture professor at the Chapingo Autonomous University, "It takes 65 years for an oyamel to reach a diameter of 30 centimeters (12 inches) and 160 years to reach 60 centimeters (24 inches)."

The oyamel, like all trees, is 50 percent cellulose. Trees from all over the region find their way to Industrias Resistol's Vikingo plant, to be turned into planks, paper, and glue. The plant is on land belonging to the Otomí community of San Felipe de los Alzati, in Zitácuaro. Its yards are stacked with wood that they claim comes from Durango, hundreds of kilometers (miles) away, although it's common knowledge that a network of middlemen buys illegal wood for the plant from *ejidos* and villages in the area. Sanitation harvesting (clearing of trees to eliminate insects or disease) in Michoacán and the

State of Mexico only serves to benefit this company. Such "culling" destroyed the forest in San Cristóbal, Michoacán. Last week a truck from Ocampo, Michoacán, loaded with timber probably headed for the Resistol plant, crashed. The only way to stop the principal purchaser of illegal wood in the region is by closing the Vikingo plant. Another paper manufacturer, Celulosa y Papel de Michoacán, has timber purchasing yards near the sanctuaries.

Local communities accused loggers of cutting most of the trees in the Chivatí-Huacal sanctuary. Members of the San Felipe de los Alzati community, part owner of the land, formed a defense committee and stopped one of the trucks. While the Conference on Monarch Butterfly Mortality was taking place in Valle de Bravo, inspectors from the Federal Attorney General's Office for Environmental Protection (PROFEPA) surprised SARH forestry technicians in the sanctuary sharing a meal with loggers, seated on the trunks of recently felled trees at the limit of the core and buffer zones.

During the latter half of November, 120 meters (394 feet) of oyamel and pine wood taken from the El Rosario sanctuary were found at Hervidero y Plancha, in the municipality of Ocampo. A tall stack of logs was piled up next to the tracks leading to Angangueo, purportedly where a boxcar "bringing wood from Durango" to Resistol is unloaded.

The army was brought in at Cerro Pelón because logging was so severe that the ground where the wood was hauled down was being eroded. Ejidatarios from Aporo invaded the buffer zone on Sierra Chincua to cut trees. The government does nothing on Chincua to halt the logging. Jesús Nazareno ejidatarios went into the El Campanario sanctuary with trailers to bring out the trees they felled.

Ejidatarios and communities that own the land on Cerro Altamirano have asked for help to fence in the core and buffer zones of the sanctuary to protect them from wood traffickers. To no avail they demand the arrest of illegal loggers who are selling timber from the hill in Atlacomulco, in the State of Mexico.

The boundary between Michoacán and the State of Mexico is also the dividing line between the core and buffer zones on Altamirano and Pelón. It's absurd to subject the same ecosystem to two differing sets of forest regulations, which forbid logging on the State of Mexico side but allow it on the Michoacán side.

The route for transporting clandestine wood in the region of the sanctuaries is notorious; now it's up to the authorities to do something about it. Forest sanitation permits are almost always a cover-up for destroying the forest.

Permits issued for logging in one sanctuary are reused in other sanctuaries. Half the wood sawn in the majority of sawmills in the region is felled clandestinely. The yards, including Resistol's, are used to "launder" lumber. Illegal wood always finds its way to a sawmill or workshop.

Now the loggers have to cut down four trees instead of one: one for the local police, one for the federal police, one for the highway police, and one to sell. Since November 1992, local communities have denounced more than 130 cases, but SARH's forestry arm doesn't notify the Public Prosecutor's Office, which means that no one is prosecuted and logging goes on. Only 20 or so cases have been investigated. Official coverups of illegal logging make it especially dangerous for those communities that dare to make accusations, and the San Cristóbal and San Felipe communities have received death threats. The peasants in Crescencio Morales who asked for official help were beaten up.

Illegal logging benefits the logger and not the peasant. If the oyamel forests disappear in the coming years, when the trees are gone local residents will be as poor as ever. The only difference will be a death sentence for the monarch butterfly, because, as William Calvert pointed out last week in Valle de Bravo, "The entire structure of the oyamel forest and the surrounding areas is of the utmost importance for the existence of the migratory phenomenon."

We can't allow another massive mortality due to deforestation such as occurred in the winter of 1992 in the sanctuaries at Piedra Herrada, Chincua, Pelón, and El Campanario, when 70 percent of the butterflies in the colonies perished. Lincoln Brower, who has studied the monarch for decades, warned during the meeting that "if a large-scale conservation plan isn't put into place to protect the monarch butterfly's habitat, we are facing the irreversible loss of the migratory phenomenon in 15 years."

Deforestation Could Lead to Their Extinction Twenty Years from Now

THE GROUP OF 100 ASKS FOR THE MONARCH'S HABITAT TO BE PURCHASED

HA, *Novedades*, January 13, 1996

The Group of 100 will propose to the governments of Mexico, Canada, and the United States the purchase of the overwintering areas of the monarch butterfly and an additional 16,000 hectares (62 square miles) on Sierra Chincua, valued at 30 to 50 million dollars, in order to preserve the monarchs' habitat, Homero Aridjis, the group's president, said, stating that should the petition be accepted, the group will provide the three countries with a list of possible donors, including foundations, federal entities, and citizen organizations.

During a press conference in Mexico City, Aridjis called on the Secretariat of the Environment, Natural Resources, and Fisheries (SEMARNAP) to reconsider the optimum boundaries of the Monarch Butterfly Special Biosphere Reserve and suggested coming to some sort of long-term rental agreement for the overwintering areas that would provide a monthly payment to local residents.

In the petition Aridjis delivered to SEMARNAP, the group demanded that rules be set for building roads and allowing grazing within the reserve's boundaries, and suggested that a center be created for regulating ecoturism. They also asked for a solution to be found for the need for firewood by inhabitants of the region, to reduce pressure on the forest.

Aridjis denied that this would adversely affect the local population and argued that the aim is to achieve ecological balance within the region and to conserve the monarch butterfly.

During the press conference he pointed out that indiscriminate logging, ignorance of the forest's biological cycle, and human settlements have seriously disturbed the monarch's habitat, and he warned that if necessary precautions are not taken, both the butterfly and the ecosystem will become more vulnerable, and the former's reproductive cycle will be in jeopardy.

Dr. Lincoln Brower, a biologist and monarch butterfly expert at the University of Florida who was also present, estimated that of the nearly half a billion butterflies that reached Michoacán this year, approximately 10 to 20 percent perished on account of unchecked logging in the region's forests, exacerbated by snowstorms, and warned that if deforestation continues in the peripheral zones, in 20 years at most the monarch will be in danger of extinction. Dr. Brower explained that the butterflies froze to death, as they were left unprotected and exposed to low temperatures by the dearth of trees.

Conspiracy against the Monarch

HA, *Reforma*, January 14, 1996

Since 1994 the National Institute of Ecology (INE) has organized 60 workshops with community leaders to discuss the Monarch Butterfly Special Biosphere Reserve, the situation of the communities, and conservation of the forests. During the meetings the communities proposed analyzing the October 9, 1986, decree (and particularly Article 8, which deals with the ban on logging in the core zones), redefining the present boundaries of the five sanctuaries, and promoting alternative sources of income (ecotourism, handicrafts, mushroom farming and collecting, habitat improvements, earnings from sale of wood, and so on). Representatives from the Mexican Network of Campesino Forester Organizations (Red MOCAF) associated with the National Union of Autonomous Regional Farmers' Associations (UNORCA) worked with the Ocampo *ejido*, which owns two hectares in a buffer zone, and the El Paso ejido, half of whose property is within a core zone. Red MOCAF held workshops with both ejidos, which led to recommendations for the entire reserve. Gonzalo Chapela, head of soil and water conservation for the Secretariat of the Environment, Natural Resources, and Fisheries (SEMARNAP), wrote up the analyses for Red MOCAF, deliberately hiding the fact that these two ejidos, unlike the other 57 that are partial landowners of the reserve, have made progress and have developed a forestry culture. INE tried to encourage medium- and long-term participation by the communities in the reserve's management, but Chapela's people took over the idea and changed it to the short term, seeking deregulation in order to get at the forest and sow social unrest in the region.

With this aim in mind, on July 22, 1995, the Alliance of Ejidos and Communities of the Monarch Butterfly Reserve (including 14 ejidos and three indigenous communities) was created, with Delfino Cruz Guzmán, commissioner of the El Rosario ejido, at its head. In reply to these machinations, Joel Delgadillo, director of the reserve, said that his job was with all 59 ejidos and 13 communities that have land in the reserve, and not with "small groups that consist only of loggers," as is the case with this alliance. Gonzalo Chapela and Rafael Hernández (an advisor to Gabriel Quadri, president of INE), are now trying to convince the head of SEMARNAP that this is a representative, democratic organization standing up for campesinos, and they are spreading the idea that all the ejidos in the reserve are behind it (although the 14 ejidos have yet to hold an assembly to discuss their participation in the alliance). Delfino Cruz, the self-proclaimed "owner of the forest," has made threats through the press that "if the authorities don't listen to us, answer our demands, and attend to our proposals, we'll move into the forest next year." Other figures in the Red MOCAF are Pascal Cigala, former forestry advisor to the municipality of Ocampo, who does logging studies for the 14 ejidos, and Jaime Díaz, the forestry technician for Resistol (now known as Rexel), the company that bought illegal timber from the sanctuaries in 1991 and played a part in the 1992 massive monarch die-off. Jaime Díaz also acts as an advisor to Guardianes de la Monarca (created in 1994 to take the place of Monarca A. C. and to manage the federal zone of Sierra Chincua with out-of-work miners from Angangueo). Another person who is involved is Silvano Aureoles Conejo, former advisor to the Melchor Ocampo Ejidos Union, which grouped together logging ejidos in the eastern part of Michoacán and monopolized logging in the forests at a time when there were no biological or ecological criteria.

These individuals peddle the fallacy that illegal logging and deforestation in the region only began when the reserve was created in 1986, when both have existed since well before the reserve came into being. In 1982 the television show *60 Minutos* aired footage of loggers chopping down trees laden with butterflies. Using the alliance to pressure President Ernesto Zedillo into taking ill-advised actions to weaken the regulations that protect the sanctuaries, Gonzalo Chapela and Rafael Hernández may be after political jobs and financial gain, since if they achieve their purpose they would control exploitation of the forest in the sanctuaries and of the ejidatarios through the alliance. And if they get what the alliance is clamoring for, that the protected area be reduced from 16,110 to 12,000 hectares (from 62 to 46 square miles), they would finish off the trees in the buffer zone. Additionally, were Article 8 of the decree to be deregulated, under the pretext that 35 percent of the core zone of the reserve is "affected by pests," the alliance would extract "dead wood" from 974 hectares (2,407 acres), providing Industrias Rexel with a cheap supply of wood from the sanctuaries.

On this matter Joel Delgadillo was quoted in a Mexico City newspaper as saying, "I have no information about how many trees are infested. It's not a disease that's certified by the National Institute of Forestry Research," and Javier de la Maza, general director of conservation and ecological resource use at INE, stated that these natural areas "are part of the ecosystem and provide food for a variety of species." But the "advisors" have won over the ejido leaders with rumors that World Bank money earmarked for conservation projects could be used by the alliance for projects of destruction. While it's true that poverty and unemployment are problems in this part of Michoacán (as they are throughout the state, including areas where logging is rampant), the butterfly is not to blame; the responsible parties are the legions of corrupt local, state, and federal officials who have infested my state for decades. I agree with SEMARNAP that conservation of the area where the monarch overwinters is not incompatible with the well-being of local communities. Yes, butterflies and communities must and can coexist together without sacrificing one for the other. What is not acceptable is that loggers use the needs of the campesinos as an excuse for destroying the oyamel fir forests and putting the monarch at risk.

Twilight of the Monarchs

HA and Lincoln P. Brower, *New York Times*, January 26, 1996

As many as 30 million monarch butterflies—perhaps 30 percent of the North American monarch population—died after a snowstorm hit their sanctuaries in Mexico on December 30. But storms are not the real threat to the monarchs, which have wintered in the cold Mexican mountaintops for more than 10,000 years.

As is true for so much of besieged nature, the real dangers the butterflies face are man-made, in this case the destruction of the oyamel fir forests in Mexico's central highlands.

About 90 percent of the world's monarchs live east of the Rockies. Each fall, they migrate 2,000 miles from as far away as southern Canada to their winter quarters in the oyamel forests—relict ecosystems of the Pleistocene era two miles above sea level. The monarchs swirl down from the sky, festooning the boughs and trunks of the trees with layer upon layer of delicate wings, patterned in white, orange, and black.

By early April, the eight-month-old butterflies migrate 800 miles back to the southern United States, where each female lays about 400 eggs on milkweed plants and then dies. The eggs turn into caterpillars, the caterpillars into jade-colored chrysalids etched with golden crowns. When they hatch, this spring generation travels 1,000 miles north to Canada. Over the summer, two or three more generations of butterflies are produced, and the great-grandchildren of those that flew north return to Mexico to repeat the cycle.

But the monarch's existence is threatened by the cutting of the remaining oyamel forests. When intact, a forest serves as an umbrella and blanket, protecting the butterflies from freezing rains. The logging creates gaps that allow rain and snow to fall through the forest canopy and onto the butterfly clusters. As the weather clears, the life-sustaining heat radiated from the butterflies' bodies leaks out through these holes in the blanket of trees and the monarchs freeze to death.

Nearly two decades of conservation efforts by private organizations in Mexico, Canada, and the United States—as well as a 1986 order by then President Miguel de la Madrid to protect five wintering enclaves—have done little to stop the destruction. The Mexican Government continues to permit logging in protected and unprotected areas. Illegal commercial cutting is rampant. Local peasants harvest trees for fuel and building materials, and cattle trample and eat the fir seedlings.

It is not too late to undo the damage. The Mexican Government and international conservation groups together should buy or lease the forests from the peasant communities, which are now allowed under Mexican law to sell their communal lands. This must be done quickly: Loggers are lobbying the Government to open up about 25 percent of the protected areas. The land could be bought for about $60 million, a small price in light of what is at stake, environmentally and economically.

Whereas logging is a one-shot deal, the local people could benefit indefinitely if they had help to create high-quality ecotourism ventures. To plan and pay for such projects, Mexico and private environmental groups and foundations need help from the United States and Canada. The three countries should be partners on environmental issues that affect all of them, in keeping with the side agreements to the North American Free Trade Agreement.

Can trilateral cooperation save the oyamel sanctuaries? Or will North America let the forests fall and these majestic butterflies disappear?

An Alliance against the Monarch

HA, *Reforma*, June 2, 1996

Ernesto Zedillo, president of Mexico, and Julia Carabias, head of the Secretariat of the Environment, Natural Resources, and Fisheries (SEMARNAT), have just struck mortal blows against the monarch butterfly reserve decreed by President Miguel de la Madrid on October 9 1986. 1) From now on, the alliance of *ejidatarios* who have been logging the forests in the sanctuaries will be in charge of managing the reserve. 2) On May 6, the National Institute of Ecology (INE), more given to breaking laws and plundering rather than preserving the environment, fired the biologist Joel Delgadillo and his technical team, who were hitherto in charge of the reserve. The government has left the guarding of 16,100 hectares (62 square miles) in five sanctuaries, spread over parts of the states of Mexico and Michoacán, in the hands of three watchmen in a cabin on the Llano de las Papas (Plain of Potatoes).

The Banality of Destruction

HA, *Reforma*, October 5, 1997

Bureaucrats at the Federal Attorney General's Office for Environmental Protection (PROFEPA) are following a perverse logic. When a citizen denounces a crime against the environment, they immediately take the side of the transgressors to shield and justify them. And that's not all: they attempt to morally disqualify the citizen who is concerned about environmental protection in Mexico, just as in corrupt public prosecutor offices throughout the country the citizen has to prove his innocence because bureaucrats, who are often in cahoots with predators of our natural patrimony, accuse him of lying.

When Lincoln Brower and I visited the monarch butterfly sanctuaries to see for ourselves what goes on when the butterflies aren't there, we discovered equipment and workers opening up a highway a few kilometers from the Sierra Chincua sanctuary, and at the foot of the highway a sawmill with stacks of full-grown oyamel trunks. We took photographs of the highway and the sawmill to show PROFEPA officials so they couldn't say we were seeing things. Five photos were published in *Reforma* on July 3. Victor Ramírez Navarro, assistant attorney general at PROFEPA, wrote in a letter to the newspaper (which was not published) that "this is an 18-kilometer highway, of which 15 are paved. It was built by the Michoacán state government in 1994 to link the towns of Angangueo and Tlalpujahua." We requested information about the highway and were given an environmental impact assessment and a permit for land use changes arranged for by the state government with INE. And so Ramírez Navarro magically showed that a highway under construction in June 1997, as proven by our photos, had been completed in 1994. The only observable traffic on the "tourist highway" is logging trucks. PROFEPA has a curious idea of tourism. Ramírez minimized the presence of the sawmill, saying that "it's not inside the natural protected area of the monarch butterfly. It's about 10 kilometers from the Reserve and not in Michoacán; it's in the State of Mexico, in the municipality of San Felipe del Progreso, at a place known as the Paraje Cevati, and the owner of said sawmill is Señor José Francisco Bastida Chávez, who showed us the document in the National Forestry Register." Ramírez moved the sawmill, which is at the foot of the Angangueo-Tlalpujahua highway (both in Michoacán), to the State of Mexico. Or could there be two, and he is referring to the other one, deliberately ignoring the existence of the one we photographed? Or as a diligent public servant, does he want to lead us elsewhere with false clues? The bureaucrat from PROFEPA also stated that "Sr. Bastida Chávez is making use of resources on his own property, which is outside the Reserve and covered by a logging permit, and the timber does not come from the protected natural area." I have no idea how this government employee determined that the oyamel logs did not come from the sanctuaries, since there is no surveillance in the area, and while at Sierra Chincua we witnessed legal logging in the buffer zone and illegal logging in the core zone. We questioned the

Secretariat of the Environment, Natural Resources, and Fisheries (SEMARNAP) employees, who knew nothing about the existence of the sawmill nor of the highway that was built in 1994.

On September 14, I climbed Cerro Altamirano, the landscape of my hometown, Contepec, Michoacán, and home to a monarch butterfly sanctuary. Although it was Sunday, and the butterflies had yet to arrive, I came upon a campesino, undoubtedly poor, illegally cutting down oyamel trees that would have sheltered the monarchs the coming winter. He would sell a donkey-load of wood for 10 pesos—three donkey-loads would suffice to carry off a tree that had taken 60 to 65 years to grow to maturity—to the brick makers, who are not so poor and are destroying the heart of the mountain to make money from resources that aren't theirs. For PROFEPA's information, one of these brick makers has already set up shop on the mountainside. Farther down the hillside, a young woman with five children in tow was gathering twigs to heat water. The campesino and the woman are two examples of the culture of poverty, both unacceptable; the man because he's despoiling nature for a pittance and breaking the law, and the woman, because it's a waste of her own potential.

If we look at this on a larger scale, we find multinational logging companies doing big business with somebody else's forests, with the complicity of local and national governments, causing incalculable environmental damage. In a recent news item about the destruction of Amazonia by Asian logging companies, it was said that "eight of these companies had bought up two million hectares in the farthest reaches of the rain forest for a mere eight dollars each, the price of three beers at a bar in Manaus." Coming back to Mexico, the loggers are finishing off the Lacandon jungle and forests on the Iztaccíhuatal volcano, the Chimalapas, the Pico del Tancítaro, the Tuxtlas Mountains, and the Chihuahua mountain range, to name a few.

And what is PROFEPA doing about the galloping destruction of Mexico's forests and jungles? Is it only interested in disqualifying members of civil society who denounce this destruction, instead of efficiently defending Mexico's natural wealth?

The Extent of the Logging

HA, *Reforma*, April 18, 1999

A few weeks ago, millions of monarchs began their return journey toward the United States and Canada after spending five months in the protected and unprotected sanctuaries of Michoacán and the State of Mexico. Now that the butterflies are gone, these spaces will be invaded by loggers taking advantage of the absence of visitors and guards to chop down oyamel trees, mostly illegally, as is evident from audits by the Federal Attorney General's Office for Environmental Protection (PROFEPA) this past January and February. Four of ten forest audits carried out on authorized sites in Michoacán identified serious violations; six, lesser ones. Seven audits were done in Ocampo, one in Angangueo, two in Aporo, and one in Zinapécuaro. Two are still pending. The forestry and campesino organizations in this area belong to the National Peasant Confederation (CNC). The worst violations occurred in Aporo, Ocampo, and Zinapécuaro. Although the Secretariat of the Environment, Natural Resources, and Fisheries (SEMARNAP) had given permission for logging 333,632 cubic feet in the three municipalities, 698,893 cubic feet were logged, 365,261 cubic feet illegally, an overexploitation of 109.5 percent on 189.97 forested hectares (469 acres). The regulations that were broken are found in Article 47, Parts III, XIII, and XIV of the forestry law. The main violations were the lack of documents attesting to the legal provenance of the wood, logging on land without SEMARNAP authorization, and use of timber marking hammers issued for other sites. Measures taken by PROFEPA included seizure of equipment, suspension of logging, financial sanctions and reforestation. *Ejidos* belonging to the CNC where the most logging occurred are the following:

- Ejido San Agustín Ucareo, in Zinapécuaro: illegal logging (unmarked), 81,605 cubic feet; overexploitation, 124,123 cu. ft.; volume illegally logged, 205,731 cu. ft.; volume authorized by SEMARNAP for 1998–99, 81,140; total volume logged, 286,868 cu. ft.; overexploitation by 253.5 percent; audited area, 68.27 hectares (168.70 acres).

- Ejido "El Rosario," in Ocampo: illegally logged, 18,686 cu. ft.; overexploitation, 88,871 cu. ft.; volume illegally logged, 107,557 cu. ft.; volume authorized by SEMARNAP for 1997–98, 171,753 cu. ft.; total volume logged, 279,311 cu. ft.; overexploitation, 62.6 percent; area audited, 81.50 hectares (201.39 acres).
- Ejido Arroyo Seco, in Aporo: illegally logged, 29,641 cu. ft.; overexploitation, 6,808 cu. ft.; volume illegally logged, 36,449 cu. ft.; volume authorized by SEMARNAP for 1997–98, 24,535 cu. ft.; total volume logged, 60,983 cu. ft.; overexploitation, 148.5 percent; audited area, 12.75 hectares (31.51 acres).
- Ejido Emiliano Zapata, in Ocampo: illegally logged, 12,510 cu. ft.; overexploitation, 3,017 cu. ft.; volume illegally logged, 15,421 cu. ft.; volume authorized by SEMARNAP for 1997–98, 56,205 cu. ft.; total volume logged, 71,732 cu. ft.; overexploitation 27.6 percent; audited area, 27.45 hectares.

The total figures for all four ejidos are: illegally logged, 142,442 cu. ft.; overexploitation, 222,819 cu. ft.; volume illegally logged, 365,261 cu. ft.; volume authorized by SEMARNAP in 1997–98, 333,632 cu. ft.; total volume logged, 698,893 cu. ft.; overexploitation, 109 percent; audited area, 189.97 hectares.

In 11 municipalities in Michoacán (including Ciudad Hidalgo, Zinapécuaro, Tlalpujahua, and Zitácuaro), the total volume illegally logged was 39,812 cu. ft., of which 29,245 cu. ft. were pine and 10,211 cu. ft. were oyamel, in addition to white cedar and oak. At five industrial sites in Angangueo, Zitácuaro, Charo, and Morelia (PROFEPA hasn't divulged the names), serious violations occurred, and 26,126 cu. ft. of illegally logged timber were discovered, including 23,857 cu. ft. of pine and 2,165 cu. ft. of oyamel.

All this goes to prove that the biggest problem facing the monarch butterfly sanctuaries is logging. It also reinforces the conclusions several researchers and I arrived at during visits to the sanctuaries this season. A growing proliferation of large and small sawmills surrounds the entire Monarch Butterfly Special Biosphere Reserve; trucks loaded with timber hog the roads of Angangueo, Ocampo, Tlalpujahua, and Zitácuaro, entering and exiting the sawmills.

Logging goes on unchecked in El Rosario, the sanctuary that profits most from ecotourism. Eight hundred feet above the area open to visitors we observed savage destruction of the oyamel forest, noted in PROFEPA's audit. Even in the tourist area we saw trees that had been hacked to weaken them and justify their felling. The sawmill we detected last year at the foot of Sierra Chincua, alongside the road to Tlalpujahua, which is officially claimed to be outside the protected area, has expanded, and large piles of oyamel timber are on the premises. The logging is worrisome, because according to official estimates, the butterfly population at Chincua and El Rosario this season was 50 percent smaller than last winter's. In Chincua, monarchs roosted in 1.9 hectares (4.7 acres) in 1998–99, compared to 2.6 hectares (6.4 acres) in 1997–98; in El Rosario the monarchs covered 6.1 hectares (15.1 acres) in 1996–97, 2.6 hectares (6.4 acres) in 1997–98, but only 2.0 hectares (4.9 acres) this winter. A colony formed on Cerro Pelón, but none on Chivatí-Huacal. In 1996–97 the butterflies roosted in 17 hectares (42 acres) of the reserve; in 1997–98 in 13 hectares (32 acres); and this year in a mere 5.5 hectares (13.6 acres).

At Cerro Altamirano, where there were two colonies this year, Benito Morales, the person from the Contepec ejido entrusted with guarding the sanctuary, sells wood to the potters in nearby Santa María Canchesdá, delivering three pickup truckloads a week of felled trees concealed under tarpaulins. Meanwhile, brick makers in Contepec buy oyamel trees to fuel their ovens instead of using natural gas. Both potters and brick makers have been reported to PROFEPA and the local mayors from the Party of the Democratic Revolution (PRD) and the Institutional Revolutionary Party (PRI), to no avail. Each load of wood is sold for 15 pesos, a pittance for a 60-year-old oyamel. Fifteen loggers are now at work on Cerro Altamirano, each felling two trees a day.

There were thousands of visitors this year to Sierra Chincua and El Rosario, the two sanctuaries open for ecotourism, bringing in substantial economic benefits. Another threat to the butterflies was posed by the ejidatarios' diversion of water essential to the monarchs to their rainbow trout fish farms. That Mexico, the United States, and Canada, the NAFTA trio, are unable to defend the physical integrity of the oyamel forests and guarantee the survival of the monarch butterfly migratory phenomenon is proof that the so-called environmental accords are merely cosmetic. Even worse, the loggers seem bent on destroying the sanctuaries before the government takes the necessary actions to protect them.

Censored Butterflies

HA, *Reforma*, March 19, 2000

For months I've been trying to find out what's happening in the monarch butterfly sanctuaries, which are being devastated at an unprecedented rate, only to be met with official secrecy. Why? Orders from higher up, people at El Rosario and Chincua tell me. Why? Because the PRI-run governments in Michoacán and the State of Mexico are swapping trees for votes. No sooner does an *ejidatario* ask permission to log than it's granted in Morelia or Toluca. To stay in power this July 2, the Institutional Revolutionary Party (PRI) government has turned into a predator of the country's natural resources, my source revealed. Simple. And that's not all: officials also covered up the massive butterfly mortalities during December and January's freezes. After repeatedly demanding a moratorium on logging in the sanctuaries, we were given a moratorium on information.

What's going on in the five sanctuaries protected by the October 9, 1986, decree? Let's take each in turn. On Sierra Chincua this year the butterflies came to the Llano del Toro, almost at the edge of the forest and near the ravine, nearly a mile lower than their usual site. We had to walk for hours over wide, dusty pathways to reach them. "I've never seen so much dust," one of the ejidatarios remarked. "This will hurt the butterflies." Lincoln Brower stated this scientifically: "The dust is going to affect the butterflies' reproductive cycle." Otherwise, we had only to leave the paths to see the logging, the stumps still rooted in the ground. On our visit one Saturday morning the sanctuary resembled a street market in Mexico City. About 25 buses had arrived that weekend. Hundreds of horses and pickup trucks were crisscrossing the paths newly opened during the last year. In the absence of public bathrooms, people were using the forest as a toilet. The horses that carried tourists during the day roamed free at night. There were no guards except for a few ejidatarios.

At El Rosario the butterflies came to the Llano de los Conejos with fewer trees and far from their usual roosting place. New roads for horses and pickup trucks have been opened. Some 200 stands selling knick-knacks and fried snacks line both sides of the concrete walkway leading up to the entrance to the sanctuary. The constant stream of visitors trampled butterflies on the trails. According to my informants, every night 30 or so trucks, each carrying three men, drive up to El Rosario to cut trees illegally. About 12:30 a.m. they start bringing the timber down to the sawmills in Ocampo. They told me that the mayor of Ocampo is a logger.

Many people visit the monarch sanctuaries with an almost religious fervor, as if on a pilgrimage to the Basilica of Our Lady of Guadalupe. Sunday afternoon, on my way to the Llano de los Conejos, I overheard this exchange: "Señorita Frauste, what did you think of it?" The woman replied, "I thank God for all this beauty, and as a human being I ask the butterflies to forgive us for the harm we're doing them." Ecotourism in both sanctuaries open to the public is out of control but could easily be regulated for the good of the butterflies and the communities. There's a charge for everything: the El Asoleadero *ejido* has a 20-peso (2 dollars) toll per vehicle; El Rosario takes in parking and entrance fees. All kinds of merchandise are sold. The income is important for the communities. Lourdes Coronel, the regional delegate of Michoacán's tourism secretariat, has announced a plan for the state to build a theme park that would include "audiovisual rooms where the migratory phenomenon will be explained, as well as ample parking lots, restaurants, cafeterias, shopping malls, and handicrafts."

There were 200,000 visitors this year who spent approximately three million pesos (about 320,000 dollars) on entrance fees alone, but the logging goes on, and not only the extraction authorized by the deforesting arm of the Secretariat of the Environment, Natural Resources, and Fisheries (SEMARNAP), but clandestine cutting as well. Trucks are transporting wood in full daylight, and dozens of trucks go by on the Zitácuaro and Maravatío-Atlacomulco highways every night. The majority have no permits or bills of lading. Logging is already degrading 70 percent of the oyamel forest inside the reserve and endangering the monarch migratory phenomenon. Ten forest audits carried out by the Federal Attorney General's Office for Environmental Protection (PROFEPA) in April 1999 on sites in the area found overexploitation of 109.5 percent beyond the authorized amount on 190 hectares (469.5 acres). The news went nowhere. New sawmills are constantly springing up in Angangueo. Almost every house in Ocampo has its own sawmill, and existing ones are getting bigger thanks to the destruction of the sanctuaries, which has increased this year. A resident of Angangueo told me, "This is the limit. The order to chop down trees must be coming from high up, because everybody is keeping their mouth shut. The trucks bring down wood all day long, especially before dawn. If the butterflies are finished, we'll be finished too."

On Cerro Altamirano the ejidatario in charge of guarding the sanctuary is still selling wood to potters, and the brick makers in Contepec are still buying oyamel trees to fuel their ovens. There are dozens of loggers on Cerro Altamirano, the worst of them from the State of Mexico. "No more butterflies on Chivatí-Huacal and Cerro Pelón," an ejidatario said. "The forests are devastated." At the beginning of the year a small colony formed on the ground at Cerro Pelón, for lack of trees.

The two main problems facing the sanctuaries are ecotourism and deforestation, the latter being the most serious. In eastern Michoacán hundreds of legal and clandestine sawmills are operating. It's common knowledge that a mafia of mid-level SEMARNAP employees in Morelia is in cahoots with the loggers. The Rexel Vikingo plant (formerly known as Resistol) is thought to be bankrolling sawmills in the mountains. Some of the loggers are armed with AK-47s, and the maximum fine that can be imposed is a ludicrous 20 times the minimum daily salary, amounting to 500 pesos (53 dollars). As SEMARNAP has announced it will redraw the boundaries of the Monarch Butterfly Special Biosphere Reserve, which now covers the 16,100 hectares (62 square miles) protected by the 1986 decree, we fear that authorized and illegal loggers are hurrying to get at the trees within and outside the sanctuaries, and not only the orginal five but also an additional eight sites that have been at the mercy of timber traffickers.

As the North American Free Trade Agreement partners have been unable to keep the forests whole and ensure the continuance of the monarch butterfly migratory phenomenon, we must spare no efforts to save this masterpiece of nature. If the Sistine Chapel—a man-made masterpiece—were under attack, there would be an international outcry. Destruction of the monarch butterfly sanctuaries merits no less. This highly charged political year in Mexico, with a presidential election coming up in four months, is crucial for taking the necessary measures. The federal government must declare an immediate moratorium on logging in the oyamel forests and regulate tourism in the reserve.

The New Monarch Butterfly Reserve

HA, *Reforma*, September 17, 2000

A few days ago the World Wide Fund for Nature (WWF) office in Mexico released revealing aerial photographs of the region where the monarch butterfly overwinters. The photos were taken in 1971, 1984, and 1999 and are part of a study carried out by the Geographic Institute at the National Autonomous University of Mexico, which concluded that the oyamel forest is gravely threatened. An analysis of 42,020 hectares (62 square miles) on vegetation maps from these three years found that 12,225 hectares (47 square miles, or 44 percent) of the initial 27,485 hectares (106 square miles) of high-quality forest had been degraded from 1984 to 1999. The study also determined that during the 28-year period the average size of the intact patches shrank by 90 percent, from 2,114 hectares (eight square miles) to 254 (one square mile). The oyamel fir forest in the Transvolcanic Belt in central Mexico is believed to have once covered 500,000 hectares (nearly 2,000 square miles). According to the analysis, what in 1971 was a nearly uninterrupted forest mass is now a series of islands separated by large swathes of degraded forest. The study warns that "long-term sustainable management of these forests will only be possible if logging is stopped and the forest is restored, regenerating the adjacent areas."

These indisputable photos and figures disprove the woodchoppers' complaints that they have been prevented from exploiting the forest since the 1986 presidential decree, although everyone knows that before and after 1986 not a single day has gone by without legal or illegal logging in the area. In fact, although the Monarch Butterfly Special Biosphere Reserve was created on October 9, 1986, in response to a specific request by myself and the Group of 100, on October 14, five days later, the Secretariat of Agriculture and Water Resources (SARH) granted annual permits for the next 10 and 12 years to log in the core and buffer zones of the very sanctuaries the Secretariat of Urban Development and Ecology (SEDUE) claimed to be protecting: Sierra Chincua, El Rosario, Cerro Pelón, Chivatí-Huacal, and Altamirano. The study found that, from 1984 to 1999, the yearly rate of forest degradation in the "protected" sanctuaries has been 3.17 percent, significantly higher than the yearly rate of 2.41 percent in the entire region. WWF warns that if degradation continues at the current rate, 20 years from now only 10,000 hectares (less than 40 square miles) of forested islands will remain, "and the greater the fragmentation, the less chance of regeneration, endangering the forest ecosytem and its watershed."

Logging affects the water supply as well as the butterflies. Local residents identify water as their principal environmental problem. Deforestation in the reserve has been so drastic that monarchs have arrived at Chivatí-Huacal but were unable to form a colony because the trees are gone. Cerro Pelón (Bald Hill) lives up to its name. On Cerro Altamirano loggers have cleared paths to the summit, and for years arriving monarchs have left for lack of trees. El Rosario and Sierra Chincua, the sanctuaries open for ecotourism, are in a deplorable state. Last winter visitors to Sierra Chincua were using surgical masks to keep out the dust raised by horses and vehicles that entered deep into the site. Illegal logging took place at night by armed gangs of outsiders.

The actual rate of exploitation is patently unsustainable; more wood is being removed than the forest can produce. The Rexel Vikingo plant alone—part of Fernando Senderos's Grupo Desc—can process 10,594,400 cubic feet a year, double the forest's production capacity. If they really want to save the reserve, WWF and the Secretariat of the Environment, Natural Resources, and Fisheries (SEMARNAP) will have to ask Mr. Senderos to cooperate; otherwise they will be fiddling while Rome burns.

During a visit to various sanctuaries in the reserve in February 1999, we learned that the monarch population at El Rosario and Sierra Chincua had been low. Several researchers reported between 50 percent to 80 percent fewer butterflies than the previous year. In light of this dire situation, and to save the sanctuaries from systematic destruction, in the September 7, 2000, *Official Gazette of the Federation*, SEMARNAP made public a project to enlarge the protected area to 56,259 hectares (217 square miles), with a three-part 13,552-hectare (52-square-mile) core zone and a two-part 42,707-hectare (165-square-mile) buffer zone. The core zone will no longer be limited to specific overwintering sites but will now include larger, contiguous areas of forest to provide corridors between the various colonies and secure alternative sites where colonies can form should their customary roosting locations be damaged by fires or other causes. In support of this conservation scheme, the Monarch Butterfly Conservation Fund would finance purchase of valid logging permits within the core zone of the new reserve from the landowners and pay for forest conservation actions mentioned in the reserve's management plan, which should be economic activities proposed by local communities that are compatible with the conservation objectives of the reserve.

In January 1996 Lincoln Brower and I published an op-ed article in the *New York Times* proposing the purchase or rent of trees from the ejidatarios as compensation for not cutting them down. We suggested that the payments be covered using the interest produced by a five-million-dollar fund that was established by the Packard Foundation. Who was against this project to preserve the sanctuaries? Which negative forces opposed it? The forestry industry and the timber-trafficking mafias, who tried to manipulate the local communities, as if the campesinos were hopelessly naïve. In classic PRI (Institutional Revolutionary Party) fashion, opportunistic politicians such as Cuauhtémoc Ramírez, CNC leader in Michoacán, maneuvered the *ejido* commissioners into "defending our rights" to log the sanctuaries. On August 29, *La Voz de Michoacán* published a resounding "No to decrees or laws that forbid rational exploitation of the forest," probably anticipating opposition on the part of Michoacán's governor, Victor Manuel Tinoco Rubí, to saving the butterflies' forests. Among other things, disagreement was expressed with "the amplification of the 1986 decree (and yes to making it smaller)," as well as a demand to "get rid of all the bureacracy in granting logging permits." Is Michoacán's governor using this to ask President Ernesto Zedillo for a licence (unfettered by laws or decrees) to destroy what remains of the sanctuaries? Could that happen? Surely millions of Mexicans, Americans, and Canadians who are concerned about the survival of one of the most extraordinary migrations taking place on planet Earth are in favor of expanding and protecting the monarch butterfly's reserve while providing significant and lasting economic benefits for the local communities in the region. Not to pass this decree would be a criminal act against the monarch butterfly and, in the long term, against the nine hundred thousand inhabitants of the region.

Butterflies in the Storm

HA, *Reforma*, February 17, 2002

Presidents paid visits, official decrees were issued, ministers and governors came and went, promises were made, photos were taken, loggers kept on logging, but the butterfly, alas, went on dying. The situation in the monarch butterfly sanctuaries is summed up by my paraphrase of César Vallejo's poem "Masses."

On Tuesday, February 12, a shocking news item appeared on the front page of the *New York Times*: "Storm in Mexico Devastates Colonies of Monarch Butterfly." Up to 250 million butterflies had frozen to death in the Michoacán sanctuaries of Sierra Chincua and El Rosario after two days of continuous rain on January 12 and 13 followed by exceptional cold. According to Lincoln Brower, who days after the storm found the sanctuaries carpeted with butterflies to a depth of up to one foot, 80 percent of the population perished in El Rosario and 74 percent in Chincua. The scientist declared that this is the greatest mass mortality in the 25 years he has been investigating the migratory phenomenon of the monarch butterfly in Mexico. The World Wide Fund for Nature (WWF) has stated that "preliminary analysis of the massive mortality of the monarch butterfly last month in its overwintering sites indicates that the probable root cause is deforestation and logging within and around the sanctuaries of the butterfly." The mounds of dead butterflies were higher where there were no trees, reinforcing the assertion that the removal of even a single tree from the umbrella of forest cover in the core zone can lead to death by freezing.

Since the official decree of 1986, legal and clandestine logging has increased. In November 2000, the reserve was enlarged and a program launched that would pay *ejidatarios* not to cut trees.

Isidro González (a member of the managing committee for El Rosario's 261 ejidatarios) says, "What has given us a real headache are the illegal loggers. We barely turn our heads and there they are, cutting down trees" (*El Universal*, February 13, 2002). González, who is also in charge of collecting entrance fees from tourists, complains that since the beginning of the season, only 15,000 people have come, although they usually have 250,000 visitors. On Tuesday, February 12, the day news of the disaster was released, there were only 10 tourists, which is not surprising, as what were people going to see? Heaps of dead butterflies? Mutilated forests? Pools of dust? Other ejidatarios could have said the same to other reporters after the butterfly die-offs in 1992, 1995, 1998, and 2001. Deforestation persists; the circumstances hardly vary. The official line in 2002, as in past years, is that weather events, specifically rain and frosts, killed the butterflies; humans had nothing to do with it.

Most dramatically, this season there were more butterflies in the reserve than there had been for years. By studying this huge mortality, Lincoln Brower and other scientists have come to believe that the density of monarch populations in the oyamel forests could reach 50 million per hectare, rather than the 10 million calculated previously, making the monarch migratory phenomenon even more extraordinary and the responsibility of our government for its conservation even greater.

Unfortunately, Mexico is a magical country, and as happens with crime, where there are murder victims but no murderers and millionaire frauds but no crooks, so in the case of the monarchs there are massive die-offs but no guilty parties. As in the past, climate is to blame, no mention of fewer trees, of loggers' destruction of the forest's microclimate, of the butterflies' exposure to the elements. Faced with the death of 250 million monarchs, officials calmly shrug their shoulders and play down the calamity, as did Roberto Solís, director of the reserve under the Institutional Revolutionary Party (PRI) and now under the National Action Party (PAN), when he declared, "This is a natural climatic phenomenon which should be seen as part of nature's equilibrium." Besides, he said, nothing happened in the other sanctuaries. As for Cerro Altamirano, I have learned that a colony did indeed form, but the butterflies died of cold. And as for the so-called protection, does the Secretariat of the Environment and Natural Resources (SEMARNAT) know that Contepec's new mayor from the Party of the Democratic Revolution (PRD) is parceling out the Cerro among ejidatarios for grazing livestock and planting corn?

With butterflies dying every year in one sanctuary or another, it's time for drastic measures. The first should be a total ban on cutting down oyamels in the core zones of the reserve and a substantial reduction in deforestation of the buffer zones surrounding the heart of the Mexican refuge of the monarch butterfly.

Should the Army Protect Monarchs?

HA, *Reforma*, February 1, 2004

Comparison of aerial photographs taken on March 10, 2001, with satellite images from January 19, 2003, shows without any doubt that in two years, in only two *ejidos* in the state of Michoacán, more than 329 forested hectares (813 acres) were illegally clear-cut within the reserve. This indisputable evidence proves that the Ejido Francisco Serrato was responsible for the disappearance of 178 hectares (440 acres) of forest in the buffer zone and 16 hectares (40 acres) in the core zone. Twelve hectares (30 acres) were also clear-cut in the adjacent ejido. In the Ejido Emiliano Zapata, 123 hectares (304 acres) were logged in the buffer zone. It is not known whether permits were granted for any of this cutting, but during overflights on January 21 and 22, 2004, researchers and members of the press saw logging taking place in Francisco Serrato at the height of the monarch season. Footage of trucks loaded with logs was broadcast on Mexican and Spanish television news.

Until recently most of the illegal logging was in the reserve's buffer zone, but now the loggers are cutting brazenly in the core zone. In the past few years the oyamel-pine forest in the core zone on the western flank of Cerro Pelón between Macheros and Campamento, in the Ejido Nicolás Romero (municipality of Zitácuaro, Michoacán), has been almost totally destroyed by small-scale but incessant illegal logging. Overwintering colonies had hitherto always been present in this forest.

Since last year there has been illegal logging in the core zone on Sierra Chincua. Loggers have felled oyamel trees, rolling them down the hillsides to the road that has been the main access for researchers and tourists since the winter of 1976–77. This winter the ejidatarios dug huge ditches in an attempt to keep out the loggers' trucks, as government officials do nothing to stop them. It remains to be seen how successful this strategy will be for protecting one of the best-preserved forests in the reserve.

In addition to upsetting the forest ecosystem, reducing the potential for water catchment and causing serious erosion, the relentless thinning and clear-cutting of the forest will lead to increased monarch mortality during the frequent winter storms that hit the region. This January a milder storm had a lesser impact on the monarchs than 2002's snows, although on Cerro Pelón, in El Capulín, there was a massive die-off, and dead butterflies have been falling from the trees for weeks. In contrast, in the Ejido El Paso, on Chivatí-Huacal, the ejidatarios went after the loggers and burned their trucks. The satellite photos show this ejido densely forested up to its borders, contrasting with the adjacent ejidos, where there are few trees.

Some ejidos and local communities have written to local, state, and federal governments asking for help to save the sanctuaries. They have also turned to nongovernmental organizations and researchers, hoping someone will pay attention and bring their petitions to public light. Out of desperation a few ejidos have even requested military intervention to stop the logging by armed mafias and protect their forests. They should be heeded, as it's unheard of for an ejido to ask the army to enter a protected area.

Ejido La Mesa is in charge of one of the four areas in the reserve that are open to tourists, as there have always been colonies in La Mesa, which is one and a quarter miles north of the deforested area in Francisco Serrato. After the fires during the 1998 El Niño, the butterflies did not return to La Mesa until 2001 and 2002. The State of Mexico and the federal government spent hundreds of thousands of dollars on tourism facilities at La Mesa, and in December 2002, with considerable media coverage, the governor opened the season in that ejido. As a result of the logging in Francisco Serrato, which has begun to move up and invade the forest in La Mesa, there was no colony this year. Instead of recuperation, permanent loss of the colony can be expected, as well as negative impacts on the watershed and the region's microclimate and a waste of investments in ecotourism and conservation.

Logging in Francisco Serrato is on the Michoacán side, and the access roads for taking out the wood go through El Rosario and Ocampo, also in Michoacán. The heavily logged forest in Michoacán contrasts with the higher-quality forest and better law enforcement in the State of Mexico. Logging and corruption in Michoacán are damaging the State of Mexico's tourism potential. The Ejido La Mesa has sent written denunciations of logging to state and federal officials. This information has been censured in the Mexican press to avoid scaring off tourism, as this is an important source of revenue for Michoacán, and the State of Mexico has refrained from publicizing the situation after investing so heavily in an area where no butterflies arrived this year.

The only solution is to decree and enforce a total moratorium on logging throughout the reserve, covering the 13,552 hectares (52 square miles) of core zone and the 42,707 hectares (165 square miles) of buffer zone. So-called sustainable logging in the buffer zone is a farce, for the forest has been clearcut in many places, and no one respects legal limits. The director of the reserve, the Secretariat of the Environment and Natural Resources (SEMARNAT), and the National Commission for Protected Natural Areas (CONANP) are empowered to suspend logging permits in the buffer zone, and they should do so.

Permanent round-the-clock surveillance on roads and highways in the region is imperative, with roadblocks to prevent the sawmills from operating. The Federal Attorney General's Office for Environmental Protection (PROFEPA) set up roadblocks last November after its raids on the sawmills were trumpeted in the media, but they were only temporary, and a few days later the sawmills were at work again and the raids had little real impact.

Inspectors must monitor the sawmills continuously, not only when an occasional order comes from above.

To further the dialogue between communities and researchers that was begun last September during the Monarch Butterfly Regional Forum, the problem of illegal logging and how to stop it must be addressed. Talk about tourism and alternative livelihoods is a waste of time while the forests and the monarch colonies are disappearing.

Or should the army step in?

Marked for Death

HA, *Reforma*, March 13, 2005

A few days ago I was filmed climbing, on horseback and on foot, the Cerro Altamirano, in Contepec, Michoacán, the town where I was born, for a documentary about the journey of the monarch butterfly from Canada to Mexico. We reached the Llano de la Mula, where during my childhood I used to see millions of butterflies year after year. In 2004 there was no colony, and that day we didn't encounter a single butterfly. What we did see were fresh axe marks on many oyamels marked for death. It's good the army has planted pine trees and put up wire to protect them, but there is no barrier that defends the oyamels against loggers coming from the State of Mexico. Nor is there any surveillance.

On February 16, the Secretariat of the Environment and Natural Resources (SEMARNAT) issued a press release under the heading "The number of monarch butterflies that arrived during the present overwintering season in Mexico declined." It noted a 75 percent reduction of the area used by the butterflies during the present season in comparison with previous years. It made reference to the report prepared by an international committee of scientists headed by Lincoln Brower. SEMARNAT concluded that the fall in the monarch population was due to bad weather in the breeding habitat in the United States and Canada during the summer of 2004, to industrial agriculture in the United States and Canada, to the cultivation of genetically engineered corn and soybean crops, among which the milkweed (*Asclepias*) that nurtures the monarch's larvae grows, the use of herbicides in their habitats, and last winter's storms in Mexico. SEMARNAT assures us that "the migratory phenomenon of the monarch butterfly . . . is not in jeopardy," boasting that "logging in the core zones has been reduced by 100 percent, and by 80–85 percent in the buffer zones." The release states, "The forests in the region . . . are healthy or in recovery."

The official bulletin omits the most serious part of the report: the accelerated loss of monarch habitat in Mexico due to illegal logging. And that the area occupied by the colonies this year was the smallest recorded over the last 12 seasons and, possibly, the smallest since annual monitoring was begun at the end of the seventies. "We are playing butterfly roulette," the committee of scientists warns. "Degradation of the overwintering habitat in Mexico by the multiplicity of effects of illegal logging, and destruction of the summer breeding habitats by current agricultural practices in the United States and Canada, need mitigation if the phenomenal migration biology of the monarch butterfly is to survive. We are of the unanimous opinion that the most pressing need is to protect the forests within the core zone of the MBBR [Monarch Butterfly Biosphere Reserve] in Mexico from further logging."

The main climate condition for the monarchs' survival in oyamel forests is a suitable and constant temperature, protecting them from excessive cold that can lead to their freezing or too much heat that would dry them out or burn up their energy reserves. The forest canopy protects them during the day and at night covers them like a blanket. Thinning the forest exposes them to cold, wind, wetting, and heat loss, increasing mortality through freezing in severe storms like the one in 2002 when the population suffered 80 percent mortality, or those in 2004 when the mortality was 70 percent. This loss of the forest is the principal threat to their survival.

The illegal logging during the past four years in the core and buffer zones is documented, as is the destruction of habitats where colonies existed previously. Last year, in Sierra Chincua, more than 100 trucks were reported bringing down illegal timber. Cutting occurred in 130 hectares (321 acres), and some 40 hectares (100 acres) were razed in the Federal Zone, supposedly under government control. Last year the former director of the reserve allowed trees that had fallen in the January storm to be taken out on the south side of Chincua, inviting illegal logging above Arroyo Zapatero, where every year there is a colony. Living and healthy trees were taken along with the dead ones. Now nearly all the large trees are gone, leaving the butterflies with no protection from the wind. Logging has also taken place in Arroyo Hondo, where the monarchs move to in the spring before they leave. The tracks for taking the timber out have degraded the forest. The sanctuary is crisscrossed with barbed wire, and there are cows everywhere, even though cattle are prohibited in the core zone. An extensive network of roads inside the reserve that reached 1,375 miles in 2003 has been documented.

In the course of the past seven years the northeast face of El Pelón has been destroyed, and logging has rendered several traditional sites on the western edge unusable for the monarchs. Only 5 percent remains wooded. Apart from the steep southern slopes, all of the historical habitat on Cerro Pelón has been degraded or destroyed in the last decade. In November and December of 2004, cut wood and boards were seen in the core zone. This year the butterflies are at the edge of the logged area. On Sierra El Campanario, the tourist site of El Rosario is managed by the *ejido* of that name. The concrete path leading up out of the parking lot is flanked by souvenir shops and rustic eateries where once there were trees, and at the site where the butterflies used to roost the necessary microclimate has ceased to exist. They have formed the main colony in the Llano de los Conejos at an altitude of 11,000 feet, too high, according to Brower, because they're at great risk of dying if there's a storm. In the winter of 2004 the estimated mortality was between 50 percent and 90 percent of the population. Weeks later the colony regrouped in some 10 trees.

Sierra Chincua belongs to Angangueo, whose patron saint is Simon the Apostle. The effigy of the saint, who is brought out in a procession on October 28, is accompanied by the attribute of a bloodied saw, since after being crucified his body was sawn into pieces. Nowadays he might be considered the patron saint of fallen trees. The town, previously a mining center for silver, lead, copper, and zinc, is now in the sights of the Minera México company, which intends to exploit the mineral resources to the tune of 13,004,305 tons. MM is part of Grupo México, a holding company that is the world's third largest copper producer. The mining concession was granted to the English company Negociación Minera de las Trojes in the mid-nineteenth century. In 1909 the silver mines came under control of the American Smelting and Refining Company (ASARCO), owned by the Guggenheim family. When you enter the town you pass a pyramidal slag heap. In April 2004, 500 residents demonstrated against the illegal logging, calling for the army to come in, since (they said) the Federal Preventive Police, the Ministerial Federal Police, and the federal prosecutor for environmental protection were corrupt. They cited the unfulfilled promise of Vicente Fox to install permanent surveillance in the zone.

Every butterfly that arrives in Mexico makes the journey from the United States or Canada for the first time and is the grandchild, or great-grandchild, of a butterfly that was here the year before. Should the brutal deforestation continue, one day the monarchs will arrive to pools of dust. This is why it is imperative for the government to declare a moratorium on the logging of oyamel trees in the reserve, because nowadays, when the butterflies go north, the loggers move in.

Gold for Monarchs

HA, *Reforma*, April 9, 2006

During a recent visit to the monarch butterfly sanctuary on Cerro Pelón, I found a wide area in the core zone, next to the Llano de los Gobernadores, where all that remained were trunks of mature oyamel trees, carpets of sawdust, and beams cut with chain saws that were waiting to be hauled away by the wood traffickers from the township of Nicolás Romero who were brazenly working in the light of day. Over the last 10 years the north face of Pelón has been cut and burned. Now the other sides are under attack.

On Sierra Chincua there was evidence of illegal and sustained felling during the last year and a half, resulting in the disappearance of a critical habitat at the headwaters of Arroyo Zapatero, an area that has regularly been an overwintering location for monarchs. The loggers invaded Zapatero from the town of Senguio, stripped pines and oyamels from the southwest slopes of the arroyo, and carted them off in trucks. Until their disappearance these magnificent trees protected the monarchs from the winter winds and storms. The area is part of the core zone of the Monarch Butterfly Biosphere Reserve. This is yet another ecological atrocity perpetrated in the region where the monarch overwinters, and it makes plain that the current protection plan is not working. When is the government going to put an end to these violations of the law? Are predators and officials waiting until environmental deterioration has finished off the sanctuaries and the entire region is undergoing a permanent water crisis to take notice of the damage? As Lincoln Brower has stressed, the loss of the monarch overwintering sites will lead to the loss of the migratory phenomenon and the possible extinction of this species.

I grew up in Contepec, Michoacán, a site of one of the five sanctuaries protected by the 1986 decree. Back then, monarchs filled the streets every winter, and in the Llano de la Mula the oyamels were laden with butterflies. Now the monarchs stop briefly at Cerro Altamirano but do not stay. The oyamels still standing are infested, but neither authorities nor local residents are concerned. Yearly payments for "conservation activities" by the Monarch Fund, administered by the World Wide Fund for Nature (WWF), to the *ejidos* owning part of Cerro Altamirano—Ejido Contepec, Ejido Pueblo Nuevo Solís, and Ejido Cerritos Cárdenas—have been in vain, as the disastrous state of the forest reveals total neglect. The Ejido Contepec used this money (about 121,000 pesos [approximately $12,000] in 2003 and 2004) to build bridges and fix roadsides. The ejidos can use the money as they see fit, although it's supposedly given for conserving the forest. Contepec suffers from a chronic water shortage, but the mayor is more interested in creating a garbage dump in a dry stream bed adjoining a residential area than he is in protecting the town's principal natural asset: Cerro Altamirano.

Another threat is hanging over El Rosario, the most visited monarch sanctuary. Industrial Minera México, a subsidiary of Grupo México (owner of the Pasta de Conchos coal mine where 63 miners are still entombed*), is seeking the approval of the Secretariat of the Environment and Natural Resources (SEMARNAT) for the environmental impact assessment it submitted for underground mining of copper, silver, lead, zinc, and gold in the municipality of Angangueo, in the the buffer zone of the reserve. César Flores García, head of Michoacán's Secretariat of Urbanization and the Environment (SUMA), stated that mining would not harm the migratory phenomenon, and a former director of the reserve, Roberto Solís Calderón (now employed by SUMA), declared that "development is compatible with conservation of natural heritage." According to Solís, "The monarch is said to be ancestral, but nobody has been able to prove it; on the other hand, what has been proved is that as of 1975, a Canadian zoologist was able to locate the site of the monarch migration. There is nothing to tell us that there were monarch colonies before the twentieth century, and, when mining rights were established in the nineteenth century, the monarchs had not yet arrived." Dr. Brower affirms that the migratory phenomenon has existed for more than 10,000 years. Officials only speak about the underground operations,

---

*A horrific accident on February 19, 2006, caused a slow and agonizing death for the 65 miners trapped underground after a methane explosion. Two of the bodies have been found, but the owners of the mine, who have been blamed for a cynical disregard for safety conditions, say that the others are not recoverable.

omitting mention of a smelting plant where the gold will be extracted through chemical processes, nor do they consider the impacts on this basically rural region of a highly polluting industrial operation. Gold mining produces lakes of poison and springs of cyanide; large numbers of birds and other wildlife have died from cyanide poisoning associated with gold mining. The dangers of polluting groundwater with cyanide are real and serious, while the accumulation of mining waste also poses threats to the population and the environment. At the entrance to Angangueo there is still a pyramid of tailings left by the former owners of the mine, but no one seems worried about groundwater and soil contamination or the public health consequences, and much less about removing the tailings. The tailings contain arsenic, bromine, and lead. It's incredible, and immoral, that someone who has been in charge of the reserve would promote and defend an industrial project that will jeopardize the monarch's overwintering habitat.

On February 24, 2006, the Federal Attorney General's Office for Environmental Protection (PROFEPA), the Federal Preventive Police, and state police dismantled five sawmills and four storage yards, confiscating lumber—mostly oyamel—with a commercial value of one million pesos (91,550 dollars). The illegal operations were located in the communities of La Cumbre, Macho de Agua, and La Dieta, all part of the town of Crescencio Morales, in the municipality of Zitácuaro, a region notorious for its logger gangs. The curious thing about this crackdown is that it took nearly 12 hours but no arrests were made, as though nobody knew who owned the sawmills.

The environment is one of the sacrificial victims of the current electoral process; neither butterflies nor trees vote, but loggers and members of organized crime do. So far, the presidential candidates have shone by their lack of an environmental agenda, showing blindness or contempt for the main element in the fight against poverty and for the future of Mexicans: a healthy environment, which can only be achieved by halting deforestation and uncontrolled development and guaranteeing enough water for a population that will soon reach 110,000,000, just as thirsty as the monarch butterfly.

UPDATE: As Mexico's ambassador to UNESCO, in 2008 I lobbied the ambassadors of the twenty-one countries sitting on the World Heritage Committee to vote in favor of adding the monarch butterfly sanctuary to the World Heritage List. The International Union for the Conservation of Nature had recommended postponing the nomination until the committee's next meeting in 2009 for the following reasons: the boundaries of the core zone are not clearly demarcated; insufficient actions are being taken to halt illegal logging; there is a need to work "with local communities on environmental protection and alternative livelihoods to logging"; and a plan for nature-based tourism must be developed. I was successful, and the vote was unanimous in favor of declaring the Monarch Butterfly Biosphere Reserve a World Heritage Site.

On February 4–5, 2010, after several days of unusually heavy rains, torrents of water and landslides surged into Angangueo, flooding the central plaza, destroying buildings, carrying away vehicles, and burying parts of town. In the muddy debris flow thick with boulders and logs, more than thirty people lost their lives and thousands were left homeless. Delfino Cruz Guzmán, former commissioner of the El Rosario ejido, was among the dead. The scope of the disaster was magnified by deforestation, pathways dug near water flows, and, above all, mine tailings and waste in rivers and streams.

During the 2011–12 overwintering season, the ten monarch butterfly colonies in the reserve occupied 2.89 hectares (7.14 acres) of forest, a decrease of 28.11 percent from the 4.02 hectares (9.93 acres) occupied during the 2010–11 season.

The Winter of the Monarch

Lincoln P. Brower and HA, *New York Times*, March 15, 2013

In the village of Contepec, in Michoacán, a few hours northwest of Mexico City, every winter day rivers of orange and black butterflies would stream through the streets in search of water, swooping down from the oyamel fir forest on Altamirano Hill. One of us, Homero, grew up with the monarch butterflies. The other, Lincoln, saw them for the first time in 1977, also in Michoacán, on a mountain called Sierra Chincua, where the branches of hundreds of fir trees were covered with butterflies that exploded into glorious flight when warmed by the sun.

Today the winter monarch colonies, which are found west of Mexico City in an area of about 60 miles by 60 miles, are a pitiful remnant of their former splendor. The aggregate area covered by the colonies dwindled from an average of 22 acres between 1994 and 2003 to 12 acres between 2003 and 2012. This year's area, which was reported on Wednesday, hit a record low of 2.9 acres.

Reasons for the decline are multiple, including out-of-control ecotourism, extreme weather and diversion of water. Two threats loom above all others: the destruction of breeding habitat in the United States because of the widespread use of powerful herbicides and genetically engineered crops, and illegal logging in Mexico's high-elevation oyamel fir forests.

Deforestation has always been a dark shadow lurking in these beautiful mountains, and it has never been adequately dealt with by the Mexican government. In the 1980s, horrified television viewers watched footage of loggers armed with chain saws felling trees covered with butterflies and log-laden trucks crushing butterflies as they drove down the mountains. That led to the establishment, in 1986, of the Monarch Butterfly Special Biosphere Reserve, within which logging was outlawed. But still it continued.

In recent years news releases from Mexico based on aerial imagery have claimed that illegal logging inside the reserve has been reduced to virtually zero. But these reports are incomplete and misleading, as they measure only visible deforestation in the core zone of the reserve, about a fourth of the protected 217-square-mile area. Forest loss in the surrounding areas is not reported, nor is the magnitude of local logging, in which individual trees are removed from the core area. This "selective cutting" is not visible in the aerial imagery, and yet it alters the forest microclimate and increases monarch butterflies' risks of starving and freezing.

Ecotourism is presenting an additional threat to the butterflies as its popularity increases. As regular visitors to the monarch colonies, we have seen the conditions in these areas deteriorate, for butterflies and tourists. Along the heavily used trails that lead to the colonies in Piedra Herrada and Sierra Chincua, extensive areas of vegetation have been killed. Excessive dust, which now rises into the air with each step, is hazardous to the butterflies because it clogs their respiratory orifices. When we visited the Piedra Herrada site this February, along with former President Jimmy Carter, a welcome sign on the trail leading to the butterflies read, "No more than 20 people in the Sanctuary." And yet we counted 24 tourist buses in the parking lot.

So what can be done? Ecotourism is an important part of the local economy, but we must make sure that its costs in habitat degradation and increased butterfly mortality don't kill the goose that lays the golden egg. The Mexican government has made strides in reducing much—but not all—illegal logging and needs to do more. The United States, for its part, should re-examine the extent to which industrialized herbicide-based agriculture is destroying the flora in the Midwestern United States that monarchs depend on in the spring and summer. In addition to all of this, we simply need better data on the butterflies.

Measuring the size, location, and survival rate of each colony that winters in Mexico is the responsibility of the World Wildlife Fund Mexico and the staff of the Monarch Butterfly Biosphere Reserve. Sites are measured in December, and the total areas in each of the major locations are reported, usually in February or March. But, although WWF Mexico has more specific data, the published reports are not detailed enough to allow scientists to review the status of individual colonies or to evaluate the butterflies' survival in relation to forest condition. WWF Mexico must release data on where the butterflies roost each year, whether each colony is increasing or decreasing in size, and what the mortality rates are at each site.

If some are doing better than others, we must learn why. If, as we fear, all are diminishing, then we should ask why the current management plans, both in Mexico and in the United States, are failing.

We are fortunate to have experienced the magnificent overwintering phenomenon over more than three decades. We hope that better stewardship will allow the monarch butterflies to continue to festoon the oyamel forests of Mexico for generations to come.

Last Call for Monarchs

HA, *World Post/Huffington Post*, February 7, 2014

MEXICO CITY—Every winter of my childhood in Contepec, Michoacán, millions of orange and black monarch butterflies magically arrived to the oyamel fir forest at the summit of Altamirano Hill. When the sun was out, rivers of butterflies would stream through the streets in search of water. Altamirano was one of the five mountain ranges protected by the original 1986 decree that created the Monarch Butterfly Special Biosphere Reserve, for which I had petitioned Mexican President Miguel de la Madrid. In 2000, another decree enlarged the reserve's size and added protection for more butterfly colony sites.

I was born in 1940 and grew up with (and wrote about) the monarchs, but it was only in 1975 that their overwintering forests in central Mexico's Transvolcanic Belt were "discovered" by Canadian scientists.

On January 29, news was released of a dramatic plunge in the monarch butterfly population that overwinters in Mexico after flying thousands of miles south from the northern and eastern United States and southern Canada. This season's population, calculated by measuring the area of occupied trees, covers a tiny 0.67 hectares [1.66 acres]—the smallest ever since these measurements began 20 years ago—and a huge drop from the 1996 high of 21 hectares [52 acres]. The population has plummeted from an estimated 1 billion in 1996 to 33 million this year, scattered over seven sites. There have been no monarchs in Contepec for years.

In the past, most of the blame for the steady decline in monarch numbers has been placed on logging in the core and buffer zones of the reserve, out-of-control tourism and devastating climate events such as the 2002 storms in Michoacán or the severe 2011 drought in Texas. Now, it has become all too apparent that industrial agriculture in the U.S. Corn Belt (and less in Canada) is largely responsible for the dizzying drop in butterfly numbers. In the last decade there has been a huge increase in additional land planted with corn to satisfy the demand for federally mandated corn-based ethanol.

The main culprits are the herbicides relentlessly applied to genetically modified corn and soybean plants (grown from Monsanto's Roundup Ready seeds, among others) that guarantee sterile fields where only the engineered crops are allowed to flourish. Ninety-three percent of total soybean acreage in the United States is now herbicide tolerant (HT), while 85 percent of corn is HT. Graphs show an alarming correlation between increased planting of HT crops and dwindling monarch populations, for milkweed—the only plant on which adult monarch butterflies lay their eggs and the only one the hatched larvae (caterpillars) will eat after devouring their own eggshells—is a main victim of these deadly glyphosate herbicides.

Common milkweed (*Asclepias syriaca*), so named for the sticky white sap that oozes from broken stalks, branches, or leaves, is a summer-blooming perennial pollinated by insects such as bees, butterflies, moths or ants that land on the fragrant pinkish-purple flowers to suck the sweet nectar. The sap itself is toxic, and when the monarch larvae feed on the leaves, they become toxic to monarch butterfly predators.

Until now the Mexican government has denied that the monarch butterfly migratory phenomenon is in jeopardy, despite warnings since the 1990s from preeminent monarch expert Lincoln Brower, but for the first time has acknowledged the possibility of its disappearance.

When I was Mexico's ambassador to UNESCO and lobbied representatives of the 21 countries on the World Heritage Committee to vote in favor of including the Monarch Butterfly Biosphere Reserve on the World Heritage List, my colleagues from the United States and Canada were reluctant to do so, alleging opposition from their governments. They finally did give their votes, as a personal favor to me, along with the other 19, and the reserve is now listed.

During negotiations for the inclusion of the environment in the North American Free Trade Agreement, as head of the environmentalist group the Group of 100, I proposed the adoption of the monarch butterfly as the ideal symbol of tri-national interdependence and cooperation. Now, on the 20th anniversary of NAFTA, I (and all who cherish the monarch butterfly) am urging Presidents Enrique Peña Nieto and Barack Obama and Prime Minister Stephen Harper to put monarch survival on the agenda of their February 19–20 summit meeting in Toluca, in the State of Mexico, a scant 30 miles from the Piedra Herrada monarch colony at San Mateo Almomoloa.

To make up for the vast loss of grasslands to crops and urban development, we need a milkweed corridor stretching along the entire migratory route of the monarch—with plantings on roadsides, in fields and ditches, along railroad tracks, in pastures and meadows and gardens, in parks and public spaces—so that successive generations of monarchs can breed during their journey north. An abundance of nectar patches with flowering plants for the great-grandchildren of the previous year's butterflies to feed on as they fly southward to Mexico should not be so difficult to arrange.

The decline in monarch population since 1994 coincides with the NAFTA years. If our three countries cannot prevent the extraordinary monarch butterfly migratory phenomenon from disappearing, then what's the point of this agreement?

We cannot allow the monarch butterfly to figure in the coming era of extinctions.

A Milkweed-Butterfly Recovery Alliance

This letter was delivered to the ambassadors of the United States and Canada in Mexico and to President Peña Nieto. Dr. Ernest H. Williams provided the graphs that follow the letter (see below), and they accompanied the letter sent to each leader and to the press.

14 February 2014

President Barack Obama
President Enrique Peña Nieto
Prime Minister Stephen Harper

Honorable Gentlemen:

Decline of the Monarch Butterfly Migration in Eastern North America.

Among the countless organisms that have evolved during the history of life on earth, monarch butterflies are among the most extraordinary. Sadly, their unique multigenerational migration across our large continent, their spectacular overwintering aggregations on the volcanic mountains in central Mexico, and their educational value to children in Canada, the United States, and Mexico are all threatened. Monitoring of the butterfly population over the past two decades indicates a grim situation. Following a long-term decline, the total area occupied by the overwintering butterflies plunged from the 20-year average of 6.7 hectares to a record low of 0.67 hectares in the current season, a 90 percent decrease. This winter, only seven of twelve traditional sites had any butterflies at all, and only one of those (El Rosario, 0.5 hectares) was substantial in size.

The decline has two main causes:

1. Loss of breeding habitat. The major summer breeding area of the monarch butterfly is in the floristically rich grasslands of central North America, where the monarch's milkweed foodplants grow in abundance. However, over the past decade the planting of corn and soybean varieties that have been genetically modified to be herbicide

resistant has risen to 90 percent. Shortly after the corn or soy seeds germinate, the fields are sprayed with herbicides that kill all other plant life including the milkweeds, the only plants that monarch caterpillars can eat. Furthermore, with economic incentives for producing corn ethanol, the planting of corn in the U.S. has expanded from 78 million acres in 2006 to 97 million acres in 2013. Fallow fields, row crops and roadsides that used to support the growth of milkweeds and substantial acreage of land previously set aside in the U.S. Conservation Reserve Program have been converted to monoculture crops. Further loss of habitat has resulted from urban sprawl and development. More generally, the current chemical-intensive agriculture is threatening monarchs and other native pollinators and unraveling the fabric of our ecosystems.

2. Degradation of overwintering habitat. Overwintering monarchs depend on the protective cover of undisturbed oyamel fir forest canopy in Mexico. While the Mexican government has largely stopped the major illegal logging that threatened the forests used by the wintering monarch butterflies, damaging small scale illegal logging continues.

What can be done? If the monarch butterfly migration and overwintering phenomenon is to persist in eastern North America, mitigation of breeding habitat loss must be initiated. As Mexico is addressing the logging issues, so now must the United States and Canada address the effects of our current agricultural policies. Managing roadsides for native plants, including milkweeds, could be a significant tool to partially offset the loss of habitat. There are 3.2 million miles of roads east of the Rocky Mountains. If 25-foot roadside strips and medians were managed to support the growth of milkweeds, then eastern U.S. roadsides could contribute more than 19 million acres of milkweed habitat. If two monarchs were produced per acre of habitat, then these roadsides could produce nearly 40 million monarchs, i.e., about one-tenth of the 20-year average number of monarch butterflies overwintering in Mexico. Within the agricultural heartland, a second mitigation effort should promote more extensive buffers of native plant communities at field margins. Collaborative exclusion of field margins in cooperation with farming communities could add substantially and help assure the continuation of the world's most revered butterfly. An incentive program to pay farmers to set aside toxin-free areas for milkweeds and pollinators could be a move in the right direction.

A milkweed corridor stretching along the entire migratory route of the monarch butterfly through our three countries must be established. This will show the political will of our governments to save the living symbol of the North American Free Trade Agreement. We the undersigned hope that you will discuss the future of the monarch butterfly during the North American leaders' Summit that will take place on February 19–20, 2014 in Toluca, State of Mexico.

Sincerely yours,

Homero Aridjis
President, Grupo de los Cien, Mexico

Dr. Lincoln P. Brower
Sweet Briar College, USA

Dr. Gary Paul Nabhan
Co-Facilitator, Make Way for Monarchs

Dr. Ernest H. Williams
Hamilton College, USA

[For the complete list of signers, see Appendix B.]

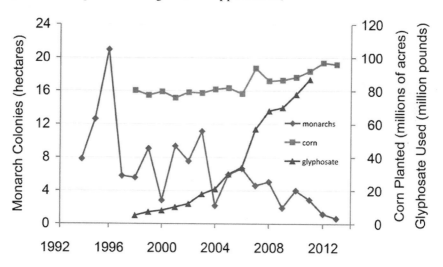

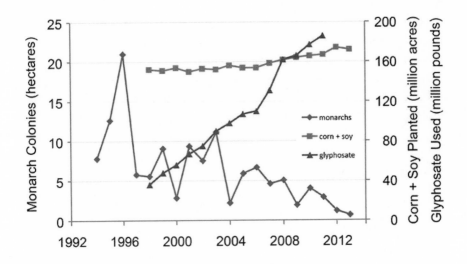

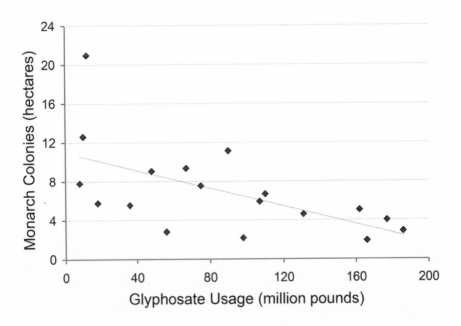

UPDATE: Our letter addressed to Presidents Obama and Peña Nieto and Prime Minister Harper received excellent coverage in the Mexican and international media, and we were successful in getting the monarch butterfly on the North American Leaders' Summit agenda.

Here is the relevant paragraph from the joint statement released at the end of the February 19 meeting in Mexico: "We will continue to collaborate in the protection of our region's biodiversity and to address other environmental challenges, such as wildlife trafficking and ecosystems at risk. Our governments will establish a working group to ensure the conservation of the Monarch butterfly, a species that symbolizes our association."

Now we will be working on the creation of a milkweed corridor along the monarch's migratory route through Canada, the United States, and Mexico.

On January 12, 2017, the EPA announced that it has authorized spraying of Dow AgroScience's Enlist Duo glyphosate and 2,4-D herbicide on genetically modified corn, cotton, and soybean crops in thirty-four states. Monsanto is now marketing its latest threat to monarchs: Roundup Ready 2 Xtend. California is issuing the world's first health guideline for Roundup Ready based on its cancer risk. The state's proposed safe level is more than 100 times lower than the EPA legal allowance. In March 2015, the World Health Organization's International Agency for Research on Cancer determined that glyphosate is "probably carcinogenic" to people.

40 Years Ago the World "Discovered" Mexico's Monarch Habitat; Today Its Survival Is at Stake

HA, *World Post/Huffington Post*, January 20, 2015

Mexico City—Forty years ago the winter habitat of the monarch butterfly in Mexico was supposedly discovered. After searching for decades, on January 9, 1975 the Canadian scientist Fred A. Urquhart, an entomologist at the University of Toronto's Scarborough College, received a phone call from an American living in Mexico City named Kenneth Brugger, married at the time to Mexican-born Cathy Aguado (known today as Catalina Trail), who told him that "We have located the colony. We have found them—millions of monarchs—in evergreens beside a mountain clearing."

The "discovery" had taken place a week earlier in northern Michoacán, in an oyamel forest on Cerro Pelón, 10,000 feet up in the mountains of Mexico's Transvolcanic Belt, and a few days later the Bruggers happened upon other monarch roosts at El Rosario and Chincua. The Bruggers were volunteer "research associates" in Urquhart's long-standing monarch tagging program, in which tiny labels reading "Send to Zoology University Toronto Canada" were stuck onto thousands of southbound migrating butterflies.

But it was only a year after receiving the news that Urquhart and his wife visited the site, and a full 20 months after the find that a stunning photo of Cathy Brugger amidst thousands of monarch butterflies perched on trees and on her, and the headline "Discovered: The Monarch's Mexican Haven" were emblazoned on the cover of the August 1976 issue of *National Geographic*.

In his article, Urquhart did not reveal the location of the monarch sites the Bruggers had told him about. When asked for details by Dr. Lincoln Brower, today the world's foremost monarch butterfly expert, and colleague Dr. William Calvert, Urquhart steered them to a bay on the Gulf Coast of Florida. Brower, Calvert and photographer John Christian figured out the general area from some clues in Urquhart's article and a paper he published in the *Journal of the Lepidopterists' Society*, and they located the sanctuaries on New Year's Eve of 1976.

Urquhart affirmed that "Cathy Brugger and her husband Kenneth discovered the site where millions rendezvous." This undisputed claim that has been widely repeated in the Canadian, U.S. and Mexican media would lead one to believe that the overwintering sites of the monarch butterfly in Mexico were unknown to Mexicans before the Bruggers made their call to Urquhart.

This January, as the 40th anniversary of the "discovery" is commemorated, isn't it time to revise the telling of history? What date should we put on the discovery—that generations of Mexicans have made for themselves—of a phenomenon that has been taking place for thousands of years?

We local residents always knew where the monarchs settled at the end of October, but we had no idea where they had come from, nor where they went each spring. The Canadian and American lepidopterists knew that. Just as the discovery of America is a misnomer—because America had been discovered ever since it was inhabited by human beings, and what Columbus so momentously initiated was a meeting of two worlds—so we can say that what occurred in January 1975 was a mutual enlightenment for people at both ends of the fabulous 3,000-mile-long migration of the monarch butterfly.

In celebration of the arrival every autumn of millions of monarchs to Altamirano Hill and the streets of Contepec, the village in Michoacán where I grew up, I wrote in the autobiographical *El poeta niño* (The Child Poet), published in 1971: "That morning thousands of monarch butterflies were crossing the village. The air, like a river, bore currents of butterflies. Through the streets, above the houses, between the trees and people they made their way south."

I have said and written many times that the presence of the monarchs in my town is part of my childhood memories (I was born in 1940), and I have described the yearly pilgrimages made by Contepec's residents to the Plain of the Mule on the summit of Altamirano to picnic and glory in the spectacle.

"Blanketing a thousand trees, monarchs converge in November on a mountain slope at 9,000 feet," wrote Urquhart 40 years ago. In *La montaña de las mariposas* (Butterfly Mountain), I marveled at the abundance of butterflies we observed during a school trip in the 1950s: "The monarchs were there, a million-strong colony in the sun-swept patches of the ancient crater." I return to these memories as if to a lost world.

In 1996, the butterfly population in the Monarch Butterfly Biosphere Reserve was estimated at one billion, occupying 21 hectares [5 acres] of forest. The 2013–14 population plummeted to 33 million, covering 0.67 hectares [1.66 acres], the lowest ever in the 20 years since measuring and counting began.

The main culprit for this precipitous decline is no longer logging in the reserve (although that still takes place) but the huge increase in land planted with genetically modified, herbicide resistant soybean and corn crops (93 percent of total soybean acreage and 85 percent of corn acreage in 2013) in the U.S. Corn Belt. Relentless spraying of glyphosate herbicides on the fields has destroyed the once abundant milkweed, the only plants that monarch caterpillars can eat. The monarch butterfly is literally being starved to death.

Before Christmas, I visited Sierra Chincua and learned that butterflies were on less than half a hectare of trees. On Dec. 29, on national television news, an official in charge of the Piedra Herrada sanctuary said that fewer than 30 trees had monarch clusters. Ejidatarios, the locals who own the land, told me the monarchs were sparse this year. In El Rosario, the butterflies were scattered, either very high up or in the ravines. Climate change is a threat throughout the monarchs' migratory route, and an unusual number of cold fronts hitting the area this year is worrying. The day after the news report, the director of the Reserve was quoted by AP as feeling "encouraged, because we've seen more." Monarch enthusiasts are anxiously awaiting release by WWF [World Wide Fund for Nature] Mexico and the Reserve of this year's winter colonies count to learn how things stand, and scientists are eager to have access to the hard data.

Meanwhile, in the wake of last year's bad news, there has been an upsurge in home planting of milkweed in the United States, but unfortunately much of it has been tropical milkweed (*Asclepias curassavica*), identified by Brower and scientists such as Dara Satterfield as a direct threat to the monarchs because it does not die back in the winter, allowing butterflies to halt their migration and breed all year round, thus making them more susceptible to the deadly protozoan parasite *Ophryocystis elektroscirrha*.

Native milkweed, specific to each part of the country, is what individuals should be planting, while we wait for action on a larger scale in the United States by the High Level Federal Monarch Working Group, which includes the Forest Service, the National Park Service, the Bureau of Land Management, the Federal Highway Administration, the Natural Resource Conservation Service, and other agencies, as well as entomologists Karen Oberhauser and Scott Hoffman Black.

The challenge is no less than restoration of millions of acres of monarch habitat.

The survival of the monarch butterfly migration will depend on measures taken in Canada, the United States and Mexico. As the U.S. Fish and Wildlife Service [USFWS] said in its December 29, 2014 response to a petition from the Center for Biological Diversity, the Center for Food Safety, the Xerces Society and Lincoln Brower, "This journey has become more perilous for many monarchs because of threats along their migratory path and on their breeding and wintering grounds."

USFWS announced it will conduct a status review of the monarch butterfly to consider listing it as a threatened species under the Endangered Species Act.

The three NAFTA leaders will meet in Canada later this year. At last year's summit in Mexico, in reply to our letter from scientists, writers and artists from around the world, the so-called "Tres Amigos" agreed to cooperate "to ensure the conservation of the Monarch butterfly, a species that symbolizes our association."

And I am left wondering if the monarch colonies will ever return to Altamirano Hill in Contepec, where they have been absent for years.

UPDATE: Regarding the petition by the Center for Biological Diversity, the Center for Food Safety, the Xerces Society, and Lincoln Brower, the U.S. Fish and Wildlife Service is now legally bound to make a decision by June 2019 as to whether the monarch butterfly will receive protection under the Endangered Species Act.

Endangered Monarch Butterflies Face Their Greatest Threat High in the Hills of Central Mexico

HA, *World Post/Huffington Post*, May 4, 2016

The monarch butterfly is now facing a potentially lethal threat to its over-wintering habitat in Mexico's oyamel fir forests.

As if it weren't enough for the migratory butterfly to contend with illegal logging in the Monarch Butterfly Biosphere Reserve, it is also facing severe depletion of the milkweed, which is indispensable for its development from egg into butterfly, caused by ever-increasing use of herbicides on genetically engineered corn and soybean crops in the American corn belt.

Extreme weather events, including drought and storms, and the unpredictable consequences of climate change are also taking their toll. Now, Grupo Mexico, Mexico's largest mining corporation, has been awarded a concession to reopen an old mine in Angangueo in the state of Michoacán, a town in the heart of the monarch reserve, that was closed 25 years ago. The company intends to mine copper, zinc, lead, silver and gold.

In April 2005, a subsidiary of Grupo Mexico filed an environmental impact assessment [EIA] for the mining project with the Secretariat of Environment and Natural Resources, also known as SEMARNAT. Michoacán's secretary for urbanism and the environment declared that mining would have no impact on the monarch migration, and a former head of the monarch reserve insisted that development is compatible with conservation, that no one can prove monarch colonies over-wintered in the area when the mining concessions were granted at the end of the 19th century.

The EIA was grossly inadequate. There was no prior consultation with affected groups, no public diffusion of information, no evaluation of the hydrologic impacts of the mine and no risk analysis or mention of risks for the human population. The EIA was only for a specific site and not regional, as is required by law, since the Reserve is part of the Lerma and Balsas Rivers watersheds and is defined as a priority hydrologic region. In order to obtain the resources, mining will extract large volumes of water from the subsoil and expel it outside the area being worked—but there is no mention in the EIA of the substantial impacts of this process.

In 2010, heavy rains led to disastrous flooding in Angangueo, destroying houses and taking lives. The mine tailings left behind when the mine closed magnified the damage. Residues of arsenic, bromine, lead, barium, cadmium, chrome and mercury have been found in Angangueo's water, and iron levels in the soil far exceed official norms. The EIA does not evaluate potential levels of toxicity from the production of sulfuric acid.

A toxic spill in August 2014 at a Grupo Mexico copper mine in the northwestern state of Sonora was labeled by the head of SEMARNAT as the Mexican mining sector's worst environmental disaster in recent history. Nearly 11 million gallons of copper sulfate spewed into the Bacanuchi and Sonora Rivers. Hundreds of miles of waterways and the water supply for 24,000 people were contaminated with copper, arsenic, aluminum, cadmium, chromium, iron, manganese and lead.

The National Water Commission blamed negligence on the part of the company, but Grupo Mexico falsely claimed the spill was caused by unexpected heavy rains that raised the level in a holding tank at the mine. It wasn't Grupo Mexico's only disaster. In February 2006, 65 workers were killed in an explosion at Grupo Mexico's Pasta de Conchos mine in the state of Coahuila. Sixty-three bodies still remain underground, and the Mexican Attorney General's office has stated that the statute of limitations for prosecuting those responsible has expired. Pasta de Conchos was run by Grupo Mexico subsidiary Industrial Minera de México, the company that owns the Angangueo mine.

In February, the governor of Michoacán met with Grupo Mexico representatives to discuss the benefits the mining project would generate, like creating jobs and increasing tourism. Angangueo's mayor has said that Industrial Minera de México is already at work in town. The reserve's management program allows for mining if all rules and regulations are complied with. However, as there is no precedent for exposing over-wintering monarch butterflies to a major mining operation, there are no studies to draw on, and so the EIA does not address the inevitable consequences to the butterflies. Water is vital for the monarch during its over-wintering in the reserve. If the mine is reopened, the impacts will become known but doubtless it will be too late for the monarchs.

Last fall, frightened local residents called me to denounce widespread illegal logging that went on unchecked from April through August 2015 on Sierra Chincua, one of the two main overwintering sites. I immediately notified Dr. Lincoln Brower, the world's preeminent expert on monarch butterflies. Brower and other scientists have since written an important and conclusive report on illegal logging on 10 hectares [24.7 acres] of forest in the Sierra Chincua monarch butterfly over-wintering area that will be the feature article in the June 2016 issue of the journal *American Entomologist*. They write: "With satellite imagery and drone photographs, we documented the location and extent of illegal logging during 2015 in what should have been one of the most protected areas within the Monarch Butterfly Biosphere Reserve in Mexico. Severe logging of 10 hectares took place from April to August. This questions the effectiveness of current strategies to protect the already precarious overwintering habitat of the monarch butterfly in eastern North America."

Curiously, the logging took place in a parcel of land belonging to the state of Michoacán, the only state-owned parcel in the entire reserve, and not in any of the neighboring communally owned *ejidos*.

On March 10 and 11, heavy rain, wind and a severe snowstorm hit the reserve, knocking down trees and tearing off roofs in neighboring towns. Officials were quick to deny any substantial harm to the monarchs. Preliminary studies by Brower and others point to a mortality rate as high as 50 percent. The investigation has been hampered by limited access to the affected areas, especially at El Rosario.

About a week after the storm a fire was deliberately set near the El Rosario site to put pressure on the reserve's acting director to authorize so-called salvage logging, presumably to remove trees after natural disturbances. Recent photos show that salvage logging has been taking place at the El Rosario site, where an alarming quantity of wood has been removed, with all the destructive impacts this process implies. There is no reliable way of telling which trees were salvaged and which were cut down illegally, as all the logging appears to have been done at once, a convenient scheme for tree laundering. There has also been salvage logging on Sierra Chincua.

In March, the Center for Food Safety and the Center for Biological Diversity filed a lawsuit against the U.S. Fish and Wildlife Service, charging the agency with failing to protect monarch butterflies under the Endangered Species Act. A recent scientific study predicts that the migratory monarch could become extinct within the next 20 years, largely due to the herbicide-resistant, genetically engineered corn and soybeans that make up 90 percent of these crops grown in the United States.

I grew up in Contepec, Michoacán, where millions of monarchs used to arrive every winter. But they no longer do. In 1986 I asked President Miguel de la Madrid to establish the Monarch Butterfly Special Biosphere Reserve, which he did. In 2008, as Mexico's ambassador to UNESCO, I convinced the 21 members of the World Heritage Committee to declare the reserve a World Heritage site.

But now I fear that the extraordinary monarch butterfly migration may not withstand the combined onslaughts of extreme weather, milkweed-killing herbicide use, illegal logging, mining, and corruption.

Dear Obama, Trudeau, and Peña Nieto: Act Now to Save the Monarch Butterfly

HA, *World Post/Huffington Post*, June 17, 2016. The letter was delivered to the ambassadors of the United States and Canada in Mexico and to President Peña Nieto on June 13 and 14

More than 200 scientists, writers and artists have signed a letter addressed to Mexican President Enrique Peña Nieto, U.S. President Barack Obama and Canadian Prime Minister Justin Trudeau in advance of the North American Leaders' Summit in Ottawa later this month.

The signers urge that swift and energetic actions be taken to save the monarch butterfly from the threats that endanger its survival. All three countries must work together to mitigate the loss of the butterflies' breeding habitat and to terminate all logging and mining in the Monarch Butterfly Biosphere Reserve in Michoacán and the State of Mexico.

President Barack Obama
President Enrique Peña Nieto
Prime Minister Justin Trudeau

Honorable Gentlemen:

At the North American Leaders' Summit held in Toluca, Mexico, on February 19, 2014, President Barack Obama, President Enrique Peña Nieto and Prime Minister Stephen Harper made the following commitment in their joint closing statement: "Our governments will establish a working group to ensure the conservation of the Monarch butterfly, a species that symbolizes our association."

The three heads of state were responding to the deep concern expressed in a letter signed by several hundred international monarch experts, scientists, writers and artists; the letter urged these leaders to address the future of the monarch butterfly and recommended the creation of a recognized breeding corridor along the monarch's migratory route through Canada, the United States and Mexico. High Level Monarch Working Groups were then established in each country; national and trinational meetings are being held; and research and monitoring of monarchs have continued.

Conservation activities to protect the monarch butterfly are underway in all three countries, but the need for effective action has become even more critical. Earlier this year, a group of scientists predicted that "the Eastern migratory population has a substantial probability of quasi-extinction," warning that this population must increase to at least 225 million to reduce the risk of extinction by half and to prevent the loss of a viable migratory population. The overwintering abundance of monarchs has shown a 20-year decline from 900 million in 1996–97 to 33 million in 2013–14. Although optimal weather conditions on the migratory route enabled the population to recover to 140 million during the winter of 2015–16, a severe and unusually late March storm reduced this winter's abundance by up to 50 percent, illustrating the risk to survival of a diminished monarch migratory phenomenon.

In the U.S., a June 2014 Presidential Memorandum established a Pollinator Health Task Force, and the Task Force launched the National Strategy to Promote the Health of Honey Bees and Other Pollinators on May 19, 2015. One of the stated goals of the Strategy is to "increase the Eastern population of the monarch butterfly to 225 million butterflies occupying an area of 6 hectares in the overwintering grounds in Mexico, through domestic/international actions and public-private partnerships, by 2020."

A principal cause of the 90 percent plunge in monarch numbers over the last 20 years is the massive use of glyphosate herbicides on land in the U.S. corn belt planted with genetically modified herbicide-resistant soybean and corn crops. Extensive spraying of these crops in the major summer breeding area of these butterflies has decimated milkweed, which is the only food plant that monarch caterpillars can eat. New-generation crops are being developed to resist additional herbicides, so the threat to milkweeds is increasing.

Concern about declining milkweed habitat led to a petition being submitted to the U.S. Fish and Wildlife Service on August 26, 2014, requesting that the monarch butterfly be listed as threatened under the U.S. Endangered Species Act. The petition described the urgent need for federal protection; consideration of the petition is underway.

In April 2015, Mexican (Grupo de los Cien, Alternare, Danaidas, Conservación y Desarrollo Sustentable, Costasalvaje and Telar Social México), American (Natural Resources Defense Council), and Canadian (David Suzuki Foundation) groups formally petitioned UNESCO's World Heritage Committee to list the Monarch Butterfly Biosphere Reserve World Heritage Site on the List of World Heritage Sites in Danger. In a letter to the World Heritage Centre, pollinator and monarch scientists endorsed the petition and asked that Mexico, the United States and Canada strengthen collaborative efforts to protect and restore monarch habitat.

In Mexico, degradation of the overwintering sites continues despite official assurances that illegal logging is under control. Recently, scientists have confirmed that 10 hectares [25 acres] of mature forest on land belonging to the state of Michoacán were severely logged in 2015. Observers have also found small-scale logging in the Reserve, with both forms of logging damaging the protective forest canopy.

Furthermore, an unusually severe snow and rain storm in March 2016 blew down numerous oyamel fir and pine trees. A week later, the Reserve's acting director authorized salvage logging; subsequent photographs have shown that salvage logging has seriously degraded the forest floor. In contrast, allowing protected areas to regenerate naturally is a preferable management option to salvage logging for this rich oyamel fir-pine ecosystem. Continuing logging activities underscore the need for enforcing year-round protection of the forest throughout the Reserve.

Monarchs are facing a new potentially lethal threat to their overwintering habitat. In 2007, the SEMARNAT [Secretariat of Environment and Natural Resources] awarded Grupo Mexico, Mexico's largest mining corporation, a concession to reopen an old mine in Angangueo, to mine copper, zinc, lead, silver and gold beneath the core zone of the Reserve. The mining process will extract large volumes of water from the subsoil and expel it outside the area being worked, but water is vital for overwintering monarchs and for maintaining the surrounding forest ecosystem. There is no precedent for exposing overwintering monarch butterflies to a major mining operation, and the Environmental Impact Assessment does not address the inevitable harmful consequences to the butterflies, which are the reason for existence of the Monarch Butterfly Biosphere Reserve.

The three North American heads of state will meet on June 29, 2016, in Ottawa, their first joint meeting since 2014. We, the undersigned scientists, writers, artists and concerned citizens, call upon President Enrique Peña Nieto, President Barack Obama and Prime Minister Justin Trudeau to take swift and energetic actions to preserve the monarch's migratory phenomenon. Success will require activity within all three countries: mitigation of the loss of breeding habitat due to milkweed-killing herbicide usage by protecting parcels of land with milkweeds and native nectar sources; termination of all logging in the Monarch Butterfly Biosphere Reserve; and a prohibition of mining in the Reserve. Leadership responding to these challenges is crucial; monarch butterflies are among the most extraordinary and iconic creatures on the planet, beloved by many, and they represent a fundamental connection of our three countries.

Sincerely yours,

Homero Aridjis—Writer; President, Grupo de los Cien; Former Mexican Ambassador to Switzerland, The Netherlands, and UNESCO; President Emeritus, PEN International; Member, High Level Monarch Working Group (Mexico)

Professor Lincoln P. Brower—Research Professor of Biology, Sweet Briar College; Distinguished Service Professor of Zoology Emeritus, University of Florida

Professor Ernest H. Williams—William R. Kenan Professor Emeritus of Biology, Dept. of Biology, Hamilton College

[For the complete list of signers, see Appendix C.]

UPDATE: In August 2016, the head of the National Commission for Protected Natural Areas (CONANP) declared that reopening the Angangueo mine would be "catastrophic" for the monarchs, admitting, however, that CONANP's opinion is nonbinding.

The number of monarchs overwintering in Mexico during the 2016–2017 season dropped by 27 percent, compared to last year's count. At a June 2017

Monarch Expert Meeting convened by the U.S. Fish and Wildlife Service, scientists Lincoln P. Brower and Pablo Jaramillo-López attributed the continuing decline of the butterflies to "forest degradation through illegal logging in Mexico . . . rapid increase of herbicide-resistant GMO corn and soybean crops in the midwestern USA that has eliminated an estimated 860 million milkweeds in thirteen midwestern states between 1999 and 2014, a decline of 40 percent from the original 2.2 billion milkweeds, and climate change." Addressing issues of collaborative research, they lament that "one research team is solely responsible for collecting most of the annually published data on the overwintering colonies" in a "near scientific monopoly [which] means that many crucial questions about forest and colony health remain unanswered. . . . A new procedure is needed to estimate butterfly density. . . . World Wildlife Fund and CONANP do not publish sufficiently complete yearly data. . . . It would be especially useful to know the year-by-year GPS locations of all the colonies. . . . Arrival and departure dates of the butterflies are currently not reported. . . . Complete GPS data are recorded each year but are usually not made available to scientific researchers." Mentioning that "most tourists access the colonies via horseback," and highlighting the damage to the forest floor caused by high foot traffic, they stress the need "to estimate an ecologically safe number of tourists that can be allowed to visit each sanctuary." As regards reforestation, "Currently there are multiple reforestation projects taking place in the Reserve. Unfortunately there is limited coordination among these efforts and no consensus about the best practices for intervening in this fragile ecosystem. We believe that all the reforestation programs should be carried out according to a master plan. Reforestation should be limited to within the buffer zone of the Reserve. . . . Oyamel fir trees are the dominant tree species at higher elevations in the core zone of the Reserve. The firs do not respond well to transplanting." With regard to governance, "Accountability should include detailed plans reviewed before and after implementation." There is insufficient "inclusion of local people in conservation efforts." Both scientists complain that "we have encountered problems obtaining bona fide access to perform research in certain colony areas. In the event that there are differences in opinion between the scientific researchers and the WWF research team, these would be resolved by collaborative discussion involving WWF, the scientific researchers and the Reserve Director. . . . It would be useful to have a yearly meeting of the Reserve Director and participating scientists."

3

Sea Turtles, a Torturous Road to Extinction

UNEXPLAINED PHENOMENA, 2

Between the moment of sleeping
and the moment of waking
time has not moved:
the same twelve o'clock at night.
It all happens inside of me,
the turtles lay eggs on the beach,
the turtles shed tears of sand,
the nest robbers are thieving eggs
as old as life itself.
My daughter, Eva, watches the long
white drapes of the Pacific Ocean
as if a goddess were girdling the continents
with turtle flippers.
It all took place in my mind
as if the memory of life itself
were approaching the same shore
after millennia of life underwater.
Along the coast, the recollections
deposit the sea turtle, which, animated
by the ancient Being,
drinks in light and is lost in the night.

HA (*translated by George McWhirter*)

Of Sea Turtles

A CAUTIONARY TALE

HA, translated by Betty Ferber, in *Hurricanes and Carnivals: Essays by Chicanos, Pochos, Pachucos, Mexicanos and Expatriates* (Tucson: University of Arizona Press, 2007)

When I was Mexico's ambassador to the Netherlands in the seventies, the embassy received letters protesting the slaughter of sea turtles in my country. I sent these letters on to President José López Portillo, because they were addressed to him, but I only provoked his anger, for he thought it frivolous of me to be defending turtles when there were more important matters at hand, such as selling Mexico's oil, uranium, and natural gas.

When I returned to Mexico I continued to hear about the massacre of turtles on the coasts of Oaxaca. I heard about the slaughterhouse at San Agustinillo, although the bureaucrats in the Secretariat of Fisheries and the conservationists assured me that everything was fine. And then, one day in October 1989, two women involved in a sea turtle conservation program in Oaxaca came to see me and admitted what they had denied until then: that a merciless slaughter of olive ridley turtles was taking place at Escobilla; that they were tired of keeping their mouths shut; that the bureaucrats charged with protecting the turtles either did nothing or were in cahoots with the mafias who were killing the turtles; and that I had to write about what was going on. One of them pleaded with me, "Homero, only you could save the turtles!" They laid a thick sheaf of confidential reports on my table and promised to bring more.

Two days later, we agreed on a strategy to save the sea turtle from extinction: first I would publish my articles in Mexico, and then foreign environmental groups would provide international support. I waded through hundreds of pages of reports from different parts of the country where sea turtle eggs were stolen or the turtles were butchered to strip their skins and shells or chop up their flesh. I saw photos of turtles being shot in the head or hacked to pieces with machetes, photos of a huge mound of shells behind the slaughterhouse, photos of dogs drinking from the streams of blood flowing from the murdered olive ridleys.

At last the five articles came out in January 1990 in a Mexico City daily newspaper, *La Jornada*. In San Francisco, Earth Island Institute supporters dressed in turtle costumes staged protests in front of the Mexican consulate, and in London Greenpeace held a protest during President Carlos Salinas de Gortari's official visit to the city. The president received over seventy thousand letters demanding an end to the slaughter, and there was talk of a tourist boycott. My telephone was cut off every Thursday and reconnected on Tuesday, only to go dead again two days later. Needless to say, my telephone was tapped on the days it was working. An American sea turtle expert who came to see me was put under surveillance by the Secretariat of the Interior.

As a writer I was blacklisted by all the official cultural bodies. The day the first article appeared, the Fisheries Secretary called me. She was furious because I had not simply passed on all the information to her, and she demanded that I reveal my sources, which were, she complained, much more reliable than her own.

There were turtles in the world before and after the dinosaurs. Seven of the world's eight surviving species nest on Mexican beaches or swim in Mexican waters on the Atlantic and Pacific coasts: olive ridley (*Lepidochelys olivacea*), Kemp's ridley (*Lepidochelys kempii*), hawksbill (*Eretmochelys imbricata*), leatherback (*Dermochelys coriacea*), loggerhead (*Caretta caretta*), green turtle (*Chelonia mydas*), and black turtle (*Chelonia agassizii*).

The conservation of these species, living receptacles of the earth's natural history, constitutes a grave responsibility for the Mexican people. Although turtles have survived the major natural catastrophes that finished off other species, they may not survive human predation. Experience has shown that of all their predators—larvae, dogs, birds, fish—the most insidious and harmful is man.

All seven species are endangered, and on paper, six were protected from capture, whereas capture of the seventh, the olive ridley, was partially banned, although any real control was nullified by a system of quotas and special permissions handed out by the Secretariat of Fisheries. The killing of sea turtles went on all year long: the olive ridley and the Kemp's ridley, the hawksbill and the leatherback, the Pacific green turtle, the Atlantic green turtle, and the Atlantic loggerhead were all at risk.

The biggest catches of hawksbills were in the Caribbean and the Gulf of Mexico, in Isla Mujeres and Cozumel in Quintana Roo, in Merida and Progreso in Yucatán, and in Campeche. Although merchants and authorities alike were fully aware that it was illegal, the trade in tortoiseshell flourished.

Approximately five and a half pounds of usable shell were taken from each adult turtle. All the sizable towns on the peninsula had shops selling craftwork, whole shells, skulls, and dried turtles. As the biggest consumer of turtle skins and shells in the world, Japan fomented the illegal trade in tortoiseshell, which is used in Japan for electronic circuits, eyeglass frames, and geisha combs.

Rancho Nuevo in Tamaulipas is of crucial importance for the nesting Kemp's ridley, for it is the only known beach in the world where this rarest of turtles comes to lay its eggs. It is estimated that fewer than one thousand turtles remain in the adult population, whereas in 1947, more than forty thousand turtles were counted on the beach in a single day. A considerable amount of money is being spent to save the Kemp's ridley from extinction, and there is a cooperative agreement between Mexico and the United States. In the Gulf of Mexico, both the Kemp's ridley and the hawksbill are further at risk from incidental capture in the nets of shrimpers and fishermen.

Perhaps my generation will be the last in Mexico to see the leatherback, for this species, the largest sea turtle in existence (weighing between 500 and 1,500 pounds) was seriously threatened by the wide-scale poaching of its nests and the slaughter of females on the beaches of Michoacán, Guerrero, and Oaxaca.

Escobilla, in Oaxaca, is the principal nesting beach for the olive ridley, the site of the greatest number of mass turtle *arribadas* and where most hatchlings are born. During the nesting season, beyond the waterline, each female digs a hole in the sand with her front flippers into which she lays between 90 to 110 golf-ball-sized eggs. After covering the nest with sand with her rear flippers she returns to the water. Fifty to sixty days later, the hatchlings push their way out of the sand and instinctively begin to crawl toward the sea. But before this can happen, the nests are in constant danger of being looted by poachers or ravaged by maggots, fungi, crabs, beetles, dogs, and birds. Only a few hatchlings will make it back to the sea, and of these, an even smaller number (perhaps two or three out of the nest of one hundred) will reach reproductive age and return to the beach of their birth in the culmination of their migratory route in the procreation of the species.

Although the sale of turtle eggs was forbidden by presidential decree throughout Mexico, egg poaching has taken place in every state with a coastline, from Sinaloa to Chiapas, from Quintana Roo to Tamaulipas. Every year approximately 10 million eggs were sold all over the country, a result of poaching or the legal and illegal slaughter of the females. A well-organized network of buyers, distributors, wholesalers, and retailers existed. Improved communications along the coast contributed to more intensive poaching than in the seventies.

The poachers from Escobilla and environs would stuff up to one thousand eggs into a sack, swarming over the beaches at night or at dawn, occasionally accompanied by the same Marines charged with guarding the nests. During the *arribazones*, or mass nestings of tens of thousands of turtles, the fisheries inspector and the marines would take bribes in exchange for not patrolling the beach, giving the poachers a free hand to steal as many eggs as they could. The going price per egg was 50 pesos, making a total of some 500 million pesos for 10 million eggs, or 57,000 dollars at the time. But in the markets of Mexico City, each egg was selling for 1,500 pesos, bringing in some 4.5 billion pesos, or the equivalent of 1,307,700 dollars. A tidy business for the middlemen, but not for the fishermen or the poachers.

The Fisheries Secretariat had set a legal quota of twenty thousand olive ridley turtles for all eight fishing cooperatives for the 1989–1990 season. This amounted to one-sixth of the turtle's entire estimated adult population. The capture had begun on August 15, 1989, two weeks after the first nesting. By mid-December thirty-five thousand turtles had been killed in the slaughterhouse alone, not to mention an estimated clandestine capture of fifty thousand more. A dozen pirate boats fished day and night right off the nesting beach, each one taking between forty and fifty turtles per day, with no interference whatsoever from the navy patrols. After cutting off the front and rear flippers, the pirates would throw the still-living turtles back in the sea.

In Escobilla the eleven marines in the camp patrolled only when the inspector ordered them to, usually because a visit from the state delegate was expected. Because they received only two thousand pesos a day (less than one dollar) for food, they supplemented their diet with turtle eggs and complained they lacked the strength to patrol the beach. The center of the olive ridley trade was in Cacalotepec, and every other day a truck came from Mexico City to take away the skins. Every restaurant on the beach at Puerto Angel had turtle meat and womb eggs on the menu. The San Agustinillo slaughterhouse was at Mazunte, about sixteen miles from Escobilla. The whole turtle was used, and the jobs at the slaughterhouse included unloading the animals; the slaughter itself; carrying away the shells, meat, and flippers; putting the eggs and innards in sacks; cleaning the skins and the meat; chopping it all up; grinding the shell; and making flour from the eggshells.

Every morning the fishermen brought olive ridleys for slaughter. Brutally piled up like boulders, one by one they would receive a .22-caliber shot in the head. On the beach, they were killed with machetes or clubbed to death. Often the womb would be slit open to extract the eggs and the turtle left to die a slow death on the sand. Near the beach was a mountain of carapaces eighty feet high. The worst slaughter took place at sea, where the pirates would lop off the flippers for the skins or slash open the stomachs to remove the eggs. The bleeding, mutilated females frequently crawled up on the beach to die. Widespread corruption allowed the massacre to go on unhindered. The members of the cooperatives were paid 23,000 pesos (about nine dollars) for each whole turtle, whereas the pirates were able to sell each pair of flippers for 40,000 pesos, almost double. A government-owned business bought and resold the skins, chiefly to Japan. The wholesale slaughter of turtles and the blatant illegal trade in turtle products was threatening the continued existence of all the sea turtles. This, then, was the situation when I published my articles.

The Fisheries Secretariat initially reacted by denying my allegations and accusing me of exaggeration and misinformation, and worse yet in their eyes, of corroborating the position taken by American environmental groups. I replied that the wanton slaughter of olive ridleys and the poaching of eggs was public knowledge on the Oaxaca coast. With financing from Greenpeace International, on April 20, 1990, the Group of 100 published a declaration addressed to President Carlos Salinas de Gortari, signed by dozens of Mexican artists and intellectuals, and endorsed by more than 100 international environmental organizations, conservation groups, universities, and scientists. We called for an immediate end to the slaughter of sea turtles on Mexican coasts, the closing of the slaughterhouses, and cessation of all trade in turtle products, because Mexico was one of the principal exporters of skins and tortoiseshell to Japan, in violation of our own laws. We argued that the real beneficiaries of this ignoble trade were, and always would be, a handful of unscrupulous individuals who, in the process of exploiting the turtles, exploited the fishermen as well.

Finally, on May 28, 1990, during an ostentatious ceremony in Chapultepec Castle, the president of Mexico signed a decree declaring a total and permanent ban on the capture of sea turtles and trade in sea turtle products.

The next fall I visited Escobilla during the nesting season. It was almost midnight when, together with my wife, Betty, my daughter Eva, and one of her friends, we ventured onto the beach, in the company of the same fisheries delegate I had denounced in my articles as corrupt. In the darkness the white waves bathed the beach. Beneath our feet crabs darted into their holes. It was easier to make out the turtle tracks on the sand if we turned off our flashlights. After walking for several kilometers, always keeping close together, we came upon the first tracks and followed them to the nesting female, who had already dug a hole and was laying her eggs. Gathered around the turtle in a circle, we carefully observed the egg laying, listening to the turtle panting and occasionally stroking her shell. We were conscious of how defenseless she was, how easily harmed. And then we watched as six more turtles appeared, deposited by waves onto the shore, and slowly advanced to dry sand, where they dug their holes, laid their eggs, and covered up the hole again, rocking back and forth on the sand to obliterate their own traces before they swung around and headed back to the sea, stopping every now and then before they disappeared into the ocean and the night.

The beach at Escobilla is still guarded by marines, and young biologists transplant some of the nests to a corral to protect them from predators. However, during two visits I made to Escobilla several years after the decree, I learned that almost all the nests between the *arribazones* are being poached, and that on all the other unprotected beaches of Oaxaca and Michoacán there is much poaching as well.

At the abandoned slaughterhouse, sea turtles are still not safe. The Group of 100 pushed for an international agreement which would protect sea turtles along their migratory routes, from Chile to Mexico and along the Atlantic and Caribbean coasts. Without such an agreement, it would be impossible to ensure the survival of one of the most ancient animals on earth, and it would be impossible to control the actions of its worst and most implacable predator: man. Ten thousand endangered sea turtles are slaughtered off the coasts of Baja California each year, making its waters the most dangerous place anywhere in the world for a sea turtle to swim. Easter week is especially deadly for sea turtles. In the spring of 2001 up to five thousand turtles were murdered for the Easter dinners of affluent Mexicans in Tijuana, Hermosillo, and Ensenada and were smuggled across the border to Mexican communities in San Diego, Los Angeles, Phoenix, and Tucson. Along with Wildcoast and the Sea Turtle Conservation Network of the Californias, in 2002 we petitioned the Vatican to make an official statement that sea turtle is red meat, not fish or sea food, to save the lives of thousands more of these animals. No nation alone can guarantee the turtles will survive, but a single nation can destroy them.

UPDATE: Ten years after we asked for protection of sea turtles in Latin America, the Inter-American Convention for the Protection and Conservation of Sea Turtles (IAC) came into force in May 2001.

Mexico Proclaims Total Ban on
Harvest of Turtles and Eggs

HA, *Marine Turtle Newsletter* 50:1–3, 1990

On 28 May 1990, the President of Mexico, Carlos Salinas de Gortari, announced a total and permanent ban on the capture of sea turtles and trade in sea turtle products. The decree covers all sea turtle species that swim in Mexico's waters and/or nest on Pacific or Atlantic coast beaches. This means the immediate cancelation of all legal quotas and closure of the olive ridley turtle slaughterhouse in Oaxaca. The presidential decree implies a substantial increase in on-site protection of remaining populations, more support for the "turtle camps" (base camps established on nesting beaches for research and conservation purposes), more support for research and training programs, and the development of alternative sources of income for local persons economically dependent on the officially sanctioned (or clandestine) exploitation of these species.

Mexico's responsibility for safeguarding those seven of the world's eight sea turtle species (including the East Pacific green turtle) which nest on its shores, and the critical role which Mexico plays in ensuring their future, have been seriously neglected in the past 15 years. This year, however, the Group of 100 and conservationists disclosed evidence of the wholesale slaughter of sea turtles and the blatant illegal trade in turtle products, which gave rise to a public outcry demanding that the government guarantee the maintenance and preservation of these species and their habitats for future generations. International support received from more than 100 environmental organizations, conservation groups, universities, and those scientists who have been endeavoring for years to achieve effective protection of the sea turtles resulted in a barrage of tens of thousands of letters addressed to the President, making him acutely aware of the intense worldwide concern to prevent the ultimate extinction of these animals.

Hitherto, more than 20 sea turtle conservation and research programs have existed in Mexico, but they were unable to prevent the over-exploitation of species and the collapse of three of the four major nesting populations of

the olive ridley. These programs, in existence now for many years and working diligently to save sea turtles in Mexico from extinction, include:

a. establishment by SEPESCA [Secretariat of Fisheries] of the first turtle
   camp in Mexico, at Rancho Nuevo, the only known nesting site for
   the world's population of Kemp's ridley turtles,
b. 1978 agreement with the USFWS [U.S. Fish and Wildlife Service] to
   protect the beach at Rancho Nuevo by officially declaring it a refuge,
c. research programs sponsored in the 1980s by the universities of
   Sinaloa, Guadalajara, Michoacán, Oaxaca, Guerrero, Tamaulipas,
   Nayarit, Veracruz, Baja California Sur, and the Universidad Nacional
   Autónoma de México,
d. beach work carried out by ProNatura in Oaxaca and the Yucatán, as
   well as ProNatura's educational programs in Chacahua and the
   pressure brought to bear to lower the quotas in 1984,
e. declaration in 1986 of 17 nesting beaches as protected zones,
f. pioneering efforts of Operación Tortuga in the early 1980's, and
g. work of CIQRO [Quintana Roo Research Center], CINVESTAV
   [Center for Research and Advanced Studies of the National Polytech-
   nic Institute], and GEMA [Grupo Ecologista del Mayab].

These efforts have enabled the turtles to survive in Mexico until now, and
they must continue if we are to be successful in restoring the turtles to their
former abundance in the oceans of the world.

What do we need now? What remains to be done? First, the government
of Mexico must provide the necessary enforcement to back up the new decree
and to put an end to the trade in eggs, meat, shells, hides, and other products. In addition, foraging habitats and nesting beaches in the Pacific,
Caribbean, and Gulf of Mexico must be preserved, their deterioration and
destruction halted and reversed. Pollution must be controlled and a wary eye
kept on tourism development; effective and sustainable alternative sources of
income for the fishermen of the fishing cooperatives must be found, with the
support of the international environmental community; environmental education programs must be implemented in the local communities, so the children will grow up wanting to protect, rather than destroy, turtles. Mexico
must act quickly to require the use of TEDs [turtle excluder devices] on its
shrimp trawlers to avoid the incidental capture and drowning of sea turtles.

Incidental catch in other fishing industries should also be examined, and appropriate mitigating measures taken.

It is imperative that as a signatory of CITES [Convention on International Trade in Endangered Species of Wild Fauna and Flora], Mexico join with other nations of the region and 105 countries worldwide to prevent laundering of turtle products from other Latin American nations through Mexico. Furthermore, Japan must drop its CITES reservations for the olive ridley and hawksbill sea turtles immediately so as to eliminate the incentive for illegal harvesting and export of these species. As long as countries like Japan buy large quantities of turtle skins and tortoise shell, conservation and protection efforts on our coasts will be futile. Tourists coming to Mexico must be dissuaded from purchasing turtle products sold locally (hair combs, shells, leather, oil). Many turtles are killed for these products, and usually the money has been spent in vain, as these items can be confiscated by customs officials when tourists return to their own country. Finally, we need an international agreement, from Canada to Chile, prohibiting commercial harvesting of sea turtles. This agreement should be ratified by all nations bordering the east Pacific. Other countries in the Americas must follow Mexico's lead, for no single nation can save the sea turtles . . . although a single nation can destroy them.

The sea turtle survived the natural disasters that caused the extinction of dinosaurs and is the repository of an irreplaceable biological memory of the origins of life on earth. It is imperative that we protect the turtle from extinction at the hands of man. Will the decree just announced bring an end in Mexico to the taking of sea turtles on nesting beaches, poaching of eggs, illegal trade in shells, skins and other products, inadequate protection of beaches and coastal waters? Will it be possible to conserve these species, and to recover them to their previous levels of abundance, if demand (domestic or international) continues for tortoise shell combs or turtle skin shoes or purportedly aphrodisiac eggs? The answer to the latter question is surely "no"; the answer to the former is a hopeful "yes." Mexico is certainly moving in the right direction and can be proud to be setting an example for the world to follow. With help and support from the international conservation community, we believe there IS a chance for survival in Mexico of Atlantic green turtles, black (East Pacific green) turtles, hawksbills, Kemp's ridleys, olive ridleys, leatherbacks and loggerheads. The time for commitment is now.

———

UPDATE: The summer after the ban, on a visit to Mazunte with Todd Steiner, founder of the Sea Turtle Restoration Project (STRP), we were approached by a thickset man in shorts who grumbled, "The greenbacks are still swimming out there, but we can't take them. I'd like to get my hands on that son of a bitch from the Group of 100." He had no idea that was me.

An End to Sea Turtles

HA, *Reforma*, October 27, 1996

The night of August 28, 1996, a guerrilla group called the Ejército Popular Revolucionario (ERP) carried out an attack in the Bahías de Huatulco tourist resort. The detachment of marines guarding the turtle camp at Escobilla was taken away from their posts, leaving the way open for 200 poachers to loot the nests and slaughter nesting females during two days. They scooped up as many as one million eggs and butchered an unknown number of females. The afternoon of October 14, judicial police and Oaxaca Federal Attorney General's Office for Environmental Protection (PROFEPA) inspectors stopped a 14-ton truck loaded with more than 526,000 olive ridley eggs, packed in 267 nylon sacks weighing 150 pounds each. The eggs, laid by five to six thousand turtles, had been poached at the unguarded Morro Ayuta beach. Two federal judicial police vehicles were escorting the truck, in exchange for the equivalent of two thousand dollars. Eighty more sacks had been unloaded by the police when the truck got stuck in a rut. The eggs would have been sold in a public market for 25 cents each, half the price of a hen's egg. The poachers on the beach get 100 pesos, the equivalent of 13 dollars, for 2,000 eggs; in Mexico City each egg sells for five pesos. Three people were arrested, and the 526,000 eggs, no longer suitable for incubation and already rotting, were destroyed at the city dump. Garbage pickers had hoped to get some of the eggs, but the sacks were crushed by tractors. Overriding the protests of Dr. Georgita Ruiz, the admirable PROFEPA delegate in Oaxaca, the detainees were released.

UPDATE: In 2016 one million olive ridleys laid more than 90 million eggs, producing 32 million hatchlings at Morro Ayuta.

Saving the Leatherback

HA, *Reforma*, July 6, 2003

A blue breeze stirs my flippers, a strange tide
churns in my breast, the green sea, the dark sea
is calling to me, the ancient ocean is crying out to
me in the sand.

LAURA LEATHERBACK, "Song of the Sea Turtle," *Searching for
Archelon: Odyssey of the Seven Turtles*

The leatherback, the oldest and largest of sea turtle species that roam the world's waters, at more than 150 million years old, is about to disappear. The rare and majestic leatherback (*Dermochelys coriacea*), with its rubbery skin and seven ridges on its carapace, has been crossing the Pacific, Atlantic, and Indian Oceans for millennia. The leatherback nests in Mexico on the coasts of Michoacán, Guerrero, and Oaxaca but is also seen in Baja California Sur, Colima, Jalisco, and Chiapas. There are crucial nesting beaches for Eastern Pacific leatherbacks in Costa Rica and Nicaragua. The largest leatherback on record was 10 feet long and weighed 2,019 pounds. Making long-distance migrations between breeding and foraging grounds, leatherbacks dive as deep as 3,300 feet in search of jellyfish, their almost exclusive diet.

The Seris (or Comcáac, as they call themselves) of the western Sonoran desert have a long-standing cultural and material link to sea turtles. Most of the remaining 800 members of the group live on communal Seri property on the mainland coast of the Gulf of California in the towns of Punta Chueca and El Desemboque. The Seri name for the leatherback is *mosnípol* ("black sea turtle"), and a ceremony is held in its honor to pacify and placate the spirit of the turtle, whom they believe to have been one of their five creators who was mourning the death of a beloved at the time of the flood. A Seri told me that when a member of the community dies, that person turns into a leatherback, and the elders say they can talk with them. Obviously, the Seri do not eat leatherbacks, but both may become extinct.

Because the leatherback is in critical danger of extinction, scientists from Mexico and elsewhere are fighting to restore its population before it's too late.

Todd Steiner (of the Sea Turtle Restoration Project [STRP]) wrote to President Vicente Fox warning him that if his government doesn't take action, the Pacific leatherback will go extinct in a few decades. Disgracefully, use of longlines by fleets fishing for shark, swordfish, and tuna are condoned by the National Aquaculture and Fisheries Commissions. "During the past ten years, leatherback numbers in Mexico have declined by 90 percent, so dramatically that it doesn't seem possible for the remaining population to recuperate the species," said Carlos Drews, a biologist with the World Wide Fund for Nature (WWF). Noting that the worldwide leatherback population has plummeted by 95 percent over the past 22 years, more than 400 scientists appealed to Kofi Annan and the United Nations to call a moratorium on pelagic longline and gillnet fisheries in the Pacific. They also requested that governments of all nations where Pacific leatherbacks nest take immediate steps to protect these sites and stop egg collection. Laura Sarti, a biologist working at the Secretariat of Environment and Natural Resources (SEMARNAT), and Mexico's top expert on leatherbacks, said that in the Mexican Eastern Pacific there were 75,000 adult leatherbacks at the beginning of the 1980s (and 115,000 in the world), but in the past season fewer than 800 females nested on Mexico's beaches.

The principal cause of this steep decline is the leatherback's incidental capture in commercial fishing gear. Longlines are fishing lines up to 60 miles long with branching secondary lines, from which dangle thousands of barbed, baited hooks, snagging whatever living creature crosses their path: dolphins, whales, sea turtles, sharks, and seabirds. Struggling to free itself from the line, the leatherback gets hooked and drowns. The boats help themselves to the bycatch: sharks (often deliberately caught to cut off their fins, after which the living animals are thrown back into the water), tuna, or swordfish. A Pew Charitable Trusts study found that every year longline fleets cast 1.5 billion hooks into the world's oceans, some 4.5 million hooks a night. More than 90 percent of these predators armed with longlines and fishing in the Eastern Pacific but roaming international waters belong to fleets from Taiwan and Korea. The Latin American fleets hail from Mexico, Costa Rica, Ecuador, Peru, and Chile.

Poaching of eggs at nesting beaches in Mexico, Guatemala, Costa Rica, and Nicaragua is another major threat, fueled by a wrongheaded belief that they are aphrodisiacs. The eggs are snack food in markets, saloons, and eateries. Despite Mexican laws forbidding this vandalism and Dr. Sarti's efforts as head of the leatherback recuperation project, each year there are fewer turtles.

Another danger is posed by the destruction of nesting areas for tourist, urban, and industrial development, as every beach harbors an imminent threat, whether at Mexiquillo, in Michoacán, Tierra Colorada in Guerrero, Barra de la Cruz and Cahuitán in Oaxaca, or the Los Cabos region in Baja California Sur. Plans have been drawn for a coastline highway between Acapulco and Puerto Escondido that would pass through olive ridley and leatherback nesting beaches. Why does the highway have to follow the coast, rather than be inland? All over the Pacific local fishermen set their nets in front of nesting beaches, posing a threat of incidental capture. Marine pollution is also a menace, as leatherbacks mistake plastic bags and balloons floating in the water for jellyfish, and choke on them.

Mexican environmental groups are urging Mexico not to cave in to the commercial fleets at the August meeting in Costa Rica of the Inter-American Convention for the Protection and Conservation of Sea Turtles (IAC). SEMARNAT should lead the way, and not the Secretariat of Agriculture, Livestock, Rural Development, Fisheries, and Food (SAGARPA), which is a willing accomplice to the depredation of our marine species.

Approval and implementation of Mexican Norm 029 to regulate shark fishing in terms that will benefit sea turtles is crucial, beginning with acceptance of circular hooks along the entire longline. In the United States, there was a 60 percent reduction in incidental capture of leatherbacks when J-shaped hooks were replaced with circle hooks. Leatherback nesting areas need more protection. The migratory routes of leatherbacks all along the Pacific coast of Mexico must be protected by enforcing the 50-mile limit for local fishermen and keeping out bigger boats. "Looks like the word is out to block any attempt to protect sharks and other species at risk, such as sea turtles, whales, seals, and even sportfish such as swordfish," Juan Carlos Cantú, a biologist at Defenders of Wildlife in Mexico, said.

After declaring a total ban in 1990 on the killing and commercialization of sea turtles, why doesn't our government take the lead in protecting the leatherback on an international scale, beginning with closing access to nesting beaches at night, as is done in other countries, to keep the poachers out? The leatherback population can't take more losses, nor can our fisheries policies take more corruption. We must put a stop to the harmful practices allowed by the National Commission of Aquaculture and Fisheries (CONAPESCA), where permissions are freely given and where Jerónimo Ramos, the national commissioner for acquaculture and fisheries, has proved to be the main enemy of marine species in Mexico since the Salinas presidency.

It would be utopian were the Mexican government to declare an immediate ban on use of longlines and gill nets in Mexico's territorial waters. A concerted effort to save one of the planet's most venerable species, the leatherback, is well worth the trouble.

UPDATE: In 2012 the US National Marine Fisheries Service established a protected area of 41,914 square miles off the coast of Washington, Oregon, and California for the leatherback.

SEMARNAT under a Carapace

HA, *Reforma*, January 18, 2004

Among the dead on the beaches of Guerrero between last September and this January are two young students from the National Autonomous University of Mexico (UNAM) Veterinary and Zootechnical School and more than 500 leatherback and olive ridley turtles, the former most probably murdered in their attempt to protect the latter. Marco Antonio Barillo and Martha Lidia Díaz Núñez came to Michigan beach, in Tecpán de Galeana, to join a group of 100 volunteers who were trying to stop human predation of nesting turtles on Pacific beaches. When their companions left on September 14, the sweethearts decided to stay on for another day, but they disappeared, until Marco Antonio's decomposed body washed up on a beach at Pez Vela, in the town of San Jerónimo. According to his father, José Badillo Camacho, "The death certificate did not say he drowned, it said he was beaten on the head, left unconscious or dead, and thrown to sea." Martha Lidia's whereabouts are unknown. Relatives trying to find out something in Guerrero about her fate learned that the two had been warned of the danger they were in from turtle traffickers (who are believed to also traffic in drugs). Their efforts were in vain, but after appearing on television they received threatening phone calls. Officials made no attempt to find whoever committed the presumed double homicide. One more example of that Mexican phenomenon, "murder victims but no murderers."

A few days ago, this newspaper published photos of the massacre on the

San Valentín beach in Petatlán of some 500 olive ridley and leatherback turtles that had been killed with machetes and clubs. Everything points to Los Nejos being responsible for the slaughter. Did this gang of delinquents who are terrorizing the region while the authorities turn a blind eye have something to do with the crime of the two interns, whose names the Secretariat of the Environment and Natural Resources (SEMARNAT) is careful to avoid mentioning, as if they never existed?

Ignoring the 1990 decree, the environmental protection attorney in Guerrero justified the massacre by saying "these people are not in the habit of preserving animal species," and the mayor of Petatlán, from the Party of the Democratic Revolution (PRD), admitted that most of the beach is a lawless area. If, as Federal Attorney General's Office for Environmental Protection (PROFEPA) employee Diana Ponce says, 22 high-risk sites have been identified, why have no crackdowns taken place and why haven't the criminals been brought to justice? Why aren't the nesting beaches closed at night? Why is a lack of personnel used as an excuse for not prosecuting violations of environmental legislation? Couldn't some of the federal government's budget for media, image and superfluous international meetings be steered to PROFEPA, to pay inspectors in every state and ensure that our natural patrimony survives its predators?

Until now, SEMARNAT's policy has been to keep its head inside a carapace, ignoring what's happening, only reacting to pressure from the media, as if bureaucrats were mere citizens surprised by the news and who "innocently" spout statistics about nesting beaches. Every year looting on Oaxaca's beaches is denounced, the illegal sale of eggs at the market in Juchitán is exposed, but nothing is done about it.

When Georgita Ruiz, current director of wildlife at SEMARNAT, was the PROFEPA delegate in Oaxaca during Diódoro Carrasco's governorship, she was powerless against the looters of a million eggs and the murderers of thousands of turtles at Escobilla in August 1996. What can she do now about gangs flourishing in Oaxaca? Will she get any help from Governor José Murat?

As for the bootmakers in León, Guanajuato, the president's home state—has he gotten too big for his boots?—they should be prosecuted for buying flippers.

Will restaurants along the Pacific coast and in Tepito be raided to arrest turtle meat and egg sellers, while a national campaign is launched to educate people not to kill one of Earth's most ancient creatures?

The authorities know all about the turtle trafficker networks, their distribution routes, their sale points, and their corrupt government accomplices. But I am afraid that the murder of two young interns and the grotesque slaughter of leatherbacks and olive ridleys on the coast of Guerrero will go unpunished, and once the storm has subsided it will be business as usual for traffickers, local authorities, and SEMARNAT bureaucrats at their desks, hiding their heads under a carapace.

God created animals, but man created the beast.

UPDATE: In 2005 Wildcoast and the Group of 100 carried out a poster campaign featuring a scantily clad model proclaiming, "My man doesn't need turtle eggs because he knows they don't make him more potent," and "Sea turtle eggs DO NOT increase sexual potency!"

All species of sea turtles in Mexican waters have been classified as "at risk of extinction" (by NOM-059-SEMARNAT) in norms issued by SEMARNAT in 2010 that specified the categories of risk for flora and fauna found in Mexico. The International Union for Conservation of Nature (IUCN) lists several of these species as critically endangered, one as endangered, and two as vulnerable. The IUCN classifies species considered at global risk.

Currently, egg poaching continues on many beaches, and there is still illegal trafficking in turtle meat and skins. The proposed General Law on Biodiversity, which would replace the General Law on Wildlife, would allow this trafficking to increase, as it would legalize commercial exploitation of sea turtles.

Louisiana's No Friend to Sea Turtle

HA and Todd Steiner, *Houston Chronicle*, March 23, 2015

For those of us who have been lucky enough to watch a giant sea turtle lumber ashore and lay her eggs, or seen baby hatchlings scamper out of their nest back to the sea, the reasons to protect these gentle creatures are clear and compelling.

One of the most fascinating and also the most endangered sea turtle in the world is the Kemp's ridley. This ancient species is the only sea turtle that arrives in mass nesting emergences during daylight hours, primarily on Mexico's Gulf Coast. Yet it spends most of its life in the coastal waters of the U.S. Gulf and Eastern Seaboard, feeding on crabs and shrimp as it migrates to places such as the Long Island Sound, storing up the nourishment it needs for its annual re-migration back to the southern Gulf to nest.

In one of our most important collaborative efforts to protect endangered sea turtles, Turtle Island Restoration Network and the Mexican Group of 100 convinced Mexico to close its notorious slaughterhouse on the Pacific Coast in 1990. This helped bring Mexico's environmental standards in line with international norms supported by U.S. policies.

Now, 25 years later the tables have turned and it is the state of Louisiana that needs to follow Mexico's lead in increasing protection for sea turtles.

In Mexico, the primary nesting site for the most endangered of all sea turtles, the Kemp's ridley, is in the state of Tamaulipas, about 400 miles southwest of Houston. Here in 1947, 40,000 Kemp's ridley nested in a single day.

Sadly, by the mid 1980s, nesting numbers had declined to about 700 in an entire year. The Mexican government increased protection of Rancho Nuevo, a major Mexican Kemp's ridley nesting beach located about 200 miles south of the U.S. border, with the assistance of the U.S. government. Equally important, both the U.S. and Mexico created no-shrimping, marine-protected areas in critical sea turtle habitat and began requiring the use of a trap door on shrimp nets to allow the sea turtles to escape drowning and entanglements in the deadly nets. Familiar to Texas shrimpers, these are called turtle excluder devices, or TEDs. These trap doors are simple, inexpensive devices that allowed the turtle population to begin to recover.

Also, in 1978 a new program began to establish a second nesting beach in the U.S. at Padre Island National Seashore in Texas. Since then, 15,875 turtle eggs from Rancho Nuevo have hatched at Padre Island and were released into U.S. Gulf waters. The success of this work helped bring Mexico's environmental standards in line with international norms supported by U.S. policies.

Then came the devastating BP oil spill five years ago. Since then, the population of endangered Kemp's ridley sea turtles has been on the decline.

Now more than ever, these small sea turtles need U.S. and international support to get back on the path of recovery. Louisiana should follow Mexico's lead in increasing protection for sea turtles.

Unfortunately, Louisiana Gov. Bobby Jindal refuses to allow state wardens to enforce the U.S Endangered Species Act TED requirements.

Without the use of TEDs, it is likely that more than 60,000 sea turtles of various species would drown every year in U.S. waters (the majority in the Gulf of Mexico). Today, most sea turtles drown in Louisiana waters and, due to ocean currents, are washed up on the Texas coast. Sadly, it seems that one is more likely to encounter a dead sea turtle than see the magnificent animals repeat their age-old nesting ritual.

Ironically, Jindal has used the Gulf oil spill as the excuse not to enforce TED laws, claiming shrimp fishers should be freed from this responsibility in the aftermath of the oil spill.

It is time for Jindal to take a lesson from Mexico, Texas, and the other U.S. Gulf states and begin to enforce TED laws and create a no-shrimping, marine-protected area in Louisiana waters.

The fate of the Kemp's ridley at this critical juncture may determine one of Jindal's most important environmental legacies as the American public considers his viability as a contender in the 2016 presidential race.

UPDATE: On July 1, 2015, Governor Bobby Jindal signed a bill that would allow Louisiana Department of Wildlife and Fisheries agents to enforce federal turtle-excluder device regulations.

4

And God Created the Great Whales

THE EYE OF THE WHALE

And God created the great whales. . . .
Genesis 1:21

For Betty

And there in San Ignacio Lagoon
God created the great whales
and each creature that moves
on the shadowy thighs of the waters.

God created dolphin and sea lion,
blue heron and green turtle,
white pelican, golden eagle
and double crested cormorant.

And God said unto the whales:
"Be fruitful and multiply
in acts of love that are visible
on the surface

only through a bubble
or a fin, flapping,
while the cow is seized on the long
prehensile penis below;

there is no splendor greater than a grey
when the light turns it silver.
Its bottomless breath is
an exhalation."

And God saw that love
between the whales
and the sporting with their calves
in the magical lagoon was good.

And God said:
"Seven whales together
make up a procession.
One hundred, a daybreak."

And the whales came up
to spot God over
the dancing gunnels of the waters
and God was sighted by a whale's eye.

And whales filled
the waters of the earth.
And the evening and the morning
were the fifth day.

San Ignacio Lagoon, March 2000

HA (*translated by George McWhirter*)

One Country against the World

HA, *Reforma*, May 30, 1994

Japan had argued that its opposition to a circumpolar whale sanctuary in Antarctica was based on democratic reasoning, because killing whales is a cultural tradition among a segment of its population. Ironically, global democracy prevailed over nationalistic democracy, favoring the wishes of dozens of countries and millions of human beings who did want the sanctuary. Speaking at the International Whaling Commission meeting in Puerto Vallarta, Mr. Kazuo Shima, Japanese commissioner to the IWC, said, "If the human species is going to survive in the future, we have to exercise more control over the human and cetacean populations." Mr. Shima put humans and cetaceans at the same level. And when a reporter from Reuters asked Mr. Shima how the Japanese see whales, he answered, "Like fish." Not like marine mammals.

To continue consuming large amounts of whale meat in Japan (in spite of the moratorium, some 3,000 tons are consumed each year), up to the last minute the Japanese tried to block creation of the sanctuary, with the support of Norway and several Caribbean countries—St. Vincent, Dominica, Grenada, and St. Lucia—and the Solomon Islands. The delegates from these countries, whose votes were bought openly by Japan in exchange for development aid, were a public disgrace in Puerto Vallarta, and until Thursday afternoon they tried to obstruct voting on the sanctuary with confusing speeches.

Japan has endlessly repeated that killing whales is a cultural tradition among its inhabitants. The reply is that there are unnatural cultural traditions that have no reason to be continued. Take the case of Mexico, whose government declared a total ban on the slaughter of sea turtles, making consumption of turtle meat illegal. The Japanese surely have many other food sources and won't die of hunger if they stop eating whale meat. Their ships are depleting fish stocks all over the world. Matsuo Basho, Hokusai, and Kurosawa are examples of what we respect in Japanese culture, not the killing of whales.

Thursday, May 26, was a great day for whale lovers, but above all for the whales themselves, when the proposal put forth by Mexico, France, and Chile to establish the Southern Ocean Whale Sanctuary, an area of 19 million square miles surrounding Antarctica, respecting Chile and Argentina's sovereignty, was passed with 23 votes in favor, one against (Japan's), and six abstentions. The Mexican delegation voted in accordance with the public announcement made by President Salinas de Gortari on May 19.

Commercial whaling is prohibited in the sanctuary, crucial for whale populations that have been overexploited close to the brink of extinction by whaling fleets. The total biomass of large whales today is thought to be only 5 percent of the total whale biomass prior to the onset of commercial whaling. More than 350,000 blue whales, the largest animal known to have existed on Earth, weighing up to 200 tons, were hunted. The global blue whale population is now estimated to range from 10,000 to 25,000. The right whale was nearly exterminated by whalers in the nineteenth century, and the current population is in the low hundreds. In the nineteenth century commercial whalers considered the minke whale too small to hunt, which explains why the population now numbers in the hundreds of thousands. However, Japan wants to capture hundreds of minkes every year. As the Brazilian delegation pointed out, "There is no maritime area large enough to afford whales the protection they deserve after decades of decimation by the pelagic whaling industry. . . . The proposal is compatible with the rights of countries with territorial seas and exclusive economic zones that are included within the Sanctuary." Nevertheless, we don't know if Chile will be a Trojan horse for Japan or Norway to continue whaling in Antarctica. We will have to monitor Chile's fishing relationship with both countries.

Mexico's stance towards whaling has been conservationist and was reiterated in Puerto Vallarta. Our whale is the gray (*Eschrichtius robustus*), which mates and gives birth in the lagoon complex of Baja California Sur during the winter season. The males reach an average body length of 43 feet, while the females average 46 feet. Males weigh approximately 16 metric tons and late-pregnant females as much as 36 metric tons. Females breed every two to four years, giving birth to a single calf after 13–14 months of gestation. The calves measure about 15 feet long at birth and remain close to their mothers up to nine months. The gray whale's average life span is unknown, but they may live to 75–80 years. The whales' presence every year in Baja California Sur was first reported in 1874 by Scammon, an American whaler who took advantage of his discovery to hunt them. In English Laguna Ojo de Liebre is called Scammon's Lagoon. Places where whales reside or migrate often bear the names of whale killers.

Exportadora de Sal, the largest solar salt producing company in the world and jointly owned by Mitsubishi (49 percent) and the Mexican government

(51 percent), operates in the Baja California Sur lagoon complex. Annual production of sea salt is above five million tons. It is a permanent threat to the gray whale habitat. Mexico decreed official protection for the whales and their habitat on January 14, 1972, when Ojo de Liebre was declared a refuge zone for whales; on September 11, 1972, when Ojo de Liebre and San Ignacio Lagoons were declared a reserve and refuge area for migratory birds and wildlife; on July 16, 1979, when San Ignacio Lagoon was declared a refuge for gravid whales, calves, and tourism; on March 20, 1980, when Manuela and Guerrero Negro Lagoons were included in protected areas; and on January 30, 1988, when the El Vizcaino Biosphere Reserve was decreed.

Towards the end of March the gray whales begin their northward migration to the Bering, Chukchi, and Beaufort Seas. After so much work by conservationists and the investment of human and financial resources, we cannot allow whaling fleets from foreign countries to slaughter them on their migratory route. The southern ocean sanctuary is indeed worthy of celebration, as is the extension of the moratorium on commercial whaling. This year Japan and Norway were defeated by a majority of countries. The danger lies in their determination to continue hunting whales. The conflict surrounding the sanctuary and the whales is none other than the conflict between arrogant and nationalistic democracy versus global democracy.

UPDATE: The support given in 1994 to the Group of 100's proposals by Emilio Azcarraga Milmo, the head of Grupo Televisa, was crucial. Azcarraga told me he would see whales swim by when he was at sea on his yacht, and he loved them. He gave orders for alerts to be broadcast throughout the day on Televisa channels asking viewers to call the Japanese and Norwegian embassies (telephone numbers were provided) and demand that their countries stop whaling, and he made sure there was ample coverage on news programs. President Carlos Salinas de Gortari took note and called the undersecretary of fisheries, who had offered me a 50,000 dollar bribe if I would back off opposing Mexico's stand with the Japanese, and instructed him to get the new Mexican position from Homero Aridjis.

The precommercial whaling biomass of large whales, including sperm whales, was 5,691,915 metric tons. The current biomass of large whales, including sperm whales, is 874,512 metric tons, according to James A. Estes, Douglas P. DeMaster, Daniel F. Doak, Terrie M. Williams, and Robert L. Brownell Jr., editors of *Whales, Whaling, and Ocean Ecosystems* (Berkeley: University of California Press, 2007).

The Silence of the Whales

HA, *Reforma*, February 21, 1995. The first public denunciation of the
saltworks project in Laguna San Ignacio was made by Homero Aridjis
in his article "Mexico Sells Whale Sanctuary" (*Reforma*, January 21,
1995). American graduate student Serge Dedina, who would later
found Wildcoast (and is now mayor of Imperial City, California),
alerted Aridjis to the imminent approval of the project's
environmental impact assessment (EIA) by the
National Institute of Ecology

Every year gray whales make a 5,000- to 6,800-mile migration south
from the Bering, Chukchi, and Beaufort Seas, proceeding down the
coast of North America (passing Alaska, British Columbia,
Washington, Oregon, and California) to their breeding and calving areas in
Mexico. The wintering lagoons of the eastern Pacific population of the gray
whale are part of the Vizcaino Desert Biosphere Reserve.

The whales are believed to gather in Laguna Guerrero Negro, Laguna Ojo
de Liebre, Laguna San Ignacio, and Bahía Magdalena because of the warmer
temperatures and greater buoyancy of the water, and for the protection the
lagoons afford from predators and the open sea. Laguna San Ignacio is the
only one of these areas still unaffected by human intervention.

This pristine breeding ground for hundreds of gray whales is now threatened by plans of Exportadora de Sal, SA (ESSA) to develop an industrial salt
production facility on the flats around Laguna San Ignacio. The company,
which is jointly owned by Mexico (51 percent) and the Mitsubishi
Corporation of Japan (49 percent), already produces upwards of 6 million
tons of salt per year at Ojo de Liebre and Guerrero Negro. Sales in 1994
totaled approximately 86 million dollars. The San Ignacio project would turn
over an additional 52,150 hectares (201 square miles) to ESSA, increasing its
annual production capacity by more than 7 million tons. Japan is the principal importer of sea salt produced in Mexico.

Each month eight oceangoing ships would dock at a mile-long pier and
loading facility jutting into Bahía de Ballenas, between Punta Abreojos and
Estero el Coyote, some 15 miles west of San Ignacio's mouth. Salt would

reach the ships by conveyor belts from a one-million-metric-ton stockpile. Two major saltwater pumping stations would be installed on the lagoon's shoreline, one at the northern end of the northern arm, the other directly across from the wildfowl refuge on Isla Pelícanos and Isla Garzas, two of the reserve's core zones. The stations would be capable of pumping nearly 6,600 gallons per second of lagoon water to the concentration and evaporation ponds. The facility would operate continuously, pumping sea water 24 hours a day, 365 days a year, and harvesting salt 16 hours a day except Sundays.

Mexico established a gray whale sanctuary in Laguna San Ignacio in 1954 and banned whaling. In 1972 the lagoon was decreed a reserve and refuge area for migratory birds and wildlife, and in 1979 a refuge for pregnant whales and calves and a tourist attraction area. In 1988 the Vizcaino Desert Biosphere Reserve (the largest protected area in Latin America) was established. Within Laguna San Ignacio are two core zones, theoretically dedicated to preserving biodiversity with no human interference. Laguna San Ignacio is also a UNESCO World Heritage Site.

Compañía Exportadora de Sal (founded in 1954 by global shipping and business magnate Daniel Ludwig and sold to Mitsubishi in 1973) began operating in Laguna Guerrero Negro in 1954 and shifted its barging operation to the larger Laguna Ojo de Liebre in 1967. Annual salt production has jumped from 50,000 metric tons in 1957 to current levels. The company has a history of environmental negligence: in 1984 nearly a million gallons of diesel fuel were unaccounted for, and in December of 1985 an oil spill was detected, covering 3.5 hectares (8.6 acres) of the salt marsh adjacent to Puerto El Chaparrito, a tank farm and distribution center within the lagoon for the approximately 4 million gallons used annually by ESSA. No official evaluation of damage to the lagoon was made, and the company's main concern was recovering the fuel in order to use it; by June 1986 400,000 gallons had been recuperated. The spill was never made public.

Between 1951 and 1977, during seven hurricanes Punta Abreojos was buffeted by winds up to 87 miles per hour. Should stormy weather make the pier unusable, an alternative loading procedure would be needed, since it is impossible to shut down operations, and storage is not available for the approximately 20,000 metric tons of salt produced daily. The probable choice would be to barge salt to Cedros Island for subsequent shipping out, as is done at Ojo de Liebre. The barges would have to be loaded inside Laguna San Ignacio, necessitating dredging both the entrance to the lagoon and a turning area within it, causing havoc for nursing whales and their calves.

An environmental impact assessment (EIA) was carried out for the salt company by the Centro de Investigaciones Biológicas de Baja California Sur. Its 465 pages consist mainly of description and general information, with a scant 22 pages devoted to mention of possible impacts, and a mere five to recommended prevention and mitigation measures. Unbelievably, the study denies the existence of any body of water in the area that would be adversely affected by the saltworks' operations. However, contrary to the EIA's sweeping dismissal of negative impacts within the lagoon, seconded by the ineffectual Secretariat of the Environment, Natural Resources, and Fisheries (SEMARNAP), extracting 462 million metric tons of water per year from it will lower the lagoon's salinity and temperature, inevitably affecting the abundance, reproduction, and growth of marine animals and plants, including the gray whale.

A total of 23 lines deal with impacts to the gray whale, as if it were just one more fish in the sea. The study suggests spacing the piles of the pier 111 feet apart to allow the whales to get to the lagoon (if they swim in single file and the sea is calm?). No mention is made of the long-term gray whale studies done in the Laguna San Ignacio area or of the potential effects of pumping, dredging, oil leaks from storage tanks, or spills from Pemex (Mexico's state oil company) tankers delivering up to 3.4 million gallons of diesel annually in as many as 25 visits, or of the noise during one year of pile-driving and from aircraft, ships, and conveyer belts. A recommendation that noise be curtailed during the four-month whale season is ludicrous, as the operation is designed to be nonstop, and storage capacity for diesel and salt is limited. Boat traffic drove the gray whales away from Laguna Guerrero Negro; none have been sighted there in the past two years.

Blithely claiming that there will be no impacts because the "affected habitats are terrestrial wastelands, with little biodiversity and no known productive use," the EIA states that only one species, the critically endangered peninsular pronghorn antelope, is potentially at risk. The appendices conveniently omit marine mammals, sea turtles, and terrestrial plants.

The company intends to cut down the mangrove swamp in Bahia de Ballenas to make room for the pier. Mangroves in Laguna San Ignacio and adjacent bays mark the northernmost limit of mangroves in the western hemisphere. The 30,000 hectares (115 square miles) of evaporation ponds will upset drainage patterns in the entire watershed, some 100,000 hectares (386 square miles), causing erosion and increasing the flow of freshwater into the lagoon. Impacts on eelgrass beds visited annually by more than

10,000 brant geese and on the large Catarina scallop fishery are not mentioned. Among other species at risk are the peregrine falcon, golden eagle, osprey, northern pintail, blue-winged teal, American widgeon, lesser scaup, and white pelican.

The EIA even recommends punching a hole in the nationwide ban on capture and commercialization of sea turtles, to allow harvesting of green turtles, which feed and mate in the lagoon. The study mentions that turtle meat is a delicacy in the area, ignoring the fact that since 1991 imprisonment is the punishment for anyone dealing in turtle products.

The EIA predicts the saltworks will operate forever, thus permanently altering 212,319 hectares (820 square miles)—its acknowledged area of direct physical impact—of the Vizcaino Desert Biosphere Reserve. During flights over Ojo de Liebre in 1988, the Group of 100 detected discrepancies between official maps and the actual area in use, indicating encroachment by the saltworks on the adjacent desert. What is to prevent expansion at San Ignacio as well?

This shameful EIA resembles many of Mexico's environmental laws: wishful thinking, followed years later (but not always) by specific norms and regulations. The official management plan allows for productive activities within the reserve as long as they do not jeopardize conservation and preservation of the various ecosystems. The proposed salt production facility makes a mockery of the concept of a biosphere reserve and, we believe, would destroy crucial core and buffer zones of Mexico's largest protected area. This is not a vacant lot or an industrial park, but one of the most fragile ecosystems in the world and winter home to the gray whale.

Government approval of this pitiful EIA, tantamount to a green light for the project, is imminent, and only afterwards will the report be made available to the public. This will be an acid test of which interests will prevail in the newly created Secretariat of Environment, Natural Resources, and Fisheries (SEMARNAP) and will indicate whether Mexico's environmental laws are window dressing for environmentally disastrous business ventures. The issue will also be a challenge to NAFTA's North American Commission for Environmental Cooperation. Does Mexico have the right to deal a lethal blow to the gray whale, a migratory species whose survival is also a legitimate concern of Canada and the United States?

We must speak for the whales before their silence in Laguna San Ignacio becomes as permanent as the saltworks will be.

Whale Meat Sushi

HA, *Reforma*, July 14, 1996

In 1982 the International Whaling Commission (IWC) adopted a global moratorium on commercial whaling. Since then the negative impacts on whales and more than 80 other cetacean species of chemical pollution, climate change, global warming, trawling, and habitat degradation and destruction by industrial and tourism projects has been amply studied and confirmed. This can be the case with the San Ignacio Saltworks, the disastrous project of the Mitsubishi Corporation and the Mexican government to build a massive saltworks at Laguna San Ignacio in the heart of the fragile ecosystems of the Vizcaino Desert Biosphere Reserve.

Nevertheless, after the moratorium was implemented in 1986, Japan and Norway continued killing whales. During the 48th meeting of the IWC in Aberdeen, Scotland, held June 24–28,1996, both countries objected to the moratorium on whaling. Each year they argue for a "management" scheme that will allow them to "harvest" whales according to population estimates, although these schemes don't take into account other threats in the ocean; not only harpoons kill whales. The minke whale, the smallest of the great whales, measuring up to 33 feet, is the main victim of the whaling industry, as it is the only whale whose population is still considered abundant. The Norwegians have been hunting increasing numbers of minkes in the northeast Atlantic, flouting worldwide disapproval. This year the Norwegians began hunting before the IWC Scientific Committee had given its verdict on the latest minke whale population estimates, and so far this season their fleet has killed approximately 400 whales.

The Norwegian delegation at Aberdeen walked out of the meeting room when the IWC passed a resolution ordering Norway to honor the moratorium and stop whaling. The country's IWC commissioner, Kare Bryn, stated that Norway would ignore the vote and continue the hunt. The French commissioner remarked, "A country that walks out of the room because it doesn't want to hear opposing points of view has a strange idea about how democracy works."

Illegal smuggling of whale meat and blubber from Norway to Japan—the main market for these products—has been exposed on several occasions.

Demand for whale sushi in Norway is low. Japan justifies its killing of minkes as "scientific research," which is permitted by the IWC, invoking a provision in the 1946 International Convention for the Regulation of Whaling that allows whales to be killed for scientific purposes. The hunt takes place in the Southern Ocean Whale Sanctuary, established at the 1994 IWC meeting in Puerto Vallarta in large part thanks to the work of organizations such as the Group of 100, the International Fund for Animal Welfare, Greenpeace, and the World Wide Fund for Nature (WWF). At the meeting Japan argued, "Scientific research is a sovereign right. We will not accept foreign scientists or observers," and again questioned the legality of the sanctuary. Japanese whalers killed 440 minkes in the Southern Hemisphere and 100 in the northern Pacific during the 1995–96 season. The Japanese government authorized a similar kill quota for 1996–97, and a week after the Aberdeen meeting four Japanese whaling boats set out for the western North Pacific to catch 100 whales, openly defying the IWC resolution that called on Japan to conduct its "scientific research" without killing whales. Makoto Ito, vice secretary of the Japan Whaling Association, said, "I eat whale meat and my father ate whale meat. . . . I don't think of whales as especially intelligent. They are just another marine resource. As long as they are abundant enough for a sustainable harvest I think it is right to catch the whale."

Whaling is extremely cruel. About 30 percent of the whales struck by penthrite explosive grenade harpoons die, the remaining 70 percent are finished off by secondary killing methods, either by rifle (the Norwegian way) or electric lance (the Japanese way). Both methods inflict suffering and intense pain to the cetaceans, whose death throes can last for up to half an hour. This year there was an attempt to seek a ban on the use of the electric lance. Britain noted, "The Berne Convention prohibits the use of electrical devices as a means of killing wild mammals, including whales." The United Kingdom–New Zealand proposal failed, with Mexico abstaining in the vote.

The United States delegation sparked the biggest controversy of the meeting with its proposal on behalf of the Makah Tribal Council's petition to kill up to five gray whales a year (whales conceived and born in Mexico) off the coast of Washington, invoking the Aboriginal Subsistence Whaling clause in the 1986 moratorium which allows certain native peoples to hunt whales to satisfy their traditional needs. While the Norwegians congratulated the United States for wanting to breach the moratorium, the environmental NGOs brought two Makah women to the meeting who testified that during the last seventy years no member of the tribe had taken part in a whale hunt and no one would know how to go about cutting up a whale. They affirmed that the petition was not supported by the majority of the tribe. When Mexico's commissioner, ambassador to the United Kingdom Andrés Rozental, questioned this lack of consensus, the head of the US delegation replied to his Mexican colleague, "I wonder how many decisions are made in his own Government that are completely unanimous." During a subsequent session, Rozental accused the American of having made remarks "which I consider to be quite offensive to my country and to my government. . . . I feel that the US Commissioner's comments about Mexico were unwarranted." The US NGOs applauded his reply. An emergency resolution against the Makah petition passed in the US Congress forced the American delegation to withdraw its unfortunate proposal.

Mexico's attacks on civil society at Aberdeen were disturbing. The first was a letter addressed to the IWC by the Mexican commissioner proposing that every member country be given the right to object to the granting of observer status to any NGO during the yearly meetings. To the contrary, the US delegation proposed that the commission work to achieve maximum openness and transparency in its deliberations. Towards the end of the meeting Mexico suggested that an intersession meeting only for commissioners be held in which various issues would be discussed during "informal brainstorming" and that NGOs could send written comments before such a meeting without being allowed to attend. Several commissioners objected: New Zealand's said, "I am concerned at the effect that could result from a total exclusion of NGOs. We would seek an open and inclusive process." The US stated, "I think the participation of intergovernmental organizations, of nonmember governments, of NGOs is a critical part of the progress of the IWC." And the UK declared, "It is important that whatever we do is open. What we must have is a credible and fully transparent process." The antidemocratic Mexican proposal also angered and worried the NGOs at the meeting. The next date for debating the fate of whales will be in Monaco in October of 1997.

Whales in the Desert

HA, *Reforma*, March 23, 1997

Each fall and winter thousands of gray whales travel 5,000 to 6,800 miles from the icy seas of the Arctic to the coastal bays and lagoons of Baja California Sur, such as Laguna San Ignacio, where they mate and calve. Recovery of the gray whale population, brought to the brink of extinction by whaling at the end of the nineteenth and first half of the twentieth centuries, is one of the great conservation achievements of our time. Hunting is no longer the main danger for the gray whale; today the principal threat is a plan by ESSA, jointly owned by Mitsubishi and the Mexican government, to build a massive saltworks at Laguna San Ignacio that will produce seven million tons of sea salt yearly in an industrial plant covering 52,150 hectares (200 square miles) in the heart of the Vizcaino Desert Biosphere Reserve. In 1995, thanks to opposition from environmentalists, the project's environmental impact assessment was rejected by the National Institute of Ecology, but it is still a threat.

Joining forces against ESSA's project, two US and one Mexican environmental group, the Natural Resources Defense Council (NRDC), the International Fund for Animal Welfare (IFAW), and the Group of 100, put together a mission earlier this month to Laguna San Ignacio with actors Glenn Close and Pierce Brosnan, environmental attorney Robert F. Kennedy Jr., and oceanographic explorer and film producer Jean-Michel Cousteau. The spectacle of the cows with their newborn calves dazzled the visitors, who not only watched but were also able to stroke the whales. During a public meeting Kennedy said, "I flew over ESSA's saltworks at Guerrero Negro and it's an industry. We don't want to see the whales in the middle of an industry. Is it too much to ask that we keep some things as they were created by God? Do we have the right to destroy something we can't create? It's going to be a long battle, but we'll fight it together." Fisherman Jorge Peón said that the saltworks is a problem for the community, and they will defend the lagoon and its resources, which are their livelihood, with all their might. Josele Varela, head of Ecoturismo Kuyima, a local whale-watching venture, claimed that the more they knew about the project the more they worried about the impact it would have on their way of life and the fishery, and he made it clear that they didn't need ESSA to create jobs, because their current activities were sufficient.

With few exceptions, the visit by celebrities and environmentalists was ignored by the Mexican media. Nevertheless, while defenders of the gray whale and the rights of local communities that depend on fishing and eco-tourism were at Laguna San Ignacio, the government organized a junket for a group of Mexican reporters to ESSA's saltworks at Laguna Ojo de Liebre, another important gray whale winter sanctuary, and to ESSA's offices in the squalid company town of Guerrero Negro. Unlike the NGO trip, this one merited entire pages in the papers, along with verbal attacks on the activists made by ESSA employees and Guillermo Mercado Romero, Baja California Sur's governor and booster of the new saltworks, who accused them of doing the bidding of "murky business interests." The mayor of Guerrero Negro disqualified the opponents of ESSA's factory in the gray whale sanctuary with a disdainful "They're poets." If the boss of Guerrero Negro meant me, I would remind him of these verses by René Char: "Obey your swine who exist. I submit to my gods who do not." In April the gray whales will start their return journey to the northern seas, ignorant of the threat hanging over the lagoon where they breed and give birth. Will they come back one day to find their refuge turned into an industrial park?

Friends of Japan, Enemies of Whales?

HA, *Reforma*, November 2, 1997

Prompted by the deplorable stance in the Mexican delegation's official statement on the first day of the Forty-ninth Annual Meeting of the International Whaling Commission (IWC), held in Monte Carlo, Monaco, October 20–24, 28 NGOs condemned what they deemed a shocking about-face in Mexico's position towards whale conservation during previous meetings. The International Wildlife Coalition, World Wildlife Fund-US, Greenpeace, International Fund for Animal Welfare, Center for Marine Conservation, Gesellschaft zum Schutz der Meeressäugetiere, Japan Whale Conservation Network, Whale and Dolphin Conservation Society, and the Group of 100, among others, interpreted Mexico's recommendation to "reaffirm the commitment made by the members of the International Whaling Commission to increase the availability of regulated species for human consumption" as support from Mexico for Japan and Norway's campaign to reopen the hunt for whales.

The reaction against its statement was so immediate and strong that the Mexican delegation rushed to issue a revised version—unheard of and unprecedented, triggering laughter among attendees—deleting the recommendation and a few others but leaving in language that emphasized "the sovereign rights of coastal states over living resources within their territorial waters . . . and over conservation and sustainable use of these resources," which means that Mexico was proposing to cede control over management and conservation of whales to individual nations, which directly contradicts the International Whaling Commission's mandate and various international conventions to which Mexico is signatory. Whales are highly migratory species and enjoy special status, as they do not belong to any particular country. Mexico also supported Japan and Norway's commercial coastal whaling, asking for a definition of the "principles, objectives, and clear applicable norms for granting quotas to aboriginal groups whose subsistence has been historically based on consumption of whale products, to respect the interests of local and aboriginal communities." By introducing the word *local*, Mexico attempted to establish a new category of tolerated whaling. Mexico's stance was confirmed by its voting. On a resolution proposed by 15 countries (including Australia, France, Germany, Spain, Sweden, Brazil, and the United States) asking Japan to stop its lethal so-called scientific whaling of minkes in the Southern Ocean (in the sanctuary decreed by the IWC in 1994 in Puerto Vallarta), Mexico voted against, along with the Japanese puppets in the Caribbean—Dominica, Antigua and Barbuda, Granada, St. Lucia, St. Vincent, and the Grenadines—and Norway, Russia, and China. The Japanese slaughter in the Antarctic last year was increased to 440 minkes. To Mexico's chagrin, the resolution against Japan was approved, although it will be ignored.

Mexico decorously abstained in the vote on a similar resolution condemning Japanese whaling in the Northern Pacific, although our delegation did vote against Norwegian whaling. After all, we are not that economically dependent on Norway. Another resolution asked for IWC member states to cooperate in quantifying stockpiles of whale meat and identifying the meat's origin using DNA testing. Mexico abstained, tacitly supporting Japan and Norway against 15 votes in favor cast by Ireland, Netherlands, New Zealand,

China, Chile, United States, and so on. The Mexican delegation also abstained in the vote on a proposal—which failed—to allow Japanese coastal communities to take 50 minke whales.

After two years of intense lobbying, the United States managed to get an annual quota of four gray whales for the Makah Indian Tribe of northwest Washington state, which has not hunted a whale since the 1920s. The quota was approved in a package along with the yearly renewal of a permit to hunt gray whales for the Chukotka Indians in the Russian Federation. Nevertheless, the resolution was amended to allow only this type of hunting by indigenous groups "whose subsistence, cultural and nutritional needs have been accepted by the IWC." The IWC has yet to recognize that the Makah have these needs, and legal challenges to their slaughter of gray whales, which may have been born in Mexican waters, have begun. In this instance the position taken by Mexican ambassador Santiago Oñate was correct.

Exportadora de Sal, S.A.'s project to build a saltworks at Laguna San Ignacio, inside the Vizcaino Desert Biosphere Reserve and one of the four bodies of water where the gray whale mates and gives birth in Mexico, was in evidence in Monaco. Exportadora de Sal, S.A. (ESSA), jointly owned by the Mexican government and Mitsubishi of Japan, sent 45 pounds of propaganda from its New York office touting the project. The Mexican delegation had no qualms about the company's displaying its propaganda on tables reserved for the NGOs so that delegates and observers could learn about the benefits of building a massive salt factory in an area protected by Mexico's environmental laws. The company has already paid 1.5 million dollars to the Universidad de Baja California Sur, the Universidad Autónoma de México, and the Scripps Institute of Oceanography (in San Diego) for doing the new environmental impact statement. All 28 NGOs that criticized Mexico's statement also declared their "total opposition" to the Salitrales de San Ignacio project.

UPDATE: As president of the Group of 100, Homero Aridjis was the only representative of a Mexican NGO with observer status at the IWC meetings held in 1994 in Puerto Vallarta, Mexico; in 1995 in Dublin; in 1996 in Aberdeen; and in 1997 in Monaco. At the Dublin, Aberdeen, and Monaco meetings the Group of 100 distributed information about the planned saltworks at Laguna San Ignacio to official delegations and NGO observers and published updates in the daily NGO newsletter *Eco*.

Heritage and Democracy in Danger?

HA, *Reforma*, September 5, 1999

Both the Party of the Democratic Revolution (PRD) governor of the state of Baja California Sur and National Action Party (PAN) congressman Victor Martínez have put aside their party differences to become garbled Cantinflas-like boosters of Mitsubishi's project, disregarding Mexico's environmental laws. The congressman juggles numbers in his ridiculous accusations that environmental groups have accepted sky-high payoffs during their campaigns. Martínez accused the Group of 100 and the Natural Resources Defense Council of launching their "misinformation campaign" in the *New York Times*. Lucky for him that he lives in a state where you can talk nonsense and break laws with impunity, because anywhere else he would already have been sued for libel. When Leonel Cota Montaño, the opportunist PRD governor and defector from the Institutional Revolutionary Party (PRI), met with Exportadora de Sal, S.A. (ESSA) executives, he was quoted as "disqualifying the so-called ecological arguments made by environmental groups for canceling the saltworks project, since this is a matter of vital importance in which we cannot accept the unwarranted interference of groups who serve foreign interests" (*Diario Peninsular*, April 23, 1999). Perhaps here the governor might have mentioned the Mitsubishi Corporation's interests. "The alleged threat to the existence of the gray whale—the main reason put forward by the ecologists for not authorizing the project in the north of the state—is no more than a myth."

The Anatomy of a Victory

THE SAVING OF SAN IGNACIO LAGOON

HA, *Earth Island Journal*, Autumn 2000

In January 1995, Grupo de los Cien (the Group of 100, a group of leading Mexican artists and intellectuals), learned of a project to build a massive saltworks at Laguna San Ignacio, the last pristine mating and calving ground of the gray whale. Our informants were two American graduate students, Serge Dedina and Emily Young, who were doing research in Baja California. The students discovered that Mexico's National Ecology Institute was about to give the green light to Exportadora de Sal S.A. (ESSA, a joint venture owned by Mitsubishi and the Mexican government) to develop 525,000 acres of the Vizcaino Desert Biosphere Reserve—Latin America's largest protected natural area—into a massive saltworks.

These protected acres would become evaporation ponds, pumping stations, conveyor belts, stockpiles, service roads, and new human settlements—complete with a mile-long pier for oceangoing freighters jutting into Bahia de Ballenas (Whale Bay), directly in the path of whales heading for the lagoon. Water was to be pumped nonstop out of Laguna San Ignacio at the rate of 6,600 gallons per second.

We immediately denounced the project to both the Mexican and international media in a statement released on January 21, 1995. After ESSA and the Mexican government refused to hand over the Environmental Impact Assessment (EIA), we obtained a copy from John Twiss, executive director of the Marine Mammals Commission in Washington. One month later, on February 21, I published "El silencio de las ballenas" (The Silence of the Whales). This was a devastating indictment of the threats posed to the gray whale, the lagoon, and dozens of marine and terrestrial plant and animal species, including the severely endangered peninsula pronghorn antelope and the northernmost stand of red mangrove in the Western Hemisphere.

The proposed saltworks threatened more than two-thirds of the Vizcaino Desert Biosphere Reserve. Also in danger were human populations at Punta Abreojos, whose prosperous lobster and abalone fisheries would be destroyed, and communities surrounding the lagoon who base their livelihood on whale watching and fishing. In return, the saltworks would provide 200 permanent jobs, mostly for skilled outsiders. Only 23 lines of the EIA (which described the fragile desert ecosystems to be flooded as "sterile wastelands") mentioned the gray whale.

Six days later, on February 27, INE [National Institute of Ecology] turned down the project on the grounds that it was "not compatible with the Vizcaino Biosphere Reserve's conservation objectives" and that "nothing can justify the permanent transformation of landscape and loss of natural environment in so large an area." So began a fight that ended only on March 2, 2000, when Mexican President Ernesto Zedillo announced that the saltworks project would be canceled.

At first the Group of 100 campaigned alone, but we soon realized that we would need many allies in Mexico and abroad to win this fight against one of the world's most powerful multinational corporations and the government of Mexico. The first involvement by other groups was a protest letter to Mitsubishi endorsing our opposition to the saltworks, dated April 19, 1995, and signed by 17 groups, including Earth Island Institute, the Sierra Club, Rainforest Action Network, and Friends of the Earth. The document was prepared by Josh Karliner of the Transnational Resource and Action Center and Michael Marx of the Coastal Rainforest Coalition.

Next, thanks to funding from the Animal Welfare Institute, Greenpeace Netherlands, and IFAW [International Fund for Animal Welfare] (and the support of Sidney Holt, Craig van Note, and Geert Drieman), the Group of 100 published a full-page ad in the *New York Times* and Mexico's *Reforma* and *La Jornada*. The ad, published on May 10, 1995, was endorsed by David Brower, Octavio Paz, Allen Ginsberg, Sir James Goldsmith, Peter Matthiessen, Lester Brown, Roger Payne, Margaret Atwood, and Günter Grass, among others, and 60 environmental organizations from around the world.

The Group of 100 then took the saltworks issue to the International Whaling Commission meeting in Dublin in June 1995 as the only Mexican NGO observer (sponsored by the International Wildlife Coalition). This action proved to be a turning point. When we returned to Mexico, environmental minister Julia Carabias asked me to recommend scientists for a committee to advise the Mexican government in their evaluation of the saltworks project. We suggested American gray whale experts Bruce Mate, Steven Swartz, and Stephen Reilly and Chilean biologist Victor Marín. All four were invited to join the committee.

Meanwhile, ESSA and Mitsubishi ran ads in American and Mexican papers trumpeting their commitment to "environmental stewardship."

We continued our strategy to get other groups and individuals involved in the issue, assembling and sending out a 100-page dossier to several dozen organizations in Mexico, the United States and Europe, gray whale experts, the World Bank, and the US Marine Mammal Commission. We formed an alliance with Mexico's Green Party and established contact with local fishing cooperatives that were seeking support for several environmentally sound small-scale projects. On August 21, a month after Minister of Trade and Industry Herminio Blanco assured a meeting of ESSA's board that the project is feasible and will go forward, we filed two suits against ESSA, charging the company with operating illegally at Guerrero Negro for lack of a valid EIA and accusing it of environmental negligence at the saltworks. As a result of our suits, PROFEPA [Federal Attorney General's Office for Environmental Protection] carried out an audit, and ESSA was forced to take 254 remedial actions.

In April of 1996 the Group of 100 held a press conference with fishermen from Laguna San Ignacio and a founder of Ecoturismo Kuyima, a local whale-watching company. A highlight of the press conference was clandestine footage showing huge tires and thousands of dead fish littering Laguna Ojo de Liebre in Guerrero Negro and highly concentrated toxic brine flowing into the lagoon. The fishermen declared that the saltworks would ruin their fishing grounds, and our campaign against the project received further support from a former director of ESSA, who denied the need for a new saltworks.

Opposition to the saltworks in the gray whale nursery at Laguna San Ignacio will go down in history as the biggest environmental battle ever in Mexico. In November 1996, for the first time a Mexican federal court acknowledged the legal right of a non-governmental organization or an individual to challenge environmental regulations. This milestone came in direct response to a suit brought by the Group of 100 against the Ministry of the Environment.

In March 1997 the first "mission" to the lagoon took place. The Group of 100, NRDC [Natural Resources Defense Council], IFAW and ProEsteros brought Pierce Brosnan, Robert F. Kennedy Jr., Glenn Close, and Jean-Michel Cousteau to see the whales and join the cause. Subsequent trips included members of the European parliament and Mexican congresspersons and senators. Even Prince Bernhard of the Netherlands took a stand in a publicized letter to President Zedillo, written at my request after he called me to ask how he could support our opposition to the saltworks.

In October of that year Mitsubishi announced that it had hired UABCS [Universidad Autónoma de Baja California Sur], UNAM [National Autonomous University of Mexico], UAM [Universidad Autónoma Metropolitana], and the Scripps Oceanographic Institute to carry out a new EIA within 18 months. The 3,000-page-long EIA was unofficially presented to the Mexican government, and this was the project that Zedillo canceled.

Toward the end of November 1997, I received the first of a series of death threats, possibly resulting from my opposition to the saltworks.

Millions of men, women, and children in Mexico, the United States, and Canada wrote to Mitsubishi and the president of Mexico asking them not to build the saltworks. The Group of 100 helped the Green Party create a congressional commission to investigate ESSA's saltworks at Laguna Guerrero Negro, where the death of hundreds of sea turtles had been covered up, and the projected saltworks at Laguna San Ignacio.

During the past year in Mexico, a broad coalition of Mexican and American groups began working together, opening websites and plastering billboards all over Mexico City. Coalition members met with a UNESCO World Heritage Committee delegation that came to Mexico in response to a petition by the Group of 100, NRDC, IFAW, and others asking that Laguna San Ignacio be declared a "World Heritage in Danger" site.

We were bowled over by President Zedillo's March 2 announcement. It was exhilarating to realize that, thanks to our efforts in January and February 1995, construction of the saltworks was not already under way. After five years of campaigning by the Group of 100, along with American, European, and other Mexican groups, the lagoon and the Vizcaino Desert Biosphere Reserve will remain as they are now. This was a great victory for environmental protection in Mexico. Had the project been completed, it would have been nearly impossible to successfully defend any species or ecosystem anywhere in the country. An undeniable precedent has been set which we hope to use on other battlefields.

Zedillo claimed the project was being canceled because it would destroy the landscape (an argument put forward by last August's World Heritage Committee delegation) and not because of any possible negative environmental impacts, least of all on the gray whales. But we learned that the real reason for the cancelation was financial. Last December, Zedillo asked Exportadora de Sal for an economic feasibility study and was shocked to learn that none existed. Then he discovered that the majority of the profits from the San Ignacio saltworks would go to Japan, and that only 50 of the 200 permanent jobs would be for local residents.

The Mexican presidential elections last July brought an end to the Institutional Revolutionary Party's 71-year stranglehold on power, and the political fallout of the saltworks controversy was undoubtedly a factor. The Mexican government was already smarting from the California Coastal Commission's resolution against the project. (Mitsubishi, meanwhile, felt the effects of the California boycotts and the negative publicity the conglomerate received.) After visiting Laguna San Ignacio the last weekend in February, Zedillo made his decision to cancel.

We must now press for legal guarantees—including cancelation of ESSA's concession to mine the salt flats at San Ignacio—that the project will not be revived by the incoming government that will take office in December 2000. ESSA must be made to clean up its saltworks at Guerrero Negro, and the company's operations must be constantly monitored to ensure the saltworks are not expanded to encroach further on the area surrounding Laguna Ojo de Liebre.

Perhaps now that the project is out of the way, the management plan for the Vizcaino Desert Biosphere Reserve will finally be approved. Bahía Magdalena, the third major gray whale breeding area, is under permanent threat of major tourist development because it is not part of the biosphere reserve. We've also heard rumors about a proposed Japanese resort.

There are other problems to be addressed at Laguna San Ignacio. The local community around the lagoon needs support in developing alternate sources of income and is asking for a local high school, electricity, and water, all of which have been denied them by the government in its attempt to force them to accept the saltworks. Poaching is out of control at the abalone fishery in Punta Abreojos, and the fishermen also need help in setting up oyster banks.

Together, we've shown how "globalization" can be used to defend the Earth, not just despoil it. The fate of the gray whale population in a remote lagoon in Baja California appears to matter to people around the globe, whether they're activists, scientists, writers, or ordinary citizens. The gray whales of Mexico have won a life-preserving victory over corporate greed, and for once the government has enforced the victory.

UPDATE: As of now, Mitsubishi and ESSA have never relinquished their concession to mine the San Ignacio salt flats. However, since 2000, Wildcoast,

Pronatura Noroeste, and the Laguna San Ignacio Conservation Alliance have helped to put 178,615 hectares (690 square miles) under protection through federal conservation concessions and ejidal conservation easements.

Mitsubishi has exclusive rights to buy ESSA's salt and sell it around the world. Government auditors said an average price of $17.50 a ton was paid by Mitsubishi in 2013, compared to prices for similar salt in America and China ranging from 50 to 100 dollars a ton. Mario Alfonso Cantú, undersecretary of mining at the Secretariat of Economy, has denied this. ESSA's former director-general, Jorge López-Portillo Basave, negotiated higher prices with other clients and was fired. He was then charged with signing an unauthorized contract to sell the salt bitterns that remain after evaporation of the salt from seawater. He has been found guilty, fined nearly 270,000 dollars, and banned from holding public office for fifteen years.

The 2017 surveys of gray whale abundance in Laguna San Ignacio were carried out beween January 19 and March 31 by the Laguna San Ignacio Ecosystem Science Program (LSIESP). The count of single adults (whales without calves) reached a maximum of 120 on March 3. The highest number of female-calf pairs was observed on March 27, with 107. The highest total of all adult whales also occurred on March 3, with 199. The overall number was slightly lower than in previous years, probably due to cooler sea temperatures.

Co-founders of LSIESP Dr. Steven Swartz and Mary Lou Jones photographed whales in the lagoon from 1977 to 1982, and in 2017 they identified five breeding females that they had photographed in that period. They write, "These are the oldest photographic identification data for any living gray whales, and clearly demonstrate the fidelity of breeding female gray whales to Laguna San Ignacio."

Save Them, Eat Them

HA, *Reforma*, May 12, 2002

Whales are sociable and intelligent mammals. Usually living in groups, they communicate across long distances using their own language of sounds. The male humpback whale's song is the longest and most complex song in the animal kingdom, a veritable song of the Earth. Every humpback has unique markings on its tail flukes which allow for identification of thousands of individuals and their activities year after year. Our gray whales, born in the lagoons of Baja California but now back in the Arctic waters of the Bering, Chukchi, and Beaufort Seas, where they spend half the year feeding, are, for the moment, safe from any new offensive by Exportadora de Sal. Their roundtrip 12,000- to 14,000-mile migration is one of the longest undertaken by any mammal. Their friendly behaviour in our lagoons affords us human beings a magical opportunity to interact with a wild species. The right whale (supposedly called "right" by whalers because it is the easiest to hunt) is another playful whale. Can the whales forgive Man for having slaughtered them so cruelly and in such great quantities?

In 1986 the world realized that whales were in danger of disappearing, having been hunted to the brink of extinction for two centuries. The International Whaling Commission imposed a ban on commercial hunting of all species of whales, and the oceans became their sanctuaries. However, Japan resumed whaling in 1987, using scientific research as a pretext, arguing a need to study the impact on marine resources of whales eating fish. Defenders of whales see this as a mere excuse for commercial hunting, since the meat of whales captured for "research" is sold for human consumption in Japan, and at high prices. Whales are protected by the Convention on International Trade in Endangered Species of Wild Fauna and Flora (CITES), which regulates international trade in their meat or products, but now Japan seeks to import up to 100 tons annually of whale meat taken by Norwegian whalers because there is no more room to store it in Norway. This doesn't sound like a good idea, as studies have shown that meat from minke whales, which are hunted by the Norwegians, contains high levels of mercury and PCBs, toxins that are especially harmful to fetuses and pregnant women.

The 54th plenary session of the IWC will take place May 20–24 in

Shimonoseki, Japan, a traditional whaling town where many stores and restaurants sell whale meat. As happens every year, there will be a proposal from Japan, now the host nation, to authorize a return to commercial whaling. The main argument of the whaling lobby is that whales are eating too much fish and therefore they should be eaten first. Shimonoseki is plastered with posters of a whale swallowing a shoal of small fish with the caption "Whales are a threat to the fishing industry." According to the FAO, the global catch rose from 70 to 80 million tons in the 1980s and to 90 million tons in the 1990s. As everyone knows, the shocking decline in the population of many species is due to overfishing and pollution, and even the FAO acknowledges that commercial fishing is depleting 80 percent of the world's fish stocks.

Under the guise of "scientific whaling," this spring Japanese whalers have already killed 440 minke whales in the Antarctic Ocean. They've announced a quota of 150 minke, 50 Bryde's, 50 sei, and 10 sperm whales in the North Pacific. Norway, the other country that has continued to whale in defiance of the 1986 moratorium, intends to kill 674 minke whales this summer in the North Atlantic. The sei is an endangered species that feeds on plankton and whose population size is unknown. Shortly before last year's IWC meeting, a Japanese fisheries official called minke whales "cockroaches of the sea." I asked him if he believed in reincarnation, and what if he returned as a minke whale. He was disconcerted and had no reply. A minke weighs up to 10 tons and can measure 33 feet in length.

When the whaling fleet returned to Japan in April, an official campaign was launched under the slogan "Save Them, Eat Them!" to encourage young people to eat whale meat, the Kyodo news agency reported, with free distribution of whale stews, breaded whale chops, and whale steaks. But it seems that the Japanese are on the verge of ending their whale-eating tradition. After World War II whale meat was eaten for lack of other protein sources, and by the 1960s it was the single biggest source of meat in Japan, accounting for 27 percent of the country's production. In 1985 this fell to 0.4 percent. Last year there was a further decline in consumption. According to a survey conducted by the newspaper *Asahi Shimbun,* 53 percent of those polled between the ages of 20 and 24 said they did not eat whale meat.

If quotas are renewed at the upcoming meeting, several indigenous whaling communities will be given the right to kill 1,940 whales during the next five years. In April the Caribbean countries that support whaling met in Antigua to defend the right to use their marine resources. We may well ask whether whales belong to any one country, or only to themselves. Whales are migratory; they cross the oceans, visiting the waters of many nations. These six island states—Antigua and Barbuda, Saint Kitts and Nevis, Saint Vincent and the Grenadines, Grenada, Dominica, and Saint Lucia—have been accused of selling their votes in favor of killing whales. An Antigua government official declared that whaling was crucial for the region in order to maintain the populations of various fish species, and he added that Antigua was in the midst of building fishing infrastructure with 16 million dollars of Japanese aid. According to *The Guardian,* other countries on the receiving end of aid from Japan for "proper utilisation of marine resources" that have joined the pro-whaling block include Guinea, Panama, Benin, Gabon, Cape Verde, Morocco, and the Solomon Islands. Last year the delegate from New Zealand accused Japan of buying votes. According to Japanese authorites, Algeria, Angola, Cameroon, Congo, Gambia, Ghana, Ivory Coast, Liberia, Zimbabwe, Tunisia, Micronesia, Palau, Mauritania, and Trinidad and Tobago could be among future joiners of the commission.

This week, during the IWC Scientific Committee meeting, 170 scientists are debating estimated population figures for several whale species. According to Australian studies, during the past decade the number of minke whales in the southern hemisphere has shrunk from 761,000 to 270,000, a claim that Norway and Japan dispute. The conclusions of the debate will be crucial to discussion of the moratorium during the plenary sessions. However, there are scientists who say that even if the populations are robust, a return to commercial hunting would be risky, because no independent monitoring of this kind of hunting exists, and especially if poor nations begin whaling to supply the Japanese market. The ban cannot be lifted without three-quarters approval by IWC member countries.

Hunting is not the only threat to whales. Pollution of the oceans with carcinogenic chemicals, huge abandoned nets, and plastic debris is increasing. The current high incidence of cancer among belugas is an example of probable impacts. With climate change—now undeniable—will come a reduction in polar ice in the Arctic and the Antarctic, reducing both habitat and food for many species and altering the underwater world. The Arctic will be more exposed to oil exploration and drilling, and in the Antarctic there will be less krill, the main food source for baleen whale species such as the blue. And while sea ice thaws, less phytoplankton, the basis of the marine food web, will be produced due to an increase in UV-B radiation entering through the hole in the ozone layer. Climate change may affect ocean currents, causing unpredictable impacts on whale habitats and even disrupting whale migrations. Harmful algal blooms will increase, and diseases that attack cetaceans will become more prevalent. Massive and inexplicable mortalities have already been observed in several species. Every year critically endangered North Atlantic right whales, whose population is down to 350 individuals, are killed in collisions with ships. Whale watching will also be on the agenda at the IWC meeting, to set guidelines for minimizing the risk of adverse impacts from noise or from interactions that can disturb whale behavior.

Instead of lifting the moratorium, more protection must be given to whales from threats posed by the biggest predator on the planet: man. At the meeting, for the fourth year in a row, Australia and New Zealand will propose establishment of a South Pacific Whale Sanctuary. For the good of whales, human beings, and every living thing on Earth, it's time to awake from the sleep of reason and destroy the monsters that indiscriminate development is spawning.

Bloody Seas

HA, *Reforma*, January 14, 2007

After it was revealed that mercury levels in the dolphin filets for sale in its stores were 13 times higher than the officially permitted level, the Japanese supermarket chain Okuwa suspended sales of dolphin meat, although this decision was made only after a series of articles was published in the *Japan Times* about the annual massacre of thousands of dolphins in Japan, commercialization of the meat, and the sale of individual dolphins to dolphinariums, aquariums, circuses, and "Swim with Dolphins" programs. It's worthwhile mentioning that a show-quality dolphin can sell for 100,000 dollars, while a slaughtered dolphin is only worth 600 dollars.

Mercury is dangerous for pregnant women, as it can damage the fetal brain and nervous system. Analyses of hundreds of samples of whale and dolphin meat for sale in Japan showed that 90 percent exceded the permissible limits for mercury, methylmercury, cadmium, and other toxic pollutants. Nevertheless, the yearly slaughter of dolphins continues in the town of Taiji, where fishermen encircle the pods in coves to slit their throats or lance them to death or capture the "lucky ones" alive. The dolphins' death agony lasts up to six minutes, while they squeal with pain and fear. Ric O'Barry, who trained Flipper at Sea World (in fact, five dolphins played the part) has been defending cetacean freedom for decades, and he and his wife Helene have made a documentary (*The Cove*) exposing the brutal capture and massacre at Taiji. The fisherman defend themselves by comparing the hunt's cruelty to the slaughter of cattle in the West.

Japanese and Islandic whalers justify the hunt by blaming whales and dolphins for depletion of fisheries stocks, but it's human beings who are to blame for the emptying of the oceans. During the last 10 years the Japanese exceeded their official quota for bluefin tuna by 100,000 tons. Over the past 42 years, yearly fish catch for human consumption has risen from 20 million to 84.5 million tons.

Research suggests that whales experience love and other emotions, based on the presence in their brains of kinds of cells that have only been found in the brains of humans and great apes. Dolphins' intelligence is evidenced by their use of tools to resolve problems and by their capacity to develop new behaviors. They live in communities where they weave familial and friendly social relationships, using more than 4,000 different whistles and other sounds to communicate. Each dolphin has its own distinctive whistle. A dolphin recognizes itself in a mirror. Whales, dolphins, and other cetaceans are no nation's property; they ignore man's artificial borders. Their destiny and their right is to swim free in the oceans and to own themselves. If humans want to get to know them and make use of them, the cetacean-watching industry exists.

Savior of the Whales

HA, *New York Times*, October 31, 2013

Some 40 years ago a poor fisherman named Francisco Mayoral, who lived on the shores of San Ignacio Lagoon, halfway down the Pacific coast of Baja California Sur, stretched out his hand to touch a gray whale that raised its head out of the water alongside his wooden panga.

Mr. Mayoral, who went by the nickname Pachico, would liken this milestone to the birth of his first child.

"I didn't seek out the whale, she came to my boat," he remembered. "I was fishing with my friend and suddenly the whale came out and curiosity got the better of me and I touched her gently and saw that nothing happened. The whale went under and came out on the other side of the boat and I felt more confident and I began to stroke her and rub her head, and nothing happened."

This transcendental encounter was, sadly, not emblematic of the troubled relationship between humans and whales.

In the 19th century gray whales—which can reach a length of 50 feet and a weight of 35 tons—fought capture so fiercely that whalers dubbed them "devil-fish." The whales were hunted nearly to extinction until the International Whaling Commission adopted a 1986 moratorium on commercial whaling.

Pachico helped to protect the whales by convincing other fishermen that they had nothing to fear from them. Soon they were ferrying tourists into the lagoon—the last pristine breeding and calving ground for thousands of gray whales that migrate every winter from their feeding grounds in the icy Arctic seas to the warm refuge of the lagoons and bays along the Baja California peninsula.

Pachico lived in a sand-floored hut with no electricity, phone service, or mail delivery, but somehow in 1994 he got information about a plan by Exportadora de Sal, an enterprise co-owned by the Mexican government and Mitsubishi, to build a giant salt processing plant on the shores of the lagoon.

He passed this information on to an American graduate student studying gray whales, who called me from Baja.

The proposed plant would produce seven million tons of salt annually, flooding 116 square miles of tidal flats and dense mangroves and pumping 6,600 gallons of saltwater per second out of the lagoon.

Each month oceangoing freighters would dock at a mile-long pier jutting into Bahia de Ballenas (Whale Bay)—right in the path of whales heading for the lagoon—to take on salt brought by conveyor belts across the desert from evaporation ponds and a million-ton salt pile.

As head of the Group of 100, an association of artists and writers concerned about the environment, I denounced the project to the press and then managed to get a copy of the project's environmental impact assessment.

I was shocked to see that a mere 23 lines out of 465 pages were devoted to the gray whale.

Six days after I published an essay entitled "The Silence of the Whales" in the Mexican newspaper *Reforma,* the government decided that the saltworks were incompatible with the conservation of the surrounding Vizcaíno Biosphere Reserve, which includes the lagoon.

But the company's owners were not about to give up. They maintained that the project could be altered to accommodate the environmentalists' concerns and kept up their fight. Meanwhile, groups like the Natural Resources Defense Council and the International Fund for Animal Welfare joined our cause.

One evening in 1997, during a visit to the lagoon, a young fisherman told me that Pachico wanted to meet me. A grizzled man with leathery skin, he shyly took my hand and related his historic encounter with the whale.

He'd say to me, "Let's go hunt whales, bring your binoculars, bring your camera, so you can take them away and leave them there."

Stroking a gray whale is among the most exhilarating experiences of my life.

The Group of 100 was about to make public a petition to the Mexican government—signed by dozens of writers and artists, including numerous Nobel laureates—when, on March 2, 2000, President Ernesto Zedillo suddenly and grudgingly canceled the plan for the salt factory.

The fight to save San Ignacio Lagoon was the greatest environmental battle ever in Mexico, but it was not the last. Although conservationists working with the government have been able to protect 150 miles of shoreline and thousands of acres of federal land around the lagoon, the gray whale is still threatened in its feeding grounds by offshore gas and oil development and by climate change everywhere it swims.

Grass-roots activism has become more perilous in Mexico, as a result of the breakdown of the rule of law in areas where the drug cartels are influential. Some advocates have defended forests, farmlands, and rivers at the cost of their own lives, with the killers never brought to justice.

On Oct. 22, Pachico, the man who used to say he would give his life to save a whale, died of a stroke at the age of 72.

This winter, when the gray whales return, his sons will be taking visitors out into the water to the thrill of watching up close—and, with luck, even touching—this magnificent creature with whom we share the oceans of the earth.

5

Our America

FRAY GASPAR DE CARVAJAL REMEMBERS THE AMAZON

Old and ailing
I have no fear of death—
I have died many times already.
Up the great river I have sailed
and seen the shadows hanging from the light
and volleys of echoes from that muffled noise
set off by the crash
of its waters into the open sea.
From the steamy branches
of the forest masking the shore
I have seen the poisoned arrow shoot
and watched fall from the sky,
like needle and brand,
the lightning and the heat.
Under every bed
there's a sleeping skeleton
and wriggling in every stream
a viper of lost memory.
It is harder to be
an old man who gets cold
in the hours before daybreak,
feeling his bones ache in the rainy season,
than to drift in a lost boat with the current
of the mightiest river on earth.
Day after day
like all men I have sailed
toward nowhere
in search of El Dorado
but like them all
I have found only
the extreme gleam of extreme passion
of this river,
which through its triple channels—
hunger, weariness and rage—
pours into death.

HA (*translated by George McWhirter and Betty Ferber*)

A Latin American Ecological Alliance

Proposal written by HA and delivered to 19 Latin American presidents, King Juan Carlos of Spain, and the prime minister of Portugal by Gabriel García Márquez and HA on the occasion of the First Ibero-American Summit, Guadalajara, Mexico, July 19, 1991. Published in *La Jornada*, July 20, 1991; in *El País*, July 21, 1991; and in the *New York Times*, July 22, 1991

On the eve of the 500th anniversary of the meeting of two worlds and two natural realms, as we near the end of the 20th century and the second millennium, the Earth is experiencing its worst ecological crisis in history—a crisis that not only threatens the existence of thousands of plant and animal species but the survival of the human species as well. For this reason the issue of the environment cannot be ignored at the first summit of the 19 Latin American presidents, nor can our countries afford to be absent when global decisions are taken to protect humankind's natural heritage. That is why we, men and women of letters from Latin America, propose that our heads of state create a Latin American Ecological Alliance whose goal is to protect and preserve our nations' biological diversity, working together in those areas where cooperation is feasible.

We know that almost half the world's tropical forests have disappeared; that between 16 million and 20 million hectares (62,000–77,000 square miles) are permanently cleared each year and a species becomes extinct every hour; that by the year 2000 three-quarters of America's tropical forests may have been felled and 50 percent of their species lost forever. What Nature created in the course of millions of years will be destroyed by us in little more than 40 years. While the world wonders if there is any future for tropical forests, we wonder if there is any future for us and for the world. An awareness of the consequences of natural resource depletion and environmental damage has already made its way into the Latin American consciousness: No nation on our continent can escape their negative effects.

Latin America has much to save: 58 percent of the world's remaining 900 million hectares (3.5 million square miles) of tropical forest are here, one-third of them in Brazil alone; Panama is home to as many plant species as the whole of Europe; the Tambopata Reserved Zone in Peru is the richest bird and butterfly habitat in the world; the plants and animals found on the *tepuis* in Venezuela are natural treasures; the Lacandon rain forest is the largest in North America; not only does one-fifth of the world's fresh water flow through the Amazon River Basin every day, but one-fifth of all bird species are found in Amazon forests. Mexico and Colombia are among the four countries in the world with the greatest diversity of flora and fauna.

Because we realize there are many environmental problems and we understand the difficulties facing our national economies, we shall limit our proposals to a few specific concerns. First and foremost is the protection of our tropical and temperate forests, threatened with destruction throughout the continent, from the *lenga* forests on Tierra del Fuego in Chile to the virgin forests in the Sierra de Chihuahua in Mexico.

One initiative that could be launched during the meeting in Guadalajara would be the creation of an Amazonian Pact among the South American countries that share the world's richest and most complex ecosystem and its most extensive genetic resources. The mere possibility of seeing this natural endowment of humankind—and especially of Latin Americans—go up in smoke and become a wasteland is intolerable. An environmental loss of that magnitude would be a catastrophe for the entire planet, for life on Earth does not recognize borders.

Mexico and Guatemala share the ruins of Mayan civilization, the Usumacinta River, and the vast tropical forest that covers the state of Chiapas and El Petén. When the Mayans flourished during the first millennium of our era, the Usumacinta River was an important means of cultural communication, and the cities on its banks controlled large areas on both shores. To ensure the preservation of the region's environment, a binational eco-archeological park should be created which would encompass both sides of the river. This park could serve as a model for other joint projects in border areas as well as complementing current conservation programs such as the Montes Azules Biosphere Reserve.

The maintenance and protection of biodiversity must be a primary objective of inter-American environmental cooperation. Within this framework an agreement should be negotiated for the protection of sea turtles along their migratory routes, for no single nation can effectively conserve these species, but a single nation can destroy them. A basic agreement would recognize the migratory nature of the sea turtle species along the east Pacific, from Chile to Mexico, and along the Caribbean and Atlantic coasts. The accord would establish a commission of marine biologists, conservationists, and government representatives charged with preparing a report on the present situation of the sea turtle, indicating what needs to be done nationally and regionally and a list of priority actions with recommendations for their implementation and support.

In regard to migratory birds, America's main flyway cuts across eastern Mexico, crosses Central America, and continues into the Amazon. A huge concentration of birds follows that route every year. Another important route extends down the Pacific Coast from Canada, and some species press as far south as Chile and Argentina. There is no country in Latin America through which birds do not fly in major migrations, including such species as the bobolink, the peregrine falcon, the blue-winged teal, Swainson's hawk, and snipes and other shorebirds. We are alarmed by the impending loss of biological diversity in our continent, and we ask our presidents to protect migrating birds by promoting the establishment of sanctuaries at the stopover sites and wintering areas of these species. Each country would determine what measures it would take to comply. The habitats in need of protection include wetlands, beaches, islands, forests, prairies, and deserts.

Every year millions of tons of hazardous wastes are exported to Latin America, which has become the favorite dumping ground for toxic wastes generated by American, European, and Japanese companies. Seventy-eight percent of these emanate from the United States. Most of the waste is shipped to countries in the Caribbean or Central America or to Brazil, Argentina, and Mexico—countries that already have enough problems dealing with their own wastes without having to cope with imports. Most of the shipments consist of nuclear waste, organic chemicals, toxic liquids, incinerator ash, heavy metals, lubricants, paint, and sludge. International waste trade is on the rise, frequently illegal and often camouflaged as "recycling"—polluting the environment and endangering human life and our ecosystems for countless decades.

Given the difficulty of monitoring the quantity, nature, and ultimate destination of these wastes, we ask that the traffic and transport of hazardous and nuclear wastes across borders be banned throughout the continent. We call for the enactment of national and international legislation on this matter. Our standards and laws should be as strict as those in the highly developed countries. Latin America must not become the waste dump of the industrialized world.

On the Earth's map it is possible to draw another map: a map of the forests and jungles that are disappearing before our very eyes. And on that map of deforestation and depredation we can draw yet another map: the map of peoples threatened by the destruction of their environment. There we find the Yanomami and the Apinayé in Brazil, the Aché in Paraguay, the Yagua and the Amuesha in Peru, the Miskito in Nicaragua, the Guaymí and Kuna in Panama, the Maya in Guatemala, the Páez and Guambiano in Colombia, the Mapuche in Chile, the Lacandon Maya and the Tarahumara in Mexico. Unrestrained logging, cattle ranching, resettlement programs, and forcible expulsion from their lands to make way for mining interests, timber extractors and ranchers, the threat of economic slavery, road building and hydroelectric schemes, mass tourism projects—all have an impact on these groups.

As we approach the quincentenary of the encounter of two worlds, the inclusion of our indigenous peoples in our governments' economic development plans must become a priority. All too often the destruction of their environment entails the violation of their human rights as they lose their habitat and their means of sustenance, their social systems, and their religious practices. Before the arrival of the Europeans, the pre-Colombian peoples from Alaska to Tierra del Fuego lived off their ecosystems without destroying them, and they have a historical right to continue doing so.

Messrs. Presidents: We are part of a global problem which requires global solutions. It is imperative that we formulate an environmental policy that will effectively protect our rich biological diversity. We are certain that whatever agreement you may reach for the creation of a Latin American Ecological Alliance, and the concomitant political decisions taken to implement such an alliance in each of your countries, will benefit present and future generations of Latin Americans. It will also serve as an example to be followed by heads of state on other continents. Environmental considerations have a place on any agenda that addresses the future of humankind.

Signed by Homero Aridjis, Carlos Fuentes, Carlos Monsiváis, José Emilio Pacheco, Fernando del Paso, Octavio Paz (Mexico); Adolfo Bioy Casares, Roberto Juarroz, Enrique Molina, Olga Orozco, Ernesto Sábato (Argentina); Jorge Amado, Joâo Cabral de Melo Neto, Nélida Piñón (Brazil); Isabel Allende, José Donoso, Nicanor Parra, Gonzalo Rojas (Chile); Gabriel García Márquez, Álvaro Mutis (Colombia); Eliseo Diego, Severo Sarduy (Cuba); Claribel Alegría (El Salvador); Luis Cardoza y Aragón, Augusto Monterroso (Guatemala); Augusto Roa Bastos (Paraguay); Emilio Adolfo Westphalen (Peru); Mario Benedetti, Juan Carlos Onetti (Uruguay); Arturo Uslar Pietri (Venezuela).

UPDATE: The Mesoamerican Biological Corridor, home to 7 to 10 percent of the world's known species, was launched in 1997, and now stretches through southern Mexico, Belize, Guatemala, El Salvador, Honduras, Nicaragua, Costa Rica, and Panama. It is intended to protect the ecological connectivity of the region and provide a natural land bridge between North and South America for migrating species and other wildlife. Today it marks the route of illegal immigrants and drug traffickers, and the movement of cocaine through Central America is driving rapid deforestation. White-lipped peccaries, jaguars, and tapirs and the forest in the Isthmus of Panama are disappearing from the section of the corridor that runs through Panama. A vital component of the corridor, the Bosawás Biosphere Reserve in northeastern Nicaragua, Central America's largest forest reserve as well as the third largest in the world, is being devoured by cattle ranching and farming, mostly subsistence. The government's aggressive promotion of extractivist activities is also threatening forests in the country's North and South Atlantic Autonomous Regions. Deforestation by cattle ranching is severe in Guatemala and Honduras.

Writers and Artists Ask Brazilian President José Sarney to Save the Amazon

HA, president of the Group of 100, letter delivered on April 3, 1989, to Brazil's ambassador in Mexico. Published in *La Jornada*, April 4, 1989

The news from Brazil about what's happening in the Amazon is alarming: large-scale investment in massive deforestation that will impact the world's climate; criminal forest fires, as in the state of Rondônia, that raze millions of hectares of tropical rain forest; clearing of the forest to make room for migrant settlers and transnational agribusiness and monoculture plantations; fiscal incentives for cattle ranchers who burn trees to make room for industrial livestock farming; extermination of ethnic groups, whose members are hunted down by the "modernizers" of agriculture to take over their lands; the disappearance of thousands of animal and plant species; projects like the plan to build a highway stretching from Rio Branco in Brazil to Pucallpa in Peru with money from Japan (a country that as a World Bank member has helped finance hydroelectric dams in Brazil that will submerge wide swathes of rain forest in order to buy up the wood from the flooded land) and construction of a hydroelectric dam at Kararao on the Xingu River, which will flood Indian lands and virgin rain forest. On top of that, transnational logging companies, always avid for tropical hardwoods, have now laid their hands and saws on Amazonia, after finishing off forest wealth in African and southwest Asian countries.

Mr. President, we, writers and artists of Latin America, believe the historic responsibility for the destruction of the Amazon jungle is great, and future generations of Latin Americans will never forgive you for not doing all in your power to avoid it. We also want to remind you that our countries, and yours in particular, cannot be absent from the decisions being taken in the world to protect the natural patrimony of humanity. Invoking national sovereignty to justify crimes against nature—such as those being committed against one of the richest and most complex ecosystems on Earth—strikes us as puerile and dishonest. Chauvinist arguments are no excuse for ecocide and ethnocide, barbaric acts in Brazil or anywhere else. An international tribunal should judge these actions in Latin America.

Given your devotion to national sovereignty, we Latin Americans would like to see you defend Amazonia from local and foreign predators as well as from those who are willing to turn the lungs of the planet into a wasteland in exchange for an irredeemable foreign debt that won't even be paid off.

Mr. President, we find it regrettable that member countries of the Treaty of Amazon Cooperation have met in support of Brazil's eco- and ethnocidal policies that only favor large companies and exporters of meat and lumber to the developed countries instead of taking joint measures aimed at protecting their ethnic groups and shared natural patrimony.

If our governments are unable to defend and conserve the indigenous and plant and animal wealth of our tropical forests, then the United Nations should take charge of them, and an international tribunal should investigate and sanction these crimes against ecological integrity which is vital for humankind.

Signed by Manuel Álvarez Bravo, Homero Aridjis, Feliciano Béjar, Fernando Césarman, Gabriel Figueroa, Carlos Fuentes, Mathías Goeritz, Eduardo

Matos Moctezuma, Ofelia Medina, Carlos Monsiváis, Elena Poniatowska, Rufino Tamayo (Mexico); Adolfo Bioy Casares, Olga Orozco, Manuel Puig, Ernesto Sábato (Argentina); Isabel Allende, José Donoso, Nicanor Parra (Chile); Fernando Botero, Gabriel García Márquez (Colombia); Guillermo Cabrera Infante (Cuba); Luis Cardoza y Aragón, Augusto Monterroso (Guatemala); Mario Vargas Llosa (Peru); Juan Carlos Onetti (Uruguay); Arturo Uslar Pietri (Venezuela).

Open Letter to President Sarney

THE FATE OF THE AMAZON

HA, *The News*, Mexico City, June 5, 1989

On June 5, 1989, World Environment Day, writers and artists from four continents have joined together in the name of humankind to ask your government for the preservation of the Amazon, the ecosystem with the greatest genetic diversity on Earth, and to request that you and the other presidents of the Amazon Pact countries formulate a plan for the protection of Amazonia which will be effective in the forest and not just on paper.

We acknowledge the fact that the eight countries in whose territory the Amazon Basin is located have the legal right to control their own natural resources and that economic pressures on their growing populations must be alleviated, and we recognize their need to defend themselves against the depredations of the consumer countries who are largely responsible for the ecological deterioration of the planet. This does not imply, however, that their bad example must be followed by contributing irrationally to the overall degradation; if we compete with each other to see who can use up nature more quickly, we will inevitably exhaust life itself. We believe that it is not possible to halt the deforestation of the Amazon as long as the Brazilian government, frequently with the support of international banks, finances the forest's destruction by subsidizing farmers, loggers, miners, and cattle ranchers and by implementing projects that have disastrous environmental consequences, such as the 2010 Plan, which envisages building 297 dams in Brazil by 2010, or the Interoceanic Highway, which would link Acre with Peru and the Pacific Coast.

We are alarmed by the logging and burning of the tropical forests that help regulate global climate by filtering carbon gases, and whose death by fire contributes significantly to the greenhouse effect. Thanks to criminal forest fires, in 1980 Brazil released 336 million tons of carbon into the air. In 1987, when 30,000 square miles of virgin forests were torched, more than 500 million tons of carbon gases entered the atmosphere. The burnings in 1988 were even more extensive.

The prospect of a ravaged Amazonia is real, and not just part of an international campaign to discredit your country. According to sources within your own government, 14 percent of the original virgin forest has already been lost, and 80 percent of this destruction has taken place since 1980. In Rondônia, some 8,500 square miles of vegetation has gone and at this pace the state will be a wasteland by 1995. The Madeira Rivera, a tributary of the Amazon and a vital link in the food chain, is being poisoned with mercury by gold prospectors.

There is not a single writer or artist among us who is not concerned about the fate of the trees in his or her own country, and for this reason it worries us that the international tropical timber trade, whose headquarters are in Yokohama, Japan, is now shifting its attention to the exploitation of the Amazon, as the total depletion of tropical forests in Africa and Asia draws near. We also understand that our compatriots must reduce their voracious appetite for tropical hardwoods and hamburger meat in order to facilitate forest survival. The issue is not to prevent development in your country, but to put an end to the skewed relationship between developed and Third World nations whereby the latter annually export 6 billion dollars' worth of raw timber and board and import 10 billion dollars' worth of processed wood products. Also, projects must be avoided that only benefit those few who enjoy political and economic power and tend to convert the traditional inhabitants of the areas in question into pariahs. The despoiled and decimated ethnic groups who know how to use these ecosystems in a rational way without destroying them must be respected. Priority must be given to conservation, reclamation, and sustainable development of the tropical forests, such as that favored by Francisco "Chico" Mendes (the rubber tapper and environmental activist who was assassinated by a rancher in December 1988), and cattle ranching, which feeds far fewer people than the jungle itself and is only profitable thanks to government subsidies, should be curtailed.

Mr. President, all considerations of narrow nationalism aside, the destruction of the richest and most complex ecosystem in the world and our greatest bank of genetic diversity impoverishes us all, and we are unable to contemplate the eventual transformation of humankind's natural patrimony into wasteland and smoke; the disappearance of thousands of plant and animal species, many of which are still undiscovered, is unacceptable. An ecological disaster of such proportions would recognize no borders, and the planet could never recover from it.

For these reasons we, artists and writers from four continents, are backing the April 3 declaration by 27 Latin American intellectuals that called for a halt to ecocide and ethnocide in the Amazon region.

[For the list of signers, see Appendix D.]

The Destruction of Amazonia

HA, *Reforma*, January 12, 1997

Governments, NGOs, and the general public are indifferent to the massive ecocide taking place on the American continent: the destruction of Amazonia, where 12 percent of its 2.1 million square miles of tropical forest has already been razed. As was noted in September 1996 at the Third Annual Meeting of the Participants of the Pilot Program to Conserve the Brazilian Rainforest, held in Bonn, Germany, 29 hectares (72 acres) of tropical forest disappear every minute, equivalent to 40 soccer fields, due in large part to fires that destroy 15.4 million hectares (59,000 square miles) of tropical forest annually around the globe. This unspeakable ecocide not only spurs the greenhouse effect and global warming, but will trigger a huge loss of biodiversity. Over 50 percent of terrestrial plant and animal species are housed in tropical forests, and the Amazon Basin, whose surface is 2.7 million square miles (of which 1.9 million are in Brazil), is home to approximately one-third of the tropical forests in the world. Devastation of the Amazon accelerated after the Earth Summit (Rio de Janeiro, 1992), where many issues were touched on but conservation of the rain forest was not discussed. According to official Brazilian government figures, in 1993–94 deforestation of this planetary treasure rose 34 percent as compared to the 1990–91 burning season.

Early in July 1996 the Italian missionary Fr. Hector Turrini revealed that four Asian companies from Indonesia, South Korea, and Malaysia had bought 3,900 square miles in the far western Amazon Basin, although they were after 34,000. They immediately began logging, especially mahogany, and trucking the timber 2,800 miles to Belem. In February 1996 President Fernando Henrique Cardoso of Brazil and President Alberto Fujimori of Peru met to discuss carving out an interoceanic highway to the Pacific Ocean, to be completed before 1999, to make it easier for foreign companies to transport the trees. In late July 1996, Cardoso announced cosmetic measures for reducing deforestation in Amazonia, but concessions to Asian companies subsequently awarded by his government reached 46,000 square miles, and policies of giving loans to ranchers and farmers who destroy the forest continued. While the Malaysian loggers Barama Co., WTK Group, and Samling Corporation are stripping pristine forests in the Amazon, the Canadian Buchanan Group has set its sights on the forests of Guyana. The latter firm is competing with Berjaya Group of Malaysia, Suri Atlantic of Indonesia, and two Chinese companies for the forests of Suriname, a country that morphed from a Dutch colony into a logging colony. Recently WTK purchased a million hectares (3,860 square miles) of forest in Brazil, near the Juruá River, and 200,000 hectares (772 square miles) near the Uatumá River.

Mobil is ready to begin prospecting for oil in the territory of the Yaminahua, relatives of the Nahua and neighbors of the Amahuaca and the Mashco-Piro. When Shell carried out oil exploration in 1985 in Nahua territory, between 50 and 100 Indians died. "In 1985, the problem was caused by the loggers who came in after the oil people. They came across a group of Nahuas and gave them diseases to which they had no immunity. Half the group died. Most of those who remain now live in misery on the outskirts of a nearby mainly white city," according to the Ecuadorian magazine *Savia*.

According to Brazil's National Institute for Space Research (INPE), during "the season of madness," the fire season in the Amazon rain forest that stretches from July to November, when farmers, ranchers, and developers set fire to fallen trees to clear land, there were record numbers of fires in 1995: 39,900 in July, 72,200 in August. Most of the fires were in the states of Acre and Rondônia, on the borders with Peru and Bolivia, countries where the Asian Tigers are seeking to expand their logging ventures. Smoke from the torched areas casts a milky haze over 2.7 million square miles, covering parts of Brazil, Bolivia, Paraguay, and Uruguay and forcing airport closures. The sun was veiled, the moon and stars hidden in the sky. At the end of September,

Amazonia was still burning. Environmentalists affirmed the fires were deliberately set. Eduardo Martins, president of the Brazilian Institute of
Environment and Renewable Natural Resources (IBAMA), admitted that
illegal burning continued unchecked, and the government's prospects for
halting the destruction were unrealistic. Alberto Setzer, a scientist at INPE,
predicted that, due to the substantial increase in fires across the Amazon
basin, and in areas where fires had not been expected, the deforestation rate
for 1996 would probably be very high. Last August, scientists from the
United States and Peru announced they were measuring atmospheric gases in
the jungle to predict the impacts of deforestation on the greenhouse effect
and global warming.

Latin America, once known for its banana republics, is now home to timber republics such as Brazil, Guyana, Suriname, and others that have morphed
into wholesalers of the jungle. Politicians and local businessmen are getting
rich at the cost of sacrificing irreplaceable biodiversity that they sell to Asian
companies already notorious for their savage plundering of forests in
Cambodia, Indonesia, the Philippines, Papua New Guinea, Borneo,
Cameroon, and Gabon. To future generations of Latin Americans they will
leave a desert where once existed one of the most extraordinary and glorious
paradises on Earth: Amazonia.

UPDATE: Deforestation in the Brazilian Amazon has been on the rise,
following enactment in 2012 of a new forest code, with a 29 percent increase
in 2016. The code granted amnesty to landowners for illegal deforestation
prior to 2008. Philip Fearnside, an ecologist at Brazil's National Institute for
Research in Amazonia (INPA), now fears that proposed changes to laws that
would weaken environmental and social restrictions on development, agribusiness, and infrastructure such as dams, highways, and railways will lead to
further deforestation and increased greenhouse gas emissions. Brazil has ratified the Paris Agreement on climate change, but reaching its carbon emissions reduction goal seems unlikely. Meanwhile, the Amazon's capacity as a
crucial carbon sink is declining. Fearnside writes, "The Brazilian government
subsidizes deforestation by providing low-interest loans for agriculture and
ranching; establishing settlements; providing extension and research to
expand soybeans, cattle pasture, and unsustainable forest management; and
building and maintaining roads and other infrastructure to transport these
products." Soybeans are Brazil's main export, and the country's largest
soybean producer happens to be the current minister of agriculture.

During the next twenty years forty large hydroelectric dams will be built in the Brazilian Amazon basin. Much of the energy from hydropower fuels the electricity-hungry mining industry, and the National Mining Plan calls Amazonia "the current frontier of expansion for mining in Brazil." Brazil's main minerals are iron, bauxite, manganese, and gold. The dam and mining megaprojects, and the associated infrastructure, can do tremendous social and environmental harm.

Throughout the Amazon basin's watershed a total of 428 dams are in operation, are under construction, or are planned. A recent groundbreaking study led by Edgardo Latrubesse of the University of Texas at Austin developed the Dam Environmental Vulnerability Index. Four of the Amazon's 19 major sub-basins—Madeira and Tapajós in Brazil, and Ucayali and Marañon in Peru—are deemed highly vulnerable.

In March 1989, the eight countries of the Amazon Pact denounced foreign pressure to protect the region, rejecting "impositions from people who try to boss us around." Today the rhetoric may have softened under the guise of sustainable development, but the relentless destruction of Amazonia continues. Is it realistic to expect that Bolivia, Brazil, Colombia, Ecuador, Guyana, Peru, Suriname, and Venezuela, grouped in the Amazon Cooperation Treaty Organization, will work together in the collective basin-wide management the study identifies as the only hope for saving Amazonia from irreparable environmental damage?

Syphilis, the Other Quincentennial?

HA, *La Jornada*, January 12, 1990

On October 12, 1992, it will be 500 years since the mutual discovery took place. Christopher Columbus and his crew encountered brown-skinned, naked people, who in turn encountered bearded, clothed men. That autumn Friday the admiral jotted down his first notes about nature in the Indies: "Trees very green, and much water, and fruits of diverse kinds. . . . I saw no beasts on the land of any kind, except parrots and lizards."

At the same time, exploration of a geography unimagined by Ptolomey or the medieval geographers, and the "destruction of the Indies," began.

Although Christopher Columbus ushers us into planetary history, he also introduces us to modern ecocide and ethnocide. More than the fall of Constantinople in 1453, the discovery of America marks the end of the ancient world and the beginning of our age.

Starting in 1492, the Old World will be enriched with the flora and fauna of the New World. As José de Acosta notes, plant species never mentioned by the Greeks or Romans will be seen for the very first time: maize, potato, avocado, tomato, cocoa—used as money in Mexico—sweet potato, chili pepper, manioc, papaya, mamey, pineapple, cotton, tobacco, beans and squash of many kinds, maguey, and prickly pear and other cacti. New species of parrots and skunks; barkless, edible dogs; vampire bats; armadillos; iguanas; boas; mockingbirds; turkey vultures; toucans; quetzals; anteaters; opossums; raccoons; condors; four kinds of flamingos; many monkey species; various pelicans, ducks, and eagles; turkeys; members of the woodpecker family and hummingbirds will figure prominently in the letters, narratives, histories, and memoirs of successive generations of explorers, conquistadors, evangelists, and settlers, the four main categories of those people who brought the Old World to the New and carried the New World to the Old.

I won't go into the fantastic zoology created in parallel by the men who roamed the Indies, from Christopher Columbus himself, who sighted three mermaids (manatees) in the Río del Oro, in Haiti, on the island of Hispaniola, to Martín Fernández de Enciso, who wrote of "the loquacious and prodigious hyena, who is female one year and male the next."

On September 25, 1493, Columbus set sail from Cadiz on his second voyage with a fleet of 17 ships, stocked with seeds and plants of wheat, barley, onions, radishes, melons, peas, broad beans, lettuce, sugar cane, scallions, and parsley, "to test the soil, which seems wonderfully good," as he noted in the *Memorandum* entrusted to Antonio de Torres for delivery to the king and queen. He also brought domestic animals: cows, mares, sheep, goats, pigs, chickens, dogs, and cats "that reproduce there in a superlative manner, especially the pigs," as Michele de Cuneo wrote in a letter to a friend about the second voyage. In the *Memorandum* Columbus requested that "every time a caravel is sent here" it should bring lambs, calves, heifers, asses, and hacks "for working and sowing, for here there is not a single animal from which a man can get use or service." American Indians had few beasts of burden for their use, and as Alfred W. Crosby remarked, "the fastest and strongest animal available for service there was man himself." The horse, useful for work and travel, would be decisive in the conquest of Mexico and Peru.

The Indians would adopt and make theirs animals and plants "which prosper better there than the Indian plants do brought into Europe," many of them flourishing abundantly on the islands and mainland of the ocean sea. Meanwhile, the Europeans adopted and made theirs various New World plants, such as maize, potatoes, tomato, cocoa, and tobacco, which became staples of their diet and a part of their habits and in some cases solved the problem of their famines. José de Acostá had this to say about the first arrival of pineapples to the Old World: "The Emperor Charles was presented one of these pineapples, which must have cost much pain to bring it from the Indies on its plant, for otherwise it could not have come. He praised the smell yet would he not try the taste."

While the explorers and conquistadors brought the sword and the cross, the Spanish language and candlelight, they also brought their "biological allies," as Charles Gibson and Alfred W. Crosby have pointed out. Between the slaughter perpetrated by "destroyers" (so called by Fray Bartolomé de las Casas) such as Pedrarias Dávila and Hernando de Soto—both given to setting dogs on Indians—Hernán Cortés, Nuño de Guzmán, Gonzalo Jiménez de Quesada, and Francisco Pizarro, and the raging epidemics, the Indies were depopulated "by infinite thousands." But if the Old World gave the New diseases that passed from man to man—smallpox, measles, pestilent fevers—the New World gave the Old one that passed from body to body: "The disease of Española."

This was syphilis, whose origin each country blamed on its enemies: the Italians and the English called it the French sickness; the French, the disease of Naples; the Portuguese, Castilian scabies; the Castilians, the disease of Española. However, Gonzalo Fernández de Oviedo argued that it should have been called the disease of the Indies, since the Europeans acquired this pox along with the gold.

Some believe it was brought to Spain by a pilot from Palos, Martín Alonso Pinzón, on his return from the first voyage, dying shortly afterwards. In his book *Fruit of All Saints against the Disease of the Island Española*, the Andalusian physician Rodrigo Díaz de la Islas relates that the sickness "easily took hold" of several of Columbus's seamen and that he himself was witness to its spread in Barcelona in 1493.

Oviedo states that "this sickness was first seen in Spain after Admiral Christopher Columbus discovered the Indies and returned to these parts. . . . Afterwards, in the year 1495, when 'The Great Captain' Gonzalo Fernández de Córdoba marched into Italy . . . he brought this sickness along with some

Spaniards." In his "Syphilis sive morbus Gallicus" (Syphilis, or the French disease, a poem in Latin hexameters published in 1530), the Veronese physician Girolamo Fracastoro coined the name by which the disease is now known.

"The disease of Española" jumped from sailors and soldiers to popes and kings, courtesans and shady women. And since a great portion of the West's universal history has been turned into art and literature, "the disease of Española" entered into the world of images and words. In 1496 Albrecht Dürer gave us the earliest known portrayal of a syphilitic, in all his misery. Afterwards Miguel de Cervantes Saavedra, William Shakespeare and Francois Rabelais wrote—often with black humor—of buboes and pustules. Francisco Delicado, author of the picaresque novel *Portrait of Lozana: The Lusty Andalusian Woman* (1528) and himself a sufferer from syphilis, refers variously in the book's 66 dialogue sequences to "the French disease," "the *mal francorum*" and "the disease of Naples," and a year later in Venice he published a treatise on its cures, *On the Use of the West Indies' Wood*, referring to guaiacum (a genus of tropical flowering plants whose heartwood is Lignum vitae). According to Antonello Gerbi, some, like Giovanni Consalvo, who broke out in buboes in Naples, sailed for the New World in search of guaiacum or lignum vitae, in the belief that whence came the disease would be found the remedy as well.

For five centuries, the inhabitants of the Old and New Worlds have not ceased to discover, and love, each other. In 1992 we will celebrate the meeting of the naked and the clothed. Will syphilis also have its own fifth centennial?

The Meeting of Two Natures

HA, *Christian Science Monitor*, April 9, 1992

Fourteen ninety-two initiated the meeting of two natures. The Old World was enriched by the flora and fauna of the New, and the latter with those of the former. As the 16th-century Jesuit naturalist José de Acosta pointed out, species of plants and animals not identified in Greek or Latin would be seen for the first time: corn, the first kernels of which Christopher Columbus brought back to Spain on his first voyage; the tomato, chocolate (which Mexicans sold ground-up or used as coins—so wrote Hernán Cortés in his second letter to Charles V), tobacco, cotton, strains of peppers and beans; papaya, pineapple, and potato. The Europeans adopted the produce from the New World and made it theirs; it became part of their diet and habits, and in some countries solved problems of starvation.

Animals such as anteaters, sloths, condors, boas, cougars, tapirs, polecats, armadillos, vampire bats, toucans, quetzals, flamingos; breeds of parrot and monkey, eagles, turkeys, woodpeckers, and hummingbirds occupied a conspicuous place in the accounts, letters, histories, and memoirs of successive generations of explorers, conquistadors, missionaries, and settlers—the four principal categories of men the New World attracted.

On Sept. 23, 1493, preparing for his second expedition, Columbus loaded aboard his fleet of 17 ships wheat seed and plants, barley, radishes, onions, peas, melon, sugar cane, broad beans, lettuce, leeks and parsley, "To try out the ground, which appears most marvelous," as he put it in his "Memorandum" to Antonio Torres.

He took on domestic animals as well: cows, oxen, sheep, goats, hens, pigs, dogs and cats, "which grew over there to a superlative degree, pigs above all the rest," according to the references made by Michele de Cuneo in his narrative of the second voyage.

And since these appeared insufficient to him, Columbus continued asking for more rams, lambs, asses, and oxen "to be shipped on any available caravel for the business of planting, there being no such animals here which a fellow might use to aid him." The horse, adaptable for travel, battle, or fieldwork, would be a deciding factor in the conquests of Mexico and Peru, and later conflicts in America.

These animals and plants the native Indians accepted and made their own "in such a way that the things of Europe take better there than the things of the Indies in Europe," according to De Acosta, the flora and fauna multiplying into a great abundance throughout the New World.

Next Oct. 12, the meeting between the Spaniards and the Antilleans will surely be commemorated. That Friday in 1492, Columbus entered his first note on the nature of the Indies: "deep green trees, ample waters and fruits of divers kinds. . . . No beasts, barring parrots, dwell on this island." So, in this geography undreamed of by Ptolemy or the medieval cartographers, began the New World's age of explorations and—as Bartolomé de las Casas, one of the first defenders of human rights in the world, revealed decades later—its destruction.

From that day forward began the only documented, history-making discovery of the continent, which Martin Waldseemüller named America by mistake on his map. From that day onward we enter into an understanding of the planet and modern times. Far more so than the fall of Constantinople into the hands of the Turks in 1453, which ended the Old World, 1492 redefined history as global. Columbus, about whom so much is known after his first voyage—and almost nothing before that—is the historic traveler who opened up the geographical exploration of America.

But now, 500 years later, what has become of the meeting and interchange of two natures? The protagonists are no longer the Old and New Worlds, but the First and Third Worlds, or the North and the South. The forests of America are disappearing at an alarming rate, victim to the insatiable desires of the First World for tropical woods, to its greed for gold and mineral wealth, sacrificed to make room for the descendants of those 15th-century cattle, often to provide hamburgers for overnourished inhabitants of the First World. In the past decades alone, 20 million hectares (77,000 square miles) of Latin American tropical rain forest have been reduced to livestock pastures.

Our flora and fauna vanish as forests, deserts, and seas are ransacked in search of birds, crocodiles, tarantulas, monkeys, cacti, and plants, to turn into pets, shoes, trinkets, trophies, or profitable patented medicines. Nothing that walks, crawls, swims, flies, or grows out of the earth seems safe from the appetites for the life forms of our continent awakened five centuries ago.

Yet we ourselves are not innocent of the depredation of our own natural wealth. Dangerous accusations of environmental imperialism are utilized to justify nationalistic plans for the rape of our remaining resources. Sovereignty is invoked, and a progress which can only be short-lived, dooming future generations to a meager inheritance in a bleak, desertified expanse stretching from Tierra del Fuego to Alaska, pocked with islands where the remaining species are kept alive in reserves surrounded by concrete and asphalt under which once-limpid rivers now carry sewage away from over-populated, chaotic urban agglomerations.

Wrong-headed, unnatural antagonisms are being formulated: people *or* trees, children *or* plants. The buzzwords "sustainable growth" are being used as a subterfuge for the eradication of forests and entire ecosystems, with scant provision for their replacement. Attempts at protecting migratory or widely distributed species are being challenged as "non-tariff trade barriers," or as cover-ups for "eco-imperialism." When a prominent Brazilian industrialist can declare that the Amazon is old and decrepit, and that no harm would be done by razing the forest and building giant dams, something is seriously wrong.

What if the will to protect the environment does not exist in a country? How can that will be nurtured? What can be given in exchange for ensuring genuine protection of irreplaceable ecosystems, treasure troves of as yet undiscovered species, regulators of climate?

The free-trade argument, that each country is responsible for its own environmental policy that reflects its own values and priorities, is a fallacy. Governmental practices are too often at variance with the real long-term interests of a country and its present and future inhabitants.

The gospel according to GATT [General Agreement on Tariffs and Trade]—that greater wealth ensures greater environmental protection—is not proven. It does not explain why the richest fifth of the world's population produces 75 percent of its pollution. If wealth is generated by cutting down forests, wiping out species, damming rivers, what environment will remain to protect with that wealth?

And what of the original inhabitants of the New World? Speaking the conquistadors' language and practicing their religion, the indigenous peoples of America carry their book of wrongs, past and present, to congresses and conventions organized around the theme of the "discovery" of America. In their terms, since that ominous day in 1492, their troubles haven't ceased; prior to that, none existed. Some reach the extreme of blaming Columbus for AIDS, the contras, the corruption of Latin American politicians, military dictatorships and all the moral, social, and economic deprivations they have endured for the past 500 years.

The truth is that the Indians' complaints are based on actual experiences and are, up to a certain point, unobjectionable. For, 500 years after having been "discovered," they continue strangers in their own land, coping with the twin havocs of ethnocide and ecocide. Their grievance against Columbus is their grievance against history.

But the lines blur between Old World and New, First World and Third, when we contemplate the potential effects of global warming: The rising seas will cover Guanahani, where Columbus first stepped ashore after his voyage, and Palos, whence he set sail. Victims of massive species extinction will include monarch butterflies in Mexico and walruses in the Bering Sea, coral reefs and mangrove swamps. We must recognize our interdependence, the fragility of the web of life, the urgency for industrialized nations to stop squandering fossil fuels if they expect the poorer nations to save trees.

It is inevitable that many things separate us, but others unite us now and always will: our language and our blood. To keep on complaining into the 21st century and the third millennium about what happened 500 years ago may be cathartic, but it is also sterile. Spain will never be able to justify what was done to the indigenous peoples, nor will it ever be possible to restore the American cultures to their original, pre-Hispanic state.

What has to bring us together is common concern about the planet Earth, about the destruction of the ozone layer, the greenhouse effect, the defiling of marine and terrestrial ecosystems, and the resulting disappearance of plant and animal species. We of the Americas must accept our *mestizo* face, bestowed on us by the embrace of Cortés and the *Malinche*. And today, just as 500 years ago, we must be aware of the oneness of the world.

One Hundred Years of Indifference

HA, *Reforma*, May 5, 1996

One hundred years of indifference to Latin America are manifest in the overview published in the April 14 *New York Times Magazine* as "A Celebration of 100 Years," where Latin Americans could find little to celebrate.

In this commemorative issue the editors sought to "give a taste of what the world has looked like, as seen on some 5,000 Sunday mornings, and to recapture moments of memorable writing. . . . Through the selection process, we were dogged by a basic question: Which should take precedence, history or writing?"

In this tasting menu of the world during the past 100 years, Mexico—which shares a nearly 2,000-mile border with the United States—doesn't exist, not its 1910 Revolution or its culture or even its natural disasters. The 1973 military coup in Chile against Salvador Allende is missing, as are other, earlier coups engineered in Latin America by the empire to the North, such as the 1954 overthrow of Jacobo Árbenz, which plunged Guatemala into decades of dictatorships and human rights violations. The editors found no author worthy of anthologizing who had written on the savage warfare in El Salvador or Nicaragua, in which the United States openly intervened. Spain is absent, with nary a word about the "splendid little war" of 1898—as Teddy Roosevelt put it—with the United States, or the 1936–39 Civil War, despite Franco's protracted fascist dictatorship and its innumerable victims, including the poet Federico García Lorca. Not even the Panama Canal, regarded as America's "lifeline" at the time of its building, made it into the issue.

Latin Americans may have signified little to the United States during the past 100 years, but American military and economic actions have had a considerable impact on Latin America. The Magazine's editors found Winston Churchill's piece on "How to Kill a Lion" more important than 100 years of Latin American culture or the fires that raged in the Amazon rain forest or the Galapagos Islands, or how the Brazilian rubber tapper Chico Mendes was killed. The Anglo-Saxon vision of history, even in a liberal newspaper such as the *New York Times*, remains biased and one-sided.

The three pieces on Latin America: Herbert L. Matthews's "An Intimate Lunch with Fidel," Jacobo Timerman's "Return to the Crime" and Nora Ephron's "Yossarian Is Alive and Well in the Mexican Desert"—about the shooting of "Catch 22," not about Mexico—aren't especially representative and give a very meager "taste" indeed of what lies south of the border.

Even though the editors of this centennial compilation strove to be ecumenical, the eurocentric ego of the United States is evident. The historical exclusion of millions of Latin Americans is patent. As Rubén Darío or José Martí could have said a hundred years ago or today, once again the United States has shown that its presence on the American continent is incidental.

Latin America's native peoples are also nonexistent, despite their struggles during the past 500 years in defense of their human rights and their present tribulations. In the centennial issue there are five articles on South Africa and three on Poland, both obviously countries culturally and geographically closer to the United States than is Mexico. The section devoted to "Race and Rights" includes 12 articles dealing with black civil rights movements in the United States but not a single word about Hispanic civil rights movements or about Cesar Chavez, who championed Hispanics laboring in American fields, or about any other citizen of the nation which relinquished half its territory to the United States in the nineteenth century. Remember Texas, lost by Mexico in 1836? And the 1848 Treaty of Guadalupe Hidalgo, in which my country "ceded" the territories of New Mexico and Upper California to "Manifest Destiny," in the wake of the 1846–48 war?

Ludwig Wittgenstein wrote that words are deeds. I find it hard to believe that no other article about Latin America or Hispanics in the 5,000 Sunday issues of the Magazine was sufficiently memorable or historic to satisfy the editors' selection criteria. It seems we Latin Americans will just have to wait another 100 years for the *New York Times Magazine* to pay attention to us.

The Demographic Reconquest

HA, *Reforma*, February 18, 2001

Whereas the Huns, Ostrogoths, and Vandals carried out an armed invasion of European countries in the Middle Ages, nowadays Third World migrants are carrying out a demographic invasion. These silent, systematic and unstoppable invasions are changing the social and cultural face of Western Europe. For us, the territorial reconquest of what was lost of Mexico in wars with Texas (at the time called "the Garden of Mexico as respected richness of soil") and the United States is demographic. As informed readers will remember, the Texas Declaration of Independence in 1836 and the 1846–48 wars with the United States have been the most humiliating episodes of Mexico's history (aside from the Spanish conquest of Mexico-Tenochtitlan). Two Texan cities are named in honor of the protagonists of Texas independence: Austin (Stephen F.) and Houston (Sam).

Invariably judged as unjust and abusive by our historians, these wars resulted in the Treaty of Guadalupe Hidalgo, by which Mexico ceded the territories of Alta California and Santa Fe de Nuevo Mexico and recognized the Rio Grande as the southern boundary of Texas. On its part, the United States agreed to pay its own citizens the money they claimed they were owed by the Mexican government, to not ask the Mexicans for compensation for the cost of a war they had begun, and to pay its neighbor to the south 15 million dollars "in consideration of the extension acquired." This land subsequently became all or part of 10 states. For all this, Antonio López de Santa Anna, intermittently president of Mexico eleven times between 1833–1855 and general-in-chief of the Mexican forces—who on April 21, 1836, was surprised with his troops taking a costly nap on the banks of the San Jacinto River, losing the Battle of San Jacinto (and Texas)—is among the worst Mexican traitors (and one of the butts of gallows humor). And this was only one of the disastrous campaigns he launched against the US army.

Apart from those bloody incidents, since the nineteenth century, love/hate and admiration/resentment relationships between our governments, and between our peoples, have been the norm. Add to this the Mexican conviction that we always end up losing in the historical relationship with the United States. All this is relevant, because during their meeting two days ago at the Fox ranch in central Mexico, Presidents Vicente Fox and George W. Bush were expected to pay special attention to migration issues, and they did delegate them to a "high level" commission. In their joint press release they acknowledged that migration is one of the ties that most closely binds the two countries together, although they should have added that it is one of the conflicts that separates them the most.

Basically, the Mexican presence in what is now the United States has gone through three phases: 1. The population that was living there when our territories were annexed; 2. The people who fled the violence of the Mexican Revolution in 1910; 3. The ongoing economic migration. Our compatriots have changed names over the course of these migrations; once they were wetbacks (as in the 1955 David Silva movie *Espaldas mojadas*); they moved on to become illegals, and now they're undocumented aliens. When they return to Mexico, immigration and customs officials, who fleece them, call them *paisanos* (fellow countrymen). Our perception of Mexicans over there has also changed; now they're chicanos, before they were *pochos*. "Tony was Mexican, but born on the other side, *pocho*, neither Mexican nor American," according to the *Dictionary of Common Spanish in Mexico* (1996).

Undocumented aliens don't have an easy situation. Despite the Nopal Wall built and extended by the United States and the border control systems, hundreds of thousands of Mexicans, and Central and South Americans, make the crossing every year in search of a job. The swelling of their numbers not only means a bonanza for the *polleros* (people smugglers) but also lays bare the impoverishment of our countryside and the lack of job opportunities in our towns and cities, both in Mexico and the rest of Latin America, and the population explosion. Today the Hispanic or Latino presence is notable in states on the border and in the most far-flung states, so that travelers from our part of the world will easily find themselves speaking Spanish in stores, restaurants, public offices, and on the streets. Hispanics already make up 13 percent of the population, and add to that millions of illegal immigrants from Latin America. About 30 million people of Mexican origin are living in the US.

In the twenty-first century the Hispanic community will make its weight felt in social, political, and cultural affairs, and Spanish will be the second-most spoken language in the US. American national identity will become increasingly more Latino, and the Hispanic vote more decisive. On a recent visit to New York I was surprised to find Mexicans not only in grocery stores run by Asians, but as cooks in the kitchen of an Indian restaurant. Does that mean our "Indians" are poorer than the "Indians" of India? Also—and this was new for me—in the subway I found myself surrounded by paisanos from our most marginalized rural areas, and for a moment I thought I was in the Mexico City Metro.

But this shouldn't be surprising, for several years ago a study done by an official at the Mexican Consulate in New York found that there were at least 600,000 Mexicans in the metropolitan area, the majority from the state of Puebla. On a visit last month to Contepec—the town in Michoacán that during my childhood produced tons of corn, wheat, beans, and barley that were trucked to other parts of the country but that now imports not only these staples but even the bread it eats, local bakers having been replaced by Bimbo and Wonder—I discovered that no less than 20 adolescents, male and female, emigrate to the United States every month. I also learned that they are not only looking for employment opportunities, but also want to see what life is like there. Of course! Why should our politicians and moneyed classes be the only ones drawn to the US for tourism and shopping? Our rural compatriots want to go up North too. Isn't it strange that the Mexican states lost culturally and productively during the wars with Texas and the United States are being recovered demographically?

In the past, the obligatory meetings between the presidents of Mexico and the United States never went beyond rhetorical declarations, while daily problems continued as usual, often without solutions. Will this meeting between Fox and Bush be different? We shall see. Meanwhile, although it's unreal to hope for the open borders proposed by Fox, our migrants will keep on crossing open or closed borders to our northern neighbor, nopal walls or not. What the politicians can do is legalize the stay of undocumented Mexicans and grant them migratory security and working rights through an agreement between governments. That kind of agreement would be an act of historical justice.

UPDATE: In 2015 Mexico was the country with the second largest number of emigrants in the world, with 12,340,000 people—nearly 10 percent of its population—living abroad.

Dear Mr. President

HA, letter to the next president of the US two days before the 2008 election. Published in *Reforma*, November 2, 2008

Two days before the election of the next president of the United States of America, not only are there political, financial, social and even cultural expectations in that country, but also concerns in the bosom of international civil society, because whatever happens in the US has global repercussions.

It is hoped that you will state in your inaugural address that the science is indeed in on climate change, global warming and humankind's role in causing them. At a time when the prestige of the US is at one of its lowest levels in history, you will have the chance to reaffirm the political and economic leadership of your country, and to raise its image internationally. You should say that the United States will accept responsibility for its share of carbon emissions and embark on a revolution in energy policy.

You might begin by replacing the existing wall between the United States and Mexico with a wall of solar panels stretching across the border to provide both nations with energy from the sun. The Wall interferes with habitat connectivity and free movement of animal species such as the Mexican gray wolf (in danger of extinction), the desert bighorn sheep, the Sonoran pronghorn antelope, the ocelot, and the American black bear, all of whose populations know nothing about borders, and it destroys the integrity of the Sonoran Desert, one of the most important desert ecosystems in the world, home to pumas, jaguars, porcupines, badgers, bison, prairie dogs, javelinas, jaguarundis, and foxes, and 560 plant species, including the saguaro cactus. The barrier at the border interferes with natural watercourses and causes erosion, flooding and sedimentation. As Robert Frost wrote, "Something there is that doesn't love a wall."

In February 2001 your predecessor chose Mexico for his first trip abroad, meeting with Mexican president Vicente Fox at his ranch in San Francisco del Rincón, Guanajuato. At the joint press conference, George W. Bush said, "Our nations are bound together by ties of history, family, values, commerce and culture. Today, these ties give us an unprecedented opportunity. We have a chance to build a partnership that will improve the lives of citizens in both countries." After September 11, 2001, the United States put Mexico on the back burner. Bring this relationship back to the fore and make it a priority.

Our history and destinies are entwined. Migrations play a huge role in our shared reality. In the early 1990s I proposed the monarch butterfly as the symbol of the North American Free Trade Agreement (NAFTA), for nothing embodies the need for our tri-national environmental cooperation more than this fragile butterfly's spectacular annual migration across Canada, the United States and Mexico. Give your full support to the North American Monarch Conservation Plan, announced in June 2008 by the Commission for Environmental Cooperation (headed by the ministers of environment for Mexico and Canada and the administrator of the US Environmental Protection Agency), to prevent further habitat loss. Free the leatherback and loggerhead turtles that swim in our countries' waters from fishing gear that threatens their survival. Gray whales migrate between Baja California and Alaska. Disturbances in the Bering Sea, where gray whales feed during the summer, endanger them. Safeguard gray whales, polar bears, caribou, migratory birds, and the entire region's wealth of animal life by opposing more oil drilling in the Bering Sea. Do not allow opening of the Arctic National Wildlife Refuge to extraction of the crude oil and natural gas on its coastal plain. Don't squander unique and irreplaceable ecosystems to get at inconsequential amounts of fossil fuel that will not solve your country's energy needs. With only 3 percent of the world's petroleum reserves, United States consumes 25 percent of the world's oil.

As for the human species, it's time for comprehensive immigration reform that will benefit rather than penalize people on both sides of the border. Recognize the vital place of immigrants in US society and ensure they are treated decently and as befits your country's democratic principles.

Corn was first domesticated in Mexico some 7,000 years ago. Mexicans say, *"Sin maíz, no hay país"*—"No corn, no country." We depend on subsidized US corn, which is cheaper than Mexican corn. But as more US corn goes into ethanol, tortilla prices rise, which led to the "tortilla riots" in the winter of 2007. Stop feeding corn to cars, stop subsidizing corn-based ethanol, and back research into second-generation biofuels from non-food biomass using woody crops and agricultural residues.

To show your commitment to combatting drug trafficking, whose consequences are so disastrous for our citizens, you should put a stop to the shameful trafficking of weapons into Mexico by strengthening enforcement of laws that control their export from your country to ours. That would be a demonstration of your willingness to support our government's fight against the violent organized crime that is overwhelming us.

Remember, Mister President, that what's good for the planet is good for the USA.

Instead of Trump's Wall, Let's Build a Wall of Solar Panels

HA and James Ramey, *World Post/Huffington Post*, December 19, 2016

President-elect Donald Trump has repeatedly called for Mexico to build a wall between our countries. There is indeed a way that Mexico could create a barrier between the U.S. and Mexico, one constructed exclusively on the Mexican side, with substantial benefits for both countries and the planet: a solar border.

Sunlight in the northern deserts of Mexico is more intense than in the U.S. Southwest because of the lower latitude and more favorable cloud patterns. And construction and maintenance costs for solar plants in Mexico are substantially lower. Thus, building a long series of such plants all along the Mexican side of the border could power cities on both sides faster and more cheaply than similar arrays built north of the border.

Solar energy is already being generated at lower prices than those of coal. With solar plants along vast stretches of the almost 2,000-mile U.S.-Mexico border on the Mexican side, a new high-voltage direct-current (HVDC) grid could be set up to transmit energy efficiently from that long, snaking array to population centers along the border. HVDC power lines lose exponentially less energy over long distances than traditional power lines. Cities that could immediately benefit include San Diego, Tijuana, Mexicali, Tucson, Phoenix, El Paso, Ciudad Juarez, San Antonio and Monterrey.

If one were to construct the equivalent of a strip of arrays one-third the width of a football field south of the entire U.S.-Mexico border, wider in some areas and narrower in others, with a wide berth allowed for populated areas and stretches of rugged terrain, sufficient energy might be produced to also supply Los Angeles, Las Vegas, Albuquerque, Dallas and Houston. For the U.S. cities, it would be a way to obtain cheaper and cleaner energy than they can from other sources.

A solar border would alleviate a range of binational problems. For one, it would have a civilizing effect in a dangerous area. Since solar plants use security measures to keep intruders out, the solar border would serve as a de facto virtual fence, reducing porousness of the border while producing major economic, environmental and security benefits on both sides. It would make trafficking drugs, arms and people all the more difficult for criminal cartels. In Mexico, the solar border would create a New Deal-like source of high-tech construction and technology jobs all along the border, which could absorb a significant number of would-be migrant workers on their way to cross into the U.S. illegally, at great physical risk.

Most importantly, it would make a significant contribution to the global battle against carbon emissions, since the electricity generated would be carbon neutral, and the purchase of so much solar technology would bring its price down further. The plants would be built using environmentally sensitive techniques for avoiding habitat loss for desert species.

Additionally, the grid could extend to the coasts, where ecologically sensitive desalination plants could be built for the production of fresh water, which could be pumped inland to cities and agricultural areas along the border that suffer from water shortages—a phenomenon bound to worsen as the effects of global warming increase desertification. This would reduce tension and food security concerns that have vexed bilateral relations for decades because of the disputed water supply of the Rio Grande and other shared water sources.

Once the solar plants are installed and prove successful, additional areas in Mexico could be added to the grid, building on the accumulated know-how generated in the new workforce by the initial construction experience. Mexico has immense potential as a solar-producing country, especially in its high central plateau deserts, which provide the most favorable combination of dry, unclouded, low-latitude and relatively cool climate for solar genera-tion. Potentially, all of Mexico could be solar-powered one day.

How to pay for it? Although it would be a major investment, the price of industrial solar generation continues to drop quickly, and because Mexican solar power is cheaper to build and maintain than comparable facilities north of the border, international investors would have strong incentives. Fortuitously, Mexico's recent constitutional reforms encourage foreign and domestic investment in the electric power sector. Construction of the solar border would go a long way toward helping Mexico achieve its mandated climate change goals, which include 35 percent renewable electricity genera-tion by 2024. Electricity exports from Mexico to the U.S. have existed for over a century and have burgeoned in recent years, which should make inter-national long-term loan guarantees for solar plants relatively easy to obtain.

If the initiative were framed as a big charismatic project that has the full backing of the Mexican government, garnering the admiration of the rest of the world, it would position Mexico as an exemplary world leader in combat-ing climate change. Mexico and the U.S. would be connected by a truly beautiful wall—a symbol of unity, visible even from space.

NOTE: James Ramey is a Professor at the Metropolitan Autonomous University, a member of Mexico's National System of Researchers, and a doc-umentary film producer.

UPDATE: On June 21, during a rally in Cedar Rapids, Idaho, President Donald Trump said, "We're thinking about building the wall as a solar wall so it creates energy and pays for itself. And this way, Mexico will have to pay much less money. And that's good right? . . . Pretty good imagination, right? Good? My idea." Not quite. The *World Post/Huffington Post* editors had sent our article to Ivanka Trump.

How a Solar Border Could Help Save the Planet

HA and James Ramey, *World Post/Huffington Post*, July 7, 2017

On June 21, President Donald Trump told a rally in Iowa about his new idea for adding solar panels to the wall he wants to build on the U.S.-Mexico border. As many news reports pointed out, we had proposed a "border of solar panels" in a December op-ed in the *World Post* that prompted more than one million social media interactions. Although we are encouraged that the president has drawn further attention to the colossal potential of solar energy in the U.S.-Mexico border region, we wish to clarify that our vision is fundamentally different from Trump's—and much more rewarding.

Rather than a concrete slab with a coating of solar panels, we propose building a conventional—but vast—series of solar parks along the Mexican side of the border: a "solar border." Instead of wasting around $70 billion on a wall that would be an ecological nightmare and easily traversed in two minutes with a handmade ladder and a rope, the solar parks we propose would create a different kind of structure between the countries, one funded by private investors that would capitalize on some of the best sunlight territory on the planet. This approach would provide copious benefits.

1. Affordable clean energy could power the cities and industries near the border and also, with the help of low-loss, high-voltage transmission lines, distant areas across North America, with an environmental footprint minuscule by comparison to fossil fuel plants of the same capacity.
2. A massive, long-term infrastructure program would provide thousands of jobs, many of them high-skilled, to potential border crossers.
3. A physical obstacle equipped with sensors and other security measures would offer an effective way to impede the illegal traffic of drugs, arms and people across the border.
4. Solar-powered desalination plants would provide freshwater for desert and agricultural areas that will be ever-more desiccated as the planet warms.

5. Enough renewable energy would make an impressive contribution toward reducing global warming, one that could enable both Mexico and the U.S. to significantly exceed their original commitments under the Paris climate change accord.
6. Unlike a wall, such a border would be a shining symbol of shared purpose and comity among neighboring nations and a model for other states of the world to emulate.

Solar parks, in contrast to walls with solar panels, can produce vast amounts of clean energy with comparatively minimal environmental impact, and they actually do pay for themselves relatively quickly. That's why, as Mexican Energy Secretary Pedro Joaquin Coldwell said earlier this year, dozens of companies have invested more than $6.5 billion in solar and wind parks in Mexico in the past year, at record-breaking low costs for consumers. These companies and others are expected to bid another $4 billion before November. If Mexico can raise over $10 billion in two years for renewable energy in parts of its territory, it stands to reason it could do the same along its northern border, especially since that energy could be sold either to Mexico or the voracious markets north of the border at lower prices than are currently available. This is because the costs of construction, maintenance and operations in Mexico are far lower than in the U.S. Southwest, and the sunlight is even more intense.

Building a strip of solar parks along the Mexican side of the border would be paid for not by taxpayers of either country but, as the Berggruen Institute's Nicolas Berggruen and the *World Post*'s editor-in-chief, Nathan Gardels, have suggested, by private investors. And since such investors would pay rent to the owners of the land on which the parks would be built, a lot of which does not currently generate revenue, they would mollify fierce local resistance to the current wall proposal and, more importantly, provide training and employment at diverse skill levels for thousands of workers, some of whom might otherwise try to enter the U.S. without permission.

Our proposal would also curb the cross-border traffic of drugs, arms and people far more effectively than a 30-foot-high wall. Solar arrays ten rows deep, surrounded by chain-link fences, are not as high or imposing as a wall, but they would constitute a much more formidable obstacle course, one that would be decisively more strenuous and time-consuming to cross over or under than a single concrete wall. Sensors in these sprawling arrays would detect crossers and give authorities much more time to arrive. Vehicles carrying heroin, cocaine and crystal meth in one direction or firearms and ammunition in the other—a major concern for communities like the Tohono O'odham tribe, whose territory spans both sides of the border and is about the size of Connecticut—would be completely cut off from border areas by the solar parks. And any tunnel dug under the solar parks would have to be at least as long as the parks are wide, requiring much more time, money and risk than a tunnel under a wall that's only a foot or so thick. In other words, to impede unauthorized crossing, we are proposing a series of broad structures, rather than a tall but thin structure. Broad structures are simply better for this purpose.

Furthermore, solar arrays have an exemplary track record in the protection of delicate ecosystems—they use mitigation techniques such as land bridges, tunnels and passing areas for threatened species, including Mexican gray wolves, jaguars and ocelots; these causeways could be carefully monitored by authorities to ensure that wildlife, but not traffickers, can pass through. And in some areas, as ethnobiologist Gary Nabhan has suggested, the solar arrays could be used to provide shade and water collection for heat-sensitive food crops, thus deriving a double economic benefit from the land.

In other areas, they could be used to create what scientists have described as a "solar reef," in which local flora and fauna avail themselves of the shade provided by the solar panels. Along the U.S.-Mexico border, such reefs could protect ecosystem vitality in habitats increasingly jeopardized by climate change. An additional benefit, one that Saudi Arabia and others have pioneered, is solar-powered desalination plants that could be placed on the coasts of the Pacific Ocean, the Gulf of Mexico and the northern Gulf of California. Via pipelines, these facilities would provide fresh water for people, agriculture and wildlife preservation, thus alleviating the worst ravages of climate change that have been forecast for the border region in the decades to come.

We have been asked why Mexico would ever want to build such a structure, since it is said that the Mexican government is eager for its people to sneak into the U.S. so they can send home remittances and is secretly delighted with the large quantities of drug money that enter Mexico from the north. But this is a distorted stereotype. The reality of modern Mexico is that government leaders from all political parties sincerely lament that thousands of vulnerable Mexicans, many of them from indigenous communities, have died horrific deaths in their attempts to cross the border.

Mexico's leaders would prefer that their 130 million citizens build good lives at home, where they have access to universal health care, tuition-free public universities and a growing economy. Furthermore, Mexico's foremost political and humanitarian crisis is the brutal drug war, which has claimed 175,000 lives in a decade. Mexican leaders are aware that reducing the porosity of the border would greatly diminish the appeal of Mexico as a corridor for drugs from South America and Asia and would also make it harder for cartels to smuggle weapons from the U.S. into Mexico, where almost all guns are illegal for civilians.

Moreover, Mexico's leaders have shown a strong commitment to reducing global warming, pledging 35 percent clean energy generation by 2024. They know that whoever builds the most powerful solar array on the planet, one servicing two economies that together represent 16 percent of the world's carbon emissions, would be feted as a hero in the epic battle against climate change and, not incidentally, benefit from an investment that solar experts Vasilis Fthenakis and Ken Zweibel argue would not only be "technically and economically feasible" but also, potentially, "wildly profitable."

The question we ask, therefore, is why *wouldn't* Mexico want to invite private investors to build the solar border? For that matter, why wouldn't the U.S. want to let them build it on the northern side? If either nation were to adopt our proposal, many of the worst problems afflicting the bilateral relationship would be ameliorated, thousands of good jobs would be created, an immense return on investment would be guaranteed and an unprecedented abundance of cheap, clean energy would be generated.

In fact, if both the U.S. and Mexico were to adopt this plan in collaboration, it would be nothing less than the deal of the millennium. Mexico doesn't need a new Wall—it needs a New Deal. Instead of a wall symbolizing enmity, the solar border would be a lasting monument to hope, friendship and the entrepreneurial spirit, a glittering strand that could be seen by an astronaut standing on the moon, and one that could help save our little blue planet.

6

Our Mexico

THE JAGUAR: *TEPEYOLLOTLI*, HEART OF THE MOUNTAINS

That one who was the image of rain,
no longer leaves trails through the jungle,
the gold discs of his eyes
no longer blink brightly.

He isn't to be seen
in the morning sun floating on a log,
down the Sacred Monkey River.
His solar pelt is a rug.

The heart of the mountains no longer wears
black and white markings on its chest
nor does the volute, cloud of speech that names things,
scroll from his molten jaws.

His mute cry
booms out
my extinction.

HA (*translated by George McWhirter*)

Montes Azules and the End of Lacandonia (Part 1)

HA, *La Jornada*, May 23, 1990

Over the past half century, deforestation has reduced the Lacandon jungle to the minimum size that would allow conservation of the integrity of its ecosystems, and only a small fragment of virgin rain forest is still intact.

Now there is a plan afoot to further reduce the protected area, leaving outside thousands of hectares for future explotation, without applying any protective norms in the so-called buffer zones surrounding the Montes Azules Biosphere Reserve to halt the frenzied rhythm of deforestation.

Anticipating issuance of a decree about the reserve, in a desperate and concerted attempt to establish rights and a de facto situation, the *ejidos* are extending their boundaries towards the reserve, and even well within it, with (although ostensibly without) support from the Secretariat of Agrarian Reform (SRA), in violation of the 1971 and 1977 decrees for the Lacandon jungle, as well as the Secretariat of Urban Development and Ecology's (SEDUE's) 1986 proposal. After all, aren't there presidential resolutions from 1989 that grant land ownership within the reserve to peasants that go against the General Law of Ecological Balance and Environmental Protection (LGEEPA)—which, by the way, is fairly useless?

During an overflight of the Montes Azules Biosphere Reserve, we saw slashing and burning of wooded areas inside and around the Reserve taking place. Most of the new clearings are in hard-to-reach areas, on hills and mountainsides, presumably with the intention of claiming land for agriculture later on—although the hills that were logged several years ago are now severely eroded and show no evidence of continued agricultural production. It's the same for pastures; seen from the air, only a few cows are visible. So you bombard a mountain to kill a spider. The waste of natural resources is huge next to the meager benefits obtained.

Meanwhile, the last remaining moist tropical forest in the northern hemisphere is being destroyed. Albert Camus wrote, "Man is not entirely guilty—he did not start history. Nor is he wholly innocent, for he continues it." Governments come and go, the same pronouncements are made over and over again, but no protective measures are taken, and destruction of the Lacandon jungle continues.

If the current president of Mexico really wants to save the rain forest for present and future generations of Mexicans, he must urgently promote an agreement between all government bodies and agencies that are active in the region (SARH, SRA, CFE, Pemex, SCT, Banrural, FIRA, FIDEHULE, SEDENA, INI, INAH, SEDUE, etc.) and ensure that measures needed to give the forest adequate protection are implemented via an official decree. These bodies and agencies should be forbidden to undertake actions and projects that threaten the integrity of its ecosystems. Without this kind of public commitment, the rest is smoke and mirrors, like the smoke from Mexico's forest fires at this time of year.

As long as people still think that the way to preserve the jungle is by putting money into "development" projects, they're only fomenting its destruction and attracting peasants from other parts of the state to settle there, causing new problems and further destruction of the forest cover. It's time to put an end to the myth that Lacandonia, the Chimalapas, and other forests in the country are a resource always at hand for solving political and social conflicts and an easy way to do business without being punished.

Judging by the deplorable state of the Lacandon jungle and other forests in Mexico, Mexicans would seem to have lost sovereignty over our natural resources as far as controlling the usage and fate of ecosystems are concerned, ecosystems that are being destroyed by irresponsible or self-serving minorities to the detriment of the majority of the population. The government must make it a priority to recover ownership of those resources for the good of the country, and guarantee effective management and conservation. I find it hard to believe that this administration does not see Mexico's biosphere reserves, which are areas of vital importance, as strategic zones.

Montes Azules and the End of Lacandonia (Part 2)

HA, *La Jornada*, May 24, 1990

One of the ministries most responsible for destruction of the Lacandon rain forest is the Secretariat of Agrarian Reform (SRA), which manipulates, encourages, and allows creation of new communities in the region. After one or two harvests of corn, beans, and chile, the fields are turned into grazing land for extensive beef cattle production, and when the soil is degraded the farmers become employees of the ranchers. Three or four out of a hundred become ranchers themselves; the rest move on to slash and burn in other wooded zones. In 1965 there were 12,000 people in the rain forest; at present there are more than 200,000, and the number keeps growing.

Right now, in anticipation of a soon to be announced decree affecting the Montes Azules Biosphere Reserve, and in a last-minute attempt to establish pre-existing rights, the *ejidos* are extending their boundaries towards the Reserve, with or without support from SRA, *and even far into the Reserve*. Some ejidos, such as Lindavista, Nueva Argentina, Villa Flores, Las Pimientas, and San Gregorio, are carving out new paths to mark new limits. Most of the applicants appear to be ersatz ejidos. For example: deep inside the Reserve at Las Pimientas, with 25 applicants, there's only one family claiming 3,000 hectares. Villa Flores has 39 applicants, but only three families actually in place to take over more than 1,600 hectares. San Gregorio, officially with a similar number of families, has 41 applicants for nearly 5,500 hectares. Most of the enlargements of ejidos in the region have no demographic justification. Another contradiction: The new inhabitants of the jungle, the majority migrants from the northern highlands of Chiapas, don't make use of its resources; they are unfamiliar with the fruits, roots, medicinal plants, and traditional ways of using the land.

A few months ago, SRA gave 300 hectares in El Ixcán and Nuevo Tenejapa, south of the Reserve, to ejidos. The property limits have already been set, and the ejidatarios are cutting down the vegetation to burn it off. This area is home to the last and largest tapir populations. Legal proceedings are underway in Mexico City at SRA, awaiting a presidential decision. Meanwhile, SRA keeps sending more landless people to the zone from different parts of Chiapas, especially from the La Corona and 13 de Septiembre ejidos. These are groups of 30 to 50 people who only know how to slash and burn.

During March and April, groups of Chol from the Nueva Palestina region invaded the northern bank of the Lacantún River, inside the Reserve. Despite already owning land, these people want a larger area and they are already clearing the jungle.

The Chols—some 200 men, plus women and children—have taken over the area near the Chajul Biology Station and are moving ahead towards the banks of the Lacantún River, within the Reserve.

This particular group consists of notorious predators who eat squirrels and other animals that traditional jungle residents don't eat, including howler monkeys and endangered tapirs, white-lipped peccary, and great curassow.

Members of this ethnic group have invaded as much land as possible to establish property rights (they could never farm all the forest they are invading), taking advantage of SRA's categorization of the forest as "idle land"; a peasant is entitled to invade this land as long as it is within three miles of his ejido.

The Chols have already stripped some 40 hectares in the areas they have moved into—across from the Reforma Agraria, Pico de Oro, Galaxia, and López Mateos ejidos, inside the Reserve—creating a serious threat to Montes Azules, because the only real boundary of the Reserve was the river they have crossed. The other limits are merely lines on a map, as no one has demarcated the Reserve.

The Chols are probably being manipulated by a politician with plans to extract mahogany and macaws and whatever resources he can from the Reserve.

The *ejidatarios* from Marqués de Comillas are angry because the government won't allow them to clear their lands, but is allowing the Chols to do so inside the Reserve. Excessive clearing is ongoing at Marqués de Comillas, and the ejidatarios exploit Guatemalan workers, paying them minimal wages. Little remains of the forest, and tapir, peccary, and jaguar populations are very low.

If the government doesn't put an immediate stop to these savage invasions and rid the Reserve of this plague of predators—and here I am referring to the heart of Montes Azules, the Sierra Caribe and Rio Negro—the whole idea and existence of the Reserve will be null and void, and we will be witnessing the end of the Montes Azules Biosphere Reserve and, with it, the entire Lacandon jungle.

Montes Azules and the End of Lacandonia (Part 3)

HA, *La Jornada*, May 25, 1990

The alleged buffer zones around the Montes Azules Biosphere Reserve are unregulated. Increased introduction of livestock these past few months, building of a highway to San Quintín near Laguna Miramar, and rapid deforestation carried out by irregular settlers are canceling any intention of protecting the Reserve.

The communities that have settled within Miramar are mostly from San Quintín and they hunt illegally. They are killing tapir, spider monkeys (to take the babies), crocodiles, and jaguar, and they continue to snare macaws. There are still jaguars in the Lacandon jungle, and they could survive if left in peace. The crocodiles are being decimated for their skins.

Illegal hunting of felines, deer, and other species is widespread in the region. In several areas this is done by professionals. In the town of Chuncerro, local residents reported that Pedro Joaquín, a pilot from Tenosique, Tabasco, recently brought in a Gaspar Garda, from Veracruz, and a Dr. Armando, from Tenosique, to hunt jaguar inside the Reserve.

The poachers had three or four feline skins when they left the Reserve. According to residents of Nueva Sabanilla, this March a person sent from Comitán, Chiapas, to carry out a census purchased and took away feline pelts. Professional traps to catch jaguar are being set near the Lindavista *ejido*. Illegal hunting is widespread within and outside the Reserve.

The region is home to many endangered species: jaguar, scarlet macaw, white-lipped peccary, northern naked-tailed armadillo, Central American river turtle, Guatemalan black howler, spider monkey, tapir, and reptiles that have yet to be studied in Mexico. Dr. Jeffrey Wilkerson believes that the basin of Rio Azul, that runs from Laguna Miramar to Río Jataté, could be a natural gathering place for naked-tailed armadillo. In terms of flora and fauna, this basin is of exceptional scientific importance and fundamental for conserving various endangered species in their natural habitat.

In addition to illegal hunting, animal trafficking is rampant in the region. The tanneries and animal pelt shops are filled with ocelot, river otter, jaguar, spotted paca, and agouti skins and hides. Indians are peddling skins in the streets; all the hotels have macaws in their lobbies. Local residents recall that

in 1987, helicopters belonging to IMSS-Coplamar [a federal program providing medical attention for rural and marginalized communities] repeatedly
flew out cargos of 40 macaws. Every high-ranking army officer who is posted
elsewhere takes with him valuable plundered birds.

Biologist Rodrigo Medellín has noted the impact of religion on
Lacandonia's fauna. In observance of Lent, inhabitants of the jungle killed
many river turtles found only in Chiapas, Tabasco, Belice, and Guatemala.
Finding little to eat in the Lacantún region, the faithful pounced on the turtles during nesting season, nearly exterminating one of the few remaining
populations in Mexico.

On the other hand, the water opossum, about which little is known, is
very abundant in this area. With more than 70 species of bats, the forest is
home to one of the most biodiverse bat communities in the world. Mexico
boasts some 135 bat species that feed on insects, fruit, nectar, fish, small
mammals, and birds and blood.

Flora and fauna in the Reserve are in serious danger from the spate of
recent settlements and from illegal hunting. However, thousands of hectares
beyond the Reserve's western boundary that are not included in the Secretariat
of Urban Development and Ecology's proposal can be recovered, and this
boundary should be extended. Many scientifically valuable threatened species
are found in this area. To make them effective, regulations must be drawn up
for the so-called buffer zones surrounding the Reserve, including a ban on
cattle ranching. Only swift and decisive action can save the Montes Azules
Biosphere Reserve.

Montes Azules and the End of Lacandonia (Part 4)

HA, *La Jornada*, May 26, 1990

The Lacandon forest is also feeling pressure from the political, social,
and economic problems of Central American countries. Every week
some 1,000 Central Americans, mostly from Guatemala, cross our
southern border illegally. All want land to build a house and to farm, and that
means clearing the forest.

Local sources say that these people pass themselves off as Mexicans, as it's hard to tell the difference in Chiapas. They wade across the narrow, shallow Suchiate River, while immigration and customs authorities turn a blind eye.

Most recently, internal migration prompted by *ejido* leaders at the Secretariat of Agrarian Reform (SRA) has followed a path from Tlaxcala and Chalco in central Mexico to Campeche and Chiapas, where SRA grants land to peasants if they clear the forest. SRA must stop calling forests "idle land" and stop handing it over legally to *ejidatarios*. The law that classifies only agricultural and ranching lands as non-idle must be changed; the policy of land grants and credits that require land clearing to be legalized is as bad as the invasions. This absurd policy is leading to the deforestation of the entire country, and is finishing off wildlife through habitat destruction.

But just as Guatemalans blend in with Chiapanecans in the Lacandon jungle, the origin of trees logged in the region is also murky. The first week of May, the Secretariat of Urban Development and Ecology's General Directorate of Ecological Protection seized six truckloads of tropical cedar and mahogany bound for MiQRoo, Maderas Industrializadas de Quintana Roo, a company known as a predator; but no one can say whether the wood came from Petén in Guatemala and was brought into Mexico illegally, or if it was from the Chiapas-Campeche tropical forest. A local Secretariat of Agriculture and Water Resources (SARH) official reported that in 1989 three buyers from Campeche were illegally trafficking 1,500,000 cubic feet of mahogany that could have come from Guatemala or been logged illicitly in Chiapas.

Last week illegal shipments of some 250 scarlet macaws crossed the Mexico-Guatemala border, presumably headed for the United States. The profusion of rural roads and the difficulty in monitoring all the truck traffic in this area of Chiapas and Campeche made seizure impossible. A scarlet macaw sells for several thousand dollars in the United States, and smugglers pay the peasants who capture the birds the equivalent of 150 dollars apiece. The United States has the most parrots and macaws in captivity of any country, so much so that veterinarian schools at American universities are training specialists for these species. Why aren't traffickers and buyers in the US punished, as they know these birds are disappearing in the developing countries, and buyers are accomplices? Buyers in the United States should be required to present documentation proving legal possession of the birds, specifying which country authorized their export and commercialization.

Getting back to the problems on our southern border, at the end of August 1988, the general director for land tenure at SRA, Jesús Mario del Valle, stated that since the Lacandon jungle covers more than one million hectares (3,860 square miles), because of its adjacency to Guatemala it is "a strategic zone for defining national sovereignty." Additionally, adducing strategic importance, and to satisfy agrarian demands, the federal government put in motion its program of colonization in Marqués de Comillas, where most of the forest is gone and the population has multiplied fivefold. Defense of national territory didn't go far, for peasants from Michoacán and Guerrero settling in Chajul told me, "Very often at night rockets fired by the Guatemalan army fall on Mexican soil and soldiers frequently cross our border in pursuit of their victims."

Montes Azules and the End of Lacandonia (Part 5)

HA, *La Jornada*, May 27, 1990

The Federal Electricity Commission's (CFE's) plan to build four dams to produce hydroelectric power on the Usumacinta River, the natural border between Mexico and Guatemala, poses another threat to the Lacandon jungle. On March 25, 1987, the Group of 100 addressed a letter to the presidents of Mexico and Guatemala condemning the project, which would have entailed flooding more than 270 square miles of jungle where the ruins of Yaxchilán stand, on the Mexican side, and Piedras Negras, on the Guatemalan side, also affecting Bonampak, Mayan for "painted walls," in the valley of the Lacanjá River, a tributary of the Usumacinta.

If CFE had gone ahead with its plan, not only would it have destroyed what has already been discovered in this vast Mayan archeological zone, but it would have permanently canceled any future findings about this unique cultural heritage of the Mexican and Guatemalan people. Additionally, it would have done irreparable damage to flora and fauna in both countries, and would have struck a deathblow against the last Lacandon Indians in the region, for whom Yaxchilán is a sacred city. Only international reactions, prompted by an article and an editorial in the *New York Times*, made CFE postpone—but not cancel—this barbaric project. Then-secretary of the Secretariat of Urban Development and Ecology (SEDUE) Manuel Camacho Solís summoned me to his office to accuse me, in front of officials from CFE, of sabotaging the good relationship between the peoples of Mexico and

Guatemala by leading opposition to this joint project between both nations. I replied that the saboteurs were the engineers at CFE who were willing to destroy our shared natural and cultural patrimony: the Lacandon jungle and Mayan civilization.

However, we know that the good intentions of the enemies of nature at CFE are not the reason why the project is on hold, but rather the lack of international credit and binational problems, as the Guatemalans are not entirely convinced of the advantages of razing Mayan ruins and part of the largest montane rain forest in North America. In his April 22, 1987, reply to the Group of 100's letter, Vinicio Cerezo Arévalo, president of the Republic of Guatemala, wrote: "I must tell you that I have always agreed with your arguments and it is one of my government's intentions to work to conserve the fauna and the culture present in the area in question. I sincerely believe that this patrimony belongs to humanity and that we must preserve it for attaining knowledge about a glorious past that can serve as a basis for building an even more glorious future." Mexican president Miguel de la Madrid did not bother to reply.

I'd like to remind the technocrats and bureaucrats at CFE and other branches of government, who see rivers and forests as their personal enemies, of this Mayan belief: the sky is held up by trees of different colors, with the green ceiba at the center; if you cut them down, the firmament will fall on our heads.

Montes Azules and the End of Lacandonia (Part 6)

HA, *La Jornada*, May 28, 1990

According to a study by Dr. Jeffrey Wilkerson, the Lacandon jungle is being destroyed at a greater rate and a faster pace than the Amazon forest, with 70 percent lost in the last 30 years. In 1875, the jungle spread over 1.3 million hectares (5,020 square miles); between 1975 and 1960 it shrank 6 percent, losing 1 percent every 14 years. However, between 1960 and 1982, this increased to 1.6 percent yearly, 22 times greater than during the previous period. From 1982 to 1990 the rate of destruction soared to 3.5 percent annually, 50 times higher than before. In 1990 only 30 percent of the original forest remains, 18.3 percent of it damaged. What took 50 years to destroy in the past now takes only one year. At this rate, the jungle is at risk of disappearing in five to ten years. What remains will be neither virgin forest nor jungle, but forest severely disfigured by human activities.

Inside and outside the Montes Azules Biosphere Reserve, direct and indirect impacts are being felt. The Marqués de Comillas jungle is going down fast and may not last more than three to five years. Little forest is left, and populations of tapir, jaguar, and peccary are in critical condition. Various official decrees have been issued to protect Montes Azules, but the boundaries of the protected area are vague and with each new regulation it becomes smaller, while some parts left out of the Reserve can't be saved. It's time for the government to precisely draw the boundaries of the Reserve and of the protective area surrounding it. There are plans and maps unrelated to the terrain and that have never been put into practice. As pioneering conservationist Miguel Álvarez del Toro noted recently, despite presidential and state decrees, logging and the killing of fauna in the Lacandon jungle and Chiapas's Sierra Madre goes on; the green horizon of 30 years ago is now bare earth and rock: "Each day brings new damage, new irregular settlements, while we spend time in meetings and congresses talking about environmental destruction. At this rate, Chiapas will soon be a barren wasteland, with the legend of once-magnificent jungles." One day, all that may remain in the world will be heavily guarded green islands, similar to museums that house masterworks; perhaps the only trace of the jaguars, quetzals, macaws, and other wildlife in the Lacandon jungle will be in photographs.

Experts on the Lacandon jungle agree that the only way to stop its ongoing destruction is for the government to ban the settlements sponsored by the Secretariat of Agrarian Reform (SRA) in the Montes Azules Biosphere Reserve, and for SRA to immediately relocate those communities that have settled in the Reserve (in Miramar, the Ocotal lagoon area, etc.) during the past few months. At the same time, the Secretariat of Agriculture and Water Resources (SARH) should cancel permits for farming and ranching in the region, and suspend credits for *ejidos* within the Reserve, because a few years after the tropical forest is cleared for planting or pastureland, the impoverishment of the soil will lead to more slashing and burning. As has happened in the Amazon rain forest countries, meager yields and low market prices will mean that farming and ranching are subsistence rather than productive activities.

Pemex [Mexico's state oil company] should call a halt to exploration and drilling, and stop polluting rivers, soil, and the air; the Secretariat of Communications and Transportation (SCT) should reconsider its projected highways in the region—between Margaritas and Ocosingo—and especially the road to San Quintín (which already has World Bank funding), because any road for oil drilling, for building dams, for logging, or for facilitating creation of new peasant communities dooms the jungle to human depredation and jeopardizes its archeological patrimony. Any archeological site near a dam project or a road is in immediate danger of looting. Yaxchilán and Planchón de las Figuras, on the Mexican side, and Piedras Negras and the Altar de los Sacrificios on the Guatemalan side, are being affected. When the jungle is despoiled, our archeological heritage also suffers. Out of prudence, no permit should be given for a hotel within the Reserve or in the buffer zone.

To safeguard the integrity of the Lacandon jungle's remaining ecosystems, a Mexican nonprofit organization with no connections to government should be put in charge of keeping an eye on human actitivities, using strategically placed monitoring stations, inside and outside the Reserve, at critical points of access such as roads and rivers. The Chajul research station, a nondestructive human presence, could be an example for siting other stations on the periphery of the Reserve to monitor, research, and protect its natural resources.

The experience of Ecuador clearly shows that nongovernmental organizations play a decisive role in the defense of tropical forests, because they are free of the pressures usually affecting decisions made by elected officials, economic groups, and international bodies. Latin America's forests should be defended from a Latin American viewpoint; their indigenous peoples, whose ancestors have lived in and from the forest for centuries without destroying it, are capable of conserving it in accordance with their cultural traditions and traditional knowledge. Over the past few years, it has become increasingly clear that preserving biodiversity is vital for improving the quality of life for human populations: humankind should not be sacrificed for the sake of the environment nor should the environment be sacrificed for the sake of humankind, for otherwise no human life is possible. A new relationship of man with nature, that balances the needs of one with the rights of the other, must be established.

Talking About the Forest
While the Forest Disappears

HA, *La Jornada*, June 24, 1990

In my series of articles "Montes Azules and the End of Lacandonia," published last month in *La Jornada*, I tried to summarize the problems facing the Lacandon jungle and the complicated mix of human and natural processes that are affecting it now. The reaction to my proposals, and to the Group of 100's June 4 letter to the president, was almost total silence, until two articles, published on June 11 in *El Nacional*, appeared to be setting the stage for an open letter from ARIC (a Rural Collective Interest Association), published June 16, five days later, in *La Jornada*.

In its letter, ARIC avoids addressing the main points of my articles, including the fact that the majority, if not the entirety, of the individuals it represents were not settlers prior to Luis Echeverría Álvarez's presidential decree of November 26, 1971. (A second decree was issued by President José López Portillo on December 8, 1977—and I am not mistaken in the date, as ARIC alleges in its letter. ARIC is referring to a 1979 decree about the buffer zone.)

The area now under ARIC's control is in and outside Montes Azules, around Laguna Miramar. Almost all the settlers come from the Chiapas Highlands. Most of the communities in this association occupy, as *ejidos*, more land, and sometimes significantly more, than what was authorized or claimed (data follows). The communities now illegally present in the heart of Montes Azules include Candelaria, Villa Flores, Las Pimientas, and San Gregorio. There is abundant evidence that persons and families who do not wish to be part of this grouping in the villages under ARIC's sway are repeatedly threatened, and the level of tension in these communities is very high. For example, in Chuncerro, *ejidatarios* who did not want to belong to ARIC were forced to leave, abandoning their land to supporters of the association. ARIC operates like a government but doesn't acknowledge state bodies, as its supporters in the Laguna Miramar region openly admit. Its radio network reports daily to headquarters in Tierra y Libertad; ARIC's president claims to be from there. The spread of these communities towards and within Montes Azules is neither spontaneous nor fortuitous, but well organized.

If ARIC is in favor of conserving and studying the Lacandon jungle, why do its people keep on moving into the Reserve illegally, and why did they detain and expel independent researchers from the jungle this past spring? There's no sign of environmental education or reforestation efforts at any of the region's schools, contrary to what is claimed in the letter. These fictitious programs, and the jungle advisory committee, look more like public relations ploys. While ARIC talks, clearing of trees, hunting, and illegal wildlife trafficking continue, and plans are still being made to bring in more ranching and to plant new communities in the heart of the Reserve.

As shown in the table, the settlements are far larger than authorized or applied for, with an excessive number of hectares per beneficiary. To date, the Secretariat of Urban Development and Ecology's (SEDUE's) unfinished study has covered 184,699 hectares (713 square miles) and identified 88 tracts of land. Nevertheless, they have already found that the ejidos possess 59,543 hectares (230 square miles) more than were granted, and the new settlements occupy 22,703 hectares (88 square miles). That's only until now and as far as the study has gone.

The artificial creation of new villages with families from different ethnic groups or peasant regions of Mexico provokes social disintegration in a catastrophic fashion; sociologist Susana Villafuerte found that this violent process is promoting the disappearance of traditional indigenous societies and is a determining factor in the progressive fragmentation of these jungle communities. Transmission of communal behaviors, traditional herbal medicine, and a striking decrease in mutual aid among women are among customs that are lost. Moreover, unfamiliarity with the new environment leads to farming practices that are bound to fail, due to climates and soils that differ substantially from those in the highlands, the original home of the settlers.

If this goes on, in 10 years Mexico will have lost the tropical forests that regulate climate in the southeast and are the watershed of the rivers that power the hydroelectric plants, as well as protecting the fragile soils of the region, with its extraordinary flora and fauna, from erosion. We will have hundreds of thousands of poor peasants living in an eroded, barren region, which will lead to yet another forced emigration to our already overcrowded cities, and as always, the sole beneficiaries will be a handful of caciques, politicians, ranchers, and loggers.

As Dr. Jeffrey Wilkerson noted, the Lacandon jungle is being destroyed at a greater rate and a faster pace than the Amazon forest and risks disappearing in five to ten years. The most recent invasions of the Montes Azules Biosphere

Reserve mean the end of Lacandonia. In ARIC's letter, a small group of people talk about the entire jungle as though it belonged to them. In the Group of 100's letter to the president, we pointed out that "We Mexicans have lost sovereignty over our natural resources as far as control of the use and fate of the nation's ecosytems are concerned. They are being destroyed by irresponsible minorities, to the detriment of the majority of our people. It is a priority for the government to recuperate possession and use of those resources and to ensure their proper management and conservation. The core zones of biosphere reserves must in all cases be *property of the nation* and form its *natural patrimony.*"

Findings about several ejidos belonging to ARIC (according to an ongoing study by SEDUE)

EJIDO	HA. GRANTED	BENEFICIARIES	HA. OCCUPIED	EXCESS HA.
Tierra y Libertad	1,560	73	4,219	2,659
Benito Juárez	3,384	63	4,572	1,188
Chuncerro la Laguna	900	37	1,652	752
Vicente Guerrero	1,280	38	2,380	1,100
Amador Hernández	2,294	40	6,679	4,385
Enlargement of Amador Hernández	800	31	1,779	979

(Ha. = hectares)

A Proposal to Save Forests

HA, speech given on September 23, 1989, at the Lacandon Rain Forest Conference held in Seattle, Washington. Printed in *The News,* Mexico City, November 12, 1989

It has been said that nothing can stop an idea whose time has come, and the time to save the rain forests must be now, or never, for all too soon only the memory may remain of the existence of rain forests on Earth.

If we believe and universally accept that these forests are the natural heritage of all humankind, of the living and those yet to be born, then people in all parts of the globe must come forward in their defense and take those measures that are necessary for the effective protection of the rain forests.

With this idea in mind, I would like to propose the creation of an international environmental safeguarding corps that would work to halt the further devastation of Lacandonia, Amazonia, and the other remaining tropical forests of the world and help preserve the wealth of biological diversity on Earth.

The corps would be composed of members from developed, developing, and underdeveloped countries, something along the lines of the United Nations peacekeeping forces. Squads of Green Helmets would work with the corps, monitoring and watching over the areas in their charge to ensure acceptance of the Green Helmets in the countries whose flora and fauna it would be their job to protect. Each group should include citizens of the country and foreigners. Ideally the citizens would be recruited among the traditional inhabitants of the rain forests, and the foreigners might be young people who are not identified with any particular economic or political interest group. They would receive the professional training necessary to carry out their task and have the means to periodically inform the rest of the world about conditions in the forests in their keep.

The corps itself must also be independent of any political or economic ties to governments or private groups, to ensure its efficient safekeeping and monitoring of the biological resources of our planet. Offices of the corps should be located in countries that possess tropical forests as well as in major "First World" cities where all facilities are available for the timely notification of fires, to coordinate international assistance, to mobilize world opinion in favor of an immediate halt to any sort of depredation, and to maintain an information bank on all tropical forests. The world headquarters might be located in Washington, DC, London, Mexico City, Rio de Janeiro, Jakarta, or Kinshasa.

I cannot say with any certainty whether this idea would work or not, but I do know that we must do something soon, for in a few years it will be too late to save the world's rain forests and their native inhabitants.

The Ravaging of Montes Azules

To Francisco Toledo

HA, *Reforma,* May 14, 2000

If the National Museum of Anthropology and History were on fire, or if the pyramids at Teotihuacán were being bulldozed, an international outcry would condemn the enormous cultural loss of these places. The Lacandon jungle, Montes Azules, Lacantún, Chankín, Yaxchilán, Bonampak, Palenque, Nahá, and Metzabok are their cultural and spiritual equivalents in the Mayan world, encompassing 421,225 hectares (1,626 square miles) of protected natural areas; 331,200 hectares (1,279 square miles) belong to Montes Azules. If Bonampak, Yaxchilán, and Palenque are masterpieces of the human spirit, the Montes Azules Biosphere Reserve is a masterpiece of nature. According to the National Institute of Ecology (INE), between January 1 and May 5 there have been 261 fires in the Reserve that have burned 24,000 hectares (93 square miles); 10 of the 66 fires in the Lacandon jungle ravaged 1,683 hectares (4,158 acres). The April 11 and 28 blazes consumed high evergreen forests. The April 22 fire in San Quintín, Tierra y Libertad and Benito Juárez destroyed 329 hectares (813 acres). The fire in Salvador Allende that started on May 5 has already burned three hectares of primary forest. Logging and fires are finishing off the Lacandon jungle. Indifference in the media and public opinion toward this environmental tragedy is inexplicable. A small number of families illegally settled in the Reserve are not only endangering the natural patrimony of an entire people, but they are reducing it to ashes. The obsolete practice of slash-and-burn agriculture to extend the limits of farming and cattle ranching is a cultural and economic aberration. And even worse, as the fires burn, uncontrolled logging and wildlife trafficking are running rampant. Neighboring Petén, in Guatemala, has also been ravaged by fires.

According to the 1990 census carried out by the National Institute of Statistics and Geography (INEGI), the Lacandon jungle had 1,879,528 hectares (7,257 square miles) and 700 communities, with a population of 263,043, which in the year 2000 has risen to half a million, thanks to a 9.5 percent annual growth rate. This huge growth rate is responsible for many of the sociopolitical, economic, and environmental problems, and no country can deal with growth of this magnitude. There are constant pressures to change land use in favor of livestock grazing and planting corn, beans, coffee, chile, and cacao, and critical protected areas such as El Desempeño, El Ocotal, Indio Pedro, Río Negro, El Jardín, Chaquistero, and Miramar are regularly invaded. Of the 32 groups that settled illegally in Montes Azules, 22 groups (comprised of 367 families) did so within the Reserve and 10 (comprised of 307 families) outside its borders. Four groups (59 families) refuse to negotiate and are actively deforesting the best-conserved part of the Reserve, where the Yanqui, El Suspiro, Ocotal, El Buen Samaritano, San Francisco, and Innominado lagoons are found.

What is at stake in the Lacandon jungle? According to the Secretariat of the Environment, Natural Resources, and Fisheries (SEMARNAP), in Mexico the Grijalva-Usumacinta is the watershed that captures the greatest amount of water. Of the 439 species of mammals in Mexico, 163 of them are found in the Lacandon jungle, or 37.1 percent. The Lacandon contains 508 of Mexico's 1,041 bird species (47.9 percent); 800, or 40 percent, of Mexico's 2,000 diurnal butterfly species, 11 percent of our reptiles and amphibians, and 10 percent of our flora. Well-known species include the spider monkey, howler monkey, jaguar, tapir, Morelet's crocodile, harpy eagle, scarlet macaw, and keel-billed toucan. Mahogany, Spanish cedar, and breadnut are among its 573 species of trees.

In 14 years, the forested area of the Lacandon jungle decreased by 41 percent, equal to 33,500 hectares (129 square miles) per year, making for a deforestation rate of 3.8 percent, the highest in the country. At this rate, by 2015 its forests and jungles will be gone. The Lacandon jungle will be Mexico's largest desert. Fires deliberately set in the Lacandon during 1998 destroyed 25,000 hectares (96 square miles) of rain forest, cloud forest, and pine-oak forest. How many hectares will be torched this year? The ecocidal aberration is simple: a few families squat in or near the Reserve and log and burn, finishing off all the plant and animal life. But with what right? In whose name? On May 2, the Group of 100 denounced the fires in Montes Azules, calling on SEMARNAP to use all the technical and human resources at its disposal to put out the fires, because the political, ethnic, and social problems in the region are making the Lacandon jungle their victim. Firefighting should take into account advice from nongovernmental organizations with sufficient knowledge and impartiality to ensure that it does not become politicized, and that environmental protection activities will not be viewed as covert military actions or a pretext for armed intervention against indigenous groups. It has been said that historical ethnocide does not justify ecocide that will make history: the future victims of this destruction will be those very ethnic groups whose permanent habitat is the Lacandon jungle. National and international indifference to the destruction of Montes Azules, one of the world's most biodiverse ecosystems, is scandalous.

UPDATE: A government source in Chiapas has revealed that the current principal cause of deforestation in the Lacandon is illegal logging under the cover of night. Once an area is shorn of trees, permissions are given to plant African oil palms. A tree takes three years to begin producing, and it reaches full production eight years after planting; one hectare of palm trees generates earnings of 100,000 pesos (about $5,500) per year, whereas a once-yearly government Payment for Environmental Services is 1,000 pesos (about $50) per hectare for the conservation of natural resources.

Inhabitants of the Ejido Boca Chajul, in Marqués de Comillas, say that the Lacandon is being cleared to sow African palm. Officials claim that planting is confined to degraded land that was used for grazing. There are plantations in the Lacandon buffer zone and in the Montes Azules Biosphere Reserve (of which 80 percent has been cleared).

In Chiapas 64,000 hectares (247 square miles) are planted with African palm, more than 70 percent of 87,000 hectares (336 square miles) in Mexico, and the state government is aiming for 100,000 hectares (386 square miles). The federal government estimates that 2.5 million hectares (almost 10,000 square miles) in Mexico are suitable for African palm, of which 400,000 are in Chiapas. There are 11,000 growers, and almost all the processing plants are in Chiapas.

African palms were first sown in Mexico in 1948. In 1983 the federal government began subsidizing planting, with 3,000 hectares (7,400 acres) in

Chiapas for small scale farmers. In 1996 SAGARPA launched a National Palm Program. In 1986 only 1,500 metric tons of palm oil were produced, but in 2000 production began to soar, reaching 110,000 tons in 2016.

The monoculture palm plantations ravage biodiversity through habitat loss; pollute air, water, and soil with herbicides, insecticides, and rodenticides; and increase carbon emissions. Palm oil is used for food, soaps, detergents, oleochemicals, and cosmetics, as well as palm oil-based biodiesel, which exacerbates climate change. An African palm researcher in Chiapas has described a plantation as a "desert of silence where there is no longer a dawn chorus."

Fox versus the Usumacinta River

All of them painted, never extinct, these are the waters of the river of monkeys, Usumacinta.
Carlos Pellicer, "The Song of the Usumacinta"

HA, *Reforma*, October 13, 2002

Like a recurrent nightmare, the plan to build dams on the Usumacinta River has resurfaced, in the cradle of Mayan civilization and within the Lacandon jungle, where the rate of deforestation is even greater and destruction swifter than in Amazonia.

In the mid-sixties, the San Carlos Boca del Cerro community was slated for a large hydroelectric dam. The project was suspended. In 1980 Mexico made an agreement with Guatemala to carry out a feasibility study for a series of dams in the Usumacinta watershed, and in 1985 a recommendation was made for Boca del Cerro to be the main dam, with four additional ones; the reservoirs would cover an area of 500 square miles. In March of 1987, the Group of 100 denounced the plan to build dams on the Usumacinta River, the natural frontier between the two countries. To carry out the project would mean flooding 270 square miles, submerging Yaxchilán and Piedras Negras, canceling future discoveries about the Mayan cultural past, and giving a kiss of death to the Lacandon forest, one of the last tropical rain forests on Earth, and to the Lacandon people living in the forest. The *New York Times* printed the news on its front page, together with an editorial entitled "Don't Flood the Mayan Vatican." The Group of 100 asked the presidents of Mexico and Guatemala to cancel the project, and Guatemalan president Vinicio Cerezo Arévalo declared his intention "to work to preserve the fauna as well as the culture" of the región, stating, "I sincerely believe that this is a common heritage of humanity, and that we must preserve it." In May 1989, at the request of the Guatemalan government, Mexico's Secretariat of Urban Development and Ecology (SEDUE) suspended the Usumacinta hydroelectric project.

The Usumacinta River is the mightiest in Mexico. In 1990 an engineer named Manuel Rubio was hired by the Federal Electricity Commission (CFE) to make a study of the terrain. He concluded that the instability of the riverbed would not allow for building a concrete curtain. Rubio was fired after telling a local newspaper that CFE should forget about the project. The group of experts which then analyzed the environmental impacts of building the dam warned that holding back the flow with a concrete curtain would entail flooding 23 communities along the river bank. Their 25,000 inhabitants would have to be relocated. Construction of the curtain would create a dead river downstream, which in turn would allow parasites to proliferate in the fish, a source of food for local residents. The microclimates in which endemic flora and fauna flourish would disappear. The ecological integrity of the Pantanos de Centla, wetlands rich in biodiversity in the delta of the Usumacinta and Grijalva Rivers on the Gulf of Mexico, would be destroyed. Migratory birds that arrive year after year would no longer find a haven. Contrary to CFE's claims that additional energy was needed to satisfy the national demand for electricity and for sale to Guatemala and Belize, experts revealed that it was Pemex [Mexico's state oil company] that hungered after more energy for further oil exploration and drilling in the area. The region was already undergoing an ecological catastrophe, and the environmental impacts of dam construction would be much costlier than finding alternative energy sources.

On February 15, 1992, during an international meeting in Yaxchilán about biodiversity that I attended, President Salinas de Gotari announced the creation of a new reserve called Yaxbé ("the green road") on the Usumacinta, supposedly to ensure continuity between the Lacandon forest and the Petén in Guatemala. A few days later, I read that CFE and the Secretariat of Energy, Mines, and State Industry (SEMIP) were planning to build dams at Boca del Cerro and other sites along the river. Once again, the Group of 100 opposed this threat to the biological and cultural heritage of Mexico and Guatemala.

We were on the point of launching an international campaign with other North American groups when, at the beginning of April, while I was in New York taking part in PrepCom IV (UNCED Preparatory Committee) prior to the Earth Summit in Rio, I received a call from Dr. Arturo Gómez Pompa (an environmental advisor to Salinas), who informed me that the president had just canceled the project. And indeed, on April 2, at a "Business Participation in Development" meeting in Tuxtla Gutiérrez, Salinas declared, "My government will not build this hydroelectric dam on the Usumacinta River, nor has it plans to carry out similar projects on the river."

Ten years have passed, and now it is President Vicente Fox who has taken up the idea of damming the Usumacinta. But this time, according to residents of Tenosique, Villahermosa, and Emiliano Zapata, rather than use the word "dams," there is talk on a local radio station of "diverting the current to take advantage of its strength." Who are they trying to fool? Just as under the Institutional Revolutionary Party (PRI) governments of the past, management of disinformation by CFE is key to its strategy of achieving its objective, which has already been thwarted several times. Construction of a dam at Boca del Cerro is the cornerstone of the Plan Puebla-Panama (PPP), the most ambitious development project of the current regime, and one that has provoked the opposition of campesinos in Oaxaca, Puebla, Veracruz, Guerrero, and Yucatán; trade unions; academics and indigenous people; and NGOs. At the end of June 2002, during the Fifth Summit of the Tuxtla Dialogue and Consensus Mechanism, held in Merida, Yucatán, the presidents of Mexico, Costa Rica, El Salvador, Guatemala, Honduras, Nicaragua, and Panama and the Prime Minister of Belize agreed to move forward on the Central American Electrical Interconnection System (SIEPAC) project. Most of these countries have already contracted for loans to participate in SIEPAC, whose initial phase would involve the interconnection of Mexico and Guatemala's power grids. Mexico cannot achieve the energy dependence of other countries on our own energy resources without building dams on the Usumacinta, and without deregulating the electricity and oil sectors. The dam at Boca del Cerro will only produce 500 megawatts, 2 percent of national demand.

The arguments against damming the Usumacinta still apply. We cannot allow the destruction of an area with the greatest concentration of biological, cultural, and archeological riches in Mexico. Eighteen archeological sites (not counting those yet to be discovered) would be submerged under 425 feet of water. As I told the *New York Times* in 1987, "The destruction that this project will cause would be worse than if there were a war in the region." Where are the environmental impact assessments? Where is the public consultation? Where is the Secretariat of the Environment and Natural Resources (SEMARNAT), the rubber stamp secretariat, to defend Mexicans' natural heritage? Why has the National Institute of Anthropology and History (INAH) failed to flatly reject this project? How can the World Bank and the Inter-American Development Bank justify their support for such a disastrous undertaking? What happened to democracy, transparency, and the right to information? Has anything changed between 1987, 1992, and 2002? What's the difference between Miguel de la Madrid, Carlos Salinas de Gortari, and Vicente Fox?

In 1991 Gabriel García Márquez and I presented a proposal from the Group of 100 to create a Latin American Ecological Alliance to the 21 heads of state gathered in Guadalajara for the first Ibero-American Summit. One of our recommendations was to establish a binational eco-archeological park that would encompass both banks of the Usumacinta River, to ensure preservation of the tropical rain forest in Chiapas and the Petén, Mayan culture, and the river itself.

Will Vicente Fox go down in history as the destroyer or the savior of the cultural and natural heritage of the Mayan world? What will he decide?

UPDATE: The Plan Puebla-Panama was strongly criticized and aroused widespread opposition. Under President Felipe Calderón, with the signing in Tabasco of the Villahermosa Declaration at the end of June 2008, PPP morphed into the Mesoamerica Integration and Development Project, or Mesoamerica Project, eliminating 95 percent of the original PPP projects. The eight countries that had signed onto SIEPAC were now joined by Colombia and the Dominican Republic. Regional security and the fight against organized crime and drug trafficking came under discussion, and parts of the Merida Initiative were welcomed. SIEPAC currently interconnects the power grids of Guatemala, El Salvador, Nicaragua, Honduras, Costa Rica, and Panama.

On December 27, 2011, presidential candidate Andrés Manuel López Obrador spoke in favor of building a dam at Boca del Cerro. In April 2016, representatives of sixty communities in Chiapas and the Guatemalan Petén met in San Cristóbal de las Casas to strengthen their opposition to the Boca del Cerro dam, which, according to CFE, would have a cement curtain 182 feet high and be one of five dams to be built on the Usumacinta over a four-year period. On December 10, 2016, during a visit to Tenosique, the governor of Tabasco, Arturo Núñez, announced that during his recent visit to Chiapas, President Enrique Peña Nieto canceled construction of the Boca del Cerro dam on the Usumacinta River.

The Giant Cactus Must Stay in Mexico

HA, *La Jornada*, March 14, 1992

A 55-foot-tall, hundreds-of-years-old giant Mexican cardon, or elephant, cactus (*Pachycereus pringlei*) is leaving Baja California on a thirty-wheeler trailer truck for a 1,900 mile, weeks-long journey across Mexico to the port city of Veracruz. From there, the 18-ton cactus will sail to Valencia, and continue to Seville by land. In Spain, the giant cardon will be just another attraction at the Universal Exposition of Seville (Expo 1992), on display outside the Mexican Pavilion. As a newspaper article noted a few days ago, the pavilion's novelty resides in its "100,000 flowering and other plants." What better way to show off our natural beauty than by looting it.

This jewel of the Mexican desert is being uprooted from the Valle de los Gigantes, and its export—for any reason whatsoever—is against the newly minted Environmental Law of the state of Baja California. However, the mayor of Mexicali, Milton Castellanos, a member of the Institutional Revolutionary Party (PRI), gave permission for its removal, his opinion prevailing over the fears of state governor Ernesto Ruffo Appel, a member of the National Action Party (PAN), that the cactus would not survive the journey.

The cardon will travel on a mobile bed, cradled in a plastic-sheathed metallic cage. After its branches are smoothed and tied, the cactus and its widespread subsurface root system will be lifted out of the ground by a giant crane. Juan Siles, an engineer who came up with and is overseeing the project, said the cage and transport would cost approximately 70,000 dollars.

The green candelabra's final fate is a mystery. No one knows if it will return one day to its natural habitat in the Baja California desert, or if it will die, rootless in a foreign land, and Juan Siles will forfeit the 100 million peso bond (33 million dollars) he gave the Secretariat of Urban Development and Ecology (SEDUE) in exchange for permission to export the cardon. The best solution would be to return it to where it was. The cactus does not belong in Expo 1992; it belongs with its fellows in the Valle de los Gigantes, and moving it risks killing it. Five hundred years ago, Christopher Columbus loaded his caravels with natives and parrots. Today, 500 years later, yet still suffering from a colonial mentality, we voluntarily send over our natural gems.

A veritable temple of a plant has been torn from its home in Mexico to be put on show at a fair, a temple that might be more venerable than the cathedrals in Mexico City and Seville, older than the quincentennial of Columbus's first voyage in search of the Indies by way of the West that happened upon the New World. How ironic that a cactus that may have survived the so-called discovery of America and the conquest of Mexico may not survive the commemoration of the Fifth Centennial of the Meeting of Two Worlds.

UPDATE: Before the cactus could reach Veracruz, Juan Siles arranged for it to be flown out of Hermosillo airport by an Antonov An-124, a Russian heavy cargo aircraft that was marooned in San Diego, California. After a stop in Miami, the plane landed in Seville the morning of March 23, and that afternoon the giant cardon was planted on the Isla de la Cartuja, in front of the Mexican Pavilion. It still stands there today, surrounded by a parking lot.

The Collapse of the Nautical Ladder

HA, *Reforma*, January 19, 2003

The so-called Escalera Náutica (Nautical Ladder), a megalomaniacal project concocted by the National Trust Fund for Tourism Development (FONATUR) to turn the peninsula of Baja California into a recreation center for boat owners from the United States, has just been the subject of an independent market research study by San Francisco-based EDAW, a respected company that does analyses of the economic and environmental impacts of tourism. The study (financed by the Packard Foundation) clearly shows that FONATUR has overestimated the demand for marina slips in Baja California and the Sea of Cortez by 600 percent. While this reliable study forecasts that in 2014 some 10,000 yachts may visit the marinas, FONATUR predicts the arrival of 61,000. The study also concludes that only 5,500 berths will be needed by then, and not the 26,500 expected by FONATUR.

FONATUR'S first victim has been Santa Rosalillita. A hillside north of the village was dynamited to get rock for building a marina big enough for fifty boats, destroying half of a valuable habitat for rare plants and damaging a wetland visited by migratory birds. I've been told by witnesses that explosives used in the quarrying were left out in the open, unguarded. FONATUR cannot guarantee that some have not been stolen and are now in the hands of terrorists or local drug dealers.

Although the Secretariat of the Environment and Natural Resources (SEMARNAT) and FONATUR promised to wait for the conclusion and approval of a regional environmental impact statement (covering the entire area of the project) before proceeding with the marina in Santa Rosalillita, work on this wrongheaded and pointless venture continues. The marina, which is not far from the officially protected Valle de los Cirios (Valley of the Boojum Trees), is being built exactly where wave action is most powerful and the water shallowest. The dredging that has severely eroded this fishing town's beach is of little use, as the sand returns to clog the marina and it would have to be dredged every year, adding to the cost of construction. The project is the laughingstock of local fishermen, and evidences FONATUR's crass ignorance of how to build a marina, confirming that it should not be allowed to construct any permanent marina on the upper Sea of Cortez or on Baja California's Pacific coast.

FONATUR has already paved 2.5 miles of the so-called "land bridge" it intends to build between Santa Rosalillita and Bahía de los Ángeles, so that yachts up to 55 feet in length can be hauled from the Pacific to the Sea of Cortez. If this dry canal that will cut through the Valle de los Cirios ever gets finished, it will scar the peninsula with a superfluous strip of asphalt. The highway is on hold for the moment, since it was begun without the environmental impact statement required by law. It cannot even claim a viability study, although the road will cross a desert buffeted by high winds during half the year. The land bridge will never be used to transport larger boats whose owners are usually the biggest spenders in Mexico. At most it could serve for small craft towed by RVs whose owners consume nothing in the way of tourist services that benefit the local population. They live in their campers or tents, and catch their own fish to supplement the food they bring from the United States. Reason dictates that what has been built so far should be demolished, and no more boojums, which are endemic to the region, should be cut down.

On the Transpeninsular Highway, starting shortly after Ensenada, there is a sign every 6 miles giving the distance left to the Escalera Náutica (184 miles, 178 miles, etc.), until the hopeful traveler arrives at mile zero and a tourist site built and abandoned by FONATUR during the presidency of Luis Echeverría, just where the road to Bahía de los Ángeles begins. The ramshackle ensemble comprises a gas station, a café, and a trailer park. Until now, the signs have served to spark rampant land speculation. To get people to leave his museum, showman P. T. Barnum posted signs reading "This Way to the Egress," and the crowds would flock towards that mysterious phenomenon which turned out to be the exit. Like signs pointing the way to something that has yet to exist, and hasn't the slightest chance of meeting people's expectations, so will be the grotesque and overblown Nautical Ladder: a road that leads to nowhere.

The Sea of Cortez, dubbed "the aquarium of the world" by Jacques Cousteau, is home to gray whales, whale-sharks, sea lions, five species of marine turtle, the vaquita (a little porpoise in acute danger of extinction), and more than 800 species of fish. The surrounding land is inhabited by 65 reptile species, 40 kinds of mammal, 134 land birds, 600 plant species, and the borrego cimarrón (bighorn sheep, also in danger of extinction). FONATUR'S bloated project will impact 40 percent of Mexico's protected natural areas, including four biosphere reserves and national parks, such as El Pinacate y Gran Desierto de Altar, the Sierra de San Pedro Mártir, the Vizcaino Biosphere Reserve, Loreto Bay National Park, and Ángel de la Guarda island.

According to John McCarthy, FONATUR's director general, the Nautical Ladder, which aims to create a chain of 22 marinas 120 nautical miles apart from each other and attract 5.3 million nautical tourists, will bring in three billion dollars and create 60,000 jobs by 2015, benefiting the states of Baja California Norte, Baja California Sur, Sonora, Sinaloa, and Nayarit. But this will not happen. The market research results and the danger of irreversible environmental damage require urgent rethinking and redrawing of the scale and objectives of the Escalera Náutica before the fragile and unique ecosystems of Baja California and the Sea of Cortez are destroyed beyond repair, and the region is littered with abandoned development projects that are not viable, leaving a trail of white elephants. The destruction wreaked on Santa Rosalillita must not be repeated, as it's glaringly obvious that there is no market for marinas on the Pacific coast of Baja California. Above all, it is imperative that SEMARNAT insist upon regional and local environmental impact statements and compliance with the law.

Energy and money should be put into places of proven tourist potential, such as Ensenada, Los Cabos, Loreto, La Paz, Mazatlán, and Guaymas-Puerto San Carlos (in Sonora). Forget about building permanent marinas on the Pacific coast, and in sensitive areas like Bahía Kino and Bahía de los Ángeles (renamed "Coronado" by FONATUR as a ruse to attract investors from the North and confuse environmentalists). Floating marinas should be used in places like Bahía de los Ángeles, Punta San Carlos, Punta Abreojos, San Juanico, and San Luis Gonzago. These have almost no environmental impact because they avoid the need for dredging or altering the coastline, and are less expensive. They're also easy to remove if they're not making money. The whole project is a joke to investors from the United States, who say Mexicans don't understand the American market. On the other hand, as Serge Dedina, executive director of Wildcoast, says: "It's incongruous for FONATUR to resort to an obsolete nationalism to attack US environmental groups which have voiced their legitimate concerns about this project, when their entire thrust is directed towards tourists and investors from that country."

In place of a destructive Nautical Ladder, we need an Ecological Ladder that would promote low impact ecotourism and sustainable sport fishing. This is a far greater market than that of millionaire yacht owners. Or have investments by government officials and their cronies moved along too far to cut back on a juicy business deal that will defraud Mexicans in the region, and destroy one of the most beautiful places on the planet which, fortunately for us, happens to be in Mexico?

UPDATE: In 2004 the Nautical Ladder was rebaptised the Sea of Cortez Project. The Nautical Ladder was cancelled in 2007 by Tourism Secretary Rodolfo Elizondo, who told the press in 2016, "I opposed the project. I always knew it would be a failure, but McCarthy thought otherwise and the president [Fox] gave it his blessing. . . . FONATUR turned into a real estate agency." In 2008 a special congressional commission found that McCarthy had neither the political nor the technical capacity to carry out the Nautical Ladder project, despite having poured 150 million dollars into it. Over the years, FONATUR has unsuccessfully tried to sell off the marinas. In May 2016, Baja California's governor and the present head of FONATUR were talking about injecting more money into the defunct Santa Rosalillita marina to resuscitate it.

The Rape of the Reef

THE THREAT TO BAJA'S UNDERWATER "RAIN FOREST"

Robert F. Kennedy Jr. and HA, *San Diego Union-Tribune*,
April 21, 2011

Coral reefs, often called rain forests of the sea, shelter a quarter of all marine fish. In February, the most detailed scientific assessment ever undertaken of these spectacular ecosystems revealed that fully 75 percent are under threat—the most immediate being local pressures for coastal development.

Cabo Pulmo Bay in Baja California—home to one of these underwater "rain forests"—is facing one of those threats. Among only three living coral reefs in North America, it lies 40 miles north of San José del Cabo, on the eastern cape of Mexico's Baja California peninsula. John Steinbeck described this 20,000-year-old reef as filled with "teeming fauna" displaying "electric" colors. When decades of overfishing threatened the reef's existence, the local community convinced the Mexican government in 1995 to protect it by declaring the area a 17,560-acre National Marine Park. In 2005, the reef became a UNESCO World Heritage Site.

Fishing was banned inside the park, and today Cabo Pulmo Reef's recovery is considered a prime example of marine conservation in the Americas. It provides refuge for 225 of the 875 fish species found in the Sea of Cortez, including marlin, manta rays, giant squid and several kinds of sharks. Whales, dolphins, sea lions and five of the world's seven species of endangered sea turtles frequent its waters. Indeed, the coral reef hosts the highest concentration of ocean life within this 700-mile long arm of the Pacific Ocean that separates Baja California from the Mexican mainland. Ecotourism (diving, snorkeling, whale watching) is thriving among the 150 residents of the coastal town surrounding this spectacular marine park.

But now Hansa Baja Investments, a Mexican subsidiary of the Spain-based real estate development firm Hansa Urbana, plans to build a massive resort complex directly north of the National Marine Park. The developer has proposed what amounts to a sprawling new city on the scale of Cancún: 10,000 acres including 30,000 hotel rooms and residential housing units, at least two golf courses, 2 million square feet of office and retail space, a 490-boat marina and a private jet port.

The construction of the Cabo Cortés project would bring in close to 40,000 workers and their families. This fragile region of desert, dirt roads and traditional small communities would be overwhelmed. Cabo Pulmo Reef would die, killed by saline effluents from the planned desalination plant, chemical fertilizers whose runoff causes eutrophication, and the city's pollution flowing south on ocean coastal currents straight toward the reef.

In early March, Mexico's Secretariat of the Environment and Natural Resources gave the go-ahead for much of Hansa Urbana's proposal: not only the marina and land developments, but also a 10.5-mile-long aqueduct and 324 acres of roads and highways. The energy-intensive desalination plant—which would discharge 132 gallons per second of salt water—and a sewage treatment plant to deal with an expected 39,000 tons a day of solid waste once Cabo Cortés is going full tilt are not yet authorized, but it is considered only a matter of time, as is permission for the pending jetties and breakwaters.

The government's approval came despite the company's woefully inadequate environmental impact statement, which claimed that pollution from the development wouldn't affect the reef because ocean currents flow only from south to north, away from the reef. Recent studies show the area's currents move in multiple directions, largely depending upon the season.

In a region of water scarcity, Hansa has been granted a concession of 160 million cubic feet per year, meaning it will suck dry the Santiago aquifer, depriving the local population of resources it has depended on for hundreds of years.

In authorizing the deal, the government is violating its own laws, disregarding the rules governing environmental impact assessments in Mexico and ignoring its zoning plan for the entire region of Los Cabos.

It is up to the Mexican government to stand by its 1995 decision to protect this flourishing and irreplaceable marine nursery. The government must cancel its authorization of the Cabo Cortés development. Only then can the Cabo Pulmo coral reef remain a stellar example of ocean conservation and sustainable ecotourism. For Cabo Pulmo and its people, it is wreck or rectify. How does Mexican President Felipe Calderón want to be remembered?

UPDATE: After an international media campaign, in 2012 Hansa's Cabo Cortés resort complex permits were revoked by President Felipe Calderón "because the company failed to provide enough proof that the project would not harm the rich biodiversity of Cabo Pulmo National Park." In March 2014, a new project, called Cabo Dorado, was put forward for the same area by a joint US-Chinese venture registered in Mexico as The BCS Rivera Development Company. Its promoters were Altavista/Leisure Partners, headed by John McCarthy, former head of FONATUR, and the Glorious Earth Group (a shell company of Beijing Sansong International Trade Group). Following another international campaign, on August 3, 2015, SEMARNAT turned down the project, pointing to its failure to comply with local and national laws protecting the environment and biodiversity.

Beyond the Legend

HA, *Reforma*, December 20, 2000. Partial translation by Harry Porter, *Artes de México* 43

In a strange coincidence, on December 21, 1994, soon after Ernesto Zedillo was sworn in as president of Mexico, the Popocatépetl volcano awoke, spewing gases and blanketing the city of Puebla in ash. That month the country also had to face the Zapatista Army of National Liberation (EZLN) barricading roads in Chiapas, a 15 percent devaluation of the peso, and elevated air pollution levels in the metropolitan area. Since then, Mexican scientists have worried that the first big eruption in 50 years may be near. The volcano is 43 miles southeast of Mexico City and even closer to Puebla, with 20 million people living in a 62-mile radius of the crater, and 200,000 in the volcano's immediate vicinity.

Six years later, with Vicente Fox in power since December 1, on Monday, December 18, at 7:35 pm, Popocatépetl erupted, spitting out superheated rock fragments, lava, and ash, and sending avalanches of mud down its flanks. The crater expanded fourfold. In his *Relaciones originales de Chalco Amaquemecan*, Domingo Francisco de San Antón Muñón Chimalpahin Cuauhtlehuanitzin wrote that wandering Nahua tribes gave the volcano its name: Popocatépetl, or Smoking Mountain (from the Nahuatl *popoca* "it smokes," and *tepetl* "mountain") during the 1345–1347 eruptions. Some scientists believe that the volcano came into being about 730,000 years ago and underwent two formative periods; during the first, the primary volcano known as Nexpayantla emerged, from which Popocatépetl, with its elliptical crater, arose. Major eruptions occurred 25,000 and 14,000 years ago, followed by a catastrophic one in AD 800. Some 20 eruptions have been recorded since then, in 1522, 1545, 1548, 1804 (observed by the German scientist and explorer Alexander von Humboldt from a vantage point at San Nicolás de los Ranchos, a good place to see the current eruption), 1827, 1852, 1919, 1927, 1946, 1947, and 1982, among others. In 1986 the exhalations of smoke and gas belching from Popocatépetl increased and there was a change in the color of the crater's lake, whose temperature rose from 84 to 149 degrees Fahrenheit. As Cecilio A. Robelo wrote in his *Náhuatl Mythology,* "The mighty volcano of Puebla was revered as a god, with its feast day in the month of Teotleco (or Pachtontli). They fashioned little monticules from amaranth dough and each put them in his home, arranged around the largest, which was Popocatépetl. They made faces with eyes on the monticules and adorned them. . . . Afterwards they tossed corn of four colors to the four winds: black, white, yellow, and mottled. At the end of the feast they held a dance. . . . They brought to the dance two young slave girls who were sisters dressed in skirts painted with twisted innards, one signifying hunger and the other satiety, and they sacrificed them both."

When the Spanish conquistadors reached the Valley of Mexico in 1519, there were exhalations, which Hernán Cortés duly noted in his *Cartas de Relación* (*The Five Letters of Relation from Fernando Cortes to the Emperor Charles V*): "Eight leagues from this city of Churultecatl, there are two tall, marvelous mountains . . . and large amounts of smoke as thick as a house pour forth from the highest one continually, not only by day, but also by night, rising up from the mountain into the clouds." Decades later, the same spectacle amazed settlers and evangelists. Fray Diego Durán wrote in his *Historia de las Indias de Nueva España* (*The History of the Indies of New Spain*): "Popocatzin, which in our language means smoking mountain, is notorious for sending up visible billows of smoke two or three times each day and many times at dusk." In his *History of the Conquest of Mexico* (1843), William H. Prescott describes the great volcano, towering 17,852 feet above sea level, noting that it surpassed by more than 2,000 feet the highest peak of the "monarch of mountains—the highest elevation in Europe" [Mont Blanc]. After 1521—the year Mexico-Tenochtitlan was conquered—ascent of the volcano continued to fascinate the Spaniards. Here the historian and ethnologist Fray Bernadino de Sahagún describes his personal feat: "There is a very tall mountain that smokes that is near the province of Chalco, called Popocatépetl, which means 'Smoking Mountain'; it is a monstrous mountain worthy to behold, and I was at the top of it. Next to it is another mountain, a snowcapped one, named Iztactépetl, which means 'white mountain'; it is monstrous to see the top of it, where there used to be much idolatry; I saw it and I was on top of it." The ascent of the volcanoes by the author of the *Historia general de las cosas de la Nueva España* (*General History of the Things of New Spain*) awakened great admiration in scholar Joaquín García Icazbalceta, who wrote in his *Bibliografía Mexicana del siglo XVI* (*Mexican Bibliography of the Sixteenth Century*) that Sahagún bettered "the feats of the conquistadors Ordaz, Montaño and Mesa, for these only climbed Popocatépetl, whereas the Father was also on the peak of Iztaccíhuatl, long deemed inaccessible."

Although on the earliest maps of Mexico City the volcanoes were drawn as shapeless hills, over time they were portrayed more realistically, until they came to dominate the visual and artistic landscape of the Valley of Mexico. Their images have defined an entire iconographic history. The earliest representations of them are found in various Mexican codices (the Florentine, Vaticanus B, Telleriano-Remensis, Xolotl, and Huamantla codices and the Linen Cloth of Tlaxcala). Later, there were others by foreign and Mexican artists such as Johann Moritz Rugendas, William Bullock, Edouard Pingret, Daniel Thomas Egerton, and José María Velasco (considered the greatest Mexican landscape artist of the nineteenth century). As for me, I was raised in the culture of Popocatépetl and Iztaccíhuatl. Every evening, at home in my living room, I had before me a painting of the two volcanoes personified as a pair of Aztec lovers, perhaps inspired by a chapbook published in 1900 in the series Biblioteca del niño mexicano: Heriberto Frias's *Historia de los dos volcanes: Corazón de Lumbre y Alma de Nieve* (*A Tale of Two Volcanoes: Heart of Fire and Soul of Snow*), illustrated by José Guadalupe Posada; or by Saturnino Herrán's 1910 triptych *La leyenda de los volcanes* (The legend of the volcanoes); or by Jesús Helguera's painting of the same name for a 1940 calendar that hung on the walls of thousands of Mexican homes; or by the Tiffany stained-glass curtain at the Palace of Fine Arts. Twentieth-century artists such as Adolfo Best Maugard, Juan O'Gorman, Diego Rivera, and Frida Kahlo also painted Popocatépetl. Innumerable photographs have been taken of the volcanoes at different periods and from a variety of vantage points. However, literary references are few, the exceptions being Carlos Pellicer and Julio Torri, who called the Popocatépetl "Mexico's most prominent citizen," and of course Malcolm Lowry's *Under the Volcano*. With Iztaccíhuatl in mind, Sor Juana Inés de la Cruz composed the following verses to the Virgin Mary: "I would compare thee, my Lady, / To this snowcapped peak / Who, although smoke be near it, / Is ever white."

One hundred years ago, General Porfirio Díaz granted a vast concession to the San Rafael Paper Company to log the pine-oak woodlands on the volcanoes' slopes. Nearly a century later, president Carlos Salinas de Gortari renewed those permits, allowing 25,000 hectares to be razed. This logging severely affected the region's fauna. Moreover, from mid-twentieth century onwards, air pollution made the volcanoes virtually invisible.

Although all of Mexico is immersed in the culture of the volcanoes, it is most vividly concentrated in the communities of the region, where Popocatépetl is familiarly referred to as "Gregorio," the nickname "Goyo," or its diminutive "Goyito," for, as Doña Anselma, a seventyish woman living in a village in the shadow of the volcano, says, "The volcanoes are like people. They're not always in their place. Sometimes they leave." And now, thousands of these villagers have had to abandon their place of residence. Until recently, some Mexicans feared an imminent eruption to coincide with the end of the millennium. It was believed it would be as catastrophic as the one in AD 820, when the volcano spewed lava and incandescent rock. In *Monarquía Indiana* (Monarchy of the Indies), Fray Juan de Torquemada wrote, "In their ancient chants, the natives of these lands warn that when the mountains catch fire and begin belching smoke from their peaks, great death and pestilence would ensue, and so it was in the year 1545, which was a year of tremendous pestilence in these lands." And he added that "principal members of Indian society—the most venerated elders—said that when the mountains expel fire, the end of the world will be near and great mortality."

Beyond prophecies and legends, Popocatépetl has been present in our history's great cycles, and will be for the foreseeable future. To Fray Bernardino de Sahagún on Popocatépetl *circa* 1545: What were you doing there, Fray Bernardino, on Popocatépetl, staring the god in his mouth? Did you listen to the history of embers and ash in its sulfurous bowels, or did you only hear the hollow voice, the aimlessness of this unfortunate land? When you watched the Nexatl River winding down the volcano like a twisted lily, to resurface elsewhere, you must have thought: "Thus is the work of man, swallowed up by time, to reappear centuries later more luminous than ever. Just like my *History*, hijacked by the king, the viceroy, and the archbishop." The Earth has swallowed you up, Fray Bernardino, but wherever you may be, I want you to know that at this moment Popocatépetl is once again belching smoke over this valley of men sacrificed by their gods, their priests, and their politicians.

Where the Sky Is Born

SIAN KA'AN, QUINTANA ROO, MEXICO

For Kjell Espmark

HA, translated by Asa Zatz, from *Heart of the Land,* ed. Joseph Barbato and Lisa Weinerman (Commissioned by the Nature Conservancy, New York: Pantheon, 1995)

Betty, my wife, César Barrios, our guide, and I drove to Sian Ka'an (*Where the Sky Is Born*) in a Volkswagen Beetle. We arrived on an October morning when the heat was not yet "halfway up the sky," as the Punta Allen fishermen say.

The Sian Ka'an Biosphere Reserve, consisting of 1,305,079 acres of tropical forest, savannahs, mangrove swamps, *petenes* (wetland islets), cenotes, keys, springs, and coral reefs lying in the state of Quintana Roo and the Yucatán Peninsula, is the third-largest reserve in Mexico. Of this area, some 296,526 acres are oceanic. The barrier reef, the second longest in the world, is over sixty-eight miles in length. The reserve contains 859 species of flora and 2,161 of fauna, including copepods (619), coleoptera, or beetles (74), dipterans such as flies, mosquitos, and gnats (310), crustaceans (276), mammals (103), native bees (90), corals (84), marine turtles (4), and birds (339), of which more than 70 are aquatic. The initial impression given by this vast reserve is that, if its Maya name is to be taken literally, the sky was indeed born of the water, particularly in the wetlands, the swampy terrain that is covered with water and life almost all year round.

Having left behind us the last of the restaurants and the archway at the entrance to the reserve, we watch a crossing of crabs so camouflaged that they seem made of sand. Momentarily surprised by the noise of the car, the crustaceans remain transfixed before losing themselves in the dense vegetation.

We recognize various types of palm trees along the shore line, among them the *chit* (*Thrinax radiate*, or Florida thatch palm), with its fanlike leaves and ivory blossoms. In the jungle, fighting the other trees to reach the light, they grow to a height of between thirty-two and thirty-eight feet but on the dunes beside the sea, they are no more than twenty feet tall. Some specimens show the scars on the trunk left by the leaves that have fallen. These palms grow slowly in the jungle and at the seaside. The demand for *chit* has increased in recent years as a result of burgeoning tourism in Quintana Roo because not only are the roofs and walls of traditional Mayan dwellings made with its leaves but hotel and restaurant proprietors use them for cabanas whose walls are built with *nakax* palm poles. Fishermen use poles made from the *chit* to make lobster traps called *sombras*.

"That one is a *kuka* palm," César points out from the car. It is the *Pseudophoenix sargentii* and is found in the lowland jungle of Quintana Roo. "That one," he indicates, "is the *xiat*." It (*Chamaedorea graminifolia*) is a variety endemic to the peninsula.

We can see the holes made by golden-fronted woodpeckers *(Melanerpes aurifrons)* in the trunks of the palms, particularly those killed by the deadly yellowing, a blight which no one knows how to keep from destroying the coconut palms. "I know," José Luis Soto, of Cabañas Ana and José, told me a few hours earlier and confided the secret: "by rubbing sulfur on the trunks." A gray fox crosses in front of us. A bright green iguana stands as though rooted to the spot. A tropical mockingbird *(Mimus gilvus)*, a bird with a talent for imitating the sound of chickens, parrots, and dogs, flies from tree to tree. We spot a vermilion flycatcher *(Pyrocephalus rubinus)*, waiting to snare insects out of the air.

On arriving at the edge of the Boca Paila lagoon, we take refuge from the sun under an almond tree. Afterwards, we begin the tour of the canals in a boat. These are not the man-made canals of Amsterdam or Venice, but canals engineered by nature. Their edifices are not palaces but formations of mangrove trees, islets of *petenes,* and structures of a vegetation that has adapted to the extreme dampness. There are 163,000 acres of mangrove swamp of the four species found in the Yucatán Peninsula: red, black, white, and buttonwood. The most abundant is the red mangrove, *xtapche* in Mayan. In his study on the wetlands, Juan José Morales compares it to an immense spider because of the long, curved aerial prop roots sprouting in all directions above the water from the trunk and branches. Anchored in the marshy soil by a tangle of multiple legs, the red mangrove seems a fantastic animal stranded in the water. As a fisherman from Isla Mujeres expressed it, "The mangrove swamps are the beginning of the sea." It is on their biotic riches that life in the open sea depends in large measure.

The boat advances through the canals fashioned by the red mangroves. The dark brown color of the water, as though steeped from tea leaves, is produced by the mangrove swamps. The bubbles upon the surface indicate that the water is breathing. We spot a blue-winged teal, *maxix* in Mayan. At our approach it hides among the reeds. In the marshes of northern Yucatán this duck is overhunted. The clouds on the horizon surround the lagoon like a ring of sheep. We come upon a great egret. It flies with its head tilted backward. In her book on the birds of Yucatán, Barbara MacKinnon wrote, "It almost became extinct at the turn of the century due to the popularity of its nuptial feathers, which were used for ladies' hats."

"There goes a kingfisher," César, the guide, points out.

We pause to listen to the song of a red-winged blackbird (*Agelaius phoeniceus*). Mangrove branches in the water form webs and reed sculptures, some crowned with leaves. Orchids and bromeliads come into view. A black vulture, *ch'om* in Mayan, passes in search of carrion, or perhaps chicks of the ibis or heron. We catch sight of a white ibis, neck outstretched. And more birds: a green-backed heron, an American pygmy kingfisher, a social flycatcher. And, all of a sudden, we come upon a mangrove trunk with a ball over a yard in diameter on it that seems to be an excrescence or mass of mud. It is a termitarium. A northern tamandua or lesser anteater *(Tamandua mexicana)* is trying to break apart the extremely hard nest with its claws and with its sticky tongue to get at the insects that feed on the dead wood.

The vegetation changes and the grass cover that forms the savannahs begins. The landscape is filled with reeds. The depths of the water are green. There is a crocodile's nest in the pasture where its young were born a few weeks before. Tiny orchids appear. The florescence on the surface lasts all year long, the bulbs remaining submerged. A snowy egret flies over the buds.

An oval-shaped petén, concentrically formed, stands out to the left of the boat. The petén is an islet covered with medium-sized trees that grow amidst reeds, grass, and mangrove swamp. The one now before us has on it palm, sapodilla, and breadnut trees, orchids, and lianas. Another smaller *petén* comes into view followed by a larger one. Some have a cenote at the center. The *petenes* are said to contribute to the biodiversity of the Espíritu Santo and Ascención bays, where lobster abounds, and to be essential for the survival of wild fauna that find their water, food, and shelter there in time of drought.

Troops of spider monkeys find fruits all year round as well as protection from their natural enemies and from man. "Fires are set by poachers around here," César informs us, "to catch the white-tailed deer." His words remind me that that animals sought here by hunters, some to the point of extinction, are: the collared peccary, the coati, the paca, the white-winged dove, the yellow-lored parrot, the keel-billed toucan, the ocellated turkey, the ocelot, the white-lipped peccary, the spider monkey, the jaguar, the American and Morelet's crocodiles, the jabiru stork, the great curassow, and the leatherback, green, hawksbill, and loggerhead sea turtles. In the water, carp and permit fish flee us.

We enter a canal along which a heavier growth of red mangroves provides cool shade. Their branches, one after another, are like pendant spears, orchids and bromeliads sprouting from them. We are able to drive a pole ten feet into the swampy soil. The water is tepid.

We are before a circular Mayan temple. This is the highest temple on the coast. Bats fly screeching out of the dark chamber. César informs us that no less than ten varieties of these creatures have been identified around the archaeological ruins of the Chunyaxché zone. The warbling of invisible birds can be heard and we peer at the limb of a ceiba felled by lightning upon an orange tree.

Our return to Playa del Carmen begins at this point. We stop at the Muyil nursery where Don Cándido Ek, about forty-seven years old (so he says), and his wife, Delfina, about thirty-two, live.

Don Cándido had been waiting for us near his hut and now, with a marked absence of ceremony, he proceeds, two sons, Ismael and Joel, trailing after him, to show us the native Sian Ka'an flora that he cultivates with skill and devotion. He tells us the names in Mayan and Spanish (one of his sons helping him in Spanish) of some forty plants he intends to disseminate among the people of the region. "Here's the vegetation and along comes the wind and scatters the seed along the road and that's how they are propagated in Sian Ka'an," he explains to us as he stands amidst his plants, shrubs, and trees. "The palm is very slow growing."

Don Cándido Ek also wants to produce honey from stingless *Melipona* bees, *Xunán kab* ('royal lady') in Mayan. "It's a honey the Maya use for a medicine," he explains. "It's used when women give birth, when children are malnourished, when the navel of a child pops out and they want to make it go back in."

"How many children do you have?" I ask. "Six," he replies, and looking at his wife Delfina, visibly pregnant under her huipil, says, "seven." "All boys?" "Four boys and two girls," he says, his white teeth bared in a smile.

His grandfather Caamal Ek (*ek* means star in Mayan), he tells us, "is ninety-five but I think he's older as he has no 'birth ticket.'"

Another day we go to Punta Allen by car, the sea following us all the way beyond the road to the left. A swallow flies over the car for a few moments. Many termitaria can be seen on the trees. Young palms are growing among the old ones that died of the deadly yellowing. A black hawk perches on a trunk.

We arrive in Punta Allen toward midday. It's a fishing village which, at first sight, appears to be poor and ugly. Its beauty lies in Ascención Bay and El Ramonal tropical forest. It is the only town in Sian Ka'an that has a potable water supply and sewerage. The reefs are less than a mile and a half away.

"A barrier reef was badly damaged by Hurricane Gilbert," we are told by Victor Barrera, a fisherman from Campeche, who has lived in Punta Allen since the age of sixteen. "The most terrible thing that happened to us was the death of the coconut palms. The coconut palms have many enemies. Fourteen, altogether. The worst is the deadly yellowing. When I first came here the coast was filled with coconut palms. For me, the death of those trees is an agonizing thing."

"'We're off to the river,' the fishermen say when they are going to the lagoon," Victor adds. He agrees, after striking a deal, to take us in his boat around Ascensión Bay, famous for its lobster.

The bay, whose waters are calm and not very deep, is located on the central coast of Quintana Roo. Its mouths empty into the open sea, it has a coral reef, and is surrounded by mangrove swamps and marshes. Once there were manatees, dolphins, and otters here, but now we don't see any.

"My twenty-three-year-old brother Eleazar died in one of these springs fourteen years ago. A Señor Rodríguez, who had the idea of harvesting black coral, was teaching him to dive. The weather was bad. He dove into the water and didn't come out. The others went for help but when they got back he'd already disappeared." Victor, upright in the boat like a Viking figurehead, tells us the story. There are many springs around.

We see five brown pelicans, a great blue heron, a double-crested cormorant, and a barracuda. The white head of an osprey with its black mask across the eyes protrudes from its nest in a mangrove swamp. We spot crocodiles at the edge. The sky has grown overcast.

We are now in a canal between mangroves. We see orchids, white herons, white ibises. The water has turned milky green. It starts raining.

"Great white herons on the right, osprey on the left, a cormorant over there to the right, a yellow-crowned night-heron, a Yucatan box turtle, a northern shoveler, green-backed herons, a roseate spoonbill, a gray hawk." Victor, accustomed to scanning the air and water, appears to see everything right away.

We move toward the shore, the water is shallow, we are in Quitacalzón. Following a hawk, we enter Key Yuyúm.

"A lot of the mangroves have died off, they're in bad shape, many are dry. This one is full of shovelers. They raise their crests during the mating season." Victor stops the boat at a mangrove. We hear clucking and flapping of wings inside. "Pelicans nest in here, too, and there are spoonbills in season. I was told that flocks of flamingos were seen in January."

The sky is black. A storm begins. Victor maneuvers his boat in an effort to evade the rainfall. Rays of sunshine filter through the darkest of the clouds. The vehicle that is to take us overland to Playa del Carmen is waiting on the farther shore.

Drenched by lukewarm, fat raindrops, the boat lifted by the swell, we are spectators of the storm. There is no lightning.

The wind carries the clouds off elsewhere. The rain stops. We approach the shore. The wondrous trip is over. The threats to Sian Ka'an are all too evident. But the possibility of keeping the reserve well protected still exists.

Ninety-nine percent of the area's land belongs to the nation. The surrounding ejidatarios scarcely number more than five hundred. Chicle tapping had been one of the traditional activities of the region, but private lumbering of cedar and guayacan was allowed as of 1935 and by now those trees are in danger of disappearing. This experience should teach us not to issue permits for forestry operations, dubious "ecotourism" developments and private construction. Currently, politicians and entrepreneurs are discussing plans for developing Sian Ka'an, with the ever-present risk, however, of opening the door to undesirable tourism projects, as has been the case in other parts of Quintana Roo.

Sian Ka'an is one of the last remaining glories of the earth and must be preserved as such. Today, man is tempted to make nature "self-sustaining" by designing overly ambitious management plans which, when ill-applied, unleash destructive forces that can neither be controlled nor stopped.

I sincerely believe that no one can make nature more "self-sustaining" than it has already managed to make itself. Nature has been quite efficiently self-sustaining for millions of years without man's help. Never in history has it been so much under assault as at the present time, now that we are "developing" it.

7

The Indigenous Labyrinth

FROM THE TEMPLE TOP MOCTEZUMA SHOWS CORTÉS HIS
EMPIRE

Whatever your eye beholds is ours
Whatever is beyond the reach of your eye is ours
cities and clouds women and stone
coyotes and ahuehuetes snakes and eagles
Our men move upon the waters
and our gods roam the night
and with a black blade
we draw from the breast of our enemies
the light that floods our days

    HA (*translated by George McWhirter*)

Slaves and Guerrillas, Forests and Blood

HA, *New York Times*, January 5, 1994

On March 12, 1545, three years after denouncing Spanish cruelty toward the natives in his *Brief Account of the Devastation of the Indies*, Fray Bartolomé de las Casas arived in Chiapas, in southeastern Mexico, bearing the New Laws signed by Emperor Charles V of Spain.

The laws forbade any further enslavement of the Indians. Upon the death of a slaveholder—*encomendero*—the Indians in his possession would come under the tutelage of the throne, to be given instruction in the Roman Catholic religion as free vassals. The encomenderos bitterly opposed the New Laws, and an attempt was made on Las Casas' life. But even on his deathbed, in 1566, the former Bishop of Chiapas implored friends to protect the Indians. So began the defense of human rights in the Americas.

The Indians' tribulations have persisted through the centuries. The guerrilla uprising that took scores of lives this past week was an echo of the Tzeltal revolt in 1712 and the Tzotzil rebellion in 1868, both of them bloody and fruitless. Little changed after the Revolution of 1910; land distribution and agrarian reform were left to the big landholders.

Today Chiapas is the poorest state in Mexico. In Ocosingo, Altamirano and Las Margaritas—the towns where the Zapatista Army of National Liberation burst to prominence on New Year's Day—48 percent of the adults are illiterate. Eighty percent of the families earn less than $245 a month. Seventy percent have no electricity.

Poverty aside, Chiapas is fertile ground for conflict. There are guerrillas from across the border in Guatemala, drug traffickers, immigrants from Central America and newcomers from other parts of Mexico. There are struggles between peasants and Indians over land ownership, and between Catholics and Protestant evangelists over religion.

In the midst of all this are timber and oil resources that are all too vulnerable to exploitation. Despite official decrees of protection, the great Lacandon rain forest has been shorn—for highways, farms, oil drilling, resettlement, even airstrips for drug traffickers—to the bare minimum necessary to keep its ecosystems from collapsing. Since 1982 its trees have been cut down at the rate of 3.5 percent a year; just 30 percent of the original 5,000 square miles remains. What once took 50 years to destroy can now be destroyed in a year.

And with the disappearance of the forest, the Indian populations have been despoiled; losing their traditions and native land, they have become pariahs. After two years of harvesting corn, beans and chilies, the peasants turn the fields into grazing land and go to work for the ranchers. A few may prosper, but the rest move on to slash and burn other parts of the forest. There were 12,000 people in the Lacandon in 1960; now there are more than 300,000.

The historical and social forces behind the insurrection are clear, but the real motives are as murky as the identity of whoever is behind them. Not only did they take towns, but they also tried to seal off the forest, where they are now taking refuge. So now war may come to the forest.

Mexico cannot permit the dismemberment of its territory or allow the violence of guerrillas and drug traffickers to establish a foothold. While the Government has managed to keep the region under control and prevent revolt from spreading, it must be wary of excesses and must avoid useless bloodshed. Now that insurgents have retreated, leaving their dead and wounded behind, the peasants and innocent Indian groups must not be made victims of reprisals; the pacification of Chiapas must not be used as an excuse for backsliding on human rights.

The solution lies in negotiation. Meeting violence with violence can only lead to still more violence. Mexico cannot hope to enter the 21st century as a full-fledged democracy without social peace. As the Government joins its North American partners in free trade, it must also look toward its peasants and Indians. Mexico must attend to the needs of first-world development, but it must also heed the call of the forest.

The Indigenous Labyrinth

HA, *Reforma*, July 31, 1994

The modern history of Mexico's Indians is the history of the destruction of their culture. In the armed conquest, and in what has been called the spiritual conquest, the Indians were dominated not only materially but also in terms of religion. The figure of Fray Bartolomé de las

Casas, the first defender of human rights, who brought the New Laws to Chiapas in 1545, keeps growing in stature. Mexico City-Tenochtitlan, which Albrecht Dürer saw as an ideal city, was razed by Hernán Cortés, and the colonial city rose on its ruins, excluding the Indians from the urban center. Thousands of natives carried the building materials on their backs, and the stones from the Aztec Main Temple were used to erect the conquistadors' church.

The Zapatista uprising has called attention to the plight of all Mexico's Indians. Mexico is torn between its attempts to be part of North America's economic future and its historical indigenous past, and under cultural pressures, for 11 million of its 90 million inhabitants are Indians. Eleven percent live in the capital, now the country's largest indigenous city. There are 2,500 indigenous communities in Mexico, and 52 languages belonging to 12 linguistic families are still in use. The most widely spoken are Nahuatl, Maya, Zapotec, Mixtec, and Otomi, with the greatest linguistic variety found in Oaxaca and Chiapas.

At a conference titled "500 Years of Indian Resistance," Professor Felipe Zermeño spoke of the North American Free Trade Agreement's (NAFTA's) impact on indigenous peoples, warning that Mexico has no chance of competing with the United States, and if the price of Mexican corn plummets, half its farmers will disappear. Mexico's indigenous peoples have always grown corn, a part of their mythology. It is written in the Popol Vuh that "of yellow corn and of white corn they made their flesh; of corn-meal dough they made the arms and the legs of man. Only dough of corn meal went into the flesh of our first fathers, the four men, who were created."

Once the shock of the armed uprising passed, it was plain to see that conflict in Chiapas did not begin on January 1, 1994, but years earlier. Both 1992 and 1993 were marred by several violent incidents between government officials and indigenous groups. On Sunday, December 27, 1992, hundreds of Tzeltals belonging to an organization known as Xi'Nich ("Ants"), massed in Palenque to protest repression they had suffered that year, demanding release of 4,000 indigenous prisoners scattered among jails throughout the country and punishment for officials who had violated their human rights. In the middle of town, the Tzeltals called the government "a murderer, because it's killing us of hunger."

On December 29, the arbitrary arrest of five Tzotzils accused of the December 9 murder in the community of Tzajalch'en of a municipal representative named Vicente Gutiérrez was reported. The Fray Bartolomé de las

Casas Human Rights Center said there are many political prisoners in Chiapas and that 109 Chols had been arrested and tortured by the police during the past year.

On March 23, 1993, two soldiers, who had been mistakenly identified as forest guards, were murdered in San Isidro El Ocotal. Their bodies were dismembered with chain saws, burned, stuffed into burlap sacks, and buried. On April 12 it transpired that the judicial police had arrested 13 Tzotzils, accused without proof of the crime. Two weeks later, the Federal Attorney General's office arrested four Tzotzils for illegally stockpiling and carrying guns. Eighteen rifles and shotguns, four pistols, and bullets of various caliber were seized. The state's attorney denied any violation of the detainees' rights.

On May 25, Tzeltals from Ocosingo reported that 1,000 soldiers, who had arrived in town in 33 trucks, were searching their houses looking for weapons. During the operation, which was backed up by three helicopters and roadblocks on the highway to Altamirano, soldiers looted in Patate Nuevo and stole and destroyed possessions of the inhabitants of La Garrucha, who had fled to the hills. The next day, the Federal Attorney General's office announced that during a shootout in the Patate Viejo *ejido* between soldiers and Tzeltals, a corporal and a second lieutenant died and two soldiers were wounded. Eight Mexicans and two Guatemalans were taken into custody as the presumed culprits, being in possession of "notes and subversive propaganda about Guatemalan guerrilla tactics."

On June 3, after twelve days of "military drills and social work" in eight Altamirano and Ocosingo ejidos, 2,000 soldiers assigned to the Seventh Military Zone withdrew. Local residents denied receiving any sort of benefit and said the soldiers kept asking them about the presence of supposed guerrillas in the región.

On June 7, 300 policemen and state judicial police captured 22 Tzeltals belonging to the Emiliano Zapata Peasant Organization (OCEZ) who were besieging the Tomás Manzur ejido. Dozens of rifles and shotguns, machetes, axes, and knives were confiscated.

On August 11, human rights groups revealed that four of the Tzeltals in custody had "serious health problems caused by torture."

Early in August, four Tzotzils, two of them children, were imprisoned in the San Juan Chamula jail for not having paid a fine levied on one of the boys for absenteeism from school. Also in San Juan Chamula, the Consejo de Representantes Indígenas de los Altos de Chiapas (CRIACH, Council of Indigenous Representatives of the Chiapas Highlands) complained that officials and caciques drove out two evangelical Indians and jailed two others, and gave a fifth two days to leave town if he didn't renounce his religion. The Council also reported that for the past 20 years the Indians have been subjected to "expulsions at the behest of local caciques, with no way yet of stopping them."

On August 18, the National Human Rights Commission (CNDH) was asked to intervene so that 32 families who had been expelled could return to their communities within 40 days and their physical safety would be guaranteed.

In mid-October, researcher Ramón González Ponciano disclosed the poverty-stricken living conditions of 200,000 indigenous peasant families in the Lacandon rain forest, one of the most important natural bastions in the Americas. He warned of high risks in the region caused by deforestation, accelerated soil erosion, inappropriate colonization, the heavy flow of migrants, and highly predatory illicit activities.

At the beginning of November, a group of Lacandon Indians headed by Carmelo Chan Bor, a Supreme Lacandon Advisor, came to see me in Mexico City to complain about violence in the jungle, where drug trafficking, kidnappings and disappearances, logging, wildlife smuggling, and land invasions into the Montes Azules Biosphere Reserve and into their own territory by hostile indigenous groups are the norm. They told me that not a single official paid any attention to them.

But as if there were not already enough reasons to fuel conflict in Chiapas, on June 4, 1994, at a military roadblock on the outskirts of Altamirano, four Tzeltal women—a mother and her 16-, 18-, and 20-year-old daughters—were stopped around 11 in the morning. Towards 2 in the afternoon, in a room with a dirt floor near the military camp, the three young women were tortured and raped by 30 soldiers. To date, no one has been charged with the crimes.

Negotiations between the government and the EZLN have broken down, and since mid-June indigenous families, ranchers, and smallholders are leaving their homes to take refuge in towns.

Since the uprising began on January 1, everything points to the Lacandon rain forest as the conflict's natural victim. The Lacandon is disappearing at a faster rate than Amazonia. In 1875 there were 3.2 million forested hectares, of which 6 percent were lost between 1875 and 1960. Since 1982, deforestation has been at a steady annual rate of 3.5 percent. In 1990 only 30 percent of the original forest remained, of which 18 percent is degraded. That is what impelled the writers, scientists, and environmentalists at the Morelia

Symposium: "Approaching the Year 2000," held during the second week of January 1994, to implore the involved parties to respect the region's inhabitants as individuals and as ethnic groups, and to refrain from targeting the cultural and natural patrimony of the area, including archeological sites such as Yaxchilán, Bonampak, and Palenque. The Group of 100 asked for permission to send an observer. There was no response from the government.

The Indians' complaints about land grabs by caciques, big landowners, and governmental bodies are so regular that they are seldom noticed in the national media, as was the case when 21,650 hectares (84 square miles) were taken away from the Tohono O'odham, descendants of the Papagos, who live in the Gran Desierto de Altar in Sonora, or when 18,000 hectares (70 square miles) were seized from the Mayos, in northern Sinaloa, in February 1994. The latter occurred during construction of the Huites Dam, which was meant to free campesinos from poverty by irrigating their plots, but these were taken over by landowners. Inhabitants of Masiaca reported that they sold their land at 500 new pesos (150 USD) per hectare, "because it's never produced anything except ruination."

Recently, governors of the Yaqui, Mayo, Seri, Guarijío, Tohono O'odham, Pima, and Kickapoo tribes founded the Consejo Tradicional de los Pueblos Indios of the state of Sonora, demanding a new relationship between their tribes and the government, in a setting of respect and equality, as they are tired of broken promises, bureacratic decisions taken without their participation, and unfeeling civil servants. They said, "Today, we have decided to keep up the fight through peaceful means, but you should know that our patience is wearing thin."

"Out-of-control logging in the Sierra Tarahumara violates the human rights of the four ethnic groups living in the región," 80 indigenous leaders charged on October 1, 1991. "The soil becomes eroded and so the groups have to emigrate from the mountains." No one paid any attention. The government's reform of Article 27 of the Constitution [putting an end to land redistribution and allowing rental or sale of collectively held ejido land] was criticized by the Apostolic Vicariate of the Sierra Tarahumara as the key that would open the door to major domestic and foreign investment for logging their land, under the pretext that it is not used productively. "They claim the right to make their own decisiones, to exercise their own justice, to choose their authorities, to have contacts with neighboring cultures as they see fit and to establish the rights of succession to the land which makes up their family patrimony, in accordance with their traditions," the Vicariate declared.

Nothing was done then. Now we read in *Excelsior* that 400 Tarahumaras have invaded the seven-acre lumber yards where the Empresa Ejidal Forestal de Chinatú stores its wood. Always ritualistic, always poor, the occupiers perform their ceremonies and *yumaré* dances "to keep hunger at bay and to create jobs in the Sierra."

As Norwegian ethnologist Carl Lumholtz wrote, "If the Tarahumara did not comply with the commands of Father Sun and dance, the latter would come down and burn up the whole world." And they still use crosses in their political protests because "When Tata Dios went away, he said, 'I will leave two crosses here.' He then put up a cross where the sun sets at the end of the world, and another where the sun rises. . . . Between these two crosses the Tarahumara live . . . and God comes to eat near these crosses. He only eats the soul or substance of the food, and leaves the rest for the people."

Another sawmill in the area, belonging to the Guazapares ejido, has been invaded by a hundred Tarahumara, who are no longer allowing trees in the forest to be cut down nor the wood to be transported elsewhere. The Jesuit Esteban de la Torre, of the Chinatú parish, said these invasions were prompted by the changes to Article 27, and that "Indians don't want caciques any more, especially in the mountains, in the southern area where they are oppressed by white and indigenous caciques." Nevertheless, the Archbishop of Chihuahua, José Fernández Arteaga, doesn't believe what has happened in Chiapas could come about in his state, saying, "The reality and people in Chihuahua are different." However, Gustavo Fierro Ruiz, an adviser to the Tarahumara Supreme Council, thinks otherwise: "The situation here is so critical that some towns are virtually lawless. In Guadalupe and Calvo there are 200 violent deaths a year. . . . In Chínipas, Uriachi and Guazapares many people are armed, and neither the police nor the army dare go in."

"The Tarahumara are starving to death." I've heard that said year after year as long as I can remember. Ravaged by sickness and squalor, they have survived in the magical territory of Mexico by turning their bodies into a ritual space. Victims of yearly famines and adverse climate conditions, the Tarahumara—exalted by Antonin Artaud during his visit to Mexico—and other ethnic groups have understood that they no longer have anything to lose and that the only way to defend themselves from their long-standing enemies is by organizing and facing up to them. The CNDH has just issued a Fact Sheet of the Rights of Indigenous Peoples, hailing "the indigenous peoples of Mexico, whose existence is the basis for the nation's multicultural makeup."

"We don't want handouts, we want support to make the most of our abundant natural resources," Ferro Ruiz said, giving voice to the clamor of Mexico's indigenous population. "There are too many requirements and pretexts for us to get funding that will allow the Tarahumara to work in conditions of justice, respect for their customs, way of life and governance, in harmony with nature."

Mexico's indigenous peoples, whose ancestors founded unique civilizations and who today are producing imaginative folk art, are now aware of their human rights, and armed with this awareness they can escape from the labyrinth of history where they have been mistreated for centuries. The years ahead will be years of their liberation. But to achieve that, along with their fellow Mexicans they must first turn the country into a real democracy.

UPDATE: On March 23, 2017, journalist Miroslava Breach, Chihuahua correspondent for *La Jornada*, was murdered outside her home. Breach reported in depth about drug gang violence, opium growing, human rights violations, corruption, and ecological devastation in the Sierra Tarahumara, and covered the January murders of Tarahumara activists Isidro Baldenegro (a Goldman Environmental Prize winner) and Juan Ontiveros.

For the Indigenous Poor, All Roads Lead to Mexico City

HA, *Los Angeles Times*, September 17, 1995

Recent economic and political turmoil has dislodged a half million native people who now lead desperate lives in the capital. Will the city explode?

Ever since the Zapatista army arose in Chiapas to fight for the human rights of the indigenous peoples of Mexico, the general living conditions of the nation's natives have worsened. They are the victims of their own demographic explosion, the pauperization of the countryside, the devastation of their environment and the economic crisis ravaging the country. The native peoples are realizing they cannot earn a living in their home states; many are being forced to migrate. And since many towns and cities are as poor as the rural areas that surround them, all roads lead to Mexico City, where every thoroughfare is swarming with mendicants and street vendors plying their informal commerce.

Mazahuas from the State of Mexico; Nahuas from Guerrero; Otomis from Hidalgo, Querétaro and Puebla; Purépechas from Michoacán; Zapotecs and Mixtecs from Oaxaca; Totonacs from Veracruz, and Triques from the highlands and lowlands of Oaxaca—all are setting up shop on the streets. Day after day, you can see women and children, sitting or standing, outside of hotels, restaurants and nightclubs, or loitering in avenues, traffic circles, markets, bus terminals.

When the stop lights change colors, legions of street vendors, among them many Indians, surround the halted cars. It is a common sight to see young children who have just learned to walk amid the traffic. Their mothers, wearing traditional garb, sell chewing gum or beg for spare change.

As a general rule, the desperately poor gravitate to the wealthier areas of Mexico City; they are often controlled by small-time mafiosi who rent them space on the streets. In Lomas de Chapultepec, one of the most affluent sectors of Mexico City, pickup trucks daily drop off Indians at intersections where traffic is heaviest. Shopping malls, hotels and up-scale restaurants are off limits to them, however.

The most recent census, taken in 1990, counted some 500,000 indigenous people in Mexico City, about 3 percent of the metropolitan area's population. According to INI [National Indigenous Institute], nearly half them speak an Indian language as their mother tongue, representing 4 percent of the twelve and a half million indigenous people nationwide whose maternal tongue is not Spanish. The institute reports that the Indians who come to the capital tend to be young couples with many children.

Daniel Camarillo is one of them. At age 25, he left a small village in Oaxaca, where he farmed corn, "to do hat" (to beg by extending a hat to receive spare change) in the big city. He positions himself outside Hotel Calinda, on Liverpool Street, in the middle of the tourist area, from 9 in the morning till nightfall. He wears no shoes. He thrusts his hat into the paths of passersby in hopes of collecting some coins.

His wife, Delia Martínez, 24, and their four children—all barefoot—sit by his side. Camarillo speaks Spanish but the rest of the family only speaks Mixteco. They subsist on corn tortillas. They sleep on cardboard boxes on the floor of a room located in an outlying area of the city. So far, Camarillo has avoided falling into the evils of delinquency, drugs and prostitution that have snared many of his younger compatriots.

"Nobody ever imagines that in Mexico City, a year, a month, or a week from now, a conflict or a social outburst could occur," warns David Cilia Olmos, coordinator of human rights at the Yax Kin Center. "But it will happen if we do not attend to the demands and problems of these marginalized people who have come to Mexico City simply to survive. Ethnocide is taking place all over the country, and those who escape from it and come to the city find themselves in the same situation."

The first problem new arrivals face is unemployment. In Mexico City, the official figure for unemployment reached 7.5 percent in the first six months of 1995. Added to those city residents who are in the informal economy, or who work fewer than 15 hours a week or only occasionally, this would mean that nearly 1 million capital dwellers will have lost their jobs this year.

The second problem is that the ancestral poverty of indigenous peoples has been perpetuated by the corruption and incompetence of near-feudal state governments. Legions of bumbling bureaucrats and decades of failed economic and social programs have prolonged their poverty.

Now Mexico City's residents are not only suffering the pains of their own devalued middle-class status, but they are also witnessing the devaluation of thousands of indigenous people streaming into their city. The worst of it is that people are beginning to feel there is little, perhaps nothing, they can do to improve the situation.

Survival of Indigenous Cultures

HA, excerpt from a talk given at the KLYS World Conference on Culture, Stockholm, Sweden, March 31–April 2, 1998

Within the past two months, in the wake of the massacre of 45 Indians slain a few days before Christmas in the Chiapas village of Acteal by pro-government paramilitary gunmen, the federal government has renewed its efforts to jumpstart the peace talks with the Zapatista guerrillas which have been stalled since peace agreements were signed in the highland village of San Andrés Larráinzar in 1996. While federal government spending on social programs in the state has increased, the threat to indigenous cultures in the region is growing again.

Tensions in Chiapas are escalating and the government is toughening its stance. After several hundred European observers visited the region, and a television reporter descended by helicopter on a Zapatista stronghold to film foreigners alleged to be working with the rebels, the government has clamped down on foreigners in the area. Recent expulsions have included a French priest with 30 years' residence in the area; over the past few years more than 200 foreigners suspected of sympathizing with the Zapatistas have been expelled. The president of the Association of Foreign Correspondents has complained of new regulations which would monitor and control the movements of foreign journalists in Chiapas.

Earlier this month, President Ernesto Zedillo sent a bill for constitutional reforms to Congress which is aimed at giving legal recognition to indigenous rights and cultures throughout Mexico.

One crucial point of the presidential bill features acknowledgement of the autonomy of indigenous peoples to practice their traditional modes of government, as well as their own forms of social, economic, political, and cultural organization, as long as this takes place within the framework of existing municipal governments. The proposed reforms would also guarantee bilingual public education and the preservation of indigenous languages and customs. Federal spokesmen claim that the reforms would not only go beyond current Mexican legislation but also surpass existing international law in broadening the rights of indigenous peoples.

Some members of congress have expressed fears that should the initiative fail—and this is a real possibility, if the Zapatista Army of National Liberation refuses to discuss and ultimately accept the proposed reforms—war may break out. The Zapatistas are accusing the government of going back on its pledges to grant Indians greater autonomy.

One thing is certain: Armed conflict cannot resolve the cultural problems of Mexico's indigenous peoples. Such conflict would polarize indigenous groups and turn them against each other, worsening their situation and posing serious threats to the survival of their cultural identity. The future of Mexico, a country with deep roots in its indigenous civilizations, depends on our ability to fully acknowledge our cultural past while responding to the present needs of all Mexicans, including the Tarahamura, the Lacandon, the Yaqui, the Nahua, the Purépecha, the Zapotec, the Tzeltal, the Mazahua, and dozens of other ethnic groups. However, we have a special obligation to our indigenous peoples to make up for the centuries of injustice they have suffered, and we cannot put off this debt any longer.

Indian Is Beautiful

With flowers You write, O Giver of Life,
With songs You give color,
With songs You shade
Those who will live on earth.
Later you will destroy eagles and tigers.
   NEZAHUALCÓYOTL (fifteenth-century poet and ruler of the city-
   state of Texcoco)

HA, *Reforma*, March 18, 2001. Translation by Russell Cobb, in *The Zapatista Reader*, ed. Tom Hayden (New York: Nation Books, 2002)

The act staged by Marcos in the Zocalo on Sunday, March 11 was full of political symbolism: the Cathedral to the right, city hall on the left, the Mexican flag in the middle of the plaza, the Zapatista high command with their backs turned to the central balcony of the National Palace (the most important political space in the country), where the president of the republic gives the traditional *Grito*, the Cry of Independence. Marcos's lyrical "cry" evoked indigenous poetry in its rhetoric. The Zapatistas' arrival in the Zócalo was by way of 20 de Noviembre Avenue, which commemorates the Mexican Revolution. In fact, the event in the Zócalo was a symbolic political taking of power. Of course, if someone (Marcos) gains political space, someone else (President Fox) loses it.

In the crowds one could see everything from government bureaucrats to high society ladies masquerading as leftists, to angry youths ready to join in the armed struggle, as well as a great many others who believe that the moment in which there should be justice for Mexico's indigenous people had finally arrived. Also in attendance were many foreign intellectuals whose revolutionary expectations were on the rise—not in their own countries, of course: "This is only a prologue to what is getting ready to happen" (José

Saramago), "And now what? The response has to be the mobilization of the masses" (Manuel Vázquez Montalbán). The Left, which had waned after the collapse of communism in Eastern Europe, could take a new turn. There is no other movement on the horizon against current globalization and materialism than this political romanticism.

Seven years ago I wrote that in 1994 the Zapatista Army of National Liberation (EZLN) not only called attention to the plight of indigenous peoples in Chiapas, but also to the plight of all the indigenous in Mexico, a Mexico torn between its indigenous past and its attempts to insert itself into the economic future of North America. With no contact among them, Yanomami in Brazil, Paraguay's Aché, Peru's Yagua, Nicaragua's Miskito, Panama's Guaymí, the Tarahumara and Huichol in Mexico, Maya from Mexico and Guatemala, Colombia's Guambiano, the Mapuche in Chile, and others, are groups affected by rural and urban overpopulation; settlements of colonizers; industrial development and toxic waste dumps; the building of highways, hydroelectric dams, and tourist complexes; military raids; and aggression from miners, ranchers, loggers, and drug traffickers who violate their rights and move into their habitat. It is imperative that Latin American governments take indigenous peoples into account in their development plans (for example: the Puebla-Panama Plan) and in their definitions of free-trade zones. If not, Latin America will become full of Chiapases.

Some time ago, people began asking me questions: Has Marcos's revolutionary rhetoric stirred up social discontent in Mexico? Could members of the far Left or far Right detonate a social bomb? Is Subcomandante Marcos, deliberately, or President Fox, subconsciously, arousing "el México bronco"— the insubordinate masses (the rebellious Mexico)? Will Mexico become a country of constant demands and threats of indigenous uprisings and invasions of land and nature reserves? Will we see the end of the Montes Azules Biosphere Reserve, now that ARIC (a Rural Collective Interest Association) has invaded 250 acres of the Lacandon village of Naha and begun cutting down trees with no hindrance whatsoever? How will Marcos spend his political capital? Will he return to Chiapas? Will he found a Zapatista political party, merging with the Party of the Democratic Revolution (PRD) with an eye toward the 2006 presidential elections? Could Fox have foreseen that he would celebrate his 100 days in office with the Zapatistas in the Zócalo? Will the Fox government have the political and economic capacity to satisfy the Zapatistas' demands and the expectations of all the indigenous peoples? Will

Marcos meet the expectations of the Mexican and international Left? Will the president be able to offer Mexicans a national plan of social justice and prosperity for the entire population—regardless of ethnic background? Mexico is waiting for answers.

Meanwhile, the Zapatista movement is changing the image of indigenous people in Mexico and Latin America. These are our compatriots whom we are used to seeing begging on city streets, in village markets, and on the roadsides. They are not the only ones in the indigenous world to have suffered abject poverty: María Sabina, the priestess of magic mushrooms and the most important visionary poet of Latin America in the twentieth century, went hungry in her childhood, and it was not the rhetorical hunger that our intellectual courtesans speak of, but real hunger lived out on a daily basis.

"Indian is beautiful," the world now says, thanks to the Zapatista movement—paraphrasing the African-American slogan. After suffering discrimination, abuse, and poverty during the conquest and the colonial period, the Independence years, Maximilian's empire, and the reign of Porfirio Díaz, and the Mexican Revolution, and under the 71-year rule of the PRI, it is time that our ethnic groups become part of the Mexican body economic and politic.

"Indian is beautiful," they exclaimed in the Zócalo on Sunday, March 11—even the children of the Institutional Revolutionary Party (PRI) political and economic bourgeoisie, always eager for exciting social happenings. Watch out: When the rebel is accepted by the bourgeoisie, he becomes inoffensive (Rilke).

Vindicating the image of indigenous people is important, as after the end of the Cold War and the collapse of communism Latin America has been of little political and cultural interest to the Western capitalist powers, beginning with the United States, a country used to seeing us as a market for its goods and a supplier of natural resources, and as an immigration and drug problem. The United States shows more interest in remote cultures—Asia, Africa, or the Balkans—than in ours, as if the USA were not of this continent. You only need watch movies or television programs made in the USA to know that the so-called "Latinos" are not part of their ethnic quotas. In the media summaries of the twentieth century and the second millennium, the indigenous world did not exist.

The historical disdain for Latin America on the part of Western countries continues, and in the eyes of some we are not even newsworthy. This disdain has been fed by the defeatism, corruption, and mediocrity of our government officials. The Zapatista movement of indigenous affirmation will have a domino effect, moving beyond national borders and eventually extending to other parts of Latin America.

This affirmation has taken centuries in the making, considering that Fray Bartolomé de las Casas, the first defender of Indian rights, denounced abuses against the native population in his *Brief History of the Destruction of the Indies* and defended them with the *New Laws* (1543) and while he was Bishop of Chiapas (1545). And Chiapas, a state with 3.9 million inhabitants of whom 1.3 million are indigenous, has only been part of Mexico since 1824; before then it belonged to Guatemala.

From now on, and deservedly, our country and the world can say, "Indian is beautiful."

UPDATE: The Indigenous National Congress and the EZLN have put forward Mexico's first indigenous woman presidential candidate in anticipation of the July 2018 election. María de Jesús Patricio, known as Marichuy, is a 57-year-old Nahua healer from the state of Jalisco who will act as spokesperson for the newly formed Indigenous Council of Government, representing 525 indigenous communities in Mexico. Throughout the country indigenous groups are at odds with government and industry over resource extraction—mining, logging, wind farms, dams—on their lands.

The Huichol versus the Miners

WRITERS AND ARTISTS ASK MEXICO'S PRESIDENT TO CANCEL MINING CONCESSIONS IN THE SACRED TERRITORY OF THE HUICHOL PEOPLE

Grupo de los Cien Internacional/Group of 100, press release, December 1, 2011

Mexico may be the world's largest silver producing country, but not all that shines is silver; countries also shine in their myths and rites, their traditions and culture, and the Huichol (or Wixáritari, in their own language) have shone in Mexico and the world by preserving their unique spiritual identity over time. The annual pilgrimage made by the Wixáritari across the sacred desert landscape of Wirikuta to Cerro Quemado, the mountain where they believe the sun was born, is internationally famous.

In November 2009, the Canadian mining company First Majestic Silver bought 22 mining concessions in the Real de Catorce area, in the state of San Luis Potosí. These concessions will allow First Majestic Silver to carry out what the company describes as "an aggressive drilling and exploration program" on 6,327 hectares (15,634 acres) of land.

The problem is that this part of San Luis Potosí is in the middle of the Wirikuta Natural Reserve. For centuries Huichol men, women, and children have made their way here from communities in the western Sierra Madre mountains in the states of Jalisco, Nayarit, Durango, and Zacatecas to carry out their religious ceremonies, accompanied and guided by the *mara'akate*, their shaman-priests.

Handing over the sacred territory of the Huichol to First Majestic Silver to be mined for its own financial gain not only betrays the colonial mentality of the politicians and bureaucrats responsible for selling silver, Mexico's most emblematic mineral resource, to foreign companies but, far worse, will entail the desecration of the ancestral lands of the Wixáritari.

First Majestic Silver operates exclusively in Mexico, at its La Parrilla, San Martin, and La Encantada mines, and expects to produce seven and a half million ounces of silver in Mexico during 2011.

Minera Golondrina, a Mexican subsidiary of the Canadian-based multinational Lake Shore Gold Corp, plans to dig an open-pit gold mine in the sacrosanct core zone of the Wirikuta Reserve, extracting gold using the highly toxic cyanide process. Both mining operations would endanger the scarce local water supply.

When many people speak of a Mexico that is greater and more enduring than the current climate of violence, they are thinking of its history and culture, and mention of Wirikuta brings to mind an ethnic group which is profoundly Mexican and respected the world over for its authenticity and creativity, whereas mention of First Majestic Silver and Lake Shore Gold Corp brings to mind rapacity and colonialism.

We ask President Felipe Calderón—who witnessed the signing of the Huaxa Manaka Pact three years ago by the governors of five states who vowed to preserve the sacred territory of the Wixárika people—to cancel the mining concessions granted to both Canadian companies. We hope that President

Calderón will not go down in history as the man who authorized the destruction of Wirikuta and its holy ceremonial sites.

[For the list of signers, see Appendix E.]

UPDATE: First Majestic is still fighting in court the injunction presented in 2012 by the San Sebastián Teponahuaxtlán community on behalf of the Huichol, charging that no prior open consultation about the project was held by the mining company and the Mexican government, as required by law.

The Huichol prepared a nomination to UNESCO's World Heritage Committee of the Huichol Route through sacred sites to Wirikuta, a 310-mile-long bio-cultural corridor. In 2015 the nomination was awaiting delivery by the Mexican delegation in Paris to UNESCO. However, according to Conservación Humana, an NGO that works closely with the Huichol, the National Commission for the Development of Indigenous Peoples (CDI) intervened with the Secretariat of Foreign Affairs (SRE) and the nomination of this ancestral pilgramage route has been blocked, bowing to pressure from official agencies seeking to benefit multinational mining corporations.

In May and June 2017, the Wixárika (Huichol) and Náyeri (Cora) indigenous councils met to publicly reaffirm their opposition to the Las Cruces hydroelectric dam that the CFE plans to build in the state of Nayarit. The dam would destroy Keiyatsita, an ancestral ceremonial center, and 14 other sacred sites. It would block the San Pedro Mezquital, the only remaining free-flowing river in the western Sierra Madre Mountains. With its 617-foot high, 2,700-foot wide and 26-foot deep concrete curtain, the dam will impact 5,350 hectares (20.6 square miles), most of that the area to be flooded. Cora and Huichol were already settled in the region before the Spaniards arrived, and authorities of both groups were adamant, stating, "We won't give up. This is our church, our future, and that must be recognized."

8

Mexico in Flames

THE JUNGLE AFLAME

The saffron skies resemble tropical Turners.
The dancing palms are kissed by voracious tongues.
The howler monkeys leap from crest to crest.
Through the billows of smoke, companies of parrots
with singed tails go searching for the sun
that watches them covertly, like a putrid eye.

HA (*translated by George McWhirter*)

Group of 100: Mexico in Flames

Nonprofit ad, *Proceso*, May 13, 1991

From January through April there have been approximately 5,000 forest fires in Mexico, 98 percent of them caused by people. According to the Secretariat of Agriculture and Water Resources (SARH), the total land area burned is 130,000 hectares (502 square miles). The worst damage was the destruction of 10,000 hectares (38 square miles) of saplings, destined for 37,000 hectares (143 square miles) of new forest; mature trees were weakened and made vulnerable to infestation. The most impacted states, in order of importance, are Chiapas, Guerrero, Oaxaca, Michoacán, Quintana Roo, Yucatán, and San Luis Potosí. The greatest number of fires has been in the State of Mexico—nearly 1,000—with 900 in Mexico City's forests, mainly in the mountainous Ajusco area. National parks have also been struck, including El Tepozteco and the Lagunas de Zempoala in Morelos, Cofre de Perote, and Pico de Orizaba in Veracruz, Pico de Tancítaro in Michoacán, and the Iztaccíhuatl-Popocatépetl in Puebla and the State of Mexico. Forests within cities have burned: more than 700 hectares (2.7 square miles) of Guadalajara's Bosque de La Primavera were scorched. There are fires that were deliberately set or due to carelessness in Morelia, Uruapan, and Zapopan. The damage to Mexico's forest wealth and fauna is incalculable; the wildlife suffers from hunger and habitat loss. There are hundreds of active fires; in San Luis Potosí, Yucatán, and Quintana Roo alone more than 6,000 hectares (23 square miles) are ablaze in each state. A fire is ongoing in the Río Lagartos wildlife sanctuary. Dozens of fires break out every day, but no one has been punished.

In years past, fires also reached disastrous dimensions, but this year will set a new record and arsonists will ravage still more of our remaining forests. Their handiwork, and that of timber traffickers, will soon turn Mexico into a silent wasteland if sufficient measures are not taken; April and May are the critical months of the wildfire season, so it's safe to say there will be more fires and a greater expanse will be affected than during the first three months of the year. On April 9 alone, 18 acts of arson were reported in Michoacán; in Patamban, firefighters were repelled by shots fired by local incendiaries. On Friday, May 3, 54 fires were reported in Querétaro and San Luis Potosí, affecting 12,000 hectares (46 square miles).

Fires in the southern part of Mexico City have intensified the Valley of Mexico's air pollution and environmental deterioration, reducing the amount of available fresh water and accelerating soil erosion. Most alarming, aside from the harm done to an entire nation's natural patrimony, is the impunity enjoyed by most of those responsible. An arsonist committing an ecological, economic, and social crime is insensible to the consequences, and usually intent on burning off pasture and trees to invigorate growth of grassland for fodder during the dry season; damaging trees to justify chopping them down; taking revenge for a land ownership disagreement; or clearing plots for planting or grazing.

We acknowledge the government's firefighting efforts. We have been told that SARH, through the Forestry Undersecretariat, has plowed more than 15 billion pesos into their programs; that there are firefighting aircraft for dropping water, nearly three dozen small planes for detecting fires, several hundred vehicles for bringing personnel to wildfire sites, and radio communication equipment; that thousands of SARH employees and many thousands of soldiers, marines, and volunteers from *ejidos* and communities take part in firefighting; and that tens of thousands of emergency food packages are distributed by the National Public Subsistence Company (CONASUPO). We also know that, regrettably, lives have been lost, such as the SARH firefighters who perished in Guerrero and Campeche.

But all this won't be enough if fires continue to be set, so we propose the following:

Draw up a clear set of laws about land use that will be put into practice, not merely stated; clarify land tenure; compensate peasants who have land rights in national parks and nature reserves, so that these areas can be devoted to conservation; promote production of forage in non-wooded areas; foster alternative productive activities for peasants so they won't destroy thousands of hectares of forest to meet their immediate needs, finding themselves as poor as they were before the fires and more uncertain about their future.

Because these fires recur year after year, municipal, state, and federal governments urgently need to count on technical and human resources to combat them efficiently.

We know that the causes that motivate the arsonists who lay waste to Mexico's natural patrimony must be resolved, but also, out of fairness to our people, those who put that patrimony at risk to satisfy their own personal, ephemeral, and selfish interests must be punished.

Where There's Fire, There's Smoke

HA, *Reforma*, May 31, 1998

Mexico harbors 10 percent of the planet's terrestrial biodiversity, placing first in reptiles, second in mammals, and fourth in amphibians and plants. Oaxaca, Chiapas, Veracruz, Guerrero, and Michoacán are the most biodiverse states, and all have been hit by the 11,656 fires that have devastated nearly 365,000 hectares (1,410 square miles) of the country between January and May. Aside from their impact on our forests and jungles and the pollution and health problems they have caused in Mexican cities (shrouded in smoke and suspended particles for weeks now), the wildfires have ravaged our fauna. Not only have they turned the habitats of many species and animal populations into ashes and smoke, they have also polluted them and will deprive the fauna of food and water. According to the National Commission on Biodiversity's Jorge Soberón, we do not know yet if the current fires will cause any species to go extinct; they must be studied individually, which could take years. What we do know now is that populations of small animals suffered the most.

According to Dr. Jesús Estudillo, this is the breeding season for birds of all sizes. Chicks in nests have been trapped by flames or died of smoke inhalation. Toucans, who are poor fliers, were an easy prey to forest fires in Puebla, Oaxaca, and San Luis Potosí. Woodpeckers, who nest in tree trunks and range from the Sierra Madre to the Yucatán peninsula, were also victims of fires, as well as populations of parrots and parakeets in low-lying areas from Guerrero to Chiapas and from San Luis Potosí to Veracruz. In Campeche, Dr. Estudillo saw anteaters crossing the highway in daylight to flee from the fire. Crown fires—the most serious—burned spider and howler monkeys to cinders; both species are already at risk due to habitat loss in Chiapas, Tabasco, Campeche, and Quintana Roo. Two crown fires in Chanal, Chiapas, ravaged 2,000 hectares (nearly 5,000 acres). Subsurface fires ravaged reptiles and small mammals. Close to 50 fires in the Chimalapas, the largest remaining tropical rain forest in North America, have been devastating. The Chimalapas, with 594,000 hectares (2,294 square miles), is fourth in the world in birds and amphibians and home to 62 reptile species. While it has not been possible to determine exactly how many hectares were lost—estimates are well above

40,000 (155 square miles)—the flames reached the cloud forest; the conflagrations were described by US Forest Service brigades who were brought in to extinguish them as "the most unprecedented and extraordinary ones of this century." The fires did not spare biosphere reserves such as Río Lagartos (one of the main pink flamingo nesting areas in the Americas), where more than 500 hectares (1,235 acres) were laid waste in April. In Michoacán, where 1,269 fires that consumed nearly 16,000 hectares (62 square miles) were reported as of May 10, there were fires in all five protected areas where the monarch butterfly overwinters: Cerro Altamirano, Sierra Chincua, Chivatí-Huacal, Cerro Pelón, and El Rosario. In San Andrés, an unprotected sanctuary, logging and fires in March were responsible for massive monarch mortality. The Maya world was particularly affected by fires, from Palenque, where tourists had to be evacuated, to Tikal, in the Guatemalan Petén.

From Mexico to Honduras approximately one million hectares (3,861 square miles) were lost, including the natural surroundings of Maya ceremonial centers. Fires in the remaining green areas of Mexico City will probably contribute to the city's ultimate environmental deterioration, and will worsen air and water pollution. Despite consensus that all the Valley of Mexico's fires were deliberate, only two arsonists have been arrested. As far as I know, the Federal Attorney General's Office for Environmental Protection (PROFEPA) has yet to investigate the origin of 12,000 fires throughout the country nor has anyone been fined, although various bureaucrats have mentioned loggers, businessmen, ranchers, farmers, and drug traffickers as guilty of sending up our natural patrimony in smoke. Thanks to arsonists and loggers, 20 years from now Mexico could be a wasteland. Federal congress's Forestry and Jungle Commission recently reported in Morelia that "out of 600,000 hectares [2,316 square miles] of forest damaged every year for diverse reasons, only 100,000 [386 square miles] will regenerate. That means we are losing 500,000 hectares [1,930 square miles] annually; if we do the math, in 20 years there won't be any forests left." According to environmental attorney Alberto Szekely, Mexican legislation on forest fires is crystal clear; the principal problem is that PROFEPA doesn't enforce it and people know that the law is a dead letter.

Requiem for a Paradise

HA, *Reforma*, June 14, 1998. Published as "Burning Forests: Arson by Developers?" *The Ecologist*, November–December 1998

While Mexico and the world were being consumed by World Cup fever, almost one-third of the Chimalapas, the most biodiversity-rich ecosystem of the Americas, was ravaged by over 60 fires. The worst fires are still raging in the Espinazo del Diablo [literally, "the Devil's Backbone"], the biological corridor that links the El Ocote Special Biosphere Reserve, a montane rain forest covering 48,140 hectares (18,573 square miles), with the moist tropical forest of the Chimalapas. The area straddles the states of Oaxaca and Chiapas and contains important archaeological sites, some of which have been flooded by the Netzahualcóyotl dam. The danger, even now, is such that, even if the rains do come to the rescue, it could be another two weeks before the larger fires are extinguished, since several— including some underground—are out of control. The carnage has not only devastated irreplaceable flora and fauna, but has also upset the economy of the people who live in the area, and whose children will know only an altered climate, charred rocks, piles of ash, and serious water shortages. In short: poverty.

Researchers Ana Luisa Anaya and Marcela Álvarez have estimated that a single hectare of undisturbed tropical vegetation in the Chimalapas may be home to as many as 900 plant and more than 200 animal species. According to the *Catalogue of Biosphere Reserves and Other Protected Natural Areas of Mexico*, the forest complex of the Chimalapas, Uxpanapa, and El Ocote is one of the most important centers of biodiversity the world, a refuge for sur-viving Pleistocene species and a valuable germplasm bank. As a habitat for threatened, rare, and endemic species, and given its unique cave and cavern systems, geological formations and archeological wealth, it is a priority con-servation zone. In El Ocote, there are over 2,000 species of plants and fungi, and 12 precious tropical hardwoods such as mahagony and the endangered *Chamaedorea* (xiate) palm. El Ocote has more than 500 species of "higher vertebrates," 3,000 species of insects and arachnids, 445 species of butterflies, 31 species of amphibians, 62 species of reptiles, and 184 mammal species, including jaguar, ocelot, and the endangered white-lipped peccary, golden-mantled howler monkey, and Geoffroy's spider monkey. The American crocodile—a vulnerable species—is also native to the area. There are 350 bird species, 38 of them migratory from the United States and Canada, two of Mexico's three species of toucan, and king vulture, harpy eagle, white hawk, quetzal and scarlet macaw.

Large groups of animals and snakes have been seen fleeing the flames, but until the fires are out we will not know the extent of mortality among these species in El Ocote and in the Chimalapas, or the negative impacts on the Grijalva and Usumacinta watersheds. If the Espinazo del Diablo is fractured by fire, and the biological corridor is fragmented, no matter how much is spent on reforestation, Mexico and the world will have lost one of their most valuable natural treasures, and many species of flora and fauna will have moved closer to extinction.

Although this zone has been an earthly paradise, it has also been the scene of reprehensible human conflict, including the long-standing border dispute between Chiapas and Oaxaca, confrontations between indigenous communities in the Chimalapas and the non-indigenous population, deforestation by loggers and cattle ranchers, ransacking of wildlife by traffickers, and the threat of government and corporate projects such as the 240-kilometer, four-lane highway between Veracruz and Chiapas that was originally planned to run through El Ocote, the northeastern edge of the Chimalapas and the easternmost part of Uxpanapa.

Looming over the region is the Coatzacoalcos, Veracruz-Salina Cruz, Oaxaca Transisthmus Project, entailing construction of a coast-to-coast high-speed rail line and a four-lane highway as an overland transit corridor linking the Gulf of Mexico with the Pacific Ocean, a "dry canal" (dreamed about by Mexican and foreign governments since the beginning of the century) as an alternative to the Panama Canal. In February 1998, Carlos Ruiz Sacristán, secretary of Communications and Transport, announced the launching this year, with an initial investment of 250 to 300 million dollars, of the Isthmus of Tehuantepec Integrated Regional Development Plan, claiming it was "by consensus" with affected communities. Miguel Robles Gil, a member of the Committee for the Defense of Chimalapas, warned that a project of this magnitude would lead to "soil impoverishment, disappearance of species, depletion of the water table, indiscriminate use of agrochemicals, high levels of pollution in water bodies, and heavy pressure on forests."

Has human indifference and greed caused this year's holocaust of nature, because the Chimalapas lie within the vast area of the Isthmus of Tehuantepec megaproject for which the Mexican government and the private sector have ambitious development plans? Rosendo Montiel, coordinator for ecological land management for the NGO Maderas del Pueblo del Sureste, says, "It's very peculiar that virgin forest, where the animals are tame and the damp vegetation is hard to burn, should have caught fire in a straight line. The Americans say that someone could have dropped so-called ping-pong balls from the air, which are balls impregnated with chemical substances used in the United States to set counter-fires and which cause flames to spring up." In Mexico, as in Brazil and Indonesia, fires have been a convenient way of getting rid of the forest. The inhabitants of the Chimalapas have not yet been able to establish a Campesino Ecological Reserve, as they would like to do. In June, during a meeting between Secretariat of the Environment, Natural Resources, and Fisheries (SEMARNAP) head Julia Carabias and people from local communities, the latter argued that it would be no use to them for the government to establish a biosphere reserve instead of a reserve managed by the peasants themselves.

"El Ocote is a biosphere reserve and it's burning, wood is being looted and people are living in abject misery." Who can blame them? Why would anyone want a paradise protected on paper but devastated by ecocidal criminals?

UPDATE: By late June 1998, after the rains had extinguished all the hot spots, experts put the number of fires in the Chimalapas at sixty-eight, with 218,000 hectares (842 square miles) damaged, of which 18,000 hectares (70 square miles) were totally destroyed virgin cloud forest.

In June 2016, a federal law was passed to create Special Economic Zones (SEZ) in the southeastern regions of Mexico, with tax breaks and other preferential benefits to promote economic growth in states such as Guerrero, Michoacán, Veracruz, Chiapas, and Oaxaca, all rich in biodiversity, forests, and indigenous cultures. This is yet another reworking of the Plan Puebla Panama, but limited to Mexico. An Interoceanic Industrial Corridor on the Isthmus of Tehuantepec, one of the designated SEZ's, would connect Mexico's largest refinery, in the Pacific coast port of Salina Cruz in Oaxaca, with the petrochemical plants in Coatzacoalcos, Veracruz, on the Gulf of Mexico. In mid-June 2017, when rains from Tropical Storm Calvin flooded the Antonio Dovalí Jaime oil refinery in Salina Cruz, where one-quarter of all the fuels used in Mexico are produced, a fire broke out and blazed for days. A leaking storage tank caught fire and half a million liters of crude oil burned, and the resulting highly toxic "black rain" polluted water, crops, and the coast, affecting 10,000 fishermen as well as shrimp and other fisheries.

9

Endangered Mexico

IN VIOLENT TIMES

There are angels in violent times
who fly over the devastated streets
as if they were wearing wings on their feet;

with the terminals of sunbeams in their hands
they materialize in seedy dives at daybreak,
searching out the grey matter of the executed;

they have no robes, nor celestial jewels on,
no glowing faces, no mellifluous voices,
racing down the highways, sounding their alarms;

from a golden footprint, or transparent fingers
caressing a mouth or bloodied breast,
you can tell they're there;

they slip through army road blocks,
the Feds' steel bracelets,
nestle in the corner of some bathroom,

or leap, like a shadow, out of the closet,
where they stack the skeletons, to give
those mown down by machineguns, water;

bearing pillows plumped with nothing
they prowl the garbage dumps of dawn,
wherever a ravished woman's head is laid to rest.

In violent times, there are angels in the nothingness.

HA (*translated by George McWhirter*)

Nuclear Sleep Produces Monsters

A LETTER FROM THE GROUP OF 100 TO PRESIDENT
MIGUEL DE LA MADRID: IF THERE'S AN ACCIDENT, THE
VICTIMS WON'T CARE WHEN YOUR TERM IS UP

Proceso, November 1986

Dear Licenciado Miguel de la Madrid:

We know that in the days to come, you, as the country's maximum authority, will bear the burden of deciding whether the nuclear plant at Laguna Verde should go ahead. We also know the decision to begin work on the plant wasn't yours, but we are hopeful that, as Mexico's president, you can stop it. Although your presidency will end in two years, the huge historic and moral responsibility of authorizing Laguna Verde will not end on November 30, 1988. Should a catastrophe occur in the future, the victims won't care when your term was up, but they will ask why a president of Mexico decided against all prudence to go ahead with the plant.

On May 12, 16 days after the Chernobyl disaster, the Group of 100 demanded that the nuclear plant in the state of Veracruz be abandoned, and that the self-interest of a small group of people stubbornly set on the project be overridden. Four months have passed with no reply from the government to the serious objections we expressed, and there have been no satisfactory clarifications of the doubts and suggestions put forward by other environmental groups, energy technicians, and many Mexican citizens who have publicly opposed the plant. The safety and well-being of Mexicans concerns us all, and when an accident happens in Laguna Verde, radioactivity will make no distinction between the governors and the governed.

It has been said that the decision to start up the Laguna Verde nuclear power plant should be left to the Federal Electricity Commission's directors, but we strongly believe that because of the political and ethical risks involved, the decision is not only a matter for them, nor for the government of Veracruz, but for the entire country, which would suffer in case of a disaster.

As Chernobyl has made plain, the negative effects of a nuclear accident can be felt thousands of miles away and in many distant countries.

According to recently published information, the accident in the Soviet Union emitted 50 percent more caesium than all previous atomic energy trials and explosions together. Caesium can remain in the environment for up to 100 years and is a known carcinogen. Last summer several European countries warned against drinking milk or eating meat and fish coming from areas affected by radioactive fallout, and in East Germany a rise of 2,000 cancer-related deaths annually was predicted. If there's an accident in Veracruz, how can we forbid Mexicans who are already suffering from the economic crisis from consuming milk, meat, and fish, which 60 percent of the population usually can't afford, not to mention all the fruits and vegetables that would have to be destroyed?

Despite all the risks, the bureaucrats in charge of the project argue that Mexico cannot afford to pass up nuclear power. We say that after the disastrous LPG explosions in San Juan Ixhuatepec two years ago and the September 19, 1985, earthquake, Mexico cannot afford to have an accident in a nuclear power plant.

To the claim that Mexico will fall behind in nuclear technology if we don't have a plant in operation by 2000, we answer that Sweden, a member, as is Mexico, of the Group of Six (formed in 1984 to promote nuclear disarmament), decided to eliminate nuclear power and close its 12 plants by the year 2010, despite currently receiving 41 percent of its energy from these plants. After more than a dozen minor accidents during its sole year of operation, Spain's Ascó 2 plant has been shut down. Social Democrats in West Germany, who were in power when 17 of the country's 20 nuclear plants were built, vowed to phase out nuclear energy. In 1978, in a referendum held in Austria, voters rejected the peaceful use of nuclear power. Arguing that radioactivity ignores borders, Austrian environmental groups are planning protests against the nuclear fuel reprocessing plant planned for construction in Wackersdorf, Germany.

Recently, the National Commission on Nuclear Safety and Safeguards (CNSNS) guaranteed that the plant is designed to withstand the impact of a plane crash. However, the Ecologists' Pact denounced a rupturing of tubes last August 15 that damaged the cooling pool to be used for radioactive waste, and quoted a plant director who resigned in 1980 after alleging construction errors due to a constant turnover of contractors and scrimping on materials. If there's an accident at Laguna Verde, does the government want a nuclear Tlatelolco?

Mr. President, our unbiased opinion is that, for the good of everyone, the best option is to follow the recommendation by environmental groups and various energy technicians to convert Laguna Verde into a natural gas-fired thermoelectric plant, and it should not be ignored by a head of state who has tried to introduce a moral commitment with the people into his governance. Leaving the possibility of a nuclear accident at Laguna Verde to future generations of Mexicans is profoundly unfair, especially coming from someone like yourself who has repeatedly claimed to put the interests of Mexico before his own and those of groups who are only after personal gain and don't care if an entire country could one day wake up to a nuclear nightmare.

UPDATE: A concession granted in the mid-2000s to Goldcorp, the largest Canadian mining company in Mexico, to operate two open-pit mines as part of the Caballo Blanco Project, less than ten miles away from Laguna Verde, was acquired in July 2016 by Candelaria Mining Corp. (also Canadian), which aims to produce more than 100,000 ounces of gold per year at the mines.

In June 2017, a delegation of US nuclear executives came to Mexico to discuss Mexico's plans to build more reactors. Mexico and the United States are negotiating a bilateral agreement for nuclear cooperation. Nuclear trade delegations from France, China, and Russia also visited recently.

Lead in Our Blood

GROUP OF 100: LEAD

Nonprofit ad, *Proceso*, May 13, 1991, and *La Jornada*, May 27, 1991

Lic. Carlos Salinas de Gortari
President of the United Mexican States

Mr. President:

Thanks to its universally notorious air, water, and soil pollution, the Valley of Mexico is a high-risk zone for our children and for ourselves. Lead is one of the most pernicious and dangerous contaminants affecting us, causing a range of health disorders, especially in children, and reducing their IQ.

Recent research by chemist Hilda Muñoz and Drs. Palazuelos, Romieu and Hernández on 150 children in Mexico City found lead levels in 38 percent of the group, well above the maximum allowed by the World Health Organization, which is 15 micrograms per deciliter of blood. The group's average was 19 mcg/dl, with some children testing at 3–4 mcg/dl, while others who live in the southwestern part of the city tested as high as 40–45 mcg/dl. Another study, carried out in January 1991 by the Children's Hospital of Mexico and covering the entire child population of the city, found an average of 22 mcg/dl. Tragically, even before birth the fetus can absorb lead from its mother. The scientific literature emphasizes neurological damage, manifested in learning difficulties; 50 percent of Mexican children don't finish elementary school, in many cases due to adverse neurodevelopment and an IQ reduction of between 5 and 12 points, depending on blood lead levels. Of course, exposure to lead also affects the adult population, increasing the risk of high blood pressure, heart disease and strokes, decreased libido, impotence, and the chance of miscarriages.

Exposure to airborne lead in Mexico comes from leaded gasoline, spilled engine oil, lead chromate in yellow road markings that are pulverized and scattered, and foundries; lead from plumbing and lead solder contaminates drinking water; lead leaches into food from improperly fired glazed ceramic pottery or from the solder in cans, an obsolete technology that is on its way out in other countries because it contaminates during processing, exposes the consumer to lead and poisons the soil when the cans are discarded. Lead solder is used for Jumex juice cans and all brands of medium-sized cans of chile, because the cans are all made by the same producer.

Wooden toys decorated with paint containing lead are common in Mexico, and children can easily swallow the paint, poisoning themselves. School supplies such as Prismacolor and Berol colored pencils don't comply with safety norms that limit lead content to three parts per million; samplings of these products have found up to 70,000 parts per million.

Large amounts are spent testing for contaminants, even when we know where they come from. That is why, Mr. President, we are asking you to protect the health of Mexico's children by:

1. Prohibiting production of lead-glazed pottery, and making easy credits available to artisans to make pottery with glazes that do not contain lead.
2. Legislating so that no product a child might eat or suck on, including painted toys and Prismacolor and Berol pencils, may contain lead.
3. Requiring manufacturers to label the lead content of their products in parts per million, or else the cans in which these products are packed—as in Jumex juices and medium-sized chile cans—so consumers will be informed.
4. Educating the public as to the risks of acquiring and using products containing lead that contaminate the air, water, soil and their own bodies.
5. Replacing lead with non-toxic tin for soldering pipes, to stop unintentional poisoning of hard-to-obtain drinking water.

Progress in getting lead out of gasoline has now made the manufacturing processes of various industries the main problem in the Valley of Mexico.

If lead is banned from gasoline, pottery, paint and cans, and foundry emissions are controlled, blood lead levels will fall and Mexico's children will have healthier bodies and minds.

UPDATE: Thanks to our campaign, leaded gasoline has been phased out, use of lead soldering for cans was halted, and lead content in pottery has been drastically reduced. WHO has revised its recommendations to state that there is no known safe blood lead concentration.

Natural Sovereignty

HA, speech given on Wednesday, June 5, 1991, during the World Environment Day ceremony presided over by Carlos Salinas de Gortari. Published in *La Jornada*, June 7, 1991

We know Carlos Salinas de Gortari has been awarded a prize by the Tierra Unida Foundation for his efforts to reduce pollution in the Valley of Mexico, a notorious example of environmental deterioration in big cities and a serious health problem for its inhabitants. We must be generous in recognizing the results of measures taken by the government, but to be honest, we have to mention that, ecologically speaking, this has been one of the most critical years for our country, and a great deal remains to be done. However, degradation of the environment was not exclusive to Mexico, but took place in the air, water, and soil of the entire planet. Our fight for healthier surroundings is part of mankind's fight for a clean Earth, where plant and animal species can live with dignity in their natural habitats.

Today, just as a year ago today, just as yesterday, at midday a faint blue toxic gas settles over the Valley of Mexico. Every afternoon residents of the metropolitan area endure ozone levels two or three times the maximum norms set by SEDUE [Secretariat of Urban Development and Ecology] and WHO [World Health Organization], norms that should not be exceeded for more than one hour a year but which we are subjected to for up to nine continuous hours a day. Heedless of the damage this pollutant causes to the human body and vegetation, every day millions of drivers take to the streets to produce these ozone concentrations, turning Mexico City into a hell of private transport.

Excessive use of private vehicles has to be curtailed, making possession of more than one car harder for owners of several, and making driving more costly and difficult for everyone who wastes gasoline on unnecessary trips. At the same time, public transport must become more comfortable and efficient, using dedicated lanes for buses that will be faster and more attractive for riders. As for the most polluting industries, it's time to build on the General Law of Ecological Balance and Environmental Protection [LGEEPA, 1988] to enact specific norms, statutes, and regulations. If the gasoline problem is resolved and air emissions by stationary industrial sources are brought under control, in a not so distant future we could be witnessing a notable improvement in air quality in the Valley of Mexico.

In an open letter to the president of the republic published a few weeks ago by the Group of 100, we detailed the severe dangers lead poses to the environment and to human health in Mexico, and most especially to children. We strongly urge that this toxic substance be eliminated as quickly as possible from all the sources we mentioned.

Municipal sewage and industrial waste are being discharged into bodies of water in Mexico City and all over the country, turning rivers, lakes, lagoons, and seas into liquid garbage dumps. Overexploitation of Mexico City's acquifers are precipitating a water crisis; every day more groundwater is pumped out faster than it can be recharged. The National Program for Environmental Protection 1990–1994 lists nine groups that are responsible for 82 percent of liquid industrial wastes, with the sugar and chemical industries contributing 59.8 percent. Here the "polluter pays" principle is imperative. And we need to rethink water use and recycling, not only because of scarcity, but because water quality is at risk.

The main cause of ecosystem devastation in Mexico is the rampant logging of forests and jungles, and the lunatic practice of burning them. This year our country held fourth place in the world in deforestation, and witnessed 7,000 wildfires—98 percent of them intentional—between January and May, reducing 200,000 hectares (772 square miles) to ashes and smoke, according to the Secretariat of Agriculture and Water Resources [SARH]. More than one million hectares (3,861 square miles) have been destroyed by fires during the past three years. This year the State of Mexico, the Federal District, Michoacán, Morelos, Puebla, Chiapas, Quintana Roo, and Yucatán had the highest number of fires. Every year, hundreds of thousands of hectares of tropical rain forest and deciduous and evergreen forests are lost to logging, and vegetation in semi-arid areas disappears. Above 90 percent of our country's swamps and mangroves are gone. Loggers and arsonists don't spare volcanoes or national parks, ravaging the Pico de Orizaba, the Malinche, the Pico de Tancítaro, Iztaccíhuatl Popocatépetl, and La Primavera forest. Destruction of Mexico's forests and jungles has negative impacts on air, soil, water, climate, and animal life. Our fauna is being exterminated. In the tropics, home to the richest biodiversity, we are losing species such as the jaguar, ocelot, jaguarundi, neotropical river otter, Geoffroy's spider monkey, harpy eagle, quetzal, scarlet macaw, and American antelope. The golden eagle, Mexico's national symbol, is close to extinction. It's hard to name a species that isn't struggling to survive, that isn't threatened, that isn't a victim of the degradation and destruction of its habitat, or of hunting and wildlife trafficking. Last year, Mexico's president promised to sign the Convention on International Trade in Endangered Species of Wild Fauna and Flora [CITES], to control the plundering of our plant and animal species.

The devastation of our forests and jungles is playing havoc with our biodiversity, one of the richest on Earth. A state of emergency must be called to rein in logging until there is a nationwide classification of land use to protect our forest ecosystems and clearly define the limits to agriculture and ranching, explicitly specifying permitted land use.

Another thing we need: reporting about, paying attention to, and not harassing Mexicans who are defending nature, such as the peasants in Peribán, Michoacán, who are fighting to save the forest on the Pico de Tancítaro, the Nahua communities in the Alto Balsas who are opposing construction of the San Juan Tetelcingo dam, the activists in Zihuatenejo who were jailed for protesting the slaughter of hundreds of crocodiles, or the residents of the Federal District, Morelia, Guadalajara, Cuernavaca, and Acapulco who are defending trees in the streets and parks of their cities.

We must educate our citizens, most especially our children, in ethical behaviors towards nature. The concepts of ecology should be taught to teachers and parents to pass on to their students and children, but, above all, should figure prominently in textbooks. And children whose parents are predators of nature should be taught to educate them.

Lastly, as negotiations for the North American Free Trade Agreement are getting underway, it is important to assure the people of Mexico that economic integration will not lead to environmental disaster, that laws will be enacted to regulate the activities of foreign companies in our country, and that LGEEPA will be amended to include more specific norms and regulations within the scope of NAFTA. Mexicans must be convinced that NAFTA will include oversight, implementation, and enforcement mechanisms compatible with our country's environmental objectives, with prior evaluation of the possible environmental impacts of the Treaty, to ensure a level playing field when negotiating with the United States. Within this framework, we are particularly concerned about import, production, and use of pesticides and chemical substances that are detrimental to human health and ecosystems, and that Mexico's already abused forests are not put on a fast track for lumber traffickers and cattle ranchers and industrial farmers, who may see NAFTA as an opportunity to finish them off.

Walking in the Smog, by Manuel Álvarez Bravo, is one of 34 photographs and paintings accompanying 34 texts in *Artistas e intelectuales sobre el ecocidio urbano* (Artists and intellectuals on urban ecocide), an anthology compiled by Homero Aridjis and Fernando Césarman and published in 1989 by the Mexico City Chronicle Council.

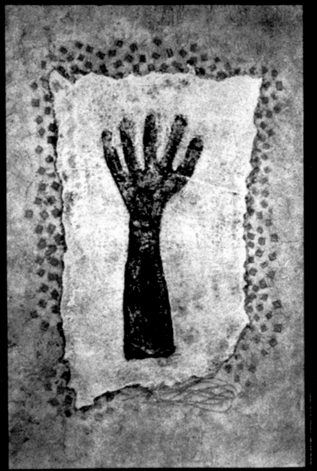

Mano negre sobre la ciudad (Black hand over the city), a poster by Rufino Tamayo for the Group of 100 exhibition held at the Foro de Arte Contemporáneo in Mexico City in April 1985.

Árbol de la vida (Tree of life), a lithograph by Pierre Alechinsky for the Group of 100's booth at the Global Forum held by nongovernmental organizations during the Earth Summit convened by the United Nations in Rio de Janeiro, June 3–14, 1992.

Grupo de los Cien

Cumbre de la Tierra

El juicio final (The last judgment), a poster by Red Grooms for the Group of 100's booth at the Global Forum held by nongovernmental organizations during the Earth Summit convened by the United Nations in Rio de Janeiro, June 3–14, 1992.

Grupo de los Cien
Cumbre de la Tierra

El cacto de la vida (The cactus of life), a poster by Roger von Gunten for the Group of 100's booth at the Global Forum held by nongovernmental organizations during the Earth Summit convened by the United Nations in Rio de Janeiro, June 3–14, 1992.

Left to right: Rufino Tamayo (in glasses), Octavio Paz, Olga Tamayo, and Homero Aridjis, representing the Group of 100 at the official closing of the Loreto and Peña Pobre paper mill's cellulose plant in Mexico City on March 17, 1986. (Photo by David Hernández, courtesy of the Group of 100.)

Homero Aridjis telling the blind writer Jorge Luis Borges about monarch butterflies during the Morelia International Poetry Festival in August 1981. (Photo by Betty Ferber.)

Filmmaker Luis Buñuel and Homero Aridjis talking about an ecological apocalypse. (Photo courtesy of Homero Aridjis.)

Homero Aridjis with artist, writer, and Group of 100 member Leonora Carrington, who used to say, "There are many animals I like. Human beings are not top of the list. In fact, they are lowest in my preferences. Humans are terrible beings who commit murder and I'm very sad to think I am one of that species." (Photo by Betty Ferber.)

Homero Aridjis and UNESCO Goodwill Ambassador Claudia Cardinale during the 34th General Conference. As Mexico's ambassador to UNESCO, in 2008 Aridjis succeeded in getting the Monarch Butterfly Biosphere Reserve listed as a World Heritage Site. (Photo courtesy of Homero Aridjis.)

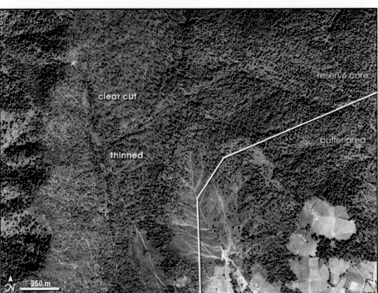

NASA photos using imagery from the commercial Ikonos satellite showing severe degradation of the forest habitat within the Monarch Butterfly Biosphere Reserve in central Mexico. The white line indicates the boundaries of the reserve's core zone, where logging is forbidden. This pair of images shows the affected area on March 22, 2004 (*top*), and February 23, 2008 (*below*). The degraded area was the site of the Lomas de Aparicio monarch colony. The circles on the image indicate the approximate positions of the colony in different seasons. The area had been largely intact since at least 1986. Scientists Lincoln Brower, Daniel Slayback, and Isabel Ramírez determined that approximately 450 hectares (1,110 acres) of forest were logged between 2004 and 2008, representing 3.3 percent of the core zone of the reserve, which comprises 13,552 hectares (33,410 acres). The majority of this logging (290 hectares, or 717 acres) occurred after March 2006. (Photo by Ikonos image © GeoEye. Caption by Dr. Lincoln Brower.)

Left to right: Homero Aridjis, Vasko Popa, Allen Ginsberg, Andrei Voznesensky, Günter Grass, and Lasse Söderberg near the Monarch Butterfly Biosphere Reserve during the First International Poetry Festival, held in Morelia, Michoacán, in August 1981. (Photo by Betty Ferber.)

Two rivers of monarchs are flying across the Llano de los Tres Gobernadores, on Cerro Pelón, on a warm clear morning. The butterflies close to the ground are heading from the colony across the Llano to an unknown water source. The butterflies higher in the sky are returning to the colony. The Cerro Pelón colonies have no free-flowing streams nearby. They drink dew off the plain in the morning, take advantage of wet seeps, and fly distances of up to three miles to streams. (Photo taken in the morning of January 13, 2006. Photo and caption by Dr. Lincoln Brower.)

Dr. Lincoln Brower (*second from left*) and Homero Aridjis (*far right*) with two *ejidatarios* on Cerro Pelón in the Monarch Butterfly Biosphere Reserve. (Photo by Betty Ferber.)

Protective Poet Finds Himself in Need of Bodyguards in Mexican Mystery

■ **Rights:** Homero Aridjis, who heads groups that guard writers and the environment, is harassed and threatened by nameless stalkers.

By MARY BETH SHERIDAN
TIMES STAFF WRITER

MEXICO CITY—Homero Aridjis had just been elected president of International PEN—the star-studded writers group—and the prominent Mexican writer was bursting with ideas.

The group would visit oppressed writers in Iran. Defend government critics in Cuba. Vigorously campaign for persecuted artists in Nigeria and China.

But a year later, Aridjis has a more urgent case on his hands.

His own.

In recent months, Aridjis has been haunted by menacing callers who wake him up at night and scar his holidays. The distinguished poet and novelist doesn't know who is behind the threats, although he suspects a political motive. He only knows they want him dead.

Suddenly, Aridjis can identify with the hundreds of jailed or threatened writers defended by the London-based PEN. He knows he isn't as badly off as some. But, shadowed by two government-supplied bodyguards, the soft-spoken poet has entered the same "culture of fear."

"You begin to limit your world," Aridjis, 58, said in an interview in his living room, a cozy clutter of books and soft chairs.

"I used to have the freedom to go out alone, to take public transport, the subway. I loved to walk. . . . It's part of my life as a writer," he said. "But now I can't do it. My mind isn't free. If I go into the street, it's in a car with two armed men, turning every which way."

Aridjis has written 26 books of poetry, fiction and essays, including "The Lord of the Last Days," his most recent to appear in English. But it is his other passion—nature—that has made him controversial.

In 1985, Aridjis founded the Group of 100, a sort of Who's Who of Mexican artists and intellectuals joined together to defend the country's imperiled environment. His activism has earned him the ~~~~~~ many business owner~~~

But ~~

KEITH DANNEMILLER / For The Times
The Aridjis family—Chloe, left, Homero and Betty—are framed in doorway at home in Mexico City.

"And you?" the caller said. "You're going to die very soon. See you soon."

Aridjis tortures himself with questions about what the callers want. Are they upset that he denounced attacks on Mexican crime reporters last fall? Are they angry at PEN's support for Brig. Gen. Jose Francisco Gallardo, a jailed critic of the Mexican military?

The only common thread, he said, is that the threats seem to come after interviews with the foreign media or speeches in which he defends freedom of expression.

International groups are mobilizing to support Aridjis. Members of PEN, including the writers Edward Albee, Nadine Gordimer, Arthur Miller and Susan Sontag, appealed to Mexican President Ernesto Zedillo late last month to protect Aridjis. The New York-based Committee to Protect Journalists did the same.

A Zedillo spokesman, David Najera, emphasized that the government has provided Aridjis with the bodyguards. "The practice of making threats is against government policy," he said. The director of the Mexican intelligence agency investigating the case declined an interview.

THE NEW YORK TIMES **ARTS & IDEAS**

SATURDAY, AUGUST 29, 1998

A16 Y

PEN Leader in Mexico Tells of Threats

By JULIA PRESTON

MEXICO CITY, Aug. 28 — The Mexican novelist and poet Homero Aridjis, who is the president of International PEN, which defends freedom of expression, said today that he had received a series of chilling death threats.

Mr. Aridjis, 58, is a leading opponent of the Mexican Government, which he has needled and challenged since 1985 as an environmentalist and newspaper columnist.

The hostile messages left on the answering machine at his home here since last November are not explicitly political. But they showed that the callers had access to information about his personal life and move-

ments that Mr. Aridjis says could have come only from Government officials tapping his phone.

In one case Mr. Aridjis received a threat hours after a telephone interview with a reporter from The Washington Post. The caller repeated several phrases drawn directly from that conversation, both Mr. Aridjis and the reporter, Molly Moore, said.

The threats have come within days after Mr. Aridjis participated in high-profile international conferences or gave press interviews in which he criticized Mexican Government policy.

Since last December, Mr. Aridjis has traveled around Mexico City followed by two bodyguards provided

for him by the Mexican Government.

"Pretty soon you are going to die like a dog," said one caller on Nov. 27. A woman left a message just after midnight on Aug. 17 threatening Mr. Aridjis's two daughters and saying, "And as for you, you are going to die very soon."

Mr. Aridjis said, "They are trying to create a perturbing psychological effect, to interrupt my work." He and his family left Mexico for several weeks in December.

Twelve writers, including Arthur Miller, Susan Sontag, Nadine Gordimer and Edward Albee, sent a letter to President Ernesto Zedillo on Thursday asking him to insure Mr. Aridjis's safety.

In 1997 and 1998, Homero Aridjis received a series of death threats and had bodyguards for a year.

Lesly Shell, de *Green Peace* y Homero Aridjis, del Grupo de los Cien, en conferencia de prensa ■ Foto: **José Luis Fuentes**

Cada dos minutos y medio muere un delfín, denuncia Homero Aridjis

Leslie Schiele of Greenpeace and Homero Aridjis, giving a press conference denouncing the incidental killing of dolphins in the tuna purse-seine fishery in the eastern tropical Pacific, May 1988. (Photo by José Luis Fuentes. Courtesy of the Group of 100.)

From Chapultepec Castle on top of Chapultepec Hill, Homero Aridjis warns, "Don't breathe today, or tomorrow," after seven days of soaring ozone levels in Mexico City. (Photo courtesy of Homero Aridjis.)

The Group of 100's advertisement addressed to the International Whaling Commission meeting in Puerto Vallarta, Mexico urging creation of a circumpolar whale sanctuary in the Antarctic and a ban on any form of commercial whaling, including for so-called scientific research. (*The New York Times*, May 10, 1994.)

The Group of 100's advertisement opposing construction of the world's largest evaporative salt facility by Exportadora de Sal (ESSA, jointly owned by the Mexican government and the Mitsubishi Corporation) at San Ignacio Lagoon, in Baja California Sur, where the gray whale mates and calves. (*The New York Times*, May 10, 1995.)

A gray whale spy hops to spot humans at San Ignacio Lagoon. (Photo by Richard Sobol.)

Pierce Brosnan and Homero Aridjis at San Ignacio Lagoon in March 1997, during the campaign by the Group of 100, NRDC, and IFAW against the saltworks project. (Photo courtesy of the Group of 100.)

Betty Ferber, Glenn Close, and Homero Aridjis at San Ignacio Lagoon in March 1997, during the campaign by the Group of 100, NRDC, and IFAW against the saltworks project. (Photo courtesy of the Group of 100.)

Joel Reynolds (NRDC), Robert F. Kennedy Jr., Homero Aridjis, and Jean-Michel Cousteau (Ocean Futures Society) celebrating the cancellation of the saltworks project at San Ignacio Lagoon and a victory for the gray whale after five years of campaigning. San Ignacio Lagoon, March 2000. (Photo by Dick Russell.)

Dick Russell, author of *The Eye of the Whale*, with Betty Ferber and Homero Aridjis at San Ignacio Lagoon in March 2000, a few days after the saltworks project was cancelled by President Ernesto Zedillo. (Photo courtesy of the Group of 100.)

Homero Aridjis stroking an olive ridley sea turtle, who is digging a hole in the sand to lay her eggs, during an *arribada* (mass nesting) on Escobilla beach in Oaxaca. (Photo courtesy of the Group of 100.)

In October 2005, Betty Ferber and Homero Aridjis help olive ridley hatchlings at Escobilla beach in Oaxaca head towards the Pacific Ocean, while Luis Fueyo, PROFEPA's director of inspections, looks on. (Photo courtesy of the Group of 100.)

Postcard from the 2005 campaign by Wildcoast and the Group of 100 to discourage consumption of turtle eggs under the mistaken belief that they have aphrodisiac properties. Argentine model Dorismar is saying, "My man doesn't need turtle eggs. Because he knows they don't make him more potent."

Betty Ferber and Homero Aridjis about to board a military helicopter that will take them to the ancient Maya city of Yaxchilán, in Chiapas, February 15, 1992. (Photo courtesy of the Group of 100.)

Homero Aridjis and President Carlos Salinas de Gortari in Yaxchilán, Chiapas, on February 15, 1992, during an international meeting about biodiversity when the president announced the creation of a new reserve called Yaxbé ("the green road") along the Usumacinta River, meant to serve as a biological corridor between the Lacandon forest and the Petén in Guatemala. (Photo courtesy of the Group of 100.)

Homero Aridjis standing in front of the dormant Iztaccíhuatl ("White Woman" in Nahuatl) volcano. (Photo by Betty Ferber.)

Homero Aridjis in the Zone of Silence, inside the Mapimí Biosphere Reserve in the state of Durango, looking for the bolson tortoise. (Photo by Betty Ferber.)

Homero Aridjis in Bonampak, a Maya archaeological site in Chiapas, during the campaign against construction of hydroelectric dams on the Usumacinta River. (Photo courtesy of Homero Aridjis.)

The Mexican giant cardon or elephant cactus (*Pachycereus pringlei)* that was uprooted from the Valle de los Gigantes in Baja California to adorn the Mexican pavillion at the Universal Exposition of Seville (Expo '92) on the Isla de la Cartuja today stands forlornly in a parking lot near the pavillion. (Photo by Nicolás Haro.)

Homero Aridjis and Betty Ferber in front of the United States Embassy on August 6, 1995—40 years after the US dropped "Little Boy" on Hiroshima—protesting against French nuclear weapons tests at the Mururoa Atoll in the southern Pacific Ocean during Jacques Chirac's presidency. (Photo by Arturo López. Courtesy of the Group of 100.)

Homero Aridjis and Kenzaburo Oe, standing together against nuclear power during the Hemingway Centennial at the John F. Kennedy Library in Boston, April 1999. (Photo by Betty Ferber.)

J. M. G. Le Clézio, Homero Aridjis, Jeffrey Wilkerson, and Peter Matthiessen during the First Morelia Symposium: Approaching the Year 2000, Morelia, Michoacán, September 1991. (Photo courtesy of the Group of 100.)

Homero Aridjis and Kjell Espmark in the oyamel fir forest at El Rosario, in the Monarch Butterfly Biosphere Reserve, during the Second Morelia Symposium: Approaching the Year 2000, January 1994. (Photo courtesy of the Group of 100.)

The governor of Oaxaca, Diódoro Carrasco (1992–1998), Francisco Toledo, and Homero Aridjis. Toledo and Aridjis asked the governor to shut down the open air garbage dump in the state capital. (Photo courtesy of the Group of 100.)

Seamus Heaney, Betty Ferber, and Homero Aridjis during the 47th meeting of the International Whaling Commission, Dublin, June 1995. (Photo by Marie Heaney.)

The Group of 100's advertisement opposing construction of a new airport in Lake Texcoco, a major migratory bird habitat. (*The New York Times*, April 11, 2001.)

Homero Aridjis, Mikhail Gorbachev, and Betty Ferber in Hollywood, 2002, where Aridjis and Ferber received the International Environmental Leadership Award from Gorbachev and Global Green USA.

Mr. President, our country's history has taught us that there is no material benefit worth the sacrifice of our national sovereignty, and our physical national sovereignty is our natural patrimony. Defending the patrimony of present and future generations of Mexicans is defending Mexico.

UPDATE: Mexico joined CITES on July 2, 1991, four weeks after my address to the president. In 1992 the LGEEPA was amended and more than 100 new standards issued. By 1997, lead was fully eliminated from gasoline sold in Mexico.

Coatzacoalcos, the River of Death

HA, *Reforma*, October 22, 1995

As it flows through Minatitlán, Coatzacoalcos, Nanchital, and Pajaritos, the Coatzacoalcos River receives sewage from these cities and all the polluting effluents from the industrial zone in the lower basin of the river. This is a troubled area from an environmental and a social perspective. The heavily contaminated Coatzacoalcos could be considered a dead river. There's no other body of water in the country so teeming with pathogens as this river, where the cholera bacillus resurfaced in Mexico in 1982.

This industrial corridor could be the most graphic example of every existing type of pollution: of water, soil, and air. Ironically, an October 31, 1984, presidential decree proclaimed this area a "Priority Zone for Environmental Improvement." "A Priority Zone for Environmental Disaster" would have been more exact. Following issuance of the decree, programs were drawn up and agreements were signed to tackle the problems, including cleaning up the receiving watercourses that converge into the river and carrying out corrective and preventive measures in the industrial facilities that discharge their waste into those bodies of water, and the realization of studies to create the infrastructure for treating sewage which was being dumped untreated into the river.

These programs and promises were never fulfilled. Pollution forced the fishermen who made their living from the river to take menial factory jobs or emigrate in search of other opportunities. Not long ago, shrimp fishermen asked for a final indemnification to stop fishing in the river, since the shrimp is inedible; everyone knows the wastewater discharged in the Pajaritos lagoon is highly toxic. Once snook was caught in the port of Coatzacoalcos, but nowadays the coastal dwellers complain that "there's no point fishing anymore."

In February 1993, the federal government announced a series of environmental audits of the subsidiary installations of Pemex (Mexico's state oil company), and of other industries in the area, to ascertain their real impact. No information was ever released publicly about the results of those audits or about the measures each industry had to take to stop polluting the river, the air, and the aquifer. Extraofficially, these results are known:

1. Water. All the Coatzacoalcos's tributaries receive contaminants from the industrial zone, where the Pajaritos, Cosoleacaque, Cangrejera, and Morelos petrochemical complexes are located, as well as the Minatitlán refinery, Celanese, Sales del Istmo, Cloro de Tehuantepec, etc. The principal contaminants are organochlorines, sulphides, benzene, toluene, hydrocarbons, caustic soda, acetic acid, phenol, ammoniacal nitrogen, ammonium sulfate, used fats and oils, and coliform bacteria. Additionally, the Minatitlán refinery discharges high temperature wastewater into the river. The Arroyo Nuevo Teapa is so heavily polluted that it's biologically dead. All these discharges violate the norms. That is also the case for water consumption permits. Several pipes registered as rain water drains are used as industrial drains—in Pajaritos, chemical substances are released into the rain water drain—and most of the industrial discharges do not comply with the legally allowed limits. Others are not even registered.

2. Groundwater. Toxic compounds found in the subsoil include lead, chrome, copper (all found at Cosoleacaque), arsenic, cyanide, chloroform, chlorinated derivatives, hydrocarbons, benzenes (a serious problem in Morelos), and toluene, among others.

3. Air. No monitoring program or inventory exists for atmospheric emissions at the petrochemical plants (Pajaritos, Morelos, Cangrejera, etc.) and other industrial sites. The principal pollutants are carbon monoxide, sulfur compounds, nitrogen oxides, ammonia, chlorinate derivatives, acetaldehyde, and light hydrocarbons. The chimneys are not compliant with the norms for analyzing gases emitted; in

Pajaritos, 95 percent of the chimneys don't comply. Natural gas flaring belches out towering plumes of smoke in a Dantean landscape. At Morelos an incinerator is emitting 200 times the allowed limits of volatile organic compounds.

4. Industrial waste (or *pajaritos del mal*, "bad little birds"). As with other kinds of waste, there are no management procedures, hazardous wastes are mixed with harmless ones, and the volume of hazardous wastes swells. There are no adequate storage factilities. Most of the wastes are exposed to the weather, allowing filtration to the subsoil and atmospheric emissions, and increasing the risk for people in direct contact with them or near by to develop cancerous and noncancerous diseases. There are no real inventories identifying and quantifying the waste. This is the case at Pajaritos, which has no permission for temporary waste storage, and where there is no monitoring of impacts on the soil and the subsoil, nor are officials informed of the end use of the waste produced. At some plants there are transformers that contain polychlorinated biphenyls (askarels, PCBs) that exceed the established norm more than 100 times. These PCBs are carcinogenic and mutagenic. All the plants lack an integral program for management, control, and final disposal of toxic wastes.

But the worst problem is at Pajaritos, where more than 9,000 tons of hexachlorides are exposed to the weather without controls or authorization. Under previous governments, two incinerators were acquired to burn these toxic wastes. They lack the technology to avoid the generation and atmospheric emission of dioxins, persistent organic pollutants that are even more dangerous than the wastes themselves. Although no official permission has been granted for their operation, trial burns for both incinerators are scheduled for November. Recent studies in the United States have found that even low levels of exposure to dioxins can cause cancer in people and animals, as well as impairment of the immune system, congenital defects, hormonal alterations, and infertility. Dioxins accumulate in the food chain, and the most sensitive to dioxin exposure are fetuses and nursing infants, as well as workers whose occupations expose them to dioxins. Who will dare to take responsibility for so much potential devastating harm to the population of Coatzacoalcos?

5. Risks. Environmental impact assessments have not been done for most of these plants. Risk analyses carried out for several installations

were incomplete, including a risk analysis for the potential release
of toxic substances. Various zones of risk have a high possibility of
accidents, as well as for potential leaks of toxic materials. Almost no
installation has an emergency plan for prompt attention to eventuali-
ties that can lead to leaks, fires, or explosions that will affect human
populations in the vicinity. For example, a leak of ammonia at
Cosoleacaque could create a toxic cloud with serious consequences
for people who live virtually at the plant's doorstep.

For quite a while everyone has known about the negative impacts on
human health and the environment caused by the contaminants released by
the industrial plants in this area, including acetaldehyde, which attacks the
respiratory and nervous systems; chromium, related to gastrointestinal, lung,
and sinonasal cancer: benzene, toluene, and xylene, aromatic hydrocarbons
that are carcinogenic and mutagenic; crotonaldehyde, that severely irritates
the eye and damages the cornea; sulfur oxides and other compounds discharged into the air, water, and soil. When will the officials in charge of rem-
edying ecocide cease drawing up programs that are never enforced? What will
happen to the agreement signed August 17 between Pemex-Petrochemical
and PROFEPA (Federal Attorney General's Office for Environmental
Protection), if there is no budget, no political will, and no appropriate technology to enforce it? Governments come and go, but things never change.
Now that the date approaches for bidding on Cosoleacaque, the first of
10 petrochemical complexes that Pemex seeks to privatize, and from whose
sale it expects to receive some six billion dollars, the burning question is, who
is going to assume the cost of the environmental passives that require reme-
diation—put by some analysts as high as 800 million dollars—of these
plants? Will the river of death be revived before all human, plant, and animal
life around it disappears?

UPDATE: The sale of petrochemical plants in 1995 was canceled. Thirty-two
people died and one hundred thirty-six were injured in an explosion caused
by a leak at a PVC plant in the Pajaritos Petrochemical Complex on April 20,
2016.

The Case of the Tainted Milk

HA, *Reforma*, December 16, 1995

On January 21, 1988, the Group of 100 held a press conference to denounce the presence in Mexico of 17,000 tons of powdered milk contaminated with radioactive fallout from the nuclear disaster at Chernobyl. The Veracruz Mothers Against a Nuclear Laguna Verde had given us information that the milk had been imported from Ireland to Mexico and that several government officials were about to make a killing off it. The most catastrophic nuclear power plant accident in history took place on April 26, 1986, and the radioactivity traveled far beyond Belarus and Ukraine, reaching countries such as Sweden, Finland, Norway, Scotland, Austria, and Switzerland. The Soviet government's first reaction was to conceal the disaster, but the scandal shook the political foundations of the Kremlin. As nuclear engineer Gregori Medvedev remarked, this accident put an end to the myth of nuclear plant safety. Over the weeks after the accident, the water and soil of Ukraine, and grass and water in various European countries, were seriously contaminated, with the consequent contamination of the cattle that ate the grass and drank the water. Milk and meat became lethal for human beings.

Many of these food products found their natural way to countries in the Third World. Venezuela sent back meat contaminated by radioactivity, and eventually several socialist and nonsocialist nations had to keep thousands of millions of dollars of exportable products for themselves. The 17,000 tons of milk imported by the National Public Subsistence Company (CONASUPO)—the number rose to 43,000 tons, although the exact amount was never known—were stored in warehouses in the port of Veracruz in June 1987. Despite the fact that the World Health Organization had notified the Mexican government that the milk was contaminated with caesium-137 and strontium-90 and its sale was forbidden, on December 26, 1987, the Secretariat of Health gave official permission for the powdered milk to be distributed throughout Mexico, stating, "It's free of radioactive contamination and safe for human consumption."

On January 11, 1988, we learned that 1,000 tons of powdered milk loaded in trucks were leaving the customs warehouses in Veracruz to be sold by LICONSA (a parastatal distributor of subsidized milk). The Group of 100 asked the Secretariat of Health to reverse its decision and order CONASUPO to immediately return the tainted milk to where it came from. The first official response to the group's denunciation was to deny that there was contaminated milk in Mexico, but on January 25, Dr. Jaime Martuscelli, undersecretary for Sanitary Regulation and Development, admitted that in June 1987, CONASUPO had bought 7,000 tons of powdered milk contaminated with caesium-137, "well above the recognized toxic limits," and he promised it would be sent back, explaining that nothing had been said about it earlier because the Secretariat of Health's policy is "to not alarm the citizenry." According to Guillermo Zamora (*Proceso*, February 8, 1988), on June 3, 1987, the ship *Adventure* docked in Veracruz carrying 5,569 tons of powdered milk and 702 drums of butter with a net weight of 136,890 kilos (301,790 pounds); on June 4 the *Tenacious* brought 5,569 tons of nonfat milk, and on November 1, the *Rumija* unloaded 5,820 tons of powdered nonfat milk and 290 drums of butter with a net weight of 56,550 kilos (124,671 pounds). The Veracruz Direction of Port Services grudgingly admitted that in 1987, CONASUPO had received 80,000 tons of powdered milk from Ireland—the second largest exporter of milk to Mexico—which had been sold to our country by the Irish Dairy Board. In March 1988, the *Pheasant* sailed from Veracruz for Ireland carrying 4,000 tons of contaminated milk powder. We have always suspected that some of the milk was pilfered by employees at the warehouse in Veracruz. It was never known what happened to the rest, and the government officials involved in the purchase and import permits—Dr. Guillermo Soberón, secretary of Health; Raúl Salinas de Gortari, head of LICONSA; and José Ernesto Costemalle, director of CONASUPO—refused to talk about the business deal that was cut short. No one ever knew who was responsible for the case of the tainted milk that was going to poison millions of unsuspecting Mexican consumers. The tainted milk scandal still stinks, an example of the rancid moral and material corruption of a handful of public officials.

UPDATE: The whistleblowers who first became aware of the milk were Vice Admiral Manuel Rodríguez Gordillo and physicist Miguel Ángel Valdovinos, both of whom subsequently suffered harassment. According to a prominent oncologist at the National Pediatric Institute, cases of childhood cancer increased 300 percent in Mexico between 1987 and 1997. There is no access to information that would allow an investigation into a possible link to the tainted milk.

The Science Teacher and the Ecologists

HA, *Reforma*, June 16, 1996

During her press conference on June 10, Julia Carabias, MSci. and head of the Secretariat of the Environment, Natural Resources, and Fisheries (SEMARNAP), lashed out at civil society, nongovernmental organizations and, in particular, me, because, in response to a submission made on January 18, 1996, to NAFTA's Commission for Environmental Cooperation (CEC) by the Group of 100, the Mexican Center for Environmental Law, and the Committee for the Protection of Natural Rights objecting to the building of a pier and a port terminal in Cozumel, on June 7 the CEC had recommended that the trinational environmental ministers' Council draw up a factual record to "consider whether the Party concerned [i.e., Mexico] has failed to enforce effectively its environmental law since . . . January 1, 1994."

Through the secretary of SEMARNAP, the current administration is attempting to cancel the right of citizens and NGOs to participate in defense of the environment, a right hard-won by Mexican civil society after years of government harassment, cooptation, and censorship. Respect for the right to participate is respect for democracy.

I can understand that Carabias is annoyed because the CEC denied her request to close the file on the Paraiso coral reef in Cozumel, since it was she who renewed the building permits as head of the National Institute of Ecology (INE) during Carlos Salinas de Gortari's presidency. The director of the CEC, veteran Mexican diplomat Victor Lichtinger, is behaving with admirable impartiality on cases submitted by civil society in Mexico, the United States, and Canada. As for defending the environment, perhaps Madam Secretary believes that biosphere reserves and other prime ecosystems in Mexico are only a matter for bureaucrats and academics, and the rest of us have no reason to concern ourselves about or fight for conservation of the natural patrimony of past, present, and future generations of Mexicans.

Does Julia Carabias think that because she's the Secretary we environmentalists should close our eyes to the frontal attacks on nature in our country and keep silent about permissions granted by INE to the Canadian swindler Barry Sendel, who planned to build a Jurassic Park inhabited by animatronic dinosaurs in the Cacahuamilpa Caves in Guerrero? Or accept trampling on human rights of Tepotzlan residents who are opposing a golf club that developers seek to build in a biological corridor? Or applaud Exportadora de Sal's planned industrial saltworks at Laguna San Ignacio, where gray whales mate and give birth, and which is part of the largest biosphere reserve in Latin America? Or that we should do nothing to prevent destruction of the Paraiso coral reef, part of the Mesoamerican Barrier Reef System, the second largest in the world? All these projects violate Mexico's environmental laws, and, ironically, NGOs have been forced to defend these laws against the officials who are charged with their enforcement. It's sad that some of these officials were once environmentalists themselves, but have now forgotten that once they stood alongside citizens and NGOs, standing up for what they are now trying to degrade: our country's environment. Prof. Carabias, always a proponent of "sustainable development," should be brought to account for the assaults on nature that are justified in the name of those travesties called "developments," built with the blessing of SEMARNAP.

Our January 18 submission, made pursuant to Article 14 of the North American Agreement on Environmental Cooperation (NAAEC), alleged a "failure on the part of Mexican authorities to enforce their environmental law effectively with regard to the totality of the works of the port terminal project in Playa Paraíso, Cozumel, Quintana Roo." The judicial standing of Mexican environmental groups is systematically denied in our country, making it necessary to have recourse to legal entities outside the country, such as the CEC. Prof. Carabias has no right to say that "Mexico has its own laws and oversight mechanisms. If there is any failure in the application of the law, it is society as a whole and the government of our country who will point that out. I cannot accept that supranational organizations tell us how to govern."

If Carabias refuses to accept them and refuses to comply, then why did the Mexican government sign the NAFTA parallel agreements on labor and the environment?

The three groups charge that the developer of the "Port Terminal Project," Consortium H, has been working on the project without having submitted an Environmental Impact Statement covering all included works; construction of the pier is already 40–45 percent complete, and the first cruise ships are expected to dock in April 1997. The beach and seafront area included in the project is within the refuge for the protection of marine flora and fauna of the western coast of Cozumel established by presidential decree on July 11, 1980. We claimed that the land on which the project will be constructed and will operate does not lie within a zone designated for "port use" on the Island of Cozumel. Rather, this zone is classified for high-density tourist use.

The environmental impact assessment submitted by Consortium H is incomplete, and only refers to impacts resulting from construction of the pier, omitting any reference to the port terminal or to impacts from associated projects such as a passenger terminal building, a means of access from the terminal to the cruise ship pier, a parking lot, and a public access road leading to the Chan-Kanaab highway. It does not address operating risks arising from this pier's proximity to the international pier, which could lead to collisions between ships and environmental damage.

I am detailing these points from the groups' suit because Prof. Carabias has mounted an attack against me for the joint denunciation made by the groups and accused me of lying, claiming I am motivated by financial interest, and not environmental concern. This makes three direct personal attacks against me by SEMARNAP during the past two weeks, leading me to believe that I am the victim of a smear campaign by the government, like those against other members of civil society, such as Jorge G. Castañeda and Adolfo Aguilar Zínser.

I ask Prof. Carabias to present evidence that I have financial—and not environmental—interests in the matter of the Paraiso coral reef. No one pays me to defend the rights of Mexicans to protected forests, rivers, and wild species, or to healthy air and water; no government or corporation pays me to defend whales or butterflies; my conscience as a human being pays me. Nor do I wave the banner of ecology to distract the public's attention. I don't have to. The distractions are concocted by governments to keep the public from thinking about the real problems. Mexico's environmental groups cannot drop their activism to please bureacrats and politicians. Their committment is and has always been to Mexico's natural patrimony. Any attempt to cancel that right is a green light to environmental pollution.

UPDATE: On April 4, 1997, the *Majestic of the Sea* cruise ship collided with the pier construction site. Despite finding that Mexico was in violation of its own law, the CEC has no power to enforce its ruling. Puerta Maya, one of three international cruise piers on Cozumel, is now operated by the Carnival Corporation.

The Children of Guanajuato

HA, *Reforma*, October 13, 1996

T he mass mortality of up to 40,000 migratory waterbirds that took place in the winter of 1994–95 at the Presa de Silva (Silva Reservoir) in San Francisco del Rincón, in the state of Guanajuato, exemplifies the terrible problem of the final destination of eight million tons of toxic waste produced in Mexico every year and its fateful effects on innocent beings. The waters of the Turbio River—which feeds into the reservoir—were not only turbid, they were lethal, because they were and are contaminated by the untreated discharges of the tanning industries and the plastic and rubber factories, by chlorinated and organophosphorous pesticides, by heavy metals such as chromium, mercury, and lead, by raw sewage from León and other nearby cities, and by slaughterhouse waste.

Dissatisfied with the explanations given by Mexican officials, on June 6, 1995, the Group of 100, the Mexican Center for Environmental Law (CEMDA), and the National Audobon Society submitted a petition requesting the Commission for Environmental Cooperation (CEC) to prepare a report under Article 13 of the North American Agreement on Environmental Cooperation (NAAEC) on the causes of this mass mortality of birds that have migrated from Canada and the United States. Mexican bureaucrats put the blame successively on chromium, endosulfan, a reddish dye found in the reservoir's sediment, and a disease the birds might have caught on their way to Mexico. The International Silva Reservoir Scientific Panel appointed by CEC concluded in September 1995 that the overriding cause of the die-off of the birds—shovelers, pintails, green-winged teal, ruddy ducks, American coot, and eared grebes—was an outbreak of botulism. Extreme pollution of the reservoir by untreated municipal sewage resulted in extreme eutrophication, which, compounded with the shallowness of the basin—on average one meter (39 inches) deep—was conducive to botulism outbreaks. The scientific panel made recommendations for proper treatment of sewage and industrial waste, monitoring of the Presa de Silva for future waterbird mortality, and preparation of a response plan should mortality occur—which would include draining the reservoir—and increasing cooperation between Canada, the United States, and Mexico.

But with the birds dead and the reservoir drained, no one mentioned the grave risks for people living near the Presa de Silva. An unpublished study carried out by Dutch researcher Marcus G. M. Terberg in Santa Rosa, San Germán, San Roque de Montes, and Silva—four communities on the León River—concluded that inhabitants' health is in danger. After analyzing sediments around the reservoir and surface water, Terberg found arsenic, hexavalent and trivalent chromium, mercury, and cadmium in concentrations far above accepted standards. The principal routes of exposure are the same in all four communities: breathing contaminated dust, skin contact with contaminated soil, water and dust, and eating milk and meat from livestock exposed to the contaminants. Cows graze on alfalfa watered with contaminated water from the river, and in Silva, due to dryness, winds, and their feeding on plants on the banks of the reservoir, cattle are exposed to an even higher concentration of contaminants than in the other three communities. The worst contamination was found in plots watered from the sewage-laden León River and within fifty meters of each bank of the river.

Children under eight are most vulnerable to contaminants. The grounds of a school in Santa Rosa were polluted by water from a canal that fed the reservoir, increasing risks to children playing outdoors. Developing fetuses of pregnant women exposed to contaminants are more likely to suffer genetic mutations. Adults working plots irrigated with contaminated water are exposed. Inhalation of chromium-laden dust can cause respiratory problems and affect the salivary glands, and drinking milk and eating meat contaminated by chromium can lead to urinary tract ailments. The Dutch researcher's statement that ingesting arsenic and lead can lead to learning disabilities and concentration problems seems like a cruel joke on local residents who are already undermined by malnutrition.

Terberg predicts a probable high incidence of illness in all the communities on the León and Turbio Rivers, including gastrointestinal ailments, thanks to the absence of sewage treatment, as well as other ills brought on by exposure to smoke, since garbage is burned outdoors in these towns. Another hazard is the plume of aerial pollution from the Química Central chromate factory. Most frustrating of all, Terberg gave the results of his research to the Guanajuato state government, but nothing is being done to protect the health of the area's inhabitants. An employee of the state Secretariat of Health who was helping Terberg was fired.

Even when the sewage treatment plant starts operating in León and the river looks cleaner, it will still be receiving chemical contamination from industries that discharge their toxic waste into it. Moreover, the tanning industry in León is expected to grow, which will increase the contaminants and the risks.

It is urgent that the municipal governments of León and San Francisco del Rincón provide information and advice to the population about existing threats to their health, and that research be carried out about real levels of exposure, including evaluation of the risks entailed by ingesting locally produced milk and meat. Root vegetables that can potentially absorb the most contaminants can no longer be grown in many plots of land, meaning lowered incomes. There is rainwater now in the Presa de Silva, but the ground is highly contaminated. Migratory birds arrived last winter [1995–96], but far fewer than in previous years. While we wait to see how many will come this winter, the reek from the León River is a permanent annoyance for the local population, and the unbearable stench wakes everyone up in the morning. Worst of all, the contamination that killed thousands of migratory birds two years ago at the Presa de Silva is still there: four communities on the León River are in danger of being poisoned. And especially the children of Guanajuato.

UPDATE: Our petition was the first to be submitted to CEC after NAFTA came into effect on January 1, 1994. In 1997 Presa de Silva was declared a State Natural Protected Area and an ecological restoration zone, and is now a Ramsar Site (Wetlands of International Importance). As of July 2017, León continues to be the center of the tanning industry in Mexico, and businesses are still being fined for discharging toxic wastes.

A Historic Legal Victory

HA, *Noticias de la Tierra* (Mexico: Random House, Mondadori, 2012)

On November 12, 1996, in response to a legal challenge by the Group of 100 to an attempt by the government to weaken rules for the submission of environmental impact assessments by industries, a federal court made a ruling in favor of the group which was the first instance in Mexico of federal courts acknowledging the judicial standing of a nongovernmental group, and of any individual concerned about the environment, to legitimately question an official act that affects the environment.

On October 23, 1995, a few weeks before Pemex (Mexico's state oil company) was supposed to start receiving bids to privatize 10 petrochemical complexes in the Papaloapan river basin in Veracruz, the Secretariat of the Environment, Natural Resources, and Fisheries published its intention to simplify requirements for environmental impact assessments. On October 30, one week later, the Group of 100 filed its suit. In the spring of 1996, the government excluded foreign buyers from majority ownership. The attempt to make it easier for potential investors in the petrochemical industry to ignore pollution issues, environmental liabilities, deficient maintenance procedures, and lax safety measures failed.

Our Flood

HA, *Reforma*, October 17, 1999

Many people cannot explain President Ernesto Zedillo's refusal to accept foreign aid from the United Nations, the United States, Finland, Spain, and elsewhere (except for cash channeled through the Red Cross) for Mexicans who have been devastated by torrential rains this month. His response was, "We can handle this ourselves." Even less explicable is the glaring incompetence of the Mexican Federal Civil Protection Service and civil protection agencies in the worst-hit states. Not only did they fail to protect residents before and during the disaster, in the aftermath of the floods they were bumbling and uncoordinated, excepting military brigades, who are working nonstop in the area and running the refuges.

Amazement grows when we compare this to how the Cuban government protected its population before hurricane Irene struck the island. Advised by experts in meteorology and civil defense, Fidel Castro ordered the evacuation of 130,000 people, closing of schools, and removal of 45,000 head of cattle from the areas that could be lashed by the hurricane. I would ask President Zedillo this: Once national and foreign meteorological services had predicted the severity of the storms heading for Mexico, why didn't he order evacuation of the population at risk?

Officials in charge of civil protection are another kind of disaster. Many residents of flooded towns are still complaining about the lack of food, drinking water, and blankets; hundreds of communities are without electricity or telephone service; prices are sky high and there's looting; 50,000 children can't go to school; aid trucked in is too little and is not getting to the victims; harvests, animals, incomes, and livelihoods are gone. Huddled in corners of their ruined or flooded homes, men and women are asking, "What are we going to live on?" As for supplies that were not distributed, the reasoning of officials such as this one from Tulancingo is questionable: "If we give stuff to one community, all the others will be bothering us and then there'll be a riot." Better keep it for yourselves, or hoard it for political candidates to hand out in upcoming elections. A president touring disaster areas with official reporters in tow to film him making promises to help is pointless; a national plan to help the victims is needed, not only for the short term but to cover the rebuilding of ruined towns and financial rescue of the victims.

Images of our flood are everywhere: "We saw people clinging to palm trees being dragged away by the river," Tecolutla's mayor reported. "The Coatzacoalcos River bore three corpses—one of them a child—all the way to the coast," and remains of cattle, horses, dogs, furniture, and lizards have washed up on the beaches. There have also been instances of solidarity, such as a resident of Zacatlán, who "put together a makeshift kitchen to feed the crowds walking for hours to food distribution centers." What no one can understand is why, once the scope of the disaster was evident, the government did not ask for help from the United States, its partner in NAFTA with wide-ranging experience of hurricanes in Texas, Louisiana, Florida, South Carolina, and North Carolina. When the roads were blocked, a fleet of helicopters from across the border could have saved many lives and eased the plight of families and communities that were stranded. Hundreds of people who took refuge on rooftops or clung to trees could have been rescued. Dr. Jeffrey Wilkerson, an anthropologist and Group of 100 member, spent two days in Gutiérrez Zamora hanging onto a tree, and lost everything when the brilliant bureaucrats at the National Water Commission and Central Light and Power opened the sluice gates of the Necaxa reservoir without warning.

By blaming the victims for their own misfortunes because "they didn't pay attention to evacuation warnings," officials in Puebla and Veracruz are adding infamy to ineptitude. President Zedillo claimed that "excellent handling" of the reservoirs prevented worse flooding in Villahermosa. While the gale-force rains may well owe their strength to global climate change, the severity of the disaster was magnified by widespread environmental deterioration in the region. Logging has been relentless in the affected states, and construction of hydroelectric dams has changed the course of rivers. Deforestation on slopes and hills, and the disappearance of vegetation and roots has upset normal hillside water flow and percolation of rainwater into the soil; soil in mountainous zones has been destabilized and silt is swept along in torrents. Deforestation created the conditions for mud and landslides that have buried people alive, including 20 schoolchildren and an entire village.

We're waiting for the Secretariat of the Environment, Natural Resources, and Fisheries (SEMARNAP) to do a survey of flora and fauna lost in the disaster area. We're also waiting for cultural officials to report on damage to archeological sites in the region, including El Tajín, one of pre-Colombian Mexico's prime ceremonial centers. A shortage of sewers in Poza Rica, Villahermosa, and other cities turned the streets into fetid rivers. In addition to flooded houses and streets, Villahermosa residents had to deal with crocodiles, poisonous snakes, and tarantulas swimming by.

The government's mindset hasn't changed since the September 1985 earthquakes, when official inertia sent Mexico City residents out into the streets to save families, friends, and strangers in admirable acts of solidarity. Once again bureaucrats are minimizing the facts; the Secretariat of the Interior (SG) puts the numbers at 360 dead and 315,094 victims. Once again we are never going to know the real numbers. The federal government should forget for a moment about the Banking Fund for the Protection of Savings (FOBAPROA) frauds and the bailing out of private toll highways and concentrate on relieving the urgent material needs of half a million Mexicans who have lost everything. Thousands of victims from the states of Veracruz, Puebla, Hidalgo, and Tabasco, now turned into economic refugees, are flooding state capitals, the Federal District, and border cities on their way to the United States, because they have no other choice but to emigrate. Gustavo Elizondo, mayor of Ciudad Juárez, complained that the 400 people who arrive daily from affected states "are causing problems because there is no housing or public services," and he asked the governor of Veracruz, Miguel Alemán Velasco, to "convince Veracruzans to stay home." I think that if a nationwide poll were to be carried out today, many Mexicans would agree that human urgency takes precedence over saving bankers of dubious moral solvency. Many of these bankers in a fix are still wealthy enough, so why does the government treat them like financial victims? Everyone knows where the real victims are: in Puebla, Veracruz, Hidalgo, and Tabasco. And that is a brief chronicle of our flood.

The Seeds of Wrath

HA, *Reforma*, November 25, 2001

Trade ministers at the World Trade Organization meeting in Qatar have discussed food safety and sovereignty. The European Union tried to get the right to prohibit genetically modified foods and meat treated with hormones. Free trade treaties often attempt to limit what a country can do to protect its environment and citizenry, alleging that national environmental laws are a nontariff trade barrier. Developing countries, such as India, oppose inclusion of the impact of trade on the environment out of fear that some day importation of Indian crops will be prohibited because their farming is detrimental to the environment. To emerge from poverty, some countries prefer to keep the right to harm their own environment, which will only lead to more poverty.

In Mexico, the Secretariat of Agriculture, Livestock, Rural Development, Fisheries and Food (SAGARPA) plans to legalize planting of genetically modified corn and other grains, giving in to pressure from agrobiotechnological companies such as Monsanto, Pulsar (Savia), Aventis, and Dupont, ignoring the opinion of producers of non-GM seeds and consumer preferences. The Intersecretarial Commission on Biosafety of Genetically Modified Organisms (CIBIOGEM) appears to be in the service of agrobioindustry. SAGARPA has floated regulations that would define the "requirements for importation, transport and release within a pilot program and eventual commercial release of genetically modified organisms for agricultural activities." Should these regulations be passed, the health of consumers and biodiversity would be jeopardized, and society's right to voice an opinion on matters that can have unknown impacts in the field and on human health would be ignored. GM tomatoes, cotton, flowers, and potatoes are already commercialized in Mexico, and authorized experimental release of alfalfa, rice, zucchini, chile, corn, canteloupe, pineapple, banana, soy, tobacco, and wheat are ongoing.

It would be ironic if corn in Mexico—where it first appeared, to be disseminated throughout the world—were to become the intellectual property of transnational corporations and for peasants to be forced to buy their seeds every year, becoming completely dependent on these companies. Is the idea to eliminate planting corn? Javier Usabiaga, the head of SAGARPA, suggested that sowers of corn in several of the most productive states should stop growing it, and live off subsidies instead, because "if he doesn't grow corn, the farmer continues to earn money from federal subsidies and purchasers can be supplied from other regions." Which regions? The United States? Mexico imports five to six tons of corn a year. Until when can a farmer receive a subsidy for not farming and still be considered a farmer and be entitled to more subsidies? Better check the paper to see if it isn't April Fools' Day.

There are 800 million undernourished or starving human beings in the world. Will it be necessary to encourage biotechnology in order to feed the growing global population, especially in the developing countries? Producers of GM seeds would have us believe that biotechnology to increase food production is the panacea for hunger. Paradoxically, there is a large surplus of food in the world, especially in the United States and the European Union. The problem lies in inequitable distribution and in the poverty that prevents the hungry from getting enough to eat. The battle around biotechnology diverts attention from how to solve the problem of world hunger, which should be through trade policies and reforms of land tenure and use.

Agrobiotechnology companies claim that GM crops are less harmful to the environment than traditional crops. Studies undertaken by the US Department of Agriculture have shown that growing Monsanto's Bt corn (resistant to the European corn borer) has not decreased use of pesticides on corn, because most corn is not treated to resist this insect.

There is a controversy over whether Bt corn is harmful to monarch butterflies. Most scientists agree that transfer through pollen of genes from GM crops to conventional crops and wild plants is unavoidable, with unforeseeable consequences. In Canada, the transfer of genes from GM herbicide-resistant crops has engendered weeds resistant to those herbicides.

Does food from GM crops pose risks for human health? Care must be taken when making gene combinations that don't exist in nature, especially when this is for food. Allergies are one of the risks associated with GMOs. If plants already contain toxic components, manipulation of a plant's genetic composition may produce new allergens whose introduction into food is risky, as well as exposing agricultural workers to asthma and other allergic reactions. That's playing vegetal Russian roulette. No one has yet to prove that GM food is harmless. And if there are some indications to the contrary, are they sufficient? Meanwhile, it's prudent not to take chances. Any food with GM ingredients should be labeled as such, so the consumer can choose and know what she's eating. Recently a spokesman for Monsanto declared to the Spanish newspaper *El País* that his company's commercial policies "are based on transparency, freedom of information, respect for cultures," but that information should only be available on the Internet, and not on the products themselves. Greenpeace revealed that Maseca (Mexico's industrial producer of corn flour) is selling flour in Mexico made from GM corn imported from the United States.

Three weeks ago the International Treaty on Plant Genetic Resources for Food and Agriculture was approved in Rome, with 116 votes in favor, while Japan and the United States abstained. The treaty, which must be ratified by 40 countries to enter into force, recognizes the right of farmers "to save, use, exchange and sell farm-saved seed and other propagating material," even when these seeds have been resgistered or patented. In 1999 an American company that had managed to patent a variety of yellow bean grown in Sinaloa was demanding a tithe on each kilo of the bean exported from Mexico to the United States.

During the forum "Transgenic corn threatens our biodiversity," the risks GMOs hold for biodiversity in Mexico, where there are some 300 varieties of corn, were discussed, and the importance of protecting our corn was emphasized, because there's no telling what the impacts of GMOs may be on all these varieties. Bending to pressure from Greenpeace, the Secretariat of the Environment and Natural Resources (SEMARNAT) admitted the presence of transgenic corn in the northern mountains of Oaxaca that was contaminated with pollen from transgenic seeds introduced into the country.

In the United States, dozens of small farmers found corn seeds contaminated with StarLink (produced by Aventis CropScience), a variety of GM corn not authorized for human consumption, due to a protein it contains that may bring on allergic reactions. The finding forced the American government to withdraw Taco Bell products from the market, at a taxpayer cost of 20 million dollars. Sale of StarLink stopped. Last April, in Germany, seeds of GM corn mixed with conventional seeds imported from Chile and Canada were discovered. The GM seeds were from an herbicide-resistant strain whose consumption is banned in Europe.

James Goldsmith, the visionary critic of multinational corporations and creator of the Chamela-Cuixmala Biosphere Reserve in Mexico, wrote in his 1993 book *The Trap*:

"In agriculture, I feel that the disadvantages [of biotechnology] greatly outweigh the advantages. Let's take the case of the most extraordinary form of biotechnology: genetic engineering, also known as recombinant DNA technology. The aim of genetic engineering is to transfer genes from one cell to another and thereby to create new forms of life. . . . The consequences of genetically altering the plant realm are far reaching. Supporters of biotechnology claim that genetically engineered seeds will produce crops which are tolerant of herbicides and more resistant to drought, frosts, disease, and pests. It is also claimed that they will reduce the need for chemical fertilizers and insecticides.

"As a result of lobbying by the biotechnology industry, it is now possible to obtain a patent on living organisms altered by genetic engineering. New life forms will become patented commercial monopolies. . . . We are playing with the fundamental elements of all life on earth."

UPDATE: A September 2013 ruling halted planting of GM corn in Mexico, even in pilot plots. On January 26, 2017, a Mexican court postponed a decision on a challenge by Monsanto and other companies to the ruling. In May 2017, the Supreme Court of Justice of the Nation refused to hear Monsanto's case for permission to plant GM corn commercially in the country. The case will now be decided in the First Collegiate Court on Civil Matters. Meanwhile, in violation of the law, GM corn is being planted in Chihuahua, Durango, Puebla, and Oaxaca.

And the Birds Will Speak

HA, *Reforma*, October 28, 2001

In a year such as this [Ce ácatl]
this new temple will be destroyed
Prodigious things will happen
the birds will speak.
NEZAHUALCÓYOTL

Next year President Vicente Fox's government will celebrate the sixth centenary of the birth of poet-king Nezahualcóyotl (1402–1472) by building an airport in historic Lake Texcoco, seat of his kingdom, and by expropriating from his descendants the lands they farm with steadfast dedication. Historian José Luis Martínez dates the birth of Acolmitzli Nezahualcóyotl to April 28, 1402 (that is, Ce Mázatl [1-Deer] in the year Ce Tochtli [1-Rabbit] according to the Aztec calendar in use at the time), in Texcoco, capital of Acolhuacan, one of the oldest realms of the Nahua world, located in the east of the Valley of Mexico and bordering the great lake.

Last Monday Secretariat of Communications and Transportation (SCT) head Pedro Cerisola announced the government's decision to build an airport in Texcoco (about 20 miles east of downtown Mexico City). While basing the choice of Texcoco over the competing site at Tizayuca, in the state of Hidalgo (about 45 miles north), on technical factors, the government ignored the social factors. The roundtable discussions mounted by the Secretariat of the Interior (SG) were a farce; they were held a full month after the SCT had asked the Secretariat of Agrarian Reform (SRA) to expropriate *ejidal* property in Texcoco for "construction of the new Mexico City airport." Flaunting the lack of democracy, Cerisola admitted that residents of the municipalities that would be affected had not been consulted, because "we didn't bother asking for people's opinions, since there was no point adding more fuel to the fire. Raising expectations would reinforce a political standoff."

Faced with a done deal, residents of San Salvador Atenco, Texcoco, Acolman, Chiconcuac, Chimalhuacán, Nezahualcóyotl, and Ecatepec protested. The mayor of Texcoco, Horacio Duarte, said, "In the 14 months Montiel has been state governor we have only spoken with him once about the airport. That was a long time ago and we told him then we were against it, and now he wants to pretend that everyone backs the project." Expropriation by eminent domain of 21 square miles of land in the State of Mexico will leave 365 *ejidatarios* and their families (and 22 private property owners) landless, after being paid six to eight pesos a square meter, rather than the 500 pesos real estate experts say the land is worth. It appears that, in violation of the constitution, the expropriation decrees were issued without giving the owners a hearing. What money the ejidatarios receive will barely be enough for the down payment on a cramped public housing apartment—perhaps built by the same speculators who are grabbing their land—in a far-flung corner of the Valley of Mexico where cement is eating away at the trees. If the ejidatarios were paid a fair price—the commercial value—and to this was added the cost of supplying the airport with water pumped in from elsewhere (because the Texcoco aquifer is overexploited) and payoffs to lease-holders of retail space at the Mexico City International Airport (AICM), as their contracts extend beyond the estimated closing date of the airport, the alleged financial advantage of the Texcoco Project would disappear, and this is one of the main "technical factors" Cerisola used to justify the decision. Our government officials resemble the sixteenth-century Spanish *encomenderos* (holders of grants of Indian labor) challenged by Fray Bartolomé de Las Casas, who famously quoted Ecclesiasticus (the Book of Sirach): "The bread of the needy, is the life of the poor: he that defraudeth them thereof, is a man of blood. He that taketh away the bread gotten by sweat, is like him that killeth his neighbour." Vicente Fox should heed those words.

Cerisola notwithstanding, the environmental objections are inescapable. The bodies of water within the Texcoco plan are home to nearly 300,000 birds, mostly migratory, who pose the threat of bird strikes for planes, as the proposed landing and take-off paths for the Texcoco airport cross their habitat. Using an argument worthy of a nonsense collection, Cerisola told members of congress that "I believe the birds have their own opinions and have made them clear. The airport was in the same place fifty years ago and the birds weren't there, it was only when Lake Nabor Carrillo was created that the birds decided they could get along fine with the planes, because that's what they and the planes decided." Cerisola neglected to mention that airports all over the world that "coexist" with birds spend millions of dollars every year getting rid of them.

"I'm surprised they claimed that both sites have the same number of risky birds," said Laura Alicia González of Cipamex (a Mexican partner of BirdLife International). "By combining the AICM with Tizayuca, they came up with the same risk as Texcoco. That's dishonest. I noticed that Gerardo Ceballos both proposed and evaluated Texcoco (acting as judge and jury). So did others in the studies favoring Texcoco. Rodrigo Medellín, Patricia Ramírez, and María del Coro Arizmendi were asked to join the university's environmental program. Apparently, all these conflicts of interest tipped the balance towards Texcoco." Several scientists who took part in the university's environmental program were advisors to the Texcoco Project, casting doubt on the results of the study.

The subsoil of the Texcoco lakebed is highly compressible clay. Jorge Moret, a researcher at the Chapingo Autonomous University, warns that "former Lake Texcoco is not suitable for any kind of construction, because it will immediately sink." It's like building on jello. Some parts sink as much as 8 inches each year. The ground is also prone to high seismic wave amplification, the zone is often foggy, and it's closer to Popocatépetl than to the AICM, increasing the chance of damage to planes from volcanic ash.

How can they jeopardize 30 years of work to recover the ancient lake network in Texcoco, part of Mexico City's Aztec-era water system and an essential area for hydraulic management in the Valley of Mexico? Cerisola told Mexico's senators that no road work or other infrastructure for the airport could begin without consent from Mexico City's government, which was consistently snubbed. Nor did he bother consulting the city government before announcing his plan to build something akin to the Santa Fe business district on AICM land once the airport is shut down. And to plant a forest! He claimed, "We have no intention of tearing down the current airport, we just stop using it and then recycle it. Everything is usable: the buildings, the runways, etc." Aaron Dychter, an SCT undersecretary, foresaw "opening a new road, surrounding it with woods . . . and laying tracks for rapid light rail transit." Fernando Martínez Cue, a National Action Party (PAN) congressman, suggested the new airport be baptised with the name of Vicente Fox.

UPDATE: After José Enrique Espinoza Juárez died two weeks after taking a beating on July 11, 2002, during a violent clash between ejidatarios from San Salvador Atenco with State of Mexico police, on August 1 the president canceled the project, blaming the ejidatarios' refusal to sell their land. One member of the Popular Front for Defence of the Land remarked, "The Secretary of Communications and Transport asked the ducks for their opinion, but not us." The rebellion of the machetes was more convincing than all the environmental and technical arguments that were raised against an airport in Texcoco. The lesson here is that peoples' rights can no longer be ignored.

In his State of the Union address on September 2, 2014, President Enrique Peña Nieto announced construction of the New International Airport of Mexico City (known by its abbreviation in Spanish: NAICM). The airport will be built on the dried up lakebed of Lake Texcoco, on federally owned land in the State of Mexico, thus avoiding conflicts over land expropriation. The environmental arguments against NAICM still exist: subsidence, flooding, disruption of the hydrological balance, bird strikes. Construction is underway, and opening is planned for 2020.

Cuatro Ciénegas

FOX'S CRIME AGAINST NATURE?

HA, *Reforma*, October 22, 2006

Anyone who lives in a desert region knows that taking care of an oasis is fundamental for survival, but in Cuatro Ciénegas, an oasis in a mountain-ringed basin in the Chihuahuan Desert in the state of Coahuila that is crisscrossed by a network of groundwater-fed bodies of water and is a wonder of the natural world, there are local, state, and federal officials, abetted by commercial interests and uninformed citizens, who are bent on drying up and destroying this oasis, in what looks to be the crime against nature of Fox's six-year term of office.

In Cuatro Ciénegas there are sedimentary rocks called stromatolites, formed by layers of single-celled, photosynthetic, lime-secreting cyanobacteria and green algae. According to researchers from NASA, the study of stromatolites and the organisms they house—colonies of primitive bacteria which show life forms that existed on the planet more than a hundred million years ago—can help in understanding conditions necessary for life on other planets.

The level of endemism within the 77 square miles of the valley of Cuatro Ciénegas, which was declared a Protected Area for Flora and Fauna in 1994, is the highest in North America, with more than 70 species of acquatic vertebrates that exist nowhere else on Earth. As a unique ecosystem, Cuatro Ciénegas is comparable to the Galápagos Islands. Its biological diversity is closely tied to more than 200 springs that feed the freshwater pools, lagoons, streams, and marshes of an interconnected hydrologic system. The aquifer harbors fossil water that is approximately 220 million years old. The valley is a refuge for species such as the Coahuilan box turtle, the American black bear, the golden eagle, the peregrine falcon, the maroon-fronted parrot, the burrowing owl, and the Mexican kingsnake, as well as more than 400 species of cacti, bats, and migratory birds. Think of fish in a desert to get an idea of how extraordinary a site this is.

But this biological treasure house harboring more than 1,000 species is threatened by industrial development, human population increase, chaotic tourism, introduction of exotic species, and, above all, by overexploitation of water.

The National Water Commission (CONAGUA) holds the main responsibility (or irresponsibility) for the crime against Cuatro Ciénegas, having handed out permits for drilling wells for farming. The increase in the number of wells and in the rate of extraction in the Cuatro Ciénegas Valley and the adjacent Ocampo-Calaveras and El Hundido valleys to grow alfalfa for milk cows for Grupo Lala and Soriana, the two companies most closely linked to the region of La Laguna, is a death sentence for this unique treasure. On its website, Lala boasts of "advances in food production for prime dairy cattle," omitting to mention that to irrigate the alfalfa fields it is milking vast amounts of water from the springs through canals. Since the opening of 50 new wells, added to 32 already operating in El Hundido Valley, 70 percent of the wetlands in Cuatro Ciénegas have dried up. One example is the virtual extinction of Laguna Churince, whose disappearance CONAGUA blames on solar evaporation.

For years there has been an unregulated garbage dump in Cuatro Ciénegas over the aquifer between the township and the pools. Pools have been polluted by nitrogen gas from the dump, and also by nutrients from human activity released into ecosystems known for their very low nutrient content. In 2004 the Nature Conservancy and the World Wide Fund for Nature (WWF) raised five million pesos (roughly half a million dollars) to move the dump, but no one knows where the money went and the dump is still there, supposedly being turned into a sanitary landfill. The gypsum dunes, essential habitat for six endemic species, are another target for plunderers; the woman in charge of Cuatro Ciénegas and her cronies want to open a gypsum mine in the valley.

In a travesty of ecotourism, a stampede has been allowed, including all-terrain vehicle races that destroy vegetation and the delicate layer of cyanobacteria. Shoddy tourist accommodations were hastily built, garbage is everywhere, and cacti and other species are being looted.

It's hard to believe that Cristóbal Jaime Jáquez, director-general of CONAGUA; Gabriel Villareal, mayor of Cuatro Ciénagas; Susana Moncada, director of the area (for which the National Commission for Protected Natural Areas, or CONANP, is responsible); and Grupo Lala and Soriana are bent on turning this fragile desert oasis into a wasteland.

Dr. Valeria Souza, a specialist in bacterial evolution and a staunch defender of Cuatro Ciénegas, fears that in five years the deadly decline of the pools and their stromatolites will become irreversible throughout the aquifer. She urges that the water be protected by means of a moratorium until just how much water is available is ascertained, taking into account the ecosystem and its needs, excluding concessions of wells, and enforcing bans on water use based on aquifer replenishment, which in the desert is almost nil. The next step would be to raise the level of protection by designating Cuatro Ciénegas a biosphere reserve, with clearly delineated regulations and permitted activities.

It's outrageous that the Mexican government is turning an area vital for astrobiological research by NASA into a wasteland and a garbage dump. The spoliation of one of the most emblematic places on the planet doesn't say much for CONAGUA, Soriana, and Lala. The milk's gone bad.

The survival of Cuatro Ciénegas is in the hands of Coahuila's governor, Humberto Moreira, and the government of Vicente Fox, who could leave an important legacy. Or does Fox want to be remembered as the man who stood by as the ecological crime of his presidency was committed, and let the last chance to understand the evolution of our planet be lost?

UPDATE: Churince was lost forever in the winter of 2017. A decree issued by President Lázaro Cárdenas for water to be channeled out of Cuatro Ciénegas to Ciudad Frontera, fifty miles away, is a continuous drain on the wetlands. The unsustainable practice of gravity-fed irrigation in and outside the valley has prevented the aquifer from recharging. The canals must be canceled.

The Sun, the Moon, and Walmart

HA, *New York Times*, April 30, 2012

A child in Mexico soon learns that corruption is a way of life, and that to get ahead in school, work and politics, "El que no transa, no avanza"—loosely, "You're not going anywhere if you don't cheat."

When I was in junior high school, my history teacher sold us lottery tickets, promising that the more we bought, the higher our grades would be. The winning number, he said, would coincide with the National Lottery winner. I happened to buy that number and received the highest grade, but because he kept the tickets, I never got the money.

Years later, as president of an environmental activist organization called the Group of 100, I was offered visits to Las Vegas (chips provided), cars (drivers included), cash, and even prostitutes in exchange for staying silent. But my most uncomfortable experience was in 1988, when I met with the Secretary of Fisheries to protest the killing of dolphins by tuna fishers. He asked me, "What's your problem?"

"I don't have any problems," I replied.

"How can I help you?"

"Make the tuna fleet stop killing dolphins."

He reached for his checkbook. "Let's talk money, how much do you want?"

So the news that Walmart may have paid $24 million in bribes for permits to open stores in Mexico was no surprise to me. When President Felipe Calderón declared he was "very indignant," I thought of Claude Rains in Casablanca: "I'm shocked, shocked to find that gambling is going on in here!"

Walmart already had a history of controversial behavior in Mexico. Most notably, in November 2004, despite widespread opposition, the company opened a 72,000-square-foot store within the boundaries of the 2,000-year-old city of Teotihuacán, which features the Pyramids of the Sun and the Moon ("the place where men became gods"—or consumers?). Walmart has also built a supermarket on forested land in the resort town of Playa del Carmen, in Quintana Roo—though the permit for the building later turned out to have been granted for another site, on the island of Cozumel. The question now is who allows this, and in exchange for what?

Will the federal investigation discover how many Walmarts were built on the quicksands of corruption? Marcelo Ebrard, the mayor of Mexico City, is carrying out his own investigation, but considering that his brothers have been Walmart executives, I don't have much hope that the truth will emerge. The other day I visited a Walmart, and one of the teenage packers, who are unsalaried and work for tips, confided in me that they had been forbidden to say anything to the press about their employer. They were told to consider themselves lucky to have a job at all.

In this country, corruption exists at all levels, from magnates to street vendors. It seems easier to get something done with a bribe than to fill out myriad forms and wait in lines to confront evasive civil servants. According to a recent study, companies shell out approximately 10 percent of their earnings to corrupt officials. In the last 30 years, the Mexican economy has lost more than $870 billion to corruption, crime and tax evasion.

The consequences of this corruption are clear. When devastating earth-quakes hit Mexico City in 1985, an alarming number of shoddily constructed public buildings—schools, hospitals and government offices—were destroyed. Our school system has been hijacked by the politically powerful teachers' union, and around 90 percent of the budget is eaten up by teachers' salaries, though many on the payroll work for the union or hold political office instead of teaching.

Extortion and protection rackets flourish alongside drug trafficking. President Álvaro Obregón, who was assassinated in 1928, once said that "no general can resist a 50,000-peso cannon blast," a precursor to today's "plata o plomo"—silver or lead, the drug cartel's offer to officials of a bribe or a bullet.

Clearly, putting an end to corruption—to kickbacks and nepotism, to crooked judges and policemen, to delinquent bureaucrats and drug lords—is Mexico's greatest challenge. In 2000, when the left-of-center Institutional Revolutionary Party lost the presidency and its 71-year grip on power, there were hopes for reform, but it remains to be seen whether increased democratization will lead to lessened corruption.

This January, when a 341-foot-tall quartz-clad tower known as the Estela de Luz was inaugurated to commemorate 200 years of independence from Spain, Mr. Calderón called it "an emblem of a new era for Mexico." And yet, the tower was finished 16 months late, at three times its planned cost. An investigation has begun; public servants have been charged with criminal offenses; protesters call it a monument to corruption.

The truth is, we have created a corrupt system that preys on both Mexicans and foreigners—how can we be outraged when an American company exploits it? At the same time, how can we hope for Mexicans to put an end to corruption when one of the most powerful and allegedly law abiding companies in the United States gives in to the same temptations? As a former governor of Chihuahua once said, after being accused of corruption, "If we put everyone who's corrupt in jail, who will close the door?"

UPDATE: Mexico ranks 123 (out of 176 countries) on Transparency International's Corruption Perception Index 2016, wedged between Laos and Moldova. Mexico is suffering an epidemic of corrupt governors who have massively looted public funds, and impunity prevails. Some are also accused of links to drug cartels. The NGO Mexicans Against Corruption and Impunity said that only seventeen out of forty-two governors suspected of corruption since 2000 have been investigated, and as of April 2017, only three were in jail. Since then, arrests have been made of Javier Duarte (exgovernor of Veracruz) in Guatemala, Tomás Yarrington (Tamaulipas) in Italy, and Roberto Borge (Quintana Roo) in Panama. Duarte was extradited to Mexico on July 17, and Yarrington and Borge are awaiting extradition. Andrés Granier (Tabasco) has been held in the medical wing of a prison since 2013. Jesús Reyna (Michoacán) is serving time for links to drug traffickers. Guillermo Padrés (Sonora) is behind bars in Mexico. Mario Villanueva (Quintana Roo) is serving a twenty-two-year sentence in Mexico for money laundering, after three years in prison in the US preceded by six years in jail in Mexico. In June a warrant was issued for the arrest of César Duarte (Chihuahua). Eugenio Hernández (Tamaulipas), Luis Reynoso Femat (Aguascalientes, free on bail in Mexico), Humberto Moreira (Coahuila), and Jorge Juan Torres López (Coahuila) are currently under investigation in the US for money laundering. Rodrigo Medina (Nuevo León) was granted an injunction after eighteen hours in prison and his case is ongoing. Jorge Herrera Caldera (Durango) was granted an injunction against arrest. Flavino Ríos (Veracruz) is free on bail. The case against Mario Anguiano Moreno (Colima) is stuck in the courts.

Migrants Ride a "Train of Death" to Get to America and We're Ignoring the Problem

HA, *World Post/Huffington Post*, July 8, 2014

The evening news in Mexico regularly features footage of a ramshackle freight train known as La Bestia (The Beast) making its way across the country bearing a cargo of illegal immigrants trying to reach the United States's southern border. One can see hundreds of men, women and children perched on the roof, crammed between the boxcars, clinging to the sides. The trains are loaded with cement, iron, quartz, wheat, corn, diesel, vegetable oil, fertilizer, or wood, but the human cattle along for the ride have no food, drink or guarantee of safety.

To reach the depot at Arriaga, in the state of Chiapas, across the border from Guatemala, from which La Bestia departs every two or three days, migrants walk for days, even skirting mountains to avoid immigration check-points and roadblocks. The U.S. border is two weeks from here on the back of the Beast. Along the way pregnant women, mothers with infants, teenagers and adults will sleep on the streets or, if lucky, in makeshift or more permanent church-run shelters. During the long journey, accidents often happen, and passengers tumbling off the roof have their limbs severed. An aid group in Honduras has counted more than 450 migrants who have returned mutilated. Derailments are common, with cars flying off the tracks, leading to injuries and death.

Murders, muggings, extortions, gang rapes of women and kidnappings (some 20,000 a year) are committed by the rapidly expanding Central American Mara Salvatrucha gangs or by Mexican drug traffickers such as the bloodthirsty Zetas. They often infiltrate the groups of travelling migrants on the trains or in shelters, selling them drugs, tricking girls into prostitution, luring boys into gangs or murdering perceived informers. And at each stop, the migrants are prey to local police, who demand bribes up to several hundred dollars a head in exchange for allowing them to continue on their way.

At crowded safe houses along the Beast's route, the migrants' smugglers may coach their charges in how to reply to questioning or fake a Mexican accent. Forged birth certificates and other documents are available at a price, either to migrants or to their traffickers. Everyone knows the road to the American dream runs through the Mexican nightmare and that many passengers on "the train of death" will either perish during the journey, disappear by the wayside or be wounded, robbed or mutilated.

Who reaps the profits from La Bestia? Why do officials turn a blind eye while thousands of women are trafficked inside Mexico or abroad? What laws are broken to allow the transport of undocumented aliens across the country by tri-national smugglers acting as travel agents, risking lives and creating a humanitarian crisis? How much do the railroad engineers charge? Human despair has been turned into a commodity, a flourishing business for illicit enrichment.

The Bestia line once belonged to Genesee & Wyoming Inc., which bought the 1,119-mile Ferrocarriles Chiapas-Mayab freight concession in 1999 during the presidency of Ernesto Zedillo, when the government-owned Ferrocarriles Nacionales was privatized. After the havoc wrought on the track by Hurricane Stan in 2005, GWI sought to end its 30-year concession and suspend freight service. The government threatened sanctions and transferred service to the semi-public Ferrocarril del Istmo de Tehuantepec, and after years of legal wrangling, extended the latter's concession to fifty years. The concession clearly states that it is for carrying freight, not passengers, so the company is in constant violation of the law.

These days many migrants prefer to take a bus and risk detection at a checkpoint, where a payoff may allow them to continue. Others are crammed into airless trucks for the trip north. A former National Migration Institute agent reported that the going fee at each checkpoint for a truckload of migrants is around 20,000 dollars, divvied up "fairly" among the employees. Coyotes and polleros (literally "chicken herders") charge upwards of 5,000 dollars per migrant to shepherd him or her across the U.S. border.

For years refugees have started their journey north by crossing the Suchiate River, the border between Guatemala and Ciudad Hidalgo, in Chiapas. Lately the number of unaccompanied children who pay $1.50 to cross on an inner-tube raft has grown, as has the business that services them. Three ad hoc unions control the crossing, and the rafters, who are also money changers, are on call 7/24 for U.S.-bound migrants or mere shoppers, as well as for running drugs, guns and cash. A Catholic priest working with migrants estimates that 60 percent of the underage children come from Honduras, mostly driven out by extortion or running from gang recruitment. These thousands of migrant children, some barely able to understand Spanish due to their Indian heritage, have been an easy prey.

In Tapachula, half an hour's drive from the border, up to 1000 migrants are held at a time (or "lodged," in official parlance) at the Siglo XXI Migratory Station prior to being "repatriated" (read: deported). Mexico deports 250,000 foreigners a year to Central America. Meanwhile countless girls, young women and boys who have been sold into prostitution are working in Tapachula, which the founder of the Center for Investigation and National Security has compared to Sodom and Gomorrha. Elsewhere in Mexico, corpses of migrants have been found with their organs harvested.

Smugglers have been spreading false rumors about lenient U.S. policies to drum up business for themselves, convincing parents that after their children turn themselves in to the Border Patrol, they will be allowed to remain in the country if they can furnish the name of a relative already in the U.S. More than 52,000 unaccompanied minors have been apprehended at the border since the start of the year, more than twice last year's total of 24,000.

Chronic illegal migration and trafficking of persons can only be tackled if the U.S., Mexico, Honduras, El Salvador and Guatemala work together on combatting the underlying causes: a reign of terror and violence imposed by organized crime, relentless poverty in the migrants' home countries, lack of opportunities and employment, and weak law enforcement and corruption at the official level. Family businesses close as owners can no longer pay off the criminals who threaten them, and even street vendors have to hand over some of their earnings. Teenagers face a future of gangs, prostitution, and drugs. Perhaps the time has come for a Central American Marshall Plan. And what about UNICEF, and the UN Refugee Program?

The situation is very complex. What are the options? Deporting 52,000 children, at least two thirds from Central American countries embroiled in violence tantamount to civil war, to become victims of gangs or sex slaves, with slim chances of survival? They are war refugees and deserve treatment guaranteed by international agreements to which the U.S. is a signatory. Or allowing them to join family members already in the United States, legally or not, sending a message that this is the way to go? And turn the U.S. border into Lampedusa?

The Obama administration has not looked south of the border at failing states. Human rights experts estimate that 10,000 undocumented immigrants are kidnapped every year during their passage through Mexico. Mexico is legally obliged to guarantee the safety of these migrants. Should Mexico close down the border crossing at the Suchiate River?

Hondurans, Salvadorans and Guatemalans escape from hell, journeying through the limbo of Mexico to be held in the purgatory of shelters at the U.S. border, always striving towards the paradise of rejoining family members in the promised land.

Is it morally acceptable—or even legal—to send thousands of children back to hell? Mr. Obama, while you ride in the comfort and safety of The Beast (as the Secret Service calls the armored presidential limousine), give some thought to the hopeful passengers on the Bestia.

UPDATE: A new route for would-be migrants has been opened on the Pacific coast from Ocós, Guatemala, a strategic drug-trafficking town, to Mazatán, in Chiapas. Fishermen take some 20 aboard their boats at 400 to 800 dollars a head for the six- to eight-hour journey through the waves of the Pacific. There have been drownings.

Enough! Mexico Is Ready to Explode

HA, *World Post/Huffington Post*, October 28, 2014

Mexico has been profoundly shaken by atrocities and high-level corruption in Guerrero. The earthquake's epicenter is Iguala, the state's third largest city.

Fifty thousand marchers thronged Mexico City's main avenues last Wednesday, and demonstrations took place all over the country. More than 80 delegates to the Inter-University Assembly have called for a nationwide halt to all educational activities on November 5, and are asking other social groups to join them. Protesters set fire to state headquarters in Chilpancingo, Guerrero's capital, and are sacking supermarkets and shopping centers.

On September 26, María de los Ángeles Pineda Villa, wife of Iguala's Mayor José Luis Abarca, of the left-leaning Party of the Democratic Revolution, was in the main square giving a speech about her accomplishments as head of the municipal social services agency, and it was rumored that she would announce her candidacy to succeed her husband as mayor in next June's election, since she is also a state PRD official.

Just as she was beginning, two busloads of students from the notoriously radical rural teachers' college in nearby Ayotzinapa, who had come to town to raise money to supplement their meager 50 peso daily allowance, headed for Iguala's central square. According to the Federal Attorney General's Office, the mayor ordered the local police chief to stop them. After a minor clash with police the students "borrowed" three buses from the local bus station to return to Ayotzinapa and later travel to this year's march in Mexico City commemorating the October 2, 1968 massacre in Tlatelolco, and were driving out of town when they were sprayed with machine gun fire by police and gunmen from the Guerrero Unidos (United Warriors) cartel.

Three students died, as well as a soccer player in a bus bringing a third division team to town that was also fired on, a taxi driver and his female passenger. One student who panicked and ran off when his classmates were rounded up by police and gang members was later found dead, his eyes gouged out and face flensed with a box cutter, in an act of gratuitous violence. Forty-three students were bundled into police cars and have disappeared.

Pineda's family had been working with the Beltrán Leyva, Sinaloa and Guerreros Unidos cartels for years, two of her brothers were gunned down in gang violence, another served time in jail, and a recently captured leader of Guerreros Unidos identified her as "the key operator" of criminal activity in and around Iguala. The Abarcas have not been seen since the mayor hastily requested a leave of absence, and perhaps they are already in one of the burial pits.

Official statements that the 38 bodies found so far in 10 makeshift mass graves are not the students have exacerbated rather than calmed public anger, as now the other question is, who are these trussed up, tortured, headless or charred corpses? Will there be an investigation to find the perpetrators? Or will time be allowed to pass until public indignation subsides, and these cases will join the roughly 98 percent of unsolved homicides in the country that have been swept under a rug as high as the Pico de Orizaba, Mexico's tallest mountain? On October 27, information given by four people arrested early in the day led to the discovery of another clandestine grave holding human remains in the municipal garbage dump in Cocula, whose mayor and police force were arrested two weeks ago.

A month after the Iguala atrocities, officials are bogged down in a quagmire of contradictory information and paralysis in the punishment of those responsible for the disappearance of the 43 students.

The collapse of the PRD [Party of the Democratic Revolution] in Guerrero, where Angel Aguirre, the governor who migrated from the ruling PRI [Institutional Revolutionary Party] to the PRD just in time to be elected, has been forced to take an indefinite leave of absence, comes after revelations of multi-million dollar irregularities in the construction of a new subway line in Mexico City during the administration of former PRD mayor Marcelo Ebrard, and ongoing violence in the PRD-governed state of Morelos, where the capital city of Cuernavaca and other towns live under the volcano in a climate of kidnappings and executions at the hands of the Beltrán Leyva and Guerrero Unido cartels.

The National Action Party has yet to recover from the stigma it acquired under PAN [National Action Party] president Felipe Calderón.

Ten days after taking office on December 1, 2006, Calderón launched a war on drugs which took more than 120,000 lives and left 30,000 persons missing in his six-year-long violence-filled presidency. Government officials claimed that most of the deaths were due to internecine fighting among cartels, or were members of security forces killed in action. However, all too many were innocent victims, in the wrong place at the wrong time, such as the 16 teenagers gunned down at a party in Ciudad Juárez by a squad of masked gunmen.

This latest episode in the ongoing Mexican horror story brings to mind gruesome brutality during the Calderón presidency, such as "El Pozolero"—"The Hominy Stewmaker"—who was charged in 2009 with dissolving the bodies of 300 members of a rival cartel in boiling lye on orders from his boss, or the massacres of undocumented Central and South American migrants making their way to the United States, abducted from buses and raped, tortured and murdered in San Fernando, Tamaulipas, by the Los Zetas cartel in reprisal for refusing to work for the cartel or pay a ransom for their release. In 2010, 72 bodies were discovered at a ranch, and a year later 193 were exhumed from mass graves.

A 14-year-old hit man arrested in Cuernavaca—the youngest yet—claimed he had tortured and beheaded more than 300 people. Throughout the Calderón years bodies were regularly found hanging from bridges, corpses—often headless—or severed heads turned up on city streets, in abandoned vehicles, in shopping centers, on public highways. Threatening messages were usually left with the remains.

In 2011, gunmen set fire to a casino in Monterrey, killing more than 50 people, many of them bingo players, presumably because the owners had refused to make extortion payments. Teachers in several states stopped working in response to threats from gunmen demanding money. In June 2011, U.S. Customs and Border Protection announced that it had arrested more than 100 of its agents since 2004 for collaborating with Mexican cartels. The PAN has yet to recover from its besmirching.

Two days after the Ayotzinapa tragedy the leader of the PAN in Guerrero was assassinated in an Acapulco restaurant by two disgruntled party members, ostensibly because they weren't given the jobs they wanted.

Not only the PRD and the PAN are in the eye of the storm. Michoacán, which borders on Guerrero and is governed by the PRI, came close to being run de facto by the Caballeros Templarios (Knights Templar) cartel, and citizen vigilante groups frustrated by police corruption and inaction took justice into their own hands.

The president appointed a commissioner to take charge and after the governor's son was outed in videos sharing a beer and chatting with La Tuta, the still-at-large leader of the cartel, the governor was replaced by the head of the state university. The vigilantes were disarmed and channeled into an ad hoc rural police force, although now dissatisfaction is prompting them to join together anew. Peña Nieto's native State of Mexico, bordering Michoacán, Guerrero and five other states, also suffers from serious problems of criminal violence in towns adjacent to Mexico City, such as Ecatepec. The Military Justice Attorney General has just convicted seven soldiers and a general for involvement in the summary execution of 22 alleged drug traffickers.

With midterm elections coming up on June 15, all three dominant political parties have fallen into disrepute, leaving Mexicans orphaned and without alternatives to purge the country of rampant corruption. The seven smaller parties are largely irrelevant.

Well before Enrique Peña Nieto took office as President on December 1, 2012, it was common knowledge that the main goals of the new PRI government would be to change Mexico's image abroad and to promote foreign investment at home. To avoid legislative deadlock, his operators cobbled together a "Pact for Mexico" by horse-trading with leaders of the main opposition parties, and an ambitious reform package was pushed through Congress.

Sweeping educational reforms—preceded by the arrest and incarceration of the powerful leader of the principal Mexican teachers' union, who had publicly challenged the president—were followed by new rules meant to encourage competition in telecommunications, presently controlled by three huge companies. However, the largest and most controversial reform has opened up the energy sector to private and foreign investment, taboo since 1938, when President Lázaro Cárdenas expropriated and nationalized all oil reserves and foreign oil companies in Mexico.

For many, one of the most worrisome aspects of energy reform is the possibility that privately owned land can be expropriated for oil and gas exploration. The reform may be challenged in a referendum called for by millions of citizens, after the courts rule on its legality.

The self-congratulatory euphoria following passage of the reforms brought to mind former President José Lopez Portillo's boast of "Fellow Mexicans, we're rich," after vast oil reserves were discovered in the Gulf of Mexico in 1978, ushering in several corruption-ridden boom years.

During the past two years a string of drug kingpins has been arrested or killed, but successors waiting in the wings quickly take their place, or control of turf shifts to other groups. The cartels have branched out, supplementing income from the lucrative drug market in the United States, where most of the weapons used by Mexican criminals originate, with extortion and protection rackets and kidnappings.

Peña Nieto put an end to Calderón's practice of parading captured criminals before television cameras, and has toned down media reports of violence. Entire municipal police forces have been disbanded. Nevertheless, every day brings news of clashes, kidnappings, and murders, and clandestine mass graves have been found in Jalisco, Tamaulipas and Veracruz.

Five years ago Ciudad Juárez, on the northern border with the United States, was widely considered Mexico's most dangerous city, but now the center of gravity seems to have shifted to Guerrero, historically one of the most violent states and an incubator of guerrilla insurgencies. After the recent discoveries in Iguala people suspect that the country may be peppered with burial pits. The Secretariat of Foreign Affairs has deluged embassies and consulates with talking points for damage control. A parody of Peña Nieto's "Saving Mexico" *Time* magazine cover portraying him as the grim reaper has been making the rounds on Internet.

It would appear that the much-trumpeted Mexican Moment does not belong to the multinational corporations greedy for a share of Mexico's oil, gas and wind energy bounty and major airport, highway and high-speed rail projects. In the current explosive situation, if the citizenry is left bereft of democratic choices to tackle political corruption, we run the risk of another 1968, when student movements put the government against the ropes shortly before the Summer Olympics were to begin in Mexico City, culminating in the massacre at Tlatelolco, when an unknown number of peaceful demonstrators were shot down by government shock troops and more than 1300 arrested.

Today all Mexico resounds with the cry, "They took them alive, we want them back alive." If the 43 are ever found, and they are dead (for why and where would their abductors be hiding them?), all hell may break loose. Are the president and his cabinet ready for a major upheaval? Police, politicians and judges have been bought off or put into office by the cartels. Mexicans are fed up with living in a pervasive state of corruption and impunity. They are losing hope. If (as Goya said) the sleep of reason produces monsters, reason has been in a coma in Mexico. What we desperately need now from Enrique Peña Nieto is a new deal that can be summed up in two words: honesty and justice.

This can be the real Mexican Moment.

Mexico's 1985 Earthquake Awoke a Social Earthquake That Is Still Roiling

HA, *World Post/Huffington Post*, September 21, 2015

Many things changed after the devastating September 19, 1985 earthquake, measuring 8.1 on the Richter scale, struck Mexico City. Mexico's president was Miguel de la Madrid, champion of a failed "moral renewal" campaign, and the city's mayor was Ramón Aguirre Velázquez, a man close to the president and a candidate to succeed him.

That September morning, the monolith that was the Institutional Revolutionary Party (PRI) began to crumble, along with tens of thousands of buildings, while the phantom of systemic corruption rose up among the ghosts of many thousand dead. "The tragedy that devastated us yesterday has been one of the worst ever in the history of Mexico. There are hundreds of dead and wounded. We don't have the exact or final numbers yet," Miguel de la Madrid said in his first message to the Mexican people, 36 hours after the earthquake struck at 7:19 a.m. Thirty years later, no one can explain why the President of the Republic kept silent for a day and a half, unless he was struck dumb morally.

In his absence, Mexico's Tenochtitlan-Federal District was taken over by its inhabitants. During the President's disappearance, people discovered that the city was vulnerable: electricity, water, gas, telephone and transportation services were all affected; people streamed into the streets to rescue relatives, friends and anyone else trapped in the ruined structures and to search for the missing. Burials of the dead began. Heroes emerged from the crowd, such as La Pulga (The Flea), who risked his life digging through the ruins to find survivors. At the Tlatelolco housing complex, among volunteers trying to find family members buried under the remains of the 13-story Nuevo Leon building's 288 apartments, Plácido Domingo dug through the rubble with his hands trying to find his aunt, uncle, nephew and grandnephew, but they had perished. On Sept. 23, the Group of 100 declared to the media that, "Now more than ever it's glaringly obvious that corruption is a disastrous builder. The number of public buildings, including government offices, public housing, schools and hospitals, that were destroyed in the earthquake is alarming. However, it's not by chance that the Historic Center in downtown Mexico City, built to last, survived both earthquakes."

That 19th of September, civil society found itself, learned to stand on its own feet and lost all fear of becoming organized and confronting government officials, who were seen as inept and corrupt. Ironically, Guillermo Carrillo Arena, Secretary of Urban Development and the Environment and the architect in charge of supervising the construction of several collapsed hospitals where hundreds had died, became head of the National Reconstruction Fund until February 17, 1986, when he was replaced as Secretary by Manuel Camacho Solís.

News flew through the streets: a building had fallen onto the Pino Suárez subway station, the Hotel Regis had crumbled and caught fire, taking guests and employees with it, hundreds of buildings were flattened, the dead were far more numerous than officials acknowledged, photos taken by various journalists had been confiscated by the government, censorship was in place. Like foul-smelling dust, rumors spread over the ruined streets, while many people were still trapped. The victims had faces and names. Survivors' stories became known. The homeless took up residence in parks. Funeral homes and cemeteries filled up. Among the grisly discoveries were bodies of prisoners who had been tortured by the judicial police and seamstresses who had been working in shocking conditions.

Thanks to the Soviet Union-style Mexican mania for concealing information, "the exact number" of the earthquake's victims will never be known. At one point the official death toll was 4,541 bodies, of which 4,032 were identified and 509 unidentified. Other figures given out ranged from 6,000 dead and 20,000 missing to as many as 48,000 to 60,000 dead, 30 to 40,000 wounded and 150,000 left homeless. The current official figure is 10,000 dead and the unofficial total given by the Unified Coordination of Earthquake Victims (CUD) is 60,000.

Since 1985, presidential power has splintered and some has trickled down to a host of political parties, including the three main parties—PRI, PAN, PRD—and the opportunistic PVEM (Ecologist Green Party of Mexico), plus a volatile offering of smaller parties. This past July's midterm elections featured the PANAL (New Alliance), MORENA (National Regeneration Movement), headed by former Mexico City mayor and two times presidential candidate Andrés Manuel López Obrador, Movimiento Ciudadano (Citizen Movement), Encuentro Social (Social Encounter), Partido del Trabajo (Labor Party) and Partido Humanista (Humanist Party), with the resulting electoral expenditures. The last two have already lost their registry, joining a dozen that have disappeared during the past 18 years. The power of Mexico's 31 state governors, who behave like feudal overlords, has increased.

In 1985, people lost their fear of and respect for government officials, regarding them with mounting distrust. Commissions were appointed to study a possible relocation of the capital, but it never got beyond the commissions. Grassroots organizations sprang up: the Neighborhood Assemblies (Asamblea de Barrios), the Unified Coordination of Earthquake Victims (CUD) and groups defending the environment and human rights. Women and indigenous peoples began standing up for themselves. There were schisms within the PRI (Institutional Revolutionary Party) and several prominent members formed the National Democratic Front (FDN), a precursor of the PRD (Party of the Democratic Revolution). In 1988, it is widely believed that the PRI lost the presidential election, but during the count "the system crashed" (the official reason) and contender Cuauhtémoc Cárdenas' victory was stolen. Hordes of protestors and street vendors took over the Zocalo, and President de la Madrid retreated from the National Palace to govern from Los Pinos, the presidential residence.

Rebelling against the Secretariat of the Treasury and the banks, on August 25, 1993, a debtors' coalition called El Barzón organized marches, rallies and sit-ins in the capital and several states in protest against voracious financial institutions. On January 1, 1994, the day the North American Free Trade Agreement came into effect, the Zapatista Army of National Liberation rose up in protest against the Mexican government, revealing two Mexicos, one that looked towards the United States and Canada, the other, composed of indigenous peoples who are marginalized and face discrimination. Mexico City became the city of demonstrations; hundreds take place every year, mostly against the government.

From the absolute power of PRI presidents, in 2000, we moved on to the virtual power of PAN president Vicente Fox, the lord of the sound bite. Never before did a sitting President of the Republic need have recourse to self-promotionals to sell his achievements to an incredulous population, all at the expense of public funds, of course. Fox was followed by fellow PAN member Felipe Calderón, who ramped up the disastrous war on drug cartels that has already claimed as many as 150,000 lives. The PRI returned to power in 2012 with Enrique Peña Nieto, and images of politicians hungry for the top spot in 2018 are already proliferating in the printed and electronic media.

Three decades later, Avenida Juárez is on the way to regaining its former splendor. Other streets in the city have never recovered, such as Chihuahua, home to surrealist painter Leonora Carrington until her death in 2011.

Across the street from her house, the remains of a ten-story building, ostensibly a solid mass, have been colonized by squatters. "It's a monument to incompetence," her husband would say. In 1995, on the tenth anniversary of the catastrophe, a congressman declared that 15,000 buildings over six stories high were "death traps." The vacant lots left by the disaster, which politicians had promised to turn into public parks, were built over by developers or invaded by social groups. That same year, the Legislative Assembly of the Federal District revealed that 1,200 homeless families were still living in 24 government-run camps and that 300,000 dwellings would be at risk during a future earthquake.

The city has never stopped moving, on the tectonic and social levels. The Michoacán fault, site of the Sept. 19 earthquake, is 125 miles long and 50 wide, and any day now could be the site of another large quake. Thanks to the densification of housing and lax enforcement of building regulations, if another big one happens there may well be more victims than 30 years ago. Although building codes have become stricter since 1985, only when the next big quake strikes will we know which of the thousands of buildings that have gone up in Mexico City during the last 30 years have been built following the rules, as they will remain standing and unscathed.

Meanwhile, during the past year, the entire country has been rocked by a major quake: the as yet unexplained forced disappearance in the state of Guerrero last Sept. 26–27 of 43 students from a teachers' college in Ayotzinapa. Former attorney general Jesús Murillo Karam's televised January 27th revelation of what he called "the historical truth," that members of the Guerreros Unidos cartel had mistaken the young men for members of a rival drug gang and had incinerated their bodies on an open air garbage dump outside the town of Cocula, pulverized the remains, stuffed them into plastic bags and thrown them into a river, has been given the lie in a report issued on September 6 by the Interdisciplinary Group of Independent Experts that has been investigating the students' disappearance and the confirmed murder of six people. Relying on expert findings, the group has stated that incineration of 43 bodies on the dump is physically impossible, and there is no evidence whatsoever on the unguarded crime scene to indicate that this took place. Satellite images of fires presented by the attorney general date from previous years or a later month last year. The "historical truth" has gone up in smoke.

Throughout the year and in every state, citizens, led by the students' families, have been publicly and massively protesting this horrific crime and demanding a full investigation, barring no holds and with questioning of the army allowed, of the events that fateful night. Next Saturday, on the anniversary of the Ayotzinapa students' disappearance, demonstrations will be held all over Mexico and abroad.

The 1985 temblor that shook the foundations of government is seen in retrospect as the detonator of the social earthquake that is still roiling Mexico City and the entire country. To achieve the changes we have been seeing, people had to wake up from centuries of civic lethargy. Nevertheless, the population is still waiting for a truly democratic and equitable Mexico to rise from the ruins of the earthquake.

UPDATES: Since 2015 the families of the forty-three students have been leading an international campaign demanding a full investigation into the students' disappearance. In 2016 the UN Human Rights Office in Mexico found evidence that at least fifty-one suspects arrested during the Ayotzinapa investigation showed signs of having been tortured.

Earthquakes on September 7 and 19, 2017, in Mexico City and six states left 471 dead and 250,000 homeless. Rebuilding housing, schools, businesses, and public buildings will cost two billion 100 million dollars.

A Letter to Donald Trump from Mexico

DON'T TURN OUR DREAMS INTO NIGHTMARES

HA, *World Post/Huffington Post*, November 11, 2016

Dear Mr. Trump:

I write to you from Mexico, where your victory has been greeted with surprise, fear, dismay and timid optimism. There is no aspect of Mexican life that is not going to be affected by your election.

This is a political earthquake for the Mexican government that will require a massive overhaul of every aspect of the relationship between our two countries. In your victory speech you said, "While we will always put America's interests first, we will deal fairly with everyone, with everyone—all people and all other nations. We will seek common ground, not hostility; partnership, not conflict." It's time to bring our countries closer together, not tear them apart.

President Enrique Peña Nieto tweeted congratulations to the United States for its electoral process, and the foreign minister declared, "The campaign is over, a new chapter is beginning in the bilateral relationship." She also stated that a wall along the U.S. border is "not in the picture" and that Mexico would not pay for it. Meanwhile, the Mexican peso plunged more than 10 percent to a new low.

Mr. Trump, your victory will impact our 2018 presidential elections. Until November 8, the frontrunner, Margarita Zavala, was banking on riding the wave of a woman's election to the U.S. presidency, and she publicly supported Hillary Clinton. Meanwhile, Andrés Manuel López Obrador, who was defeated for the presidency in both previous elections and is second in the polls, had a reassuring message. He said there's no reason to worry about Trump's victory and migratory problems can be resolved amicably, without recourse to a wall. Last month opposition party lawmakers compared him to Trump, calling them "as alike as two drops of water."

Don't forget, Mr. Trump, that thanks to Mexico's invitation, your visit to Mexico and the televised press conference on August 31 with President Peña Nieto was the first time you were given presidential treatment outside your country. Luis Videgaray, the architect of that visit, was trounced by public opinion and obliged to resign from his post as treasury secretary. Videgaray's chances of running for governor of the State of Mexico have now suddenly revived, and there's even talk of a presidential candidacy for the sole Mexican politician who allied himself with you.

In the run-up to the election, cartoonists and commentators in Mexico went haywire, calling you a fascist and comparing you to Hitler, Mussolini and Berlusconi. They were enraged by your remarks about Mexicans. Last June, you said, "When Mexico sends its people, they're not sending their best. They're not sending you. They're sending people that have lots of problems, and they're bringing those problems with us. They're bringing drugs. They're bringing crime. They're rapists. And some, I assume, are good people."

As you get to know us better, you will find that Mexicans and Americans share many values, among them family, hard work, aspirations, a desire for justice and strongly held religious convictions. Don't judge or penalize 122 million people for the behavior of a few thousand criminals.

Mr. Trump, do not turn the dream of young immigrants to the U.S. into a nightmare. Your ascent to the presidency is a political version of the proto-typical American Horatio Alger myth. The "dreamers" are inspired by that same myth. Don't echo the Queen of Hearts by shrieking, "off with their heads."

During the debate between George H. W. Bush, Bill Clinton and Ross Perot on October 15, 1992, three weeks before the election and 14 months before the North American Free Trade Agreement took effect, Perot famously declared: "If you're paying $12, $13, $14 an hour for factory workers and you can move your factory south of the border, pay a dollar an hour for labor have no health care . . . have no environmental controls, no pollution con-trols and no retirement, and you don't care about anything but making money, there will be a giant sucking sound going south."

Bush, your fellow Republican, was negotiating NAFTA with Mexico and Canada, and in the debate he said, "We want to have more jobs here and the way to do that is to increase our exports . . . I believe in free and fair trade."

But you have called NAFTA "the worst trade deal in history." More than 80 percent of Mexico's exports are to the United States, and 7 million jobs in Mexico depend on NAFTA. In 2015, Mexico exported $316 billion worth of goods and services to the United States. Mexico is America's third largest trading partner in goods, and Mexico is America's second largest export mar-ket for goods. Millions of jobs in the U.S. depend on this trade.

If you follow through with your threat to demolish NAFTA, it will be a devastating blow to Mexico's economy. Does the U.S. want a neighbor in turmoil, in the grips of a recession where unemployment will soar and pres-sure to go north will build up more than ever? Must getting America's jobs back mean taking them away from Mexicans?

Remittances sent home have replaced oil as Mexico's main source of for-eign income, due to the reduction in the volume of oil being exported and the huge drop in oil prices. Your plan to hold remittances for ransom until Mexico forks over money to pay for the wall would sink the economy, but I doubt that it's legal.

As you know, a barrier consisting of fences and walls, punctuated by many large gaps and "virtual" fences, already spans about 650 of the 1,989 miles of the border running between Mexico and the United States, crossing cities and deserts from the Pacific Ocean to the Gulf of Mexico. Its main purpose is to stop illegal immigrants and drugs from entering the U.S. However, accord-ing to the DEA, Mexican cartels move most of their drugs across the border as freight or concealed in vehicles and it's almost impossible to carry out thorough inspections. The best "wall" is economic prosperity on both sides of the border, with no need for desperate men, women and children to risk everything to reach the land of opportunity.

The present wall also interferes with habitat connectivity and free movement of animal species such as the Mexican wolf, the desert bighorn sheep, the Sonoran pronghorn antelope, the ocelot and the American black bear, whose populations know nothing about borders, and it destroys the integrity of the Sonoran Desert, which is home to pumas, jaguars, porcupines, badgers, bison, prairie dogs, javelinas, jaguarundis and foxes, and hundreds of plant species, including the saguaro cactus. This marvel of nature is one of the most important desert ecosystems in the world, but it is also a place where hundreds perish each year trying to enter your country. It's time for comprehensive immigration reform that will benefit rather than penalize people on both sides of the border. Mr. Trump, recognize the vital place of immigrants in U.S. society today and ensure they are treated decently and as befits your country's democratic principles.

And speaking of borders, how are you going to deal with the upcoming expiration of the crucial water rights agreement that shares the water of the Colorado River between Arizona, California, Colorado, Nevada, New Mexico, Utah and Wyoming—and Mexico—and the treaty now being negotiated by the International Boundary and Water Commission. Do you know that available river water is way down because of lengthy, multiyear drought? Mr. Trump, whatever happens in your country has global repercussions. It is hoped that in your inaugural address you will admit that science indeed identifies climate change and our role in causing it as real. Instead of pulling out of the Paris climate agreement, as you have threatened to do, you should promise that the U.S. will accept responsibility for its share of carbon emissions and embark on a revolution in energy policy. Remember, what's good for the planet is good for the U.S.

You might begin by replacing the existing barriers between the U.S. and Mexico with a wall of solar panels stretching across the border to provide both nations with energy from the sun. Now that would be a truly beautiful wall, and I am sure my country would be happy to pay for half.

In February 2001, George W. Bush chose Mexico for his first trip abroad and met with President Vicente Fox at his ranch in Guanajuato. At a press conference, Bush said, "Our nations are bound together by ties of history, family, values, commerce and culture. Today, these ties give us an unprecedented opportunity. We have a chance to build a partnership that will improve the lives of citizens in both countries." They acknowledged that migration is one of the ties that most closely binds our countries together, although they should have added that it is one of the conflicts that separates them the most, too.

After 9/11, the United States put Mexico on the back burner. Mr. Trump, bring this relationship back to the fore and make it a priority.

Our history and destinies are entwined in many ways. Migration plays a huge role in our shared reality. In the early 1990s I proposed the monarch butterfly as the symbol of NAFTA, for nothing embodies the need for North American environmental cooperation more than this fragile butterfly's spectacular annual migration across Canada, the U.S. and Mexico. Gray whales, which migrate between Baja California and Alaska, are endangered by disturbances in the Bering Sea, where they feed during the summer. Mr. Trump, safeguard the gray whales, as well as polar bears, caribou, migratory birds and the entire region's wealth of animal life by opposing more oil drilling in the Bering Sea. Do not allow opening of the Arctic National Wildlife Refuge to extraction of crude oil and natural gas. Don't squander unique and irreplaceable ecosystems to get inconsequential amounts of a fossil fuel that will not solve your country's energy needs. Do not heed the siren song of "drill, baby, drill."

To demonstrate your commitment to combatting the drug cartels, whose activities in Mexico and the United States are lethal for our citizens and yours, you should put a stop to the shameful trafficking of weapons into Mexico by strengthening the enforcement of laws that control their export from your country to ours. That would show your willingness to support our government's fight against the violent organized crime that is overwhelming us with an epidemic of feminicides, kidnappings, brutal murders and trafficking of adults and children.

There has been a significant Mexican presence in what is now the U.S. at three historical moments: when a large population was living there at the time Mexican territories were annexed in 1848; when people fled the violence of the Mexican Revolution in 1910; and during the modern, ongoing economic migration. Undocumented aliens don't have an easy time of it. Yet despite the present barrier, hundreds of thousands of Mexicans—and Central and South Americans—make the crossing every year in search of a job and a better future. The swelling of their numbers not only means a bonanza for the *polleros* (people smugglers) but also lays bare the impoverishment of our countryside and the lack of job opportunities in our towns and cities.

We all know that Mexico must change. So much of its wealth from natural resources and the hard work of its population is skimmed off by corrupt politicians and greedy business leaders. We must root out corruption and impunity, demand more accountability and drastically reduce the poverty rate of around 45 percent by correcting the grotesque income inequality that keeps nearly half the population living precariously and in need.

Mr. Trump, with Republicans in control of the presidency, the House, the Senate and a majority of state governors, you will wield tremendous power. The time has come to make a new deal with Mexico, and you can do it. Now that would be an act of historic justice.

10

The Global War on Animals

GRAY WHALE

Gray whale, once there is no more left of you than an image
of the dark shape that moved on the waters
in animal paradise,
once there is no memory,
no legend to log your life and its passage
because there is no sea where your death will fit,
I want to set these few words
on your watery grave:
"Gray whale,
show us the way to another fate."

HA (*translated by George McWhirter and Betty Ferber*)

Defendir[...]

HA, *New York Times*, O[...]

For reasons scientists do not understand, schools of yello[...] below dolphin herds in the eastern tropical Pacific. In t[...] fishermen started using huge circular purse-seine nets o[...] to catch the tuna below. Since 1959, more than seven million[...] died, a slaughter that the U.S. tuna industry initially, and the[...] Venzuelan industries subsequently, sought to conceal and legitir[...] real official protest.

In 1972, the U.S. mandated the gradual reduction and even[...] tion of the killing of dolphins by the tuna fleet. The Marine Mar[...] Act was later amended to bar imports of tuna caught by nations th[...] certain limits on dolphin deaths, and late last year a Federal court[...] embargo on Mexican tuna under the law's provisions.

The Mexican Government challenged this ruling before th[...] Agreement on Tariffs and Trade, and in August a GATT panel sai[...] tions of the U.S. law that led to the embargo constituted an illegal[...] rier. The ruling says a GATT member-nation has no right to obstr[...] detrimental to the environment beyond its borders.

If the full GATT council adopts this ruling, it could virtually i[...] many environmental treaties and conventions. Protection of tropical[...] migratory and endangered species, ocean ecosystems and the ozone[...] well as control of toxic wastes and chemicals, would become impossib[...] the dolphins would continue to be slaughtered.

At a meeting of the GATT General Council set for tomorro[...] Mexican Government, pointing to its recent measures to protect the do[...] will ask for postponement (but not withdrawal) of the ruling. There is r[...] to believe that this decision was made in exchange for a promise[...] American officials to pressure Congress to weaken the Marine Mar[...] Protection Act. This is a dangerous precedent and one more reason[...] Congress should insist that environmental issues be an integral part of [...] on the U.S.-Mexico free-trade pact.

Defending dolphins in Mexico has been a risky business. I have recei[...] death threats and been attacked in the press. Criticizing the slaughter[...]

patriotic: the dolphin, after all, has no country, belonging to itself alone
and to the Earth. But the Mexican tuna industry is "patriotic," claiming that
challenges to it are tantamount to criticizing the Mexican people.

President Carlos Salinas de Gortari recently announced a plan to protect
dolphins and other marine species. Yet there are measures in his 10-point
plan that raise concern. One stipulates that the Secretariat of Fisheries oversee
the placement of observers on tuna boats. The observers, however, are not
required to limit the dolphin deaths, merely to count them. Another measure
calls for a million-dollar research program to develop techiniques to "reduce
and abate" the dolphin deaths. But a solution already exists: stop the practice
of setting nets on dolphins, as Ecuador and Panama have done.

Recently a European Parliament panel passed a resolution that would ban
the European Community's import of tuna caught with purse seine nets. If
Mexico agreed to phase out the deliberate encirclement of dolphins, it could
keep this market and also recover the U.S. market. Killing dolphins has
become a losing proposition: the market for tuna caught with purse seine
nets has plummeted, partly because of the embargo.

Although a measure of the Mexican Government's plan states its intention of postponing tomorrow's discussion of the GATT ruling favorable to
Mexico, tabling the ruling is not enough. Mexico should propose that GATT
bylaws be reformed so that all trade decisions take environmental effects into
account. Only then can the dolphin—and the global environment—be
protected.

UPDATE: On February 6, 1995, the Group of 100 revealed that as of January
24, 352 dolphins, nine whales and 151 sea birds had been found dead in the
Upper Gulf of California, most of them between San Felipe and Bahía San
Luis Gonzaga, in Baja California. A preliminary report issued in March by
the Federal Attorney's Office for Environmental Protection blamed the use of
a cyanide-based phosphorescent chemical, known as Natural Killer-19 or
NK-19, by drug traffickers to mark the spot where planes should drop their
loads of drugs at night for pickup in the dark by boats. Since 1995, high
concentrations of cyanide have been detected in various cetacean species in
the Gulf.

On April 25, 2017, a World Trade Organization arbitrator validated
Mexico's complaint that US "dolphin friendly" tuna labeling rules are unfair,
allowing Mexico to impose annual trade sanctions of $163.23 million against
the United States. The secretary of economy said that immediate action

would be taken, perhaps sanctioning imports of US high-fructose corn syrup. The US will appeal and a final WTO ruling is expected in the fall.

Animal Rights

HA, *El Financiero*, March 1994

Although it took Mexico nearly 20 years to sign the Convention on International Trade in Endangered Species of Wild Fauna and Flora (CITES), the convention has yet to be implemented here, and trafficking of flora and fauna is more prevalent than ever. While CITES is by no means a panacea, and it won't be able to solve all the problems of trafficking because controls, legislation, and organizational infrastructure of the member states are often inadequate, it does provide minimal measures for the nations that adhere to it. It also requires each country to set up an internal administrative and scientific authority, as well as to identify a limited number of entry ports so that control can be effective.

Mexico has yet to designate a scientific authority, and because entry ports have yet to be chosen, trafficking into and out of the country goes on at more than 300 existing ports. Customs officials have had no preparation for identifying wild species or their parts and products, nor are they able to tell the difference between legitimate and false permits.

Mexico chiefly exports endemic and native species, and in recent years has become a hub for laundering species from Africa, Australia, and elsewhere in Latin America. The CITES permits and certificates issued in Mexico not only fail to meet CITES criteria, but violate them. For example, export permits are issued for species threatened with extinction that are listed on Appendix 1 whose trade for commercial purposes is prohibited, without any study of population status or impact on the species, as required. This would be the task of the nonexistent scientific authority.

Making matters worse, in 1992 responsibility for controls and surveillance was transferred to the Secretariat of Agriculture and Water Resources (SARH) and the Secretariat of Fisheries (SEPESCA), while issuance of permits was left to the Secretariat of Social Development (SEDESOL), now shorn of authority to follow up on its own actions.

In Mexico, the magnates of plant and animal trafficking have operated with impunity, counting on political influence and official indifference. Most trafficking takes place in Veracruz, San Luis Potosí, Chiapas, and Sonora. In Mexico City, species are trafficked legally and illegally at the Sonora market, pet stores, zoos, on highways and in the street, and by phony breeders. Our plundered flora and fauna have made their way to the United States, Austria, Belgium, Germany, Italy, Spain, Japan, and elsewhere. However, illegal sales within Mexico play a large part in the assault on wildlife.

The most heavily trafficked species are macaws, parrots, cockatoos, toucans, songbirds, birds of prey, owls, crocodiles, freshwater and terrestrial turtles, monkeys, felines, snakes, iguanas, small mammals, and tarantulas. Brownsville, Texas, is a principal entry point for Mexican plant species, as well as a main US market for parrots. Traffic (USA), World Wide Fund for Nature's wildlife trade monitoring program, believes that 100,000 birds—mostly parrots—are smuggled across the border into the US every year; the U.S. Fish and Wildlife Service (USFWS) estimates that 25,000 parrots are brought into Texas, where they are openly sold at flea markets all along the border. From there they are taken to other cities where they fetch higher prices.

Traffic claims the retail market for parrots in the US, imported or bred as pets, brings in as much as 300 million dollars a year; 100,000 to 300,000 of these birds are smuggled in. Japan and several European countries also import huge numbers of parrots, 90 percent of them caught in their native habitat. As many birds die during capture and transit as reach selling points alive. Import into developed countries, coupled with trade in national markets, are endangering the survival of several species.

This year, 1994, is of prime importance for future control of wildlife trading in the world. Far-reaching decisions will be taken within CITES to strengthen or weaken the criteria for listing and protecting wild species. In Mexico, the constant turnover of bureaucrats, changes in their functions and in environmental policy, along with a reluctance to take decisions during the current electoral year may lead to widespread looting of species. We are convinced that if the Mexican government does not act efficiently within CITES, curtailing wildlife trafficking, and if it doesn't put a halt to the irrational destruction of the natural habitat of so many species, the country is on track to suffer irreversible biodiversity losses.

The animals that have shared Earth with man since time immemorial are now relentlessly pursued by the most predatory animal on the planet, man, and no longer have a place to live. Pollution, habitat destruction, legal and illegal hunting, and wildlife trafficking are dooming them to disappear. Soon we will only know them in photographs, documentaries, and as taxidermied specimens in natural history museums. We rational animals who have fought for our rights for centuries must now fight for the rights of animals, while they still exist, so they can live in safety and dignity on this planet which is as much theirs as ours.

UPDATE: The Scientific Authority for CITES in Mexico is the National Commission on Biodiversity (CONABIO), charged with advising the Secretariat of the Environment and Natural Resources (SEMARNAT) on the effects of trade on the status of species. SEMARNAT is the management authority in charge of the licensing system for issuing import and export permits for international trade. The Federal Attorney General's Office for Environmental Protection (PROFEPA) is the enforcement authority responsible for certifying the legal validity of transit and import permits and for wildlife law enforcement. Since 2000, the three authorities have been working together.

The Eliminate, Neutralize, and Disrupt (END) Wildlife Trafficking Act, to combat poaching and trafficking globally, was passed by the US Congress in 2016. Illegal wildlife trade across the US-Mexico border is still rampant, and the main points of entry are El Paso, Laredo, San Diego, and Nogales.

The Global War on Animals

HA, *Reforma*, January 20 and February 3, 2002

While scientists are warning that glaciers in Antarctica are undergoing intense melting and thinning out, Kilimanjaro, Africa's highest mountain, may lose its snowcap by 2015, and the Greenland ice sheet is melting at a record rate, phenomena that point to global warming of the atmosphere. In this age of globalization in commerce, prostitution, organized crime, and terrorism, a global war against animals, themselves victims of climate change, is also underway.

Pollution, habitat destruction, and wildlife trafficking are decimating thousands of species worldwide, abetted by widespread indifference and governmental inaction. On the contrary, in the name of development, governments are among the main promoters of those assaults on nature.

Animals have always been victims of human conflicts, as was recently the case for migratory Siberian cranes that traveled the Central Asian Flyway through Afghanistan on their way to India, or the casualties from disputes between India and Pakistan. In Afghanistan, Sheraga Omar, director of the Kabul Zoo—whose principal building and ancient aquarium were destroyed by bombing—is remarkable for his care of the animals in time of war. Sheraga Omar devotedly kept alive Marjan, a one-eyed lion, the remaining resident of the lion's den. "He's older than I am. The lion is 25, but 88 in human years, and I'm 48. The poor animal lost his mate. He's aging fast, traumatized by his contacts with death." The lion lost his eye after the Russians left Afghanistan in 1992. A soldier jumped into his den to impress his friends and the lion mauled him. Next day, the reckless man's brother threw a grenade at the lion in revenge, blinding him in one eye. Marjan died on January 25, 2002, three months after Kabul was freed from the Taliban. The director of Kabul's zoo will survive in the annals of solitary heroism.

But it's not always like this. In China, the repugnant practice of extracting bile from bears continues in hundreds of so-called "bile factories." Thousands of Asiatic black bears, also known as moon bears, are crammed into tiny cages and a catheter is implanted into their abodominal wall and gall bladder. They are milked twice daily for their bile, which is used in the treatment of fever, liver ailments, hemorrhoids, and delirium. Experts in traditional Chinese medicine assure us that there are herbs which have the same supposed medicinal powers, and synthetic bile is readily available. Conditions are so horrific that bears routinely gnaw their own paws to withstand the pain.

For decades, fishermen in Futo, Japan, have been using boats and nets to round up hundreds of dolphins, selecting the best for sale to acquariums and swim-with programs and slaughtering the rest for meat. In Africa, the killing of black and white rhinoceros continues unabated. In Kenya, where only 460 rhinos remain, three adults and a calf were killed recently for their horns, sought after in Asia as aphrodisiacs. Buyers might as well eat their own hair and fingernails.

Recently several traffickers in the US were seized with tigers they planned to sacrifice for their parts. Tigers are killed for their skins, bone, skulls, teeth, and claws, even their whiskers and eyeballs, for mindless collectors and to supply traditional Chinese medicine. The penis, which is thought to possess aphrodisiacal properties, is eaten in pricey soups. In the twentieth century, this infamous demand has reduced the world's tiger population in the wild from 100,000 to between 5,000 and 7,000.

The annual fires in Brazil and Indonesia—nearly always deliberately set—and the three-week-long Black Christmas bushfires in New South Wales, Australia, have caused massive death of fauna. Animal experts have estimated that hundreds of thousands of mammals, birds, and reptiles died in the recent fires in Australia, with few survivors. The fire wiped out the habitat of koala bears, who were trapped in the trees, and many kangaroos were burned to death. People's behavior was exemplary, caring for, feeding, and comforting the survivors. The forest conflagrations were the first environmental tragedy of the twenty-first century.

A new study of satellite images taken between 1993 and 2000 has shown that Mexico is losing its forest lands twice as fast as was previously estimated, making it the country with the second highest rate of deforestation in the world, divested of some 500,000 hectares (1,930 square miles) per year, through fires, logging, and the expansion of farms and ranches, as was revealed by Victor Lichtinger, head of the Secretariat of the Environment and Natural Resources (SEMARNAT). In three years 1.12 million hectares (4,324 square miles) have disappeared. Brazil has the highest rate of deforestation, followed by our own country and Indonesia. "The situation is doubly critical, because the loss of forests is not just a matter of plants, but loss of fertility, water retention, oxygen production," Lichtinger pointed out. We would add the serious and substantial loss of animal habitat. According to SEMARNAT, among the states most affected by logging are Campeche, which has lost nearly 100 percent of its forests, Tabasco, Veracruz, and Nayarit. Chihuahua, Michoacán, Durango, Yucatán, Quintana Roo, and, above all, the Lacandon rain forest and the Chimalapas in Chiapas should be added to the list. Unbridled logging of the forests surrounding the Popocatépetl and Iztaccíhuatal volcanoes, and devastation of Ajusco have brought the *teporingo* or *zacatuche,* a rabbit endemic to the volcanic environment, closer to extinction.

A few positive steps have been taken in Mexico. Last November SEMARNAT confiscated 2,917 cubic meters (103,013 cubic feet) of wood, enough to fill 300 trucks, and closed 15 sawmills in the monarch butterfly region. Also, the Monarch Fund, endowed with six million dollars, began paying *ejidatarios* and private landowners to conserve trees in the area. Monarch specialist Bill Calvert predicted that this will be one of the biggest and most spectactular monarch seasons in many years. In Mexico City, a new law passed banning minors from bullfights has angered bullfighting promoters.

According to the Brazilian NGO National Network to Fight the Trafficking of Wild Animals (RENCTAS), what Colombia is for cocaine, Brazil is for the traffic in animals, the world's third most lucrative illegal business after drugs and arms. RENCTAS estimates that animals are a 15-billion-dollar a year industry and that Brazil is the principal supplier, providing 37 percent of the world demand. In the Amazon city of Belém, products from endangered species like the manatee, the river dolphin, and the Amazon turtle, and many live animals, especially tiny monkeys and a great variety of parrots, are freely available. Every year 38 million creatures, from beetles and butterflies to lizards, monkeys, and felines, are snatched from their habitat, the majority from the Amazon rain forest, the planet's largest repository of biodiversity. The annual deforestation rate in Amazonia during the last five years of the twentieth century soared to two million hectares (7,722 square miles). The devastation is compounded by intentional fires and development projects, including 4,971 miles of highways, gas pipelines, and dams. One of the megaprojects will be construction on the Xingu River (a major Amazon tributary) of the world's third largest hydroelectric plant, to increase Brazil's generating capacity by 15 percent, despite opposition from the region's indigenous groups and riverside dwellers, who face displacement. Brazil is home to one quarter of the world's plant species—some have been used for thousands of years by forest dwellers to cure a range of sicknesses—and shamans have asked the government to "create punishments to deter the theft of our biodiversity," proposing "a total moratorium on commercial exploitation of traditional knowledge of genetic resources" until a more equitable system can be created.

Deforestation in Latin America is having a crushing impact on the future of animals and birds. The general lack of a culture of conservation, and the practice of trapping birds and mammals to sell in markets and at roadsides as pets or for food, are leading to the disappearance of various species. Steve N. Howell and Sophie Webb, authors of *A Guide to the Birds of Mexico and Northern Central America,* predict that 20 years from now the scarlet macaw and the yellow-headed parrot will be creatures of the past in Mexico.

BirdLife International warns that 10 percent of Africa's endemic birds may disappear, with land use shifting from forests to agriculture in many key areas that are not protected by international law. The NGO states that "bird species are found to be in a state of substantial decline in Africa, among them 218 of the 2,313 species recognized as threatened."

Lions may vanish from central and west Africa in the next decade because populations have been fragmented and remnant groups as small as 50 have little chance for survival. There are only 2,000 lions in the Senegal-Chad region, with 200 in each of the biggest groups, one in Cameroon and the other along the Senegal/Mali/Guinea border. "Lions won't go extinct in this century, but they will only exist in a dozen national parks," warns University of Leyden expert Dr. Hans Bauer. Dr. Bauer puts the current population of the continent's top carnivore between 10 to 30,000 in all of Africa.

Colonies of Adélie penguins in Antarctica are at risk, as increasing sea ice in the Ross Sea means penguins must walk—rather than swim—from their open water feeding grounds to the colonies to feed their chicks. There are fewer than 130 thousand pairs of penguins in the Cape Crozier Adélie colony. Emperor penguin expert Gerald Kooyman, of the Scripps Institution of Oceanography, feared that 1,200 Emperor penguins had not been able to feed their young.

Exploitation of natural resources in Indonesia is out of control. According to the United Nations Environment Program (UNEP), Indonesia has the third largest tropical forest in the world, after Brazil and the Congo. Illegal logging has increased since the fall of Suharto in 1998, with the eager participation of politicians, police, and the military. The province of Central Kalimantan, on the island of Borneo, is home to orangutans, sun bears, gibbons, and apes, but also to the Dayaks, descendants of the original inhabitants of Borneo. The orangutan (*Pongo pygmaeus* and *Pongo abelii*, from the Malay "person of the forest") is only found in Borneo and Sumatra, and the joint total population is estimated at 15,000 individuals. More than 80 percent of orangutan habitat in Borneo was destroyed in the latter half of the twentieth century, with one third of the population perishing during the fire disasters of the 1990s. The orangutan's chief enemies are deforestation, hunting, and the pet trade. Will orangutans survive in the wild by the mid-twenty-first century?

Under the pretext of "scientific research," the Japanese whaling fleet, equipped with cannon that fire grenade-tipped harpoons which explode inside the whale, has sailed for the North Pacific Ocean with a quota to kill hundreds of minke whales and 60 "big whales." Many do not die immediately. The Japanese government, which opposes the South Pacific Whale Sanctuary and the moratorium on commercial hunting of whales, has put out a cookbook featuring delicacies such as fried testicles and whale blubber ice cream. DNA tests on whale meat sold in Japan have found humpback and gray whale—most probably conceived and born in Mexico.

All species of sea turtles are at risk, facing threats from fishing nets, water pollution, and human predators after their skin, flesh, shell, and eggs. More than 30 thousand green turtles (*Chelonia mydas*) are killed every year in Baja California, despite the 1990 ban in Mexico and the 1978 US Endangered Species Act. Politicians, soldiers, and police are among those feasting on turtle during Easter Week, when the killing is in full swing. The number of mature females returning to nesting beaches in the state plummeted from 1,280 in 1990 to 145 in 2000.

Last year British scientists warned that humanity will be responsible for a mass extinction of plant and animal species similar to the catastrophic disappearance of dinosaurs sixty-five million years ago. The present rate of extinction is 1,000 to 10,000 times faster than the natural background rate of extinction. There is little doubt that we are in the midst of the sixth great wave of extinction in the history of life on Earth. Unlike the previous five, this time we humans have ourselves to blame. A North American Commission for Environmental Cooperation (NACEC) report stated that half the regions of greatest biodiversity in North America are being degraded by habitat fragmentation and deforestation, putting many migratory species in jeopardy. The report warned that the monarch butterfly is threatened by construction on the coast of California and logging of oyamel forests in Mexico, while the vaquita (*Phocoena sinus*), an extremely rare small porpoise endemic to the northern part of the Sea of Cortez, is a victim of bycatches and teetering on the verge of extinction.

At the dawn of the twenty-first century, everything points to humanity's losing the war to save our earthly paradise. Generations yet to come will live in a devastated Eden. The global war against animals continues its relentless course with the daily extinction of species. Only by committing ourselves, individually and collectively, to saving the planet's biodiversity can we avoid the approaching disaster.

UPDATE: The Belo Monte dam on the Xingu River, in the state of Pará, is slated to become fully operational in 2019. Up to 100 hydroelectric projects are envisaged in Brazil's National Energy Plan 2030.

On December 1, 2017, an agreement to create the world's largest Marine protected area will enter into force. The Ross Sea Region Marine Protected

Area covers 598,000 square miles, in which no fishing or krill harvesting is permitted in 432,000 square miles. The area is home to 32 percent of the world's Adélie penguins, 26 percent of emperor penguins, 30 percent of Antarctic petrels, and half of Ross Sea killer whales. Up to 72 percent of South Pacific Weddell seals live there year-round.

Borneo lost 39 percent of its forests between 1973 and 2010, and a further 37 percent of habitat suitable for orangutans will most likely be converted to agricultural use by 2025. In Sumatra 60 percent of orangutan-suitable habitat disappeared between 1985 and 2007. Unless deforestation is stopped, by 2025 both species will have decreased in numbers by over 80 percent.

Despite a two-year ban on gillnet fishing in the Upper Gulf of California, only thirty vaquitas are thought to remain, according to an acoustic survey of their clicking noises in the summer of 2016, down from an estimated population of 600 in 1997. Vaquitas become entangled in nets set illegally for totoabas, a six-foot-long 200-pound fish found exclusively in the Upper Gulf of California whose dried swim bladder fetches 20,000 dollars a kilo in China and other Asian markets, where it is known as maw and erroneously thought to have medical benefits. In March 2017, there were clashes between fishermen and government inspectors, and protesters threatened to burn two Sea Shepherd vessels patrolling the Gulf—in partnership with the Mexican government—to protect the vaquita and the totoaba. On June 7, Leonardo DiCaprio and Mexican billionaire Carlos Slim met with President Peña Nieto to commit funding from their foundations for a permanent ban on gill nets, retrieval of "ghost" gill nets in the vaquita's habitat, and support for local communities with alternative fishing techniques. The government has been fundraising for a four million dollar rescue plan to set up sea pens and a sanctuary for a captive breeding program, and as of October 2017 trained bottlenose dolphins will be used by the US Navy Marine Mammal Program to aid in locating and capturing the critically endangered porpoises. No one knows whether a vaquita would survive capture and captivity. Will this last-ditch attempt to snatch the vaquita from the brink of extinction be successful? On June 30, 2017, a permanent ban on gillnet fishing in the northern Gulf of California was enacted. However, this ban does not apply to boats fishing for the Gulf weakfish (*Cynoscion othonopterus*), a vulnerable and heavily overfished species, and the gillnet ban only applies to small boats fishing in the Upper Gulf of California. The only hope for the vaquita is a total ban on any kind of fishing in the vaquita refuge.

The Absence of the Bees

HA, *Reforma*, April 22, 2007

Where did all the honey bees go? Last winter in the United States almost all the bees in a huge number of hives suddenly disappeared, leaving behind the queens, eggs, and a few immature workers. Bee loss ranges from 60 percent on the Pacific coast to 70 percent on the Atlantic coast and Texas. Beekeepers in 27 states were alarmed to discover that millions of bees were missing, leaving no trace in front of or inside the hives, where they usually leave the corpses of their fellows.

The mass disappearance starkly highlights the link between food and bees. Each year in the United States bees pollinate 14 billion dollars worth of crops, and one-third of what gets eaten depends on that pollination. Crops such as almonds, avocados, kiwis, cranberries, melons, pears, and peaches are endangered. The bees leave their hives in search of pollen and nectar and never return, and nobody knows for certain why.

Among possible causes for their absence are viral diseases, fungi, genetically modified crops, malnutrition, and the accumulation of insecticides in their bodies. Exposure to certain miticides used to kill parasitic Varroa mites that weaken bees and shorten their lives is believed to lessen the ability of queens to produce. There are those who blame climate change. Another significant factor is the stress bees suffer when they're trucked all over the country. Beekeepers are nomads, bringing their bees to pollinate crops. They earn more from pollinating than from honey, and the owner of a colony of 15 to 30 thousand bees collects up to 180 dollars for one pollinating service.

Pressures on honey bees are growing. As voracious urban development eats away at the countryside, there are fewer places where bees can forage for the nectar essential to their health and their activities. To supplement their food, beekeepers feed them artificial pollen, protein supplements, and even high fructose corn syrup, akin to fattening chickens in overcrowded poultry factories. Neither birds nor bees roam free. And there are some farmers who deny bees access to nectar, to avoid pollination of certain crops.

Bees are also mysteriously disappearing in Europe. In Spain, in 2005, in a few months 290 billion honey bees vanished and no remains were found, in what was then called "the debeeing syndrome." The hives were full of honey and pollen, but in some parts of the country depopulation reached 50 percent, when a normal mortality rate in the hives at the onset of winter is around 4 percent.

Colony Collapse Disorder has spread to the United Kingdom, and beekeepers associations are asking people to grow native pollen- and nectar-rich flowers to help bees survive. In France, use of the broad spectrum insecticide fipronil and the systemic insecticide imidacloprid—marketed as "Regent" and "Gaucho"—has been partially banned for years because of their harmful effect on bees. Imidacloprid belongs to the class of insecticides known as neonicotinoids, which impact the central nervous system of insects.

In 1923 the Austrian Karl von Frisch, who 50 years later would share the Nobel Prize for Physiology or Medicine with Konrad Lorenz and Nikolaas Tinbergen, students like himself of animal behavior, described communication among bees. When a bee finds a field in flower, or a new feeding place, it returns to the hive to inform the others of the location of the source by means of a "round dance," or a "waggle dance" for more distant food sources. Frisch also discovered that bees use the sun as an orientation tool. Curiously, Egyptian mythology held that the tears of the sun god Ra falling to Earth became bees.

If bees cannot feed freely, if they cannot fly by using the sun as a compass, and if they are too disoriented to find their way home, perhaps all they can do is die.

In Mexico beekeeping existed long before the coming of the Spaniards, who introduced the European honey bee (*Apis mellifera*), which differs from the native bee (*Melipona beecheii*, or *xunan kab*, its Mayan name) in that it has a stinger. In the Mayan region, where bees were cultivated in log hives, honey was used to sweeten food, for medicinal purposes, and in intoxicating beverages. The bees featured in religious ceremonies in conjunction with Ah-Muzen-Cab, the Mayan god of bees and honey. This stingless native bee is in danger of extinction due to deforestation, insecticide use in the forest, and competition from feral African bees, first spotted in Mexico in 1986 in Chiapas. Beekeepers in the Mayan area of Quintana Roo reported a 93 percent decrease in hives during the past 25 years. There are some two million hives in the country, and Mexico is the world's third largest exporter and fifth producer of honey. However, pesticide use is also on the increase, as well as unchecked construction in natural areas. As for climate change, its impact on a host of species and ecosystems is already evident, altering the patterns of life.

A spurious quote attributed to Albert Einstein warns, "If the bee disappeared off the face of the Earth, man would only have four years left to live." Whether he said it or not, it's more than food for thought. Is this the bitter future ahead for humankind? Today is Earth Day.

UPDATE: A permit granted to Monsanto in 2012 allowing commercial planting of Round-up Ready soybeans in Yucatán was withdrawn in 2014 by a state judge who cited threats posed by GM soy crops to honey production in the Yucatán peninsula. European Union rules require labelling of honey containing genetically modified pollen, severely limiting import of Mexican honey. Monsanto has been fighting back in the courts, and the Supreme Court of Justice of the Nation is now expected to make a final ruling on the suit brought by local beekeepers.

Agricultural uses across Europe of the bee-toxic neonicotinoid pesticides imidacloprid, clothianidin, and thiamethoxam were temporarily banned in 2013 because of their high toxicity to bees. On January 12, 2017, the EPA released its preliminary pollinator-only risk assessments for neonicotinoids marketed in the US, noting that clothianidin, thiamethoxam, and dinotefuran can kill bees and their larvae individually, but that in "most approved uses" they "do not pose significant risks to bee colonies" at the exposure levels expected to be found on fields. The agency's review of pollinator, ecological, and human health risk assessments for these insecticides, incorporating public comment, will be completed in 2018.

Two large-scale field studies carried out in Europe and Canada have confirmed that neonicotinoids are harmful to bees. Published in *Science* at the end of June 2017, both show that neonics diminish bee health and affect reproduction. Toxic residues linger in soil, water, and dust and get into untreated plants as well. France's prime minister has ruled that neonicotinoids will be banned from September 1, 2018, as scheduled. EU members are expected to vote before year's end on extending existing bans. In Mexico, Bayer markets clothianidin as Poncho and imidacloprid as Jade. Syngenta sells thiamethoxam as Cruiser FS, Actara 25WG, and Engeo. Will these latest findings help Mexican bees to survive?

Requiem for a Dolphin

HA, *Reforma*, August 7, 2007

Man has accomplished a great feat: the first human-caused extinction of a cetacean species. After six weeks of an extensive search throughout the 3,915 miles of the Yangtze River, the only known habitat of the baiji (*Lipotes vexillifer*), or Chinese river dolphin, an international team confirmed that the baiji has become functionally extinct.

One of four species of freshwater dolphins, baiji survived in the Yangtze for 20 million years until *Homo sapiens*, with his polluting industrial waste, his lethal fishing nets, his electrofishing, his boat and ship traffic, his dredging of the riverbed, his noise pollution, his multitudes (10 percent of the world's population lives in the Yangtze valley), and his towering Three Gorges Dam could finish them off.

Sixty years ago, 6,000 baiji swam in the Yangtze and its tributaries. Its tiny eyes and poor vision evolved over time, as sight wasn't of much use in the murky and turbid waters of the Yangtze, and it relied on a sonar system and echolocation for navigation, socializing, and expressing emotions. Recent attempts at breeding with a male, Qi Qi, failed, because the three females captured during Qi Qi's 22 years as the sole resident of the Baiji Dolphinarium died from the stress of captivity. Qi Qi died in 2002. Traditionally worshipped as the "Goddess of the Yangtze," and declared a National Treasure of China, during the Great Leap Forward launched by Mao Tse-Tung in 1958 the baiji's status as a divinity was repudiated, allowing it to be hunted for its meat and skin, the raw material for purses and gloves, until the population rapidly dwindled.

Another freshwater dolphin, the boto or pink river dolphin (*Inia geoffrensis*), lives in the Amazon and Orinoco basins, where it swims as easily through a flooded forest as in rivers and lakes. The largest of river dolphins, with the male reaching a maximum of 8.4 feet and 408 pounds, the boto has a small head, a long thin snout, and a highly flexible neck, and feeds on more than 50 species of fish. This pinkish grey dolphin is often solitary, and is vulnerable because the traditional beliefs that kept people from killing it are disappearing, and because fishermen view it as a competitor. In Bolivia, where it swims in the upper Madeira River, it is known as the bufeo, and it is said that while a dolphin can save a fisherman's life, he who kills a dolphin will drown.

Traditional folklore has it that the boto (or encantado) can shapeshift into human form, sometimes kidnapping women and men and taking them to the Encante, their underwater city. Meanwhile, trade in boto flourishes in Amazonia. Dolphin jaws replete with teeth are for sale in the outdoor market in Belem, and men buy the eyes as a charm to attract women and money. The powdered penis is considered an aphrodisiac.

Fishermen harpoon the dolphins and hang them live from trees, killing them when they are needed as bait. Deforestation, rampant development, increasing river traffic, pollution by agricultural pesticides and toxic chemicals used in gold mining, climate change, and a shortage of fish all threaten the survival of the pink river dolphin, and its precarious conservation status is a reliable indicator of the general condition of the region where it is found.

In July 2007 Globo TV broadcast a video of Brazilian fishermen who caught 83 tucuxi dolphins (*Sotalia fluviatilis*) in their nets and suffocated them under water, preventing the dolphins from surfacing to breathe. The slaughter took place near the mouth of the Amazon. A Brazilian Institute of Environment and Renewable Natural Resources (IBAMA) researcher on board had a camera, and he saw the fishermen laugh when one of them said, "We'll all be in the clink after this filming." IBAMA denounced the fishermen, who planned on selling the flesh as bait for shark fishing.

In 2007 more than 100 nongovernmental organizations in 28 countries, with a joint membership surpassing 15 million people, addressed a letter to the president of the Dominican Republic asking him to deny permission for importation from Japan of 12 dolphins destined for a water park, arguing that the dolphins were survivors of the annual massacre at Taiji, Japan, of more than 20,000 dolphins. The signatories charged that representatives of the water park, dolphinarium, and aquarium industry subsidize this slaughter by paying anywhere from 45,000 to 100,000 dollars for an animal suitable for a "swim with dolphins" program. They pointed out that this massacre, known as "drive fishing," is extremely violent, because the dolphins are chased to the point of exhaustion and driven into a bay, which is then closed off by a large net, and after the dolphins to be sold are selected the rest are speared to death. A water park may charge 145 dollars per person for half an hour in the water with two dolphins and eight other people. A 100,000-dollar dolphin working four shows a day to packed audiences will earn back its owner's investment in less than two weeks, but the dolphin will never get back to the ocean, to its family, and to freedom. The World Association of Zoos and Aquariums has condemned the Taiji massacre. Meat from slaughtered dolphins is sold for human consumption, although last month several supermarkets in Japan removed the meat from its shelves when two assemblymen tested samples and found extremely high mercury and methylmercury levels in meat from pilot whales (a species of dolphin). Dolphin meat is often used for school lunches. The assemblymen described the meat as "toxic waste," and wrote to the Dominican Republic's environment minister protesting importation of the 12 dolphins.

The Mediterranean common dolphin (*Delphinus delphis*), depicted on ancient Greek pottery giving rides to Nereids, celebrated in mythology for its friendship with humans, messenger of the god Poseidon, sacred to Apollo and Aphrodite, savior of Odysseus's son Telemachus, is endangered. Prey depletion resulting from overfishing, coastal development, and exposure to endocrine-disrupting chemicals are among the culprits for the steep decline in its population. Can we imagine a Mediterranean without dolphins?

Dolphins have lived in the world's seas and rivers for more than six million years, and their 40 species range in length from 5.6 to 31 feet, weighing between 110 pounds to 11 tons. All are carnivores, feeding mainly on fish and squid. About 50 million years ago, dolphins and whales began to evolve from four-footed land animals such as *Mesonyx*, sharing common ancestors with their relative the hippopotamus. Dolphins are highly intelligent and sociable animals, moving in pods of a dozen up to several hundred. The United Nations has declared 2007 "The Year of the Dolphin," to call attention to the myriad threats endangering these mammals. Will it do any good?

The baiji is the first large vertebrate driven to extinction by human activity since the disappearance of the Caribbean monk seal in the 1950s. Not only a species has been lost, but an entire evolutionary family. A branch has fallen from the tree of life.

UPDATE: In October 2016 amateur Chinese conservationists claimed to have spotted a baiji. Now it is the Yangtze finless porpoise that is critically endangered, at risk of following the baiji into extinction.

Japanese researchers studying a delphinid fossil have concluded that the earliest dolphin species may have lived on Earth 8.5 to 13 million years ago.

During the 2016–2017 six-months-long killing season at Taiji, hunters slaughtered 569 dolphins and captured 235 for sale to aquariums and dolphin shows in China, Korea, Russia, and the Middle East. The 2017 season began the first week of September with the slaughter of 20 adult pilot whales and the taking of three juveniles for sale.

A Jump Backwards

HA, *Reforma*, November 16, 2008

Alarmed that frog populations have taken a huge jump backwards, a coalition of conservationists dubbed 2008 "The Year of the Frog." Amphibians seem to be going the way of dinosaurs, and the Global Amphibian Assessment (2004) found that their populations are declining faster than those of birds or mammals. Of 5,743 known species of amphibians, including frogs, toads, salamanders, newts, and caecilians, one-third are threatened with extinction, and 129 have gone extinct since 1980. There are at least 630 species in Mexico, the Mesoamerican country with the greatest amphibian biodiversity, and 208 of those species are endangered. Soon we may lose the Chiricahua leopard frog (*Lithobates chiricahuensis*), inhabitant of the Sky Islands of the southwestern United States and northwestern Mexico; Stuart's mushroomtongue salamander (*Bolitoglossa stuarti*), native to Mexico and Guatemala; Tlaloc's leopard frog (*Lithobates tlaloci*), last seen in the Chichinautzin Biological Corridor; the mountain stream siredon (*Ambystoma altamirani*), scarce now in the high-elevation pine oak forests in the Valley of Mexico; and Anita's false brook salamander (*Pseudoeurycea anitae*), only known in San Vicente Lachixio, in the Sierra Madre del Sur near Oaxaca City.

Four thousand four hundred seventy species of frogs and toads have been identified in the world, of which 230 are found in Mexico. Frogs can change color in response to variations in temperature, intensity of light, or fear of a predator. With their long, powerful hind legs they can jump up to ten times their own length. They are all carnivores, and insects are their main diet, although some eat vertebrates such as other frogs, lizards, or small mammals. A toad can eat 1,000 ants in a day, and will also eat its own skin after moulting. Secretions produced by glands in its skin can be highly toxic for its enemies such as bacteria, fungi, or snakes.

Frogs evolved during the Triassic Period, and the oldest known fossil, found in Madagascar, is 240 to 245 million years old. But neither their prolonged life on Earth, nor their prodigious fertility, nor their poisonous defenses, nor their high jumps can guarantee their survival.

Why are they disappearing so precipitously? The threats are multiple: acidification and eutrophication of streams and lakes; habitat loss and fragmentation as a consequence of deforestation, wetland destruction, and urban development; wildlife trafficking; introduction of alien invasive species; and pesticides and environmental toxins, such as spraying of crops with the herbicide atrazine, traces of which have even been found in the polar regions. Atrazine has been detected in 57 percent of streams in the United States. Males exposed to miniscule concentrations of atrazine developed female sex characteristics. Atrazine is used widely in Mexico on sugar cane and corn crops, but there is no Mexican safe standard for its residual presence in drinking water. Atrazine is a persistent organic pollutant, and continued exposure in humans has been linked to breast and prostate cancer. Additionally, water pollution from agricultural runoff is fueling deformities among amphibian populations in the United States.

Some scientists have blamed the chytrid fungus *Batrachochytrium dendrobatidis* for the loss of nearly 200 amphibian species since 1980. An epidemic of chytridiomycosis in the tropics is emptying streams where dozens of species formerly flourished. Chytrid fungus infects and thickens the skin, preventing breathing. Researchers in Central and South America, where two-thirds of the 110 known harlequin or stubfoot toad species vanished during the 1980s and 1990s, have concluded that global warming is a key factor in the mass extinctions of amphibians, by altering transmission of the fungus. J. Alan Pounds, a scientist at the Monteverde Cloud Forest Reserve Tropical Science Center in Costa Rica, said, "Disease is the bullet killing frogs, but climate change is pulling the trigger. Global warming is wreaking havoc on amphibians, and will cause staggering losses of biodiversity."

A devastating drop in the population of blotched tiger salamanders, boreal chorus frogs, Colombia spotted frogs, and other amphibians has occurred in Yellowstone National Park, where ponds have dried up because of human-induced climate change. In 35 years, 75 percent of the amphibians at La Selva Biological Station in Costa Rica have disappeared, possibly for lack of dead leaves in which they mate. Global warming again.

Their metamorphosis from egg to tadpole to frog has led them to be seen as symbols of transformation and fertility. The Egyptian hieroglyph for 100,000 is a tadpole, and with the second plague, Egypt was overrun with frogs. In the *Rig Veda* frogs croaking in a puddle are likened to intoxicated priests intoning prayers. In many cultures, the croaking of frogs is thought to attract rain. Chalchiuhtlicue, "she of the jade skirt," the Aztec goddess of water, storms, and oceans and patron of childbirth, often received offerings of frog figures; the toad Tamazolin and the frog Atepocatl fused in Diego Rivera, who signed letters to Frida Kahlo with "Tu principal sapo-rana" ("Your chief toad-frog"). In the Middle Ages, frogs and toads were associated with witchcraft. *Macbeth*'s witches threw "eye of newt, and toe of frog" into their bubbling cauldron. Eighteenth-century French writer Nicolas Chamfort cautioned that "one must swallow a toad every morning, when one had to go out into the world, so as not to find anything more disgusting during the day." Fairy tales and legends abound with princes or princesses turned into frogs in search of someone who can return them to human form. If we continue to destroy them, the only frog children will know is Sesame Street's Kermit.

Amphibians live in the Himalayas, in tropical and temperate forests, in deserts, savannahs, trees, streams, even underground, but there's nowhere they can escape from man. Listen to the frogs. "Brekekekex koax koax" croaks the frog chorus that Dionysus meets as Charon ferries him across Acheron to Hades to find Euripides in Aristophanes' *The Frogs*. And joyous frogs they are: "We'll sing on all the more— / if we've ever hopped on shore / on sunny days through weeds and rushes / rejoicing in our lovely songs / as we dive and dive once more, / or as from Zeus' rain we flee / to sing our varied harmonies / at the bottom of the marsh, / our bubble-splashing melodies." [Translation by Ian Johnston]

Like the canary in the coal mine, amphibians, who are so sensitive to changes in air and water and breathe through their skin, are sentinel species and the barometer for ecosystems they inhabit. If you throw a frog into boiling water it will jump right out. Better to put it in cold water and raise the heat slowly, one degree at a time, and before the frog knows what's going on it will be cooked. That's what's happening to us, but the vast majority of Earth's 6.8 billion inhabitants don't have a clue. Listen to what the frogs are telling us.

UPDATE: Atrazine, manufactured by Syngenta and banned in the European Union, is the second most widely used weed killer in the United States. In June 2016, an Environmental Protection Agency risk assessment concluded that "aquatic plant communities are impacted in many areas where atrazine use is heaviest, and there is potential chronic risk to fish, amphibians, and aquatic invertebrates in these same locations." For decades biologist Tyrone B. Hayes has been saying that atrazine causes sexual abnormalities in frogs, and potentially in humans as well, as it is widely found in drinking water. Since the early 2000s Syngenta has been discrediting Hayes and attacking his credibility. Under its current leadership, is there any chance the EPA will restrict atrazine use?

China National Chemical Corp., or ChemChina, completed its 43 billion dollar takeover of Syngenta at the end of June 2017, the largest overseas purchase in Chinese history.

The Earth Belongs to Everyone

THE DESIRE TO BE ONESELF

(*After Kafka*)

If you could be a horseman riding
bareback through the winds and rains
on a transparent horse
constantly buffeted
by the velocity of your mount
if you could ride hard
until clothes were cast off far behind you
because there is no need of clothes
until reins were done with
because there is no need of reins
until your shadow was cast far behind you
because there's no need of a shadow
and then you might see countryside not as countryside
but a fistful of air
if only you could cast the horse far behind you
and ride on on yourself

HA (*translated by George McWhirter*)

The Rights of Nature

HA, *La Jornada*, August 28, 1989

At this critical moment in the natural history of Earth, two hundred years after the Declaration of the Rights of Man (1789) was adopted in prerevolutionary France and forty-one years after the United Nations proclaimed the Universal Declaration of Human Rights (1948), it is time for the world community to embrace a global covenant that sets forth the fundamental Rights of Nature.

We might wonder how countries that have yet to officially recognize or fully honor human rights can be expected to respect the Rights of Nature. Yet the struggle for the safekeeping and survival of thousands of animal and plant species is an integral part of the struggle for the safekeeping and survival of the human race. An environmentally degraded planet degrades humankind because our physical and spiritual welfare depend on the health of our natural environment.

Since the origins of life, and as evolution progressed, the destiny of human beings and the flourishing of nature have been inextricably linked. Nature can survive without humans, but humans cannot survive without nature. The vertiginous disappearance of species from the face of the planet is unprecedented in history and points the way toward our own extinction. It is not enough to preserve a select fraction of the world's flora and fauna in zoos and botanical gardens; all species must be kept alive in the places where they are born, thrive, and reproduce. Their *oikos*, their habitat, must be their sanctuary. From a divine or a natural point of view, an animal or plant species is no individual's property, nor is a species the property of any particular country; no person or group has the right to lay down conditions that limit a species' right to life. Each is a creature of Earth and is entitled to reside on it with dignity.

The world has room enough for all existing life forms, but every day humans increase in number and claim more space to satisfy their needs and greed. To get what they want, humans raze temperate conifer forests and tropical rain forests; pollute and depredate rivers, lakes, and oceans; poison the soil and wreak havoc on wetlands, coral reefs, and deserts—indiscriminately destroying the habitats of whatever walks, swims, flies, crawls, or grows. This relentless encroachment on the natural world must be seen as negative development, as humanity's march toward death. And it must be stopped.

The excessive enrichment of a small number of individuals or groups impoverishes us all. Earth must not become a silent, sterile desert, the dark garden of our worst imaginings. It is up to humans, who are rational animals with a moral conscience, to defend the right to exist of other creatures, and of plants—and not to be their executioners.

The Greek Stoics believed that man was connected with the Universe and was meant to play a part in it. They saw the Universe as a living organism with a soul, the embodiment of deity. That deity was the universal Law of Nature. The individual logos, the principal of rationality, was the universal Logos of Nature. Today more than ever, humans must perceive losses in nature as our own personal losses. We must reflect on the denaturalized life that threatens to be ours, for we are an organic part of the natural world. We must recognize the interconnectedness of human rights and the Rights of Nature, and cherish the living masterpieces around us, because, as Parmenides said, "All is full of Being."

A Letter to the Pope about the Blue Planet

HA, *La Jornada*, May 6, 1990, on the occasion of Pope John Paul II's second visit to Mexico, May 6–13, 1990

Welcome, oh Pope, *ad hanc urbem pollutissimam*, where every day, at every hour, the children of God receive their airborne, liquid, and solid portion of pollutants. Welcome to this overpopulated valley, where people have colonized volcanic slopes and ravines, burying rivers and mowing down forests over the centuries.

Welcome to this country where lakes and rivers are being poisoned, while the fishermen and peasants who depend on them are losing their livelihoods.

Welcome to this land of forests and jungles where trees are torched and hewn down by man, trees God created on the third day, as the Old Testament has it, trees that hold up the sky, according to the Mayans, and if felled the firmament will collapse on us.

Welcome to this country, whose ample geographical diversity harbors vast biotic wealth: first on the planet in reptiles, second in mammals, fourth in amphibians, and rich in birds; all fauna created on the fifth day along with the great whales, as is written in early versions of the Bible in Spanish.

Animals can no longer find a place on earth to live; their habitats are destroyed, they are hunted down; species are trafficked illegally. Victor Hugo said, "Animals run no risk of going to hell. They are already there." And hell is here in Mexico, where some of the world's worst animal traffickers are in business.

Vital links are falling from the chains of life everywhere on the planet. There are holes in the ozone layer in the stratosphere and the oceans have become a dump for toxic waste.

In spiritual terms, the terracide we are committing is an attack on God's work. On the eve of the third millennium, the blue planet is threatened by a biological holocaust brought about by man, who, according to Genesis, God created on the sixth day to "have dominion over the fish of the sea, and over the fowl of the air, and over every living thing that moveth upon the earth." To have dominion over, not to exterminate.

All this brings me to ask Your Holiness: When will the Catholic Church take a more active and energetic part in the defense of God's work, which was created before man in the mythical beginnings of life? When will the Church muster its moral authority to defend that most beautiful virgin, Mother Earth, whom Saint Francis of Assisi addressed as his Sister in *The Canticle of the Creatures*?

If we who are alive during the final years of the twentieth century and the start of the third millenium do not staunchly defend the present paradise we have inherited, which we are morally obligated to pass on to future generations, then during the Last Judgment, as the medieval Flemish mystic Ruysbroeck wrote, "Fire will purify the elements, it will renew them and return them to their quintessence."

UPDATE: On June 18, 2015, Pope Francis issued his encyclical "Laudato Si'," or "Praise Be to You," calling for radical changes worldwide to confront climate change and environmental degradation, and warning of "unprecedented destruction of ecosystems, with serious consequences for all of us." Stating that "enforceable international agreements are urgently needed," the Pope obviously hoped to influence the United Nations summit on climate change that would take place in Paris the following December. He declared that "the ecological crisis is essentially a spiritual problem," and consequently, "the Church must introduce in its teaching about sin, the sin against the environment—ecological sin." The Pope appeared to be echoing Ecumenical Patriarch Bartholomew I, the spiritual leader of the Orthodox Christian Church, who declared in November 1997 during a seminar in Santa Barbara, California, that "to commit a crime against the natural world is a sin." Bartholomew affirmed that "for humans to cause species to become extinct and to destroy the biological diversity of God's creation, for humans to degrade the integrity of the Earth by causing changes in its climate, stripping the Earth of its natural forests, or destroying its wetlands . . . for humans to contaminate the Earth's waters, its land, its air, and its life with poisonous substances—these are sins."

The Morelia Symposium

APPROACHING THE YEAR 2000: THE MORELIA DECLARATION

Group of 100 ad, The Morelia Declaration, *New York Times*, October 10, 1991

A unique exchange has taken place. For the first time environmentalists, scientists, representatives from the native tribes of North and South America, political activists and writers from 20 countries have spent a week in Mexico discussing the state of the world as we approach the end of the millennium. Independently, but without exception, each participant expressed concern that life on our planet is in grave danger.

- 24 billion tons of topsoil from cropland are being lost every year. If deforestation and other forms of land erosion continue at the current rate, the scientists present stated that by the end of the decade the earth will have no additional farmland but nearly a billion new mouths to feed.
- The nuclear disaster of Chernobyl 1986, which in varying degrees has

subjected over 35 million people to radioactive assault, was only one of more than a hundred nuclear accidents which took place over the last decade. At the conference the scientist responsible for the cleanup of Chernobyl stated his belief that at least three nuclear catastrophes on the scale of Chernobyl are likely to take place by the year 2000 A.D.

- 70% of the world's population lives within 100 miles of the sea. The profligate use of fossil fuels by the industrialized world is rapidly and irreversibly changing our climate. Experts stressed that continued rising sea levels and global warming will lead to massive flooding of coastal areas, creating millions of new environmental refugees on an even greater scale than we witness annually in countries like Bangladesh.
- Human survival depends on biological diversity. At current rates of environmental destruction, especially the wanton destruction of tropical forests in the Americas, Asia, and Africa, we will lose at least a million species within the next ten years and a quarter of all living species within the next fifty years.

I. We the participants of the Morelia Symposium urge the leaders of the world at the Earth Summit to be held in June 1992 in Brazil to commit themselves to ending ecocide and ethnocide, and we propose the creation of an International Court of the Environment modeled on the International Court of Justice at The Hague.

II. 20% of the world's population consumes 80% of its wealth and is responsible for 75% of its pollution. We believe there is sufficient knowledge and technology available to reduce the obscene disparity of wealth. We demand a genuine transfer of knowledge and resources from North to South, not the dumping of obsolescent and inefficient technologies and products. There must be an immediate end to the international traffic in toxic waste, urgent reduction of the pollution of rivers and oceans by industrial waste and human sewage, an end to the unprincipled export of banned pesticides and other chemicals to the economically desperate countries of the Third World, and the immediate availability of information and means to allow people to individually and voluntarily pursue the goal of population stabilization.

III. Traditional societies are generally the best managers of biodiversity. For the last five hundred years the knowledge and the rights of the

Native American peoples have been ignored. We believe that respecting the interests of indigenous peoples, both in the Americas and throughout the rest of the world, who have become exploited minorities in their own countries, is crucial for the preservation of biological and cultural diversity. We deplore the cultural pollution and loss of tradition which have led to global rootlessness, leaving humans, through the intensity of mass-marketing, vulnerable to the pressures of economic and political totalitarianism and habits of mass-consumption and waste which imperil the earth.

IV. At the Earth Summit of June 1992 we demand that world leaders sign a Global Climate Change Convention. Industrialized countries must make a minimum commitment to a 20% reduction of their carbon dioxide emissions by the year 2000 A.D. We insist on rigorous implementation of the Montreal Protocol on Protection of the Ozone Layer. We also demand the signing of a convention to protect biological diversity, and the evidence of concrete progress in negotiations for a global forests treaty.

V. The proven economic folly of nuclear power coupled to the probability of environmental catastrophe necessitate the urgent substitution of nuclear energy by clean, safe and efficient energy systems. The military establishment must cease the proliferation of nuclear, biological and chemical weapons and convert a significant proportion of military expenditure to expenditure on environmental security. To ensure this, we demand an end to secrecy and a right to freedom of information in all matters concerning the world's environment.

VI. The participants at this conference wish to stress that environmental destruction cannot be confined within the boundaries of any nation state. We urge our fellow writers, environmentalists, scientists, members of indigenous minorities, and all concerned people to join us in demanding the creation of an International Court of the Environment at which environmentally criminal activity can be brought to the attention of the entire world.

If the latter half of the 20th century has been marked by human liberation movements, the final decade of the second millennium will be characterized by liberation movements among species, so that one day we can attain genuine equality among all living things.

NOTE: The Morelia Declaration was written jointly by participants in the symposium.

[For the list of signers, see Appendix F.]

UPDATE: The Morelia Declaration, signed by writers, scientists, artists, and representatives of indigenous groups from fifty-seven countries, was presented at the Earth Summit held in Rio de Janeiro in June 1992.

The Age of Ecology/The Earth Sun

HA, speech delivered at the Open Speakers Forum during the Global Forum at the UN Earth Summit, Rio de Janeiro, June 9, 1992

Fourteen ninety-two marked the end of the Middle Ages and the beginning of modern times. Five centuries later the modern age is coming to an end, to give way to the age of ecology, the age of planetary awareness. On the brink of one of the most serious natural crises in history we are returning to our origins, we are reflecting once more on the Earth.

Because Christopher Columbus sought to reach the Indies from the West and happened upon Guanahaní Island, we entered into a period of geographical, natural, and cultural discoveries that transformed the worldview of medieval man.

After five hundred years the protagonist countries of the so-called "discovery of America" have scarcely changed camps. We no longer identify them as part of the Old and New Worlds, but as members of the First and Third Worlds, of the North and the South. Economics and politics pit them against each other, ecology binds them together: due to the potential effects of global warming, the islands of the Mediterranean are as likely to disappear beneath the waves as are the islands of the Pacific or the Caribbean.

The nations in these two worlds suffer from basically different environmental problems. The northern countries, whose resources have been largely depleted, are experiencing the effects of unchecked industrialization. The southern countries, where industrialization is more chaotic, are experiencing the destruction of their natural resources.

Beyond national interest, which is the rhetorical barrier erected by politicians who do not wish to commit themselves to the honest protection of the Earth, it is absurd to deny that the harm done to our planet does not affect human beings as well, and that if we do not take opportune measures to preserve it, we are headed towards collective suicide. The destruction of the ozone layer, the greenhouse effect, the despoliation and pollution of marine and terrestrial ecosystems, and the accelerating disappearance of animal and plant species herald our own extinction.

Nowadays, after the collapse of communist ideology, a new humanism is spreading throughout the world, and its name is ecology.

It is not the humanism of the Italian Renaissance, focussed on the study of classical Greco-Roman culture, but the discovery by humankind of moribund nature, of nature abused in the name of unlimited growth, of a nuclear peace that stubbornly refuses to eliminate the arsenals which can spark a terricide.

It is the idealism of men and women committed to the defense of the linked strands of life at a time when biological extinction is taking place every hour of every day, at a time when we realize that the Earth is a living organism and that we are its intelligence, its memory and its poetry—and as far as we know, it is the only planet in the Universe graced with life forms.

Even in 1989, we writers gathered together in Maastricht, Holland, at the World PEN Congress, did not align ourselves into ideological blocks replicating East-West confrontation, as had happened at previous literary meetings. In between the working groups and the poetry readings we began talking about the denaturalization of life, about Amazonia and Lacandonia, about Lake Baikal and Lake Pátzcuaro, about Copsa Mica and Cubatão, about Chabařovice and Katowice, about Mexico City and Athens, about the Coatzocoalcos River and the Mediterranean Sea, about palm trees and elephants and sea turtles and giant cacti.

And there, on the eve of the Third Millennium, we agreed that the final years of the twentieth century would be decisive for the salvation of Earth: either we would learn to live with Nature or we would embark upon the irreversible destruction of the elements, of species, and of ourselves. For even as we seek for the origins of life in space, launching complex and costly rockets and spaceships, here on Earth we are blindly destroying that life. This is true for sea turtles, animals with a biological memory spanning millions of years, that are slaughtered for the few dollars earned from the sale of their shell, skin, and eggs.

A few months ago Vaclav Havel declared that the collapse of communism had brought to an end one of the most significant ages of humankind. He said, "The modern age has been dominated by the belief, expressed in different forms, that the world—and Being as such—is a wholly knowable system governed by a finite number of universal laws which man can understand and rationally manipulate for his own benefit." Havel dates the beginning of this era to the Renaissance, and it has been characterized by rational and cognitive knowledge. But Havel forgot to mention that both before and after the collapse of totalitarian ideologies a new global humanism had arisen, the humanism of ecology, a humanism which unites human beings of all races, religions, languages, and ages, a humanism that is active but nonviolent, and which, in its commitment to defending the rights of the Earth, is also protecting the right of human beings to live in a healthy and safe environment.

Havel, as a survivor of the repressive system of his own country, Czechoslovakia, points out that "this age has created the first global, or planetary, technological civilization, which has now reached the limits of its potentiality, the point beyond which the abyss begins. The end of Communism is a grave warning for all humankind." Here I would like to emphasize what is missing: that this same technological civilization is nearing the limits for destruction of terrestrial and marine ecosystems, and that it is the annihilation of the biotic wealth of the planet which is a grave warning for humankind, because we cannot hope to survive in a world in which those elements which are essential for life—water, air, and soil—are polluted. A future that includes the destruction of the ozone layer and disastrous climate change is where the abyss gapes open.

We have reached a chapter of history where wars will be ecological, where catastrophes and famines will be the result of environmental depredation, in a denatured world that has yet to be adequately described in any work of fiction. But this world is no longer a vision, this future is already here with us, we can observe it in many parts of the world.

A few years from the end of the Second Millennium, we are entering the Age of Ecology, an age in which we will reread history and our past from a different perspective, just as we are now reinterpreting the "discovery of America" in terms of ethnocide, ecocide, and biological exchanges.

Economics, politics, science, technology, education, all future human activities will have to take the environment into account, our relationship with Nature will have to change, our children, no matter where they live, will have to be thinking abut the Earth at all times.

No, we are not looking for what Vaclav Havel identifies as "new scientific recipes, new ideologies, new systems of control, new institutions, new instruments to eliminate the terrible consequences of our previous instruments, recipes, ideologies, institutions, systems of control." We are looking for something more urgent, something more prosaic, something less grandiose but more essential, something harder to achieve: the preservation of the Earth on which human beings have found life and its marvels ever since we came into existence, an Earth on which we want to live until the end of history.

The Aztecs divided their past into five solar periods. The name of each new Sun also specified its characteristics, and the way it would die. According to Aztec mythology, the Fifth Sun, called Nahui Ollin, which is the Sun of the present era, will be brought to an end by earthquakes. From its ashes, and from its elements, the future Sun must be born, the Sixth Sun, the Earth Sun.

Earth Rights and Human Rights

HA, presentation at the conference "Earth Rights and Responsibilities: Human Rights and Environmental Protection," Yale Law School, April 3–5, 1992

Now, if instead of thinking of the Earth as just one more planet in the universe, we must think of the Earth as a natural universe in which human life has been possible, then we must agree that human rights and the rights of nature are inextricably intertwined. The violation of nature is a violation of humankind, for there is no significant abuse of nature that will not eventually and adversely affect the human species.

I would venture to say that, for many of us, the defense of the rights of nature is an implicit defense of the rights of human beings. An ecologically degraded planet degrades humankind, since our physical and moral well-being depend on the health of our environment.

It seems clear to me that those who are responsible for global warming, for the destruction of the ozone layer, for the pollution of land and water, for the razing of temperate and tropical forests, for the vertiginous disappearance of species from the face of the Earth, and for the manufacture of weapons of mass destruction are directly threatening the possibility of survival of the human species. They are, in fact, violating the rights of present and future generations, and most particularly, their very right to existence.

Because crimes committed against nature which have global repercussions must be seen as crimes against humankind, these crimes should be brought before an International Court of the Environment, a tribunal for the prosecution of ecocides, whether they are countries, economic entities, or individuals. The Gulf War, the devastation of Amazonia, Exxon Valdez, under-or above-ground nuclear testing, and the less spectacular but more frequent crimes which are perpetrated daily all over the world, come to mind.

I also believe it would be beneficial to create an information alert network through which human rights violations related to the environment could be made known quickly and internationally so that support would come rapidly. The majority of such cases are not reported in the media; they remain unpunished or are not divulged outside the local context in which these abuses are perpetrated by government officials, business interests, or unscrupulous individuals. For the most part, the victims are members of indigenous groups, peasant communities, or the rural or urban poor in countries of the South, although these violations obviously occur in the North as well. The victims seldom have adequate financial and legal resources for their own defense, much less for the defense of their immediate environment.

Although many of these human rights violations in the countries of the South result from a lack of democracy in those countries, they are also due to the absence or lax enforcement of specific environmental laws to which citizens can have recourse, if the need arises.

One of the frequent contradictions we encounter is that our governments carry out public campaigns to make citizens aware of the value of plant and animal species, of forests, of bodies of water, presenting them as the natural patrimony of the inhabitants; but at the same time they repress these very same citizens—as if they were political saboteurs or social agitators—when they speak out and take action to defend those species, those forests, those lakes and rivers, which they had been encouraged to cherish and preserve.

And it is often necessary to defend ecosystems from projects undertaken by government officials, or their business partners, which makes the struggle between protectors and predators of the environment wildly unequal.

We have frequently observed in many countries of the South that lurking behind almost every environmental problem one can discover the financial interests of an individual or group that is associated with the government, and that the destruction of the environment is often caused by small economic and political groups who are misusing their power. In many instances, these groups invoke social benefits or national sovereignty to justify the exploitation of their country's natural resources, but all too often the only beneficiaries are themselves, while their compatriots—frequently peasants or indigenous peoples—continue to live in the same poverty as before, although now their natural patrimony has been impoverished as well: the trees have been felled and the land flooded.

In Mexico, the Group of 100 constantly receives phone calls from citizens of all strata of society who are desperately seeking help to prevent trees being cut down on their street, who are trying to ensure that the forests in national parks are duly protected, who are threatened by the siting of waste dumps in their neighborhoods, or who endeavor to protect endangered species from being captured, killed, or collected by hunters, smugglers, or developers of mass tourism projects.

Oddly enough, in most of the cases brought to our attention, it is the defenders of nature who are harassed, threatened, arrested, fined, or jailed (or even murdered), while the predators get away with their plundering and pillaging; the law seems to be on the side of the ecocides. For this reason, I believe that if the problems of democracy are not resolved in our countries, it will be very difficult to resolve the problems of the environment. The gap between the laws as written and their enforcement in practice still yawns wide, and without rights to information and to fair participation in the judicial process, it will be impossible to guarantee the right to a healthy environment, no matter how many decrees or proclamations are issued by our leaders.

The practice of democracy, like respect for the environment, cannot be enforced by decree: it must be a responsible behavior, a daily conviction, as much for government officials as for all citizens.

None of the 20 countries in the world most seriously affected by deforestation are in the North: nine are in Latin America, seven in Asia and four in Africa, palpable proofs of environmental colonialism. Most of these countries are heavily in debt and their creditors take due advantage of the fact. Over the course of years the rape of their natural resources will turn them into deserts—not the deserts we know, which have their own ecosystems, but into wastelands—and the utopias of the past will become the dystopias of the future—and the debt will never be paid off.

And what of indigenous peoples threatened by the destruction of their environment?. Unchecked logging, intensive ranching, agribusiness, exorbitant development schemes, and expulsion from their own lands have had a devastating impact on these groups. Invariably this destruction violates their human rights, as they lose their traditional habitat and livelihoods, their social structure and religious practices, even their spirituality. What of the rights of these peoples to live on their lands, rather than becoming environmental refugees and pariahs in the sprawling cities of the Third World?

Millions of tons of radioactive wastes, chemicals, toxic liquids, heavy metals, incinerator ash, paint, sludge, and lubricants are exported to Latin America every year. Legal or clandestine shipments, often disguised as "recycled" materials, poison our ecosystmes and endanger human lives. The victims are usually kept ignorant of the potential health risks to which they are exposed or the nature of the substances being dumped in their midst. Surely we have the right *not* to be the repository for garbage which is not of our own making; perhaps if the wastes had to remain *in situ* or be disposed of close to the place of their manufacture, it would be a sufficient incentive for source reduction of both household and industrial wastes. The right not to receive someone else's garbage is a corollary of the responsibility for disposing of one's own garbage.

In the coming years when we speak of human rights we will be talking about our elemental rights to clean air and water, of the right of women to bear children free from lead, of each individual's right to information and the means for making personal decisions which can lead to population stabilization, of the right of future generations to live with dignity on a planet rich in biodiversity—and of each person's responsibility for making this possible. We must stop quibbling over scientific uncertainties or conflicting scenarios of global survival, debating over the expendability of species or arguing about cancer rates attributable to ozone depletion. We must make a leap of faith and acknowledge that our planet is in grave danger. We must understand that "business as usual"—the excuse given by many political and business leaders in the North and South for putting short-term national, and even personal, interests above global imperatives—will not ensure enjoyment of human and environmental rights by our descendants.

The Second Morelia Symposium

APPROACHING THE YEAR 2000: OVERPOPULATION

Group of 100 ad, *New York Times,* February 25, 1994

In September 1991, writers, scientists, environmentalists and representatives of native peoples came together at the first Morelia Symposium in Mexico. They signed a declaration that was a call to action for the leaders of the world who met at the Earth Summit in Brazil in June 1992.

Together for a second time in January 1994, we are struck by how little progress has been made on global environmental issues. The situation has been made worse by unsustainable economic policies and exacerbated by the stresses of poverty, military conflict, gender inequity, natural resource mismanagement, and population pressures. Most governments and industries have adopted pro-environmental rhetoric behind which they continue to prevent reform.

We are stretching the environment's capacity to support human life. In some places productivity has already collapsed. Soil degradation, increasing scarcity of fresh water, marine pollution, global warming, and the impoverishment of biological diversity are examples of what happens when societies live beyond their means. Our rates of population growth and accelerating levels of consumption threaten the global environment's capacity to support future generations.

In Cairo in September 1994, world leaders will gather for a major conference on population and development sponsored by the United Nations. With the prospect of the world population doubling to 11 billion within a century, can we finally cast aside our profound denials of reality and face the need for fundamental changes? Will the Cairo conference be yet another exercise in providing the comfort of rhetoric to those who thrive on inaction?

These facts confront us:

- Three people are born every second, 180 every minute, 250,000 every day. This is the fastest increase in human population in history. Each year there are more than 90 million new mouths to feed. Millions are hungry and 1.2 billion have no access to safe drinking water.

- The growth in global food production is slowing, and the world's farmers can no longer be counted on to feed the projected additions to our numbers. Achieving a humane balance between food and people now depends more on family planners than on farmers.
- Population growth is a major factor in increased pollution and destruction of forests, wetlands, and marine environments.
- Climate change threatens communities, agriculture, and biodiversity everywhere, yet carbon dioxide and other greenhouse gas emissions continue to increase.
- Habitat destruction is often discussed purely from the point of view of human physical survival as though this were our exclusive right.
- Extinctions are occurring at a rate unprecedented in recent geologic history. Up to a fifth of all species on Earth are likely to have disappeared within the next 30 to 40 years. Innumerable species are lost even before they have been recognized and named.
- Millions of women throughout the world lack freedom of choice in reproductive matters as well as access to health care, adequate food, education, employment, land ownership, credit or leadership roles.
- Everyone needs clean air and water, shelter, proper nutrition, and contact with the rest of nature. Yet 20 percent of the world's population is responsible for 80 percent of its resource consumption and the majority of pollution. An equal portion lives in absolute poverty, too poor to escape hunger and disease.
- The global cost of military expenditures is now $600 billion a year, hundreds of times what is spent on environmental protection or voluntary family planning services worldwide.
- For thousands of years, most traditional societies and tribal peoples have lived in closer balance with nature than we do. We continue to ignore and destroy their cultures.

We and our leaders must ask ourselves:

- How can we consider environmental protection to be a luxury?
- What will happen if we continue to insist on dominance instead of balance, at the expense of every other species?
- Will a child of the next century see a monarch butterfly, a tiger, or a blue whale, or walk in a forest in Malaysian Borneo, Mexico's Lacandon wilderness, or anywhere in West Africa?

- Why is the production of a machine gun treated as economically desirable while cleaning a river from which people must drink is considered a costly extravagance?
- How realistic are official environmental policies that ignore the overconsumption and population crises?
- Why are we afraid to offer adequate information and reproductive health services to our youth?
- What will our money be worth when we have turned the Earth into a wasteland?
- Do you think these questions have anything to do with you? If so, what will you do about it?
- We approach the end of the millennium faced with the prospect of massive species extinctions and environmental disasters. The Earth, our planetary home, is truly finite. In order to survive we will have to move forward with both intelligence and compassion.

NOTE: The Second Morelia Declaration was written jointly by participants in the symposium.

[For the list of signers, see Appendix G.]

UPDATE: As of June 2017, the world's population has been put at 7.6 billion. The United Nations estimates it will reach 8 billion in 2023, 9.8 billion by 2050, and 11.2 billion by 2100, with India and China the most populous nations. According to the UN, global population growth is concentrated in the world's poorest countries.

El Niño of the Century

HA, *Reforma*, December 28, 1997

Thanks to a few more degrees, the raging reappearance of "El Niño" has turned the planet's climate upside down. It was thus baptized by Peruvian fishermen towards the end of the nineteenth century, when they began to note its effects in December, soon before the Christ Child's birthday. This time the phenomenon promises to be the strongest of the century, more like the child Hercules. The warm ocean current that raises water temperatures around the Pacific Rim and along the coasts of Latin America is already responsible for forest fires, severe droughts, and agricultural disasters in Indonesia, Australia, India, Pakistan, Thailand, the Philippines, Papua New Guinea (where drought has left a quarter of a million people without food), and southern and central Africa, and floods in Somalia and Ethiopia due to the warming of the Indian Ocean. On this side of the Pacific, in Chile, Ecuador, Peru, Argentina, Uruguay, Bolivia, and Mexico, it has brought hurricanes, freezes, torrential rains, floods. In Western New Guinea, in Borneo, and in the Moluccas there are famines in consequence of the worst drought in half a century, while sea lions and seals are dying of hunger in California.

If the 1992 El Niño (considerably weaker than the 1982 event) was able to cause the death of 70 percent of the monarch butterflies that were overwintering in the oyamel forests in Michoacán and the State of Mexico, what will happen this season after the incessant logging in the sanctuaries? As Dr. Lincoln Brower has stressed, the forest is already a blanket full of holes that can't protect the butterflies from inclement weather. We mustn't forget that a small variation in temperature can give rise to a mass mortality.

No one agrees on how long El Niño will last. Some meteorologists believe it will continue to be powerful until February, and then rapidly lose power. Others predict it could stretch on through April or May. Whatever happens, El Niño has already warmed the tropical waters of the Pacific to their highest temperatures of the century; in November alone they rose to 3.6°C. The situation in northern Mexico has been grim. The cold wave brought on by El Niño led to dozens of deaths in Baja California, Coahuila, San Luis Potosí, Zacatecas, Nuevo León, the State of Mexico, and Chihuahua, where, as every year, the Tarahumaras paid for the freezing temperatures with their lives. Saltillo and other cities were left incommunicado by snowstorms, and nearly the entire country has been buffeted by freakish weather, chill blasts from the North, cold fronts, freezes, and snow. As always, the poor are the worst hit. In Mexico, similarly to wherever El Niño runs wild, economic losses will be considerable and harvests will be lost. It's quite likely that El Niño will increase the number of tropical storms on the Pacific coast; should these occur in upper Baja California Sur, they will be a timely warning to Exportadora de Sal that it should not build a saltworks around Laguna San Ignacio, where the gray whale mates and calves.

Amazonia has suffered a severe drought that caused gigantic fires in the jungle. In Argentina, thousands of people had to be evacuated because of floods, and entire towns were submerged beneath the waters. In Peru, which, with Ecuador, has suffered most from El Niño, rivers have overrun their banks, houses have collapsed, crops have been destroyed, and thousands of people displaced, but further devastation is expected this coming year. There will be rains, rough seas, and floods in Ecuador. Torrential rains led to the evacuation of thousands of families in Bolivia, while on the high plateau elevated temperatures and drought have killed thousands of cattle and sheep. Up to 20 percent of corn, rice, and bean harvests in Central America will be lost this year, due to drought. Public health problems will come on the heels of rains and droughts, leaving a trail of infectious diseases such as yellow fever and malaria.

Europe has not escaped the irascible infant: flooding last summer in Germany, Poland, and the Czech Republic was attributed to El Niño, which also is bearing the blame for atypical snows in England, France, and Spain, and for the historic cold—the worst in the last 115 years—being braved in Moscow. The criminal fires in Indonesia and Malaysia that shrouded the entire Southeast Asian region in a smoky, acrid haze became so massive thanks to the late arrival of the monsoon season, but excessive logging contributed to the fires' spread. Eighty thousand inhabitants of the Molucca Islands could die of hunger because of the persistent drought.

Christmas Island has suffered a major coral bleaching, but El Niño is not alone in heating up the atoll's waters. Studies indicate that the impact of global warming on the oceans could be equivalent to having El Niño as a permanent guest. El Niño is a recurring natural hazard, so what are the most effective responses governments and individuals can take? Experts have mentioned more accuracy in forecasting and more precision in forecasting for specific regions, information sharing, raising public awareness, taking security measures, estimating expected risks, advance planning for disaster reponse, and mitigation of impacts of extreme climate events. There's evidence that this climate pattern of sea surface temperatures across the central and eastern equatorial Pacific Ocean becoming much warmer than normal, with a mass of warm water moving to the western coast of South America, is becoming stronger and more frequent. Some scientists suspect that El Niño is feeding on greenhouse gases, although much more research is necessary to discover what might be the relationship between a destructive phenomenon of nature and a destructive phenomenon that is man's doing. But even without reaching a consensus about the possible consequences of accelerating emissions of those gases, especially carbon dioxide, on El Niño, researchers agree that a small variation in water temperature has repercussions on the climate in parts of the world very distant from each other. This truth should warn us about the vast potential effects of global warming. Until quite recently in human history, it was soothsayers and priests who ventured to interpret enigmatic and inexplicable phenomena of nature. Today it's scientists with their computerized models who predict what may happen. Either we heed their predictions or we blindly risk disaster.

The World's Thirst

HA, *Reforma*, March 31, 2002

In 1993, in my novel *Legend of the Suns*, I foreshadowed a city without water in 2027, when the next New Fire ceremony to prevent the end of the world will occur, performed by the Aztecs every 52 years on the Cerro de la Estrella (Hill of the Star), where now the Passion of Christ is enacted every year.

Meanwhile, global water consumption doubles every 20 years. According to the United Nations, more than one billion people, one-sixth of the world's population, have no access to drinking water, and five million die every year from drinking polluted water. If we go on like this, in 2025 five billion human beings—65 percent of the predicted population—will suffer from a severe water shortage or a total lack of drinking water. The majority will be in Africa and southern Asia, where the worst poverty and hunger on Earth are now found.

Citizens, scientists, and political leaders all over the world are worried about the pollution and loss of wetlands, lakes and rivers, coral reefs, seas and oceans—where fisheries are reaching their limits—but little is being done. Competition for water in those parts of the world where it is scarcest is growing. With climate change and unquestionable global warming (a sign of which is the recent breakup and shattering into thousands of icebergs of 1,250 square miles of the Larsen B Ice Shelf in the Antarctic), the water crisis can only become more acute. The impact of water shortages is becoming a destabilizing force. In the Middle East, the previous king of Jordan once said that he would only go to war with Israel over water, as Israel controls Jordan's water supply. Regions where water is now most contested are the Sea of Aral, the Ganges, the Jordan and Nile Rivers, and the Tigris-Euphrates river system. If water-sharing agreements can't be reached, there will be disputes and even armed conflicts.

Mexico has paid off a debt with the United States that existed since 1992 for water from the Rio Grande, Colorado, and Tijuana Rivers, leaving northern Mexico, where drought has reached a critical level, with a water shortage. Authorities in Texas report that the lack of this water cost the state a billion dollars during the past 10 years, and more than 30,000 jobs.

The growing industrialization and urbanization of the world, both in countries of the North and in the developing world, have raised industrial and urban demand for water. But where will this water come from? From farming? That could bring about a decrease in agricultural production. Transferral of water to cities could undermine the world's ability to feed itself, although in the industrialized world there's less plundering of agricultural water for urban use because demand rises more slowly. Everywhere allocation of water is decided by political and economic powers. In the United States and elsewhere, transference of water rights exists, affecting people who are not involved in the sale of those rights. This transference can have a negative impact on employment, stability of rural communities, and the environment. When a country's renewable supply of water falls below 60,035 cubic feet per person, there is not enough water to satisfy the population's alimentary, domestic, and industrial needs. Grain imports rise, to save water for domestic and industrial use. Today 34 countries in Africa, Asia, and the Middle East are in this situation.

The most common way to increase water supply has been by building dams that are highly destructive to local populations and to the environment. During the past 51 years, the number of dams in the world has risen from 5,000 to 38,000. It has been said that water will be for the twenty-first century what oil was for the twentieth, and that the big question will be: Who owns the water and how much can they charge for it? Privatization of water is already a 400 billion dollar a year business. The water multinationals expect to earn even more, taking advantage of international commerce agreements and investment to control the flow and offer of water.

Governments used to believe that public services such as water, health, and education were fundamental human rights and had no place in commercial agreements. These rights have been eroded since the North American Free

Trade Agreement came into being in 1994. The possible expansion of the treaty to the entire continent, imposing its failed model of privatization and deregulation on 34 countries in the Americas and the Caribbean, would establish the largest free trade zone in the world, encompassing some 800 million people. Canadian activist and water rights expert Maude Barlow warns that such an agreement would entail opening up all public services to multinational competition, whose principal interest is making a profit, and not giving public service. Private corporations would have the right to operate free of government regulation. As far as water is concerned, national or local governments would be forbidden from giving preference to national providers of water and sewage services. Privatization's defenders argue that a free market system is the only way to distribute water, but it has been shown that marketing water does not satisfy the needs of the poor. Privatized water goes to whoever can pay for it. Water flows toward money. Barlow says that in the northern hemisphere privatization of water has lead to higher prices and less access, unfulfilled promises to improve hydraulic infrastructure, the loss of indigenous groups' rights to water access, unemployment, lack of information about water quality, and juicy profits for the privatizing companies.

Part of Mexico City's water is already in private hands, some of them foreign. Instead of building an aberrant second story over the Periférico (a ringway) and the Viaducto (a freeway), which will disfigure the city and condemn the metropolitan area to a hell of selfish private transport, the Federal District's government should be investing in works that will remedy our considerable water deficit (5,818 gallons per second), improving distribution systems to avoid the widespread leakage that wastes 37 percent of the current supply, recycling sewage, and implementing efficiency and conservation in water use. The city continues to sink, thanks to excessive depletion of the water table, and what was once a fertile metropolis of lakes and lagoons in Aztec times now threatens to die of thirst.

Twenty-five years from the next New Fire ceremony, everything seems to indicate that not only are we moving toward the future, but the future is already here.

UPDATE: Early in 2012, 54 percent of the country suffered its worst drought of the past seventy-one years, which caused severe shortages of water and food and killed thousands of head of cattle. Nearly half of our protected natural areas were at risk.

Currently, one-fifth of Mexico's 653 aquifers are overexploited.

The Fifth Sun, the Earth Speaks

HA, *Reforma*, January 2, 2005

Nowadays, when climate change is melting ice in the Arctic and the horrific threat of nuclear weapons is returning, and while the world is deeply shaken by the death of more than 150,000 people and the huge number of missing and displaced (the toll of victims keeps rising and at least five million have been left without food, water, or shelter) in Thailand, Sri Lanka, Indonesia, Malaysia, the Maldives, Myanmar, India, and several African countries, as well as tourists mainly from Sweden, England, Italy, Norway, Denmark, Germany, and Australia, the legend of the suns inevitably comes to mind. And the assumption that our rampant destruction of nature increased the severity of the tidal wave's impact.

The apocalyptic earthquake beneath the Indian Ocean on Sunday, December 26, 2004, that triggered a tsunami that destroyed hotels, homes, boats, and entire towns, will surely go down in history as one of the worst natural disasters on record, but it also casts doubt on our future life on the planet. When the Earth speaks, man is like an insect or a blade of grass, and the apocalypses foretold by the Fifth Sun and the Book of Revelation can become reality.

According to Mexican apocalyptic tradition, the Fifth Sun, the present solar era of which we are inhabitants, whose sign is Nahui-Ollin (4 Motion), also called Ollin Tonatiuh, the Sun of Movement, will come to an end with earthquakes. In the creation epic Legend of the Suns, it is said that a sun will perish on the same day it is born. Our sun came into being in the year 13 Reed, and from the day of its birth this sun carries within the elements of its own destruction, for it is fashioned from the remains of the four previous cosmic ages: Nahui-Ocelotl (4 Jaguar), Nahui-Ehécatl (4 Wind), Nahui-Quiahuitl (4 Rain), and Nahui-Atl (4 Water). In his *The History of the Indies of New Spain*, Fray Diego Durán recounts that twice a year the ancient Mexicans held a feast in honor of Nahui-Ollin, on March 17 and December 2. Fray Bernardino de Sahagún relates that in the first movable feast the sun was honored when it was in the 13-day period beginning with Ce Ocelotl. "During this feast they offered quail to the image of the sun and burned incense and they slew captives before the image." The day Nahui-Ollin was the sign of the sun, the day of human sacrifice, as the hearts of the victims were offered up to the sun. Durán relates, "The Temple of the Sun stood on exactly the same place now occupied by the Cathedral of Mexico and because of its nature was called Cuacuauhtinchan, which means the House of the Eagles."

In Teotihuacán, where mythology has it that the gods gathered in the heart of night to sacrifice themselves and create the Fifth Sun, the most recurrent hieroglyph is a figure of four cardinal points united by a center, the quincunx. "As Eduard Seler pointed out, five is the number of the center and this is the point of contact between the sky and the earth," anthropologist Laurette Séjourné writes. "Here all the characteristics of the Fifth Sun—the heart of the sky—expressed in mythology are brought together in one sign."

As in the sacred geography of ancient Greece the omphalos of the world was located in Delphi, we could very well say that the heart of the world—the place where the Earth beats—is found in the Valley of Mexico. And that place is called Tocititlán, a seismic zone in today's Federal District. A shrine dedicated to the goddess Toci, Our Grandmother, was located about one mile south of the Great Temple. Durán writes: "A woman, not too old and not too young—about forty or forty-five years of age—was sacrificed forty days before the occasion of this festivity. This woman was purified and washed like the other slaves who represented deities. On her purification she was given the name of the goddess Toci, Mother of the Gods, Heart of the Earth. Behold why she was called Heart of the Earth: it is said that, when she so desired, she made the earth tremble." In the shrine "stood a wooden idol representing an old woman. Above the nose the face was white, and from the nose down it was black. . . . All her attire was white."

When the Earth speaks we must listen. The earthquakes in Bam, Iran (December 26, 2003) and exactly one year later in Sumatra, Indonesia (the island closest to the massive quake's epicenter), bracketed deadly earthquakes in Morocco (February 23) and the island of Honshu, Japan (October 23), a massive quake off Macquarie Island in Antarctica (December 24), and a strong quake along the Parkfield section of the San Andreas Fault—the tectonic boundary between the Pacific Plate and the North American Plate—in central California (September 28). The Mount St. Helens volcano in the state of Washington erupted in October, in the wake of increasing seismic activity underneath the volcano, and Mexico's own volcanoes, Popocatépetl and Colima, are continually active and threatening to erupt. Ferocious hurricanes lashed the Caribbean islands during the 2004 Atlantic hurricane season. And what about violence by the hand of man, such as the March 11 Islamist terrorist attack in Madrid or the Iraq War, as if in the midst of natural catastrophes and our condition as mortal organisms at the mercy of disease and death, we have to guard against the hatred of humans for other humans.

Although the last New Fire ceremony took place in 1507, for the Spanish conquistadors abolished the ceremony also known as the "binding of years," the next could happen in 2027, a ritual date that appears in my novel *The Legend of the Suns*. As I wrote in *Apocalypse with Figures*, no one knows the date when earthquakes will bring the Fifth Sun to an end, but whoever lives in Mexico City and experienced the 1985 earthquakes knows that myths can come true.

Now inhabitants of European countries, southwest Asia, and Africa can join us in planetary fears. And religious extremists in the United States, who in 1996 expected that a great earthquake in the bed of the Pacific Ocean would bring about the end of the world, can reread their Bible. According to their reading of Apocalypse (Revelation 6:12–14) the end will come about with earthquakes: "And I beheld when he had opened the sixth seal, and, lo, there was a great earthquake; and the sun became black as sackcloth of hair, and the moon became as blood; And the stars of heaven fell unto the earth, even as a fig tree casteth her untimely figs, when she is shaken of a mighty wind. And the heaven departed as a scroll when it is rolled together; and every mountain and island were moved out of their places."

The future will write the myths of the past, for doubtless in the coming years we will see more earthquakes, more tsunamis: it's only a question of guessing where the next "big one" will happen, and some scientists believe the "big ones" come in pairs. But while we prepare for the next one, what happened in Colombo, Sri Lanka, is still astonishing, for while human beings were dying, the animals were saving themselves. Deputy director of the Wildlife Department H. D. Ratnayake said, "The strange thing is we haven't recorded any dead animals. No elephants are dead, not even a dead hare or rabbit. I think animals can sense disaster. They have a sixth sense. They know when things are happening."

Get Close to the Stars

HA, *Reforma*, January 25, 2009

The expanding universe fits into our minds,
into our expanding minds fit all the stars,
our mind is a verse towards the universe, said the poet.
HA (translated by George McWhirter)

Since time immemorial, the daily appearance of the Sun in the firmament (and its replacement by the moon) was seen as the principal element of stability in the life of human beings, a constant in a world of unpredictable events and of changes with or without apparent causes. This helps us to understand the deification of the Sun in so many cultures, at times in simultaneous or successive manifestations, now feminine, now masculine. Thus we see Utu/Shamash in Sumeria; Sól, goddess of Norse mythology; Ra/Horus/Amun-Ra among the Egyptians; Helios and Apollo in the Greek pantheon; the Sol Invictus (and Mithras) of the Romans; Surya, the Hindu solar god; Inti, the Inca sun god; Tonatiuh, the Fifth Sun of the Aztecs, who feeds on human blood; and Amaterasu, the Japanese solar goddess. In general, the solar deity repeated its daily crossing of the sky in some sort of boat or in a chariot drawn by horses. Where did the Sun go at night? To the underworld, or to an underground passageway, in some mythologies.

Pre-Hispanic civilizations observed and worshipped the celestial bodies, giving events in the sky a preponderant place in their daily life and their destiny. In *Skywatchers of Ancient Mexico*, Anthony F. Aveni writes that "the sophisticated astronomical and mathematical achievements of the people of ancient Mesoamerica followed logically in the evolutionary development of a civilization which intensely worshipped the heavens and steadfastly associated the phenomena they witnessed in the celestial environment with the course of human affairs." By observing the firmament, the Maya established the most complete and precise calendar of their time. Aveni notes, "For the Maya, a single word, *kin*, signified time, day, and the sun. Its meaning and glyphic form suggest that the art of timekeeping was intimately connected with the practice of astronomy."

We would know more about skywatching among the Maya if Diego de

Landa, the inquisitorial Bishop of Yucatán, had not burned their books, declaring, "There was nothing in them that was not superstition and lies of the devil." Only four Mayan codices have survived all or in part, containing lunar and solar almanacs, a table listing the ephemerides of Venus, and other astronomical knowledge. The Aztecs also paid close attention to what was going on in the heavens. Fray Diego Durán writes that after observing a great comet, Moctezuma summoned Netzahualpilli, the astrologer king of Texcoco, to explain its meaning. The king replied, "That brilliant star appeared in the heavens many days ago. It comes out of the east and is directed toward Mexico-Tenochctitlan and this whole region. It is an ill omen for our king-doms; terrible, frightful things will come upon them. . . . Death will domi-nate the land! All our dominions will be lost. . . . You will be witness to these happenings because they will take place in your time." The comet presumably predicted the fall of the Aztec empire.

For Aristotle the Earth was the center of the universe. In the sixteenth century, Nicolaus Copernicus placed the Sun at its center and the Earth as a planet revolving around the Sun, initiating a genuine scientific and philo-sophical revolution. Although a German-Dutch lens grinder sought to patent a rudimentary telescope in 1608, it was in 1609 that Galileo Galilei built a telescope sufficiently powerful to make astronomical observations such as viewing the mountains and craters of the moon, discovering four satellite moons of Jupiter, and locating stars and nebulae in the Milky Way. In 1610 he published his discoveries in *Sidereus Nuncius* (*The Starry Messenger*) and went on to confirm Copernicus's heliocentric hypothesis of the solar system.

Do the stars have a place in the lives of twenty-first-century human beings? Electric light and clocks have replaced the sky; the starry night is hid-den behind light pollution. Who pays attention to the times of the rising and setting of the Sun? Occasionally one catches sight of a few stars or the Moon, and takes note of its phase. Will our devotion to the Sun return as burning of fossil fuels is gradually replaced by solar energy?

There is no credo or religion that forbids looking at the sky. Get close to the stars.

Development and Sustainability:
How Much, for Whom, until When?

HA, *Ibero*, Universidad Iberoamericana, Mexico,
December 2009–January 2010

Mahatma Gandhi said it: "There is a sufficiency in the world for man's need but not for man's greed." But how many needy and greedy are seeking satisfaction?

The world's population doesn't stop growing. Since 1950 it has jumped from 2.5 billion to the current 6.8 billion, and the United Nations predicts it may reach 9.2 or even 10.5 billion by 2050, depending on fertility rates.

According to the Food and Agriculture Organization (FAO) of the United Nations, today 1.2 billion people go hungry, and the number rises every year. The hungry (who are usually thirsty too and lack medical care) are mostly found in developing countries (where misery seems to be the only thing developing), although that label encompasses the poorest nations on the planet—Mali, Niger, Guinea-Bissau, Burkina Faso, Sierra Leone—as well as China, since 2007 the world's largest emitter of carbon dioxide, the principal greenhouse gas, thanks to its industrial boom.

On what does a country's ranking on the prosperity scale depend? According to the World Trade Organization (WTO), countries themselves decide whether they want to group themselves with the developed or the developing world. And lagging far behind is a third category: the "least developed countries," identified as such by the United Nations Conference on Trade and Development (UNCTAD), which receive special concessions in multilateral trade, preferential conditions for development financing, and priority for technical advice. At last count, in 2007, 49 countries were recognized by the WTO as least developed, most of them in Africa, several in Asia or the Pacific, and only one on the American continent: Haiti.

Ever since I attended nongovernmental organization (NGO) meetings prior to the first Earth Summit (the UN Conference on Environment and Development)—which in 1992 brought to Rio de Janeiro 108 heads of state or government and their entourages and 20,000 representatives of civil society (although the two groups were conveniently lodged and held their meetings and events nineteen miles from each other)—I have pointed out that within every "Third World" country there are "First World" enclaves. These are made up of leaders and high-level functionaries and their relatives and cronies—to whom the most lucrative contracts are funnelled—along with members of the reining military hierarchy.

The most important result of the Earth Summit was the Framework Convention on Climate Change (UNFCCC), precursor of the Kyoto Protocol, which was drawn up by participating countries in Japan in 1997 and only came into effect in 2005 after enough countries (but not the United States) had ratified it. Kyoto specifies binding targets for greenhouse-gas reductions, and its first commitment period ends in 2012. Its successor is being negotiated now on the eve of the XV United Nations Climate Change Conference to be held in Copenhagen December 7–18, in which 192 countries will take part. The declared goal of the meeting is "to achieve a legally binding comprehensive climate agreement in the first few months of 2010, coming into force on 1 January 2013."

At the end of October, the European Union's 27 countries estimated that by 2020 the yearly amount needed to help developing nations reduce their carbon emissions would reach 150 billion dollars, money that would come partly from governments and partly from the industrial sector. Due to economic inequality within the EU, no agreement was reached about who would pay how much. Less prosperous countries from Eastern and Central Europe wonder why they should subsidize development in Brazil or China, for example, when these large emerging economies are substantially wealthier than they are but resist committing to a reduction in their greenhouse gas emissions. And who would guarantee compliance with this kind of agreement, and through what mechanisms? The EU countries have put numbers and dates to their promised reductions of CO_2 emissions, but the United States, which never signed the Kyoto Protocol, has yet to commit itself to concrete measures, despite President Obama's good intentions. Only the pigheaded and dishonest still dare to deny the existence of climate change, or that human activity has brought us to where we are and that action must be taken now.

A United Nations study warns that by 2050 there could be 200 milion climate refugees. Environmental disasters will give rise to social catastrophes and fuel new conflicts within or between countries. Climate change magnifies the scarcity of water, food, and arable land and creates new sources of violence. Hurricane Katrina, perhaps the most destructive storm in the history of the United States, displaced some 150,000 people. Many scientists agree that climate change increases the destructive power of hurricanes.

Henceforth, environmental deterioration will be a causative factor of war. As desertification advances through overexploitation of soil, deforestation, drought, and floods, rivalry between social groups will worsen, as is happening now in Sudan, where nomadic herders are fighting over resources with farmers from other ethnic groups. Here in Mexico government officials blamed climate change for recent heavy rains in Mexico City and the flooding that ensued. In the Himalayas, on the roof of the world, glaciers across the Tibetan plateau are melting fast, and are predicted to lose two-thirds of their mass over the next 40 years, bringing about an enormous water shortage and prompting conflicts among countries that compete for water from rivers that have always been fed by glaciers.

I do not believe that man will rest until he has extracted the last drop of oil from the planet, whether it be from the vast reserves in Saudi Arabia, from wells drilled 10,000 feet beneath the water and seabed in the Gulf of Mexico, or from shale oil deposits in Canada. Nor will he stop using coal, which accounts for 25 percent of the world's energy consumption, and whose reserves could satisfy demand for the next 133 years.

China is now building six vast wind farms, the largest in the world. Investment in solar energy is on the rise, and on a smaller scale, alternative sources such as burning agricultural waste are being developed. Nevertheless, 70 percent of China's energy comes from coal, and even though old plants are being shut down and replaced with less polluting ones, Chinese coal-burning capacity is growing. Additionally, the wind farms will be accompanied by new coal burning plants to have in reserve when the wind doesn't blow. And so air pollution will continue to increase, and it is the regions richest in coal, such as Shanxi province—where highly polluting industries have been located to be near the coal supply—that have the highest rates of birth defects. Coal is not only lethal for the climate, but deadly for human health.

We are at a critical moment for the Earth. Climate change, the precipitous loss of biodiversity, and shrinking water, forest, and fishing resources threaten the survival of life as we know it. There are those who argue that resources must be sacrificed to combat poverty, but that would amount to squandering the present at the expense of the future.

American author and environmentalist Edward Abbey said, "Growth for the sake of growth is the ideology of the cancer cell." Growth cannot be infinite. It's not a question of stopping investment for development but of ensuring that investments respect the authentic sustainability of natural resources and aim for equitable sharing of the benefits. Horizontal growth, reaching the poorest, is preferable, not vertical growth, which only further enriches the wealthiest. But neither will be possible if corruption can't be reined in. That applies as much to the G-20 countries (19 of the world's largest economies and the EU) as to the least developed nations. The current negotiations are complicated, but their resolution is urgent. Nevertheless, I believe that to halt humanity's disastrous race towards the environmental catastrophes that are already ravaging the Earth's ecosystems and its animal and plant inhabitants, the only hope lies in a collective change of consciousness and behavior. This requires convincing society that environmental degradation affects us all, but that people do have the power to bring about change, each individual in his own life and together pressuring governments into action. Educating children from the earliest possible age to understand the consequences of their own acts is crucial, and children should learn to question the actions of their parents, teachers, and society in general and ask them to stop wasting resources (if they have access to them) and blindly consuming (if they have the money to do so).

UPDATE: The 2009 Copenhagen Accord was a disappointing nonbinding political agreement, which at least acknowledged that a rise in global average temperature should be limited to below 2° C above preindustrial levels. In December 2015, representatives of 195 countries meeting in Paris adopted the Paris Agreement on climate change, which went into effect on November 4, 2016. The Paris Agreement is the first universal agreement to cut carbon emissions, on the basis of "nationally determined contributions." However, these are not considered legally binding.

On June 1, 2017, President Trump announced that he was withdrawing the United States from the Paris Agreement, stating, "I was elected by the citizens of Pittsburgh, not Paris."

Approaching the End of the Millennium

HA, presentation at the Inter-American Development Bank in
Washington, DC, on September 26, 1995, as part of the IDB
Cultural Center Lectures Program

In the year 776 AD, Mayan astronomer-priests met in the holy city of
Copán to synchronize their two calendars: a sacred calendar representing
the time of the gods, and a secular calendar measuring human time. The
participants in this event were portrayed in a stone sculpture hewn into one
of the altars in the city. Today, over twelve centuries later, the astronomers
have long since turned to dust, their mythologies are long dead, and their
system of measuring and tabulating time with *tunes* and *katunes* has been
replaced by the Gregorian *calendarium*, with Christian religious festivals
based on the phases of the moon and European seasons. We can clearly see
that the ruination that overtook Copán came not from the heavens but from
the earth, not from the gods but from men.

In our own day, the Lacandon forest in Mexico has become a natural victim of human greed, discord, violence, and a population explosion. At the
present rate of deforestation, whatever remains of it is doomed to disappear
by the end of this century. Given the climate of ethnic, religious, economic,
political, and social conflict, combined with the standoff between the
Zapatista Army of National Liberation and the Mexican government, it is
unlikely that any feasible ecological solution to this problem will be found
any time soon.

The admonition of Heraclitus the Obscure that "the sun must not over-
step its boundaries or it risks punishment by the Furies, the ministers of justice," also applies to Copán, the Lacandon forest, and Mexico City, because
in their own ways and in their own times, these are all places whose natural
resources have been overexploited and whose limits of growth have been
exceeded. With the ritual count of 260 days abolished, we can say that
Copán, like Teotihuacán, Monte Álban, Chichén Itzá, and other pre-Hispanic sites from which people through the ages have observed the heavens, is
simply slipping back into the past, into the endless night.

We are about to turn the corner of the millennium, to enter the year 2000
as marked on the Gregorian calendar, which was adopted in 1582 by Italy,

France, Spain, and Portugal. It is now said to be in use "universally," although it would be more modest to say "worldwide." As is known, the Gregorian calendar replaced both the Roman Julian calendar, whose year started in May and which served Europe for over fifteen centuries, and the ancient systems of measuring time by the stars, the sun and moon, the creation myths, or the major happenings in the lives of religious prophets.

Our knowledge of ancient history is very relative where dates are concerned, because before 1492, for example, it is very difficult to know if events were dated according to the year of Christ's Incarnation, the year of his Passion, or the year of his resurrection.

The basic problem is that the histories or biographies of Jesus mention his birthplace, his parents, even his genealogical tree, but they cannot state with accuracy the year in which he was born. Certain scholars even have doubts about his birthplace. If, as James P. Mackey notes, we have to analyze the New Testament texts on the resurrection in order to explain the myth of Jesus' death, then we are making Western history conditional on three spiritual dates that took place at times which cannot be precisely identified. Also, the practice of dividing history into before and after Christ arose in the Middle Ages.

Will the Jews, whose lunisolar calendar puts the presumed year of the world's creation at 3761 BC, and the Muslims, whose era starts with the Hegira or the migration of Muhammad from Mecca to Medina in 622 AD, be as enthusiastic as Westerners in celebrating the year 2000? In India, where the Gregorian calendar is used for secular purposes and religious life is governed by the Hindu calendar, will people also go out into the streets to celebrate the advent of the third millennium?

Personally, I detest New Year festivities, and I'm afraid the celebrations ushering in the year 2000 will simply be two thousand times more depressing as far as I am concerned.

Eusebius of Caesarea, in his *Ecclesiastical History*, attempted to incorporate the history of the Church into the framework of the history of the world, starting with Abraham. If the Church was founded by the apostles, and the apostles talked about Jesus, then it was obvious that time should be divided into pre- and post-Christ eras. But if the birth of Christ, as Jaroslav Pelikan reminds us, had more to do with the world of mystery than the world of nature, and if the Gospels of Matthew and Luke which describe Jesus' childhood are seen more as Christologies, how can we all agree on a system for dividing time into regular divisions for dating events?

According to Rudolf Bultmann, the oldest narratives of a people are not yet history, they are *myths*. Their themes are not human experiences or deeds but theogonies and cosmogonies. Even Herodotus recounts historical facts as if they were a succession of stories. Thucydides was perhaps the first man to look upon history as a form of knowledge. What is said about history could be said about the way in which some ancient peoples measured time: the Mexicans linked it to mythology and the Christians to Christology.

We know that in the hypothetical year 221, Julius Africanus undertook the impossible task of producing a history of the world, beginning, of course, with creation. He set the Incarnation of Jesus in the year 5500 (from the creation of the world), and his return in the year 500. History would last 6,000 years. Fortunately, his calculations turned out to be wrong.

The *Estoria de España* (or *Primera crónica general de España*), a history of Spain commissioned by King Alfonso X of Castile "the Wise" in the thirteenth century, began by describing how Moses wrote the book of Genesis. It included Bible stories and drew on Greek, African, Roman, and Gothic sources up to the time of the Spanish kings. The confusion between history, religion, Christology, mythology, legend, and fable was quite poignant. Thus many of the ancient histories started not only with Jesus but with God Himself.

In the twelfth century, Joachim of Fiore divided history into three periods: the Age of the Father (Old Testament), the Age of the Son (New Testament, in which we are now living), and the Age of the Holy Spirit (the Millennium). Perhaps we owe to this belief one of the masterworks of the visual arts: *The Garden of Earthly Delights* by Hieronymus Bosch.

Within the Eurocentric context of culture, in the commemorative accounts of the year 2000 there will be Gothic cathedrals and the splendors of major tourist destinations such as Venice, Paris, London, and New York; geniuses of art, literature, philosophy, and music, such as Dante, Michelangelo, Da Vinci, Dürer, Shakespeare, Cervantes, Rembrandt, Vermeer, Spinoza, Velázquez, Goya, Sor Juana Inés de la Cruz, Bach, Mozart, Beethoven, Goethe, Carroll, Flaubert, Dickens, Machado de Assis, Proust, Dostoyevsky, Tolstoy, Kafka, Joyce, Borges; and personages such as Columbus, Bartolomé de las Casas, Bernardino de Sahagún, Galileo, Copernicus, Newton, Marx, Edison, Einstein, Freud, Pasteur, Marie Curie, and Fleming. Alongside these luminaries, we do not know how to gauge the architects of the pyramids and temples of the non-Christian world, or of Tenochtitlan, Dürer's ideal city. Into what context can we place the visionaries and shamans like Milarepa and

María Sabina, among saints and Christian mystics like Ruysbroeck, Hildegard von Bingen, Saint Francis of Assisi, Saint John of the Cross, and Saint Teresa of Avila?

Culture as an ecosystem is not only created by the great, but by a host of little people whose names are never known or known only to a few, and who are now barely remembered or completely forgotten. It was those little people, with their ideas and labor, who were the movers and motivators of the physical and spiritual structures of their day. Those familial and social fabrics have disappeared, but they were decisive in shaping the cultural ecosystem.

And speaking of ecosystems, I wonder whether this hypothetical thousand-year review, which will have so much to say about the masterworks of man, will find room for acknowledging the masterworks of nature. In what museum, if not the Earth, could they find a place, and what critic will possess the biological or aesthetic judgment to evaluate the branches of an ash tree, the colors of a coral reef, the plumage of a macaw, the skin of a tiger, or the wings of a butterfly?

People living in the year 1000 saw the upheavals of nature and human life as acts of the devil, a devil jealous of the works of God. Today we see those upheavals as acts of men, men heedless of the works of God.

The Judeo-Christian tradition of the Apocalypse, which starts with Ezekiel and continues through St. Paul and St. John of Patmos, up to Beatus of Liébana and other medieval visionaries, has changed. After World War II and the experience of the Holocaust, followed by the nuclear arms race, we now believe that the Apocalypse will be the work of man, not of God.

The concept of nature held by the poets and artists of the second half of the twentieth century has also changed. The natural world is no longer considered idyllic, as in the Homeric *Hymns to the Earth*, the *Eclogues* of Virgil, a medieval Book of Hours, or through the eyes of the romantic poets of the nineteenth century. The way of looking at water, air, and earth is different. The brotherhood evoked in the beautiful *Canticle of the Creatures* by Saint Francis of Assisi has been shattered. We have passed from an attitude of contemplation to an active or fearful mind set. The gardens, parks, and woods that used to delight people's hearts are now either sick or dying of cancer, just as human beings are. The people of today have turned against the very idea of the tree and, by extension, have even destroyed the enchanted forests of fairy tales.

As the twentieth century draws to a close, we still have not cast off the medieval terror of life or, even worse, the terror of death. Sometimes I have the feeling that man's conscience is like the obsidian mirror of the Aztecs, reflecting the living body in a corpse-like state.

We have also abandoned our anthropocentrism. In our smallness and in our greatness, we are no different from—nor are we the same as—those people who lived in the year 1000, or those who probably will exist in the year 3000. One thing will inevitably continue to unite the human beings of the three millennia: the awareness of the death of the body. A minority will be aware of something else—of the ecological deterioration of the Earth and of the dizzying speed with which plant and animal species are disappearing.

For the year 2000, the media will of course engage in their collective rituals: they will review the history of the past ten centuries, bombard us with stories of deeds done, and with examinations of conscience from which we shall always come out looking bad. The heroes of history, and of culture and civil society, will be people we already know, people who have become famous during ten centuries of Eurocentrism. After all, aren't the skeletons of Vikings in archeological museums larger than those of Mesoamericans?

National histories will merge into world histories. In these totalizing histories, constructed in the First World and repeated in the Third, Latin America (to which the Europeans brought their religion, language, and calendar) will virtually cease to exist. And if it does exist, it will be because of its natural disasters, its violations of human rights, its social conflicts, or the lack of safety on its streets and highways. Amazonia could become the world's largest desert during the next millennium. Certain Latin American cities, such as Mexico City—overpopulated and polluted, with an insufficient water supply, its natural resources destroyed—will become the scenes of frequent environmental emergencies. Others will become the locales for crime, prostitution, drugs, and kidnappings. Devalued by economic crises, we Latin Americans will find ourselves fighting against a new kind of slavery.

"The Third World is dead, long live the First World!" After the fall of the Berlin Wall this became the cry of the poorer countries that once abhorred the idea of aligning with the superpowers. These nations had been searching for a historical alternative, linked not by similar economic, environmental, or joint cultural relations, but by their shared status as victims of underdevelopment and exploitation.

It is common knowledge that the "Third World" concept did not come from the Third World itself, but was an invention of French journalists during the 1950s. It acquired political life at the Bandung, Indonesia, Conference in 1955, in which Nehru, Nasser, Zhou Enlai, Nkrumah, and Sukarno were participants. Unfortunately, the true nature of the relations between the First and the Third Worlds rapidly put an end to the dream of political solidarity among countries not aligned with the opposing sides in the Cold War.

Although the concept of Third World has weakened over the years, the problems of underdevelopment, unsustainable exploitation of natural resources, corruption, and failure to embrace democracy have not disappeared from our planet, and nor has their outcome, poverty. Out of this Third World has come a Fourth World (which includes Somalia, *inter alia*), and a Fifth World (the world of immigrants), and also a Second World, in which countries like Mexico struggle along.

What do those countries that used to belong to the Third World, and that used to attend useless conferences and gatherings, still have in common, apart from a tendency to dwell on the old economic, social, environmental, and political problems and to export human beings to the First World? They still retain the old colonial mentality, assuming that the solution to their problems will come from outside, from other countries and other people, and not from their own government or from their own populations. What we failed to learn between the Bandung Conference and the fall of the Berlin Wall was that our countries not only have to defend themselves from each of the superpowers in turn, but from their own political vices, and that the only possible solution to our problems lies in our capacity to be free. And for us to be free, our heads of state must learn to govern democratically and without corruption, and, above all, without betraying their peoples' dreams.

Immersed in multicultural and enumerative commemorations, many people will retrace the route of the dead, believing they are following the paths of time, but in the end they will have achieved a present full of absence. No one knows what paintings and books, what buildings and cities, and what other works of man will still be accessible or still be standing during the coming millennium. No one can tell what items currently referred to as art will roll around the world as bits of organic matter until they end up as forgotten garbage.

The libraries are full of the works of divine poets, princes of poets, who were extolled in their day by rhetorical critics from both East and West. In the twenty-first century, in the West, thousands of copies of books that were once bestsellers are going to end up as trash at second-hand bookstores. Those literary geniuses, titans, and giants who received lavish praise in the reviews and major newspapers of the United States will perhaps become nothing more than lists of interchangeable names. The media that idolized them, assuming those media still exist, will not remember what it was they used to praise, and will move on to exalt other shooting stars. All man's attempts to escape death through literature, painting, music, and science are in vain. At the end of time, not only man, but also his works, will disappear into the black hole of oblivion. And even those acts of love by which a man and a woman seek to perpetuate themselves and live forever will also vanish in an instant into that same black hole.

Over the map of the Americas another map may be superimposed, that of the forests and jungles that are fast disappearing. And over that map of deforestation yet another map may be drawn, one pinpointing ethnic groups threatened by environmental destruction. The Yanomami of Brazil, the Aché of Paraguay, the Yagua of Peru, the Miskito of Nicaragua, the Guaymí of Panama, the Tarahumara of Mexico, the Maya of Guatemala, the Guambiano of Colombia, the Mapuche of Chile—all these groups have been affected by the advent of settlers, military incursions, forced displacement from their land by miners, ranchers, lumbermen, highway construction, hydroelectric dams, and tourist resorts. In this, the decade of the fifth centennial of the meeting of two worlds, it is urgent that our governments take their native populations into consideration when preparing development projects or defining their free-trade areas. If they don't, Latin America will see many repetitions of the Chiapas uprising.

In 1970 the Villas-Bôas brothers, who spent decades trying to save the indigenous peoples of Central Brazil, said that all that remained of the extinct tribes of the High Xingu were their names and the sad accounts of their final disasters. The same can be said about many ethnic groups throughout the world and about their habitats.

"Of the six to nine million Indians who originally lived in the Amazonian rain forest, only about 200,000 now survive. There were 300,000 Aborigines in Australia when the First Fleet put into Botany Bay; a century later 60,000 remained. Every single Carib Indian on the island of Hispaniola was killed or deported by the Spanish colonialists, to be replaced by slaves from Africa," notes the *Atlas of the Environment*. As J. Eric Thompson wrote over three decades ago, "the disintegration of native cultures in the wake of 'civilization' is a sad thing, because material progress does not bring greater happiness nor compensate for the loss of spiritual values."

In the chronicle of human births and deaths over the past millennium that we expect to hear in the year 2000, the plant and animal species that have disappeared from the face of the Earth must be included.

In this cemetery of nature we will find such illustrious dead as the dodo bird, the painted vulture, the Bali tiger, many mammals, reptiles, birds, and fish and extensive forests in the Americas, Africa, Asia, and Europe. We cannot even mention those organisms that passed away silently and unnoticed, for we never had any names for them.

Faced with this vast natural graveyard, the twenty-first century will become a century of ecological Noahs, of men and women who are driven to create biotic arks to save those ecosystems and species that are vanishing in a flood of extinction.

Like the character in *Sophie's Choice* who has to decide which of her two children to save, the moral dilemma of this *homo ecologicus* will lie in choosing which places and which creatures to select, on what knowledge and wisdom to base the choice, in light of which social and economic conditions, which criteria to use—biological, scientific, economic, aesthetic, moral?— and how to convince other people to preserve life.

And who is this *homo ecologicus,* to decide on the fate and the right to exist of other creatures and forms of life, whose mystery surpasses his own intelligence and capacity for action or thought? Isn't there a chance that he will get lost in the labyrinth of eschatology, the doctrine of last and final things, as so many writers and visionaries before him have gotten lost in the practice of their art or religion?

It is not enough to preserve individual survivors of over-exploited species in botanical gardens or in zoos—they need to be preserved in the places where they are born and reproduce, where their life support is found. Their habitat must be their sanctuary. From natural and moral standpoints, the earth's flora and fauna belong to no person or country, and no group or nation should determine or place conditions on their right to life. Invoking national sovereignty and territorial domain to justify crimes against nature is both childish and dishonest, as has already been said about the destroyers of Amazonia and Lacandonia, the killers of whales, sea turtles, and dolphins, and the loggers of forests that are home to the monarch butterfly.

History is biting its own tail. Eras and suns are born and die. Just as the Copán River carried away a bit of the building called the Acropolis every rainy season—as Thompson noted—time sweeps along and wipes out cultures, leaving in their stead nothing but oblivion.

Mexican mythology has it that we are now living in the era of the Fifth Sun, 4-Ollin, Sun of Movement, a sun that is approaching its death, to be caused by earthquakes. As in the past, on the occasion of previous destructions, we place our hope in the next Sun, yet to be created, which, like Heraclitus' bird of the resurrection, is scavenging in the ashes of the dead suns.

This hope, which we hold on to even though we know it to be misplaced, is strengthened by the impermanent permanence of the past and by small private rituals, such as mine when, in a Dublin museum one day in May 1995, I touched the concentric circles of an ancient stone, the rings of the Stone of Time. With my idling hand I sought to caress four thousand years of oblivion.

I put a date to that encounter with the illusive present, but looking back from any year in the future, it will not matter whether that chance act of mine took place in 1995, in 1900, or in 1321.

Mircea Eliade has said that modern man, in contrast to *homo religiosus*, "regards himself as the sole subject and agent of history. . . . He will not be truly free until he has killed the last god." I am certain the last god to be killed will be Earth itself. Free of his mythological gods, man, who has created a pantheon of ephemeral gods in his own image, is now turning against the biological gods and destroying the ark of biotic wealth.

Plutarch puts the death of Pan in the first century AD, during the reign of Tiberius, after the lesser Greek gods had already died. According to Christian legend, his demise happened the day Christ was crucified. In my view, the god of Nature has had a lengthy biological death, and is still dying every day, every hour, every minute in the sphere of life.

In the Mayan religion, the sky is held up by trees of different species and colors (red in the east, white in the north, black in the west, yellow in the south) with a green tree, the ceiba, in the center. If we cut down the ceiba, the firmament will collapse upon us.

Novalis evokes distant epochs when poets played upon marvelous instruments whose strange sounds could awaken the secret life of forests and revive dead seeds in barren land. I urge all human beings to join together in letting the mythological Orpheus sing among us again in the next millennium.

Ecology, like poetry, should be practiced by all.

Signers of "A Declaration Signed by 100 Intellectuals and Artists Protesting Air Pollution in Mexico City"

Antonio Alatorre, Manuel Álvarez Bravo, Homero Aridjis, Juan José Arreola, Alejandro Aura, René Áviles Fabila, Juan Bañuelos, Huberto Batis, Hilda Bautista, Feliciano Béjar, Arnold Belkin, Fernando Benítez, Alberto Blanco, Ruben Bonifaz Nuño, Juan de la Cabada, Federico Campbell, Marco Antonio Campos, Emilio Carballido, Leonora Carrington, Francisco Cervantes, Fernando Césarman, Joaquín Armando Chacón, Alí Chumacero, Arnaldo Coen, Sandro Cohen, José de la Colina, Pedro Coronel, Raul Cosío, Elsa Cross, Rogelio Cuéllar, José Luis Cuevas, Joaquín Diez-Canedo, Felipe Ehrenberg, Salvador Elizondo, Helen Escobedo, Betty Ferber, Guillermo Fernández, Fernando Gamboa, Jomí García Ascot, Gabriel García Márquez, Fernando García Ponce, Juan García Ponce, Gunter Gerzso, Bernardo Giner de los Ríos, Alberto Gironella, Margo Glantz, Mathias Goeritz, Juliana González, Arturo González Cosío, Ulalume González de León, Roger von Gunten, Raul Herrera, David Huerta, Bárbara Jacobs, Enrique Krauze, Ethel Krauze, Mario Lavista, Vicente Leñero, Miguel León Portilla, Daniel Leyva, Luis López Loza, Elva Macías, Maka, Eduardo Matos Moctezuma, María Luisa Mendoza, Pedro Miret, Silvia Molina, Sergio Mondragón, Carlos Monsiváis, Marco Antonio Montes de Oca, Álvaro Mutis, Francisco Nuñez, Edmundo O'Gorman, Marta Palau, Cristina Pacheco, José Emilio Pacheco, Tomás Parra, Octavio Paz, Elena Poniatowska, Mariano Rivera Velázquez, Vicente Rojo, Juan Rulfo, Alberto Ruy Sánchez, Martí Soler, Rufino Tamayo, Raquel Tibol, Francisco Toledo, Gerardo de la Torre, Cordelia Urueta, Edmundo Valadés, Roberto Vallarino, Mario del Valle, Josefina Vicens, Margarita Villaseñor, Vlady, Verónica Volkow, Ramón Xirau, Gabriel Zaid, Francisco Zendejas, Eraclio Zepeda.

Endorsed by Alfonso Ciprés Villarreal (president of the Mexican Ecology Movement), José Fernández Unsáin (General Society of Mexican Writers), Juan Helguera (League of Concert Music Composers), Arturo Lomelí (Mexican Association for Consumer Defense Studies).

APPENDIX B

Signers of "A Milkweed-Butterfly Recovery Alliance," Grupo de los Cien Internacional and Make Way for Monarchs

Monarch Butterfly Scientists—USA: Dr. Alfonso Alonso (Smithsonian), Dr. Sonia M. Altizer (University of Georgia), Dr. Lincoln P. Brower and Dr. Linda S. Fink (Sweet Briar College), Dr. Stephen B. Malcolm (Western Michigan University), Dr. Karen Oberhauser (University of Minnesota), Dr. Robert M. Pyle (founder, Xerces Society), Dr. Daniel Slayback (Science Systems and Applications, Inc.), Dr. Orley R. Taylor (University of Kansas), Dr. Stuart B. Weiss (Creekside Center for Earth Observation, CA), Dr. Ernest H. Williams (Hamilton College). Canada: Dr. Barrie Frost (Queens University), Dr. Jordi Honey-Roses (University of British Columbia). Mexico: Dr. Pablo F. Jaramillo-López (UNAM Michoacán), Dr. Isabel Ramírez (UNAM Michoacán). Germany: Dr. Michael Boppré (University of Freiburg). UK: Dr. Dick Vane-Wright (Natural History Museum, London). Australia: Dr. Myron P. Zalucki (University of Queensland).

Writers and Artists—USA: Kwame Anthony Appiah, John Ashbery, Paul Auster, Deirdre Bair, Russell Banks, Rick Bass, Magda Bogin, Sarah Browning, Christopher Cokinos, Robert Darnton, Alison Hawthorne Deming, Junot Diaz, Rita Dove, Lawrence Ferlinghetti, Alexandra Fuller, Ross Gelbspan, Sue Halpern, Sam Hamill, Robert Hass, Tom Hayden, Edward Hirsch, Siri Hustvedt, Jewell James (Lummi Tribe), Robert F. Kennedy Jr., George Kovach, Nicole Krauss, Norman Manea, Peter Matthiessen, Michael McClure, Bill McKibben, Askold Melnyczuk, Michael Palmer, Janisse Ray, Jerome Rothenberg, Dick Russell, Michael Scammell, Grace Schulman, Alex Shoumatoff, A. E. Stallings, Judith Thurman, Melissa Tuckey, Chase Twichell, Rosanna Warren, Eliot Weinberger, Alan Weisman, Terry Tempest Williams, Michael Wood, City Lights Books. Mexico: Homero Aridjis, Lucia Álvarez, Juan Domingo Argüelles, Chloe Aridjis, Eva Aridjis, Alberto Blanco, Coral Bracho, Federico Campbell, Marco Antonio Campos, Ana Cervantes, Jennifer Clement, Elsa Cross, María José Cuevas, Ximena Cuevas, Pablo Elizondo, Laura Esquivel, Manuel Felguérez, Betty Ferber, Paz Alicia Garciadiego, Emiliano Gironella, José Gordon, Hugo Gutiérrez Vega, Bárbara Jacobs, Daniel Krauze, León Krauze, Mario Lavista, Paulina Lavista, Silvia Lemus de Fuentes, Soledad Loaeza, Pura López Colomé, Jean Meyer, Sergio Mondragón, Angelina Muñiz-Huberman, Carmen Mutis, Gabriel Orozco, Carmen Parra, Fernando del Paso, Marie-José Paz, Elena Poniatowska, Arturo Ripstein, Vicente Rojo, Cristina Rubalcava, Juan Carlos Rulfo, Pablo Rulfo, Alberto Ruy Sánchez, Isabel Turrent, Juan Villoro, Roger von Gunten. Canada: Katherine Ashenburg, Margaret Atwood, Wade Davis, Gary Geddes, Graeme Gibson, Terence Gower, Emile Martel, Yann Martel, George McWhirter, Michael Ondaatje, Nicole Perron,

John Ralston Saul, Linda Spalding. Elsewhere: Nicholas Jose (Australia); Hasna Moudud (Bangladesh); Pierre Alechinsky, Ivan Alechine (Belgium); Lélia Wanick Salgado, Sebastião Salgado (Brazil); Yves Bonnefoy, Alejandro Jodorowsky, Lucy Vines (France); Prof. Dr. Klaus Kropfinger, Dr. Helga von Kügelgen, Fred Viebahn (Germany); Maneka Sanjay Gandhi (member of Parliament, India); Gioconda Belli, Sergio Ramírez (Nicaragua); Gloria Guardia (Panama); Breyten Breytenbach, André Brink (South Africa); Kjell Espmark (Nobel Committee for Literature), Lasse Söderberg, Tomas Tranströmer (Nobel Prize), Per Wästberg (chairman, Nobel Committee for Literature) (Sweden); Orhan Pamuk (Nobel Prize) (Turkey); Jonathon Porritt, Simon Schama, Ali Smith, Hugh Thomas (UK).

Scientists and Environmentalists—USA: Jo Ann Baumgartner (Wild Farm Alliance), Scott Hoffman Black (Xerces Society for Invertebrate Conservation and IUCN Butterfly Specialist Group), Lester Brown (Earth Policy Institute), Serge Dedina (Wildcoast), Arturo Gómez-Pompa (University of California Riverside), Laura Lopez Hoffman (University of Arizona), Elizabeth Howard (Journey North), Diana Liverman (Institute of the Environment, University of Arizona), Claudio Lomnitz (Center for Mexican Studies, Columbia University), Amory B. Lovins, Gail Morris (Southwest Monarch Study), Dr. Gary Paul Nabhan (Make Way for Monarchs, University of Arizona), Wallace J. Nichols (California Academy of Sciences), Scott Slovic (Interdisciplinary Studies in Literature and Environment, University of Idaho), Garrison Sposito (University of California Berkeley), Ina Warren (Make Way for Monarchs), Jack Woody (U.S. Fish and Wildlife Service, retired), Lummi Tribe, Native American Land Conservancy (including tribal communities Chemehuevi, Kumeyaay, Cahuilla, Navajo, Paiute). Mexico: Joaquín Bohigas Bosch (Instituto de Astronomia, UNAM), Eduardo Farah (EspejoRed), Daniel Gershenson (Alconsumidor AC), Eduardo Nájera (Costasalvaje), Georgita Ruiz and Manuel Grosselet (Tierra de Aves A.C.), Dr. José Sarukhan (CONABIO), Valeria Souza (UNAM). Canada: Don Davis (Monarch Butterfly Fund).

APPENDIX C

Signers of "Dear Obama, Trudeau and Peña Nieto: Act Now to Save the Monarch Butterfly"

Monarch Butterfly Scientists—USA: Dr. John Alcock (Arizona State University), Dr. Alfonso Alonso (Smithsonian), Dr. Sonia M. Altizer (University of Georgia), Dr. Lincoln P. Brower and Dr. Linda S. Fink (Sweet Briar College), Dr. Stephen B. Malcolm (Western Michigan University), Dr. Karen Oberhauser (University of Minnesota), Dr. John Pleasants (Iowa State University), Dr. Robert M. Pyle (founder, Xerces Society), Dr. Daniel Slayback (Science Systems and Applications, Inc.), Dr.

Stuart B. Weiss (Creekside Center for Earth Observations, CA), Dr. Ernest H. Williams (Hamilton College). Mexico: Dr. Pablo F. Jaramillo-López (UNAM Michoacán), Dr. Isabel Ramírez (UNAM Michoacán). Canada: Dr. Barrie Frost (Queens University), Dr. Jordi Honey-Roses (University of British Columbia). Germany: Dr. Michael Boppré (University of Freiburg). UK: Dr. Dick Vane-Wright (Natural History Museum, London). Australia: Dr. Myron P. Zalucki (University of Queensland).

Writers and Artists—USA: Kwame Anthony Appiah, John Ashbery, Paul Auster, Deirdre Bair, Russell Banks, Magda Bogin, Christopher Cokinos, Robert Darnton, Alison Hawthorne Deming, Rita Dove, Lawrence Ferlinghetti, Patrick Flanery, Francisco Goldman, Mimi Gross, Jessica Hagedorn, Sue Halpern, Sam Hamill, Robert Hass, Tom Hayden, Brenda Hillman, Edward Hirsch, Siri Hustvedt, Ilya Kaminsky, Robert F. Kennedy Jr., Nicole Krauss, Jonathan Levi, Roberto Lovato, Norman Manea, Amy Evans McClure, Michael McClure, Bill McKibben, Jeff McMillan, Molly Moore, David Rieff, Velcrow Ripper and Nova Ami, Diane Rothenberg, Jerome Rothenberg, Dick Russell, Michael Scammell, Alex Shoumatoff, A. E. Stallings, Judith Thurman, Melissa Tuckey, Chase Twichell, Gwynedd Vetter-Drusch (Moving for Monarchs), Chuck Wachtel, Rosanna Warren, Alan Weisman, Terry Tempest Williams, City Lights Books. Mexico: Lucia Álvarez, Juan Domingo Argüelles, Chloe Aridjis, Eva Aridjis, Homero Aridjis, Alberto Blanco, Miguel Calderón, Marco Antonio Campos, Jennifer Clement, Elsa Cross, María José Cuevas, Ximena Cuevas, Laura Esquivel, Manuel Felguérez, Betty Ferber, Rubén Gallo, Emiliano Gironella, José Gordon, Roger von Gunten, Barbara Jacobs, Gabriela Jauregui, Daniel Krauze, León Krauze, Pura López Colomé, Jean Meyer, Marina Meyer, Matías Meyer, Pablo Meyer, Humberto Musacchio, Margarita de Orellana, Carmen Parra, Fernando del Paso, Paulina del Paso, Elena Poniatowska, Vicente Rojo, Betsabeé Romero, Cristina Rubalcava, Juan Carlos Rulfo, Pablo Rulfo, Alberto Ruy Sánchez, Francisco Segovia, Isabel Turrent. Canada: Margaret Atwood, Ann Eriksson, Gary Geddes, Graeme Gibson, Terence Gower, Emile Martel, Yann Martel, George McWhirter, Michael Ondaatje, John Ralston Saul, Linda Spalding, Alison Wearing, Barbara Williams. Elsewhere: Luisa Valenzuela (Argentina); Jean-Claude Masson (Belgium); Lily Michaelides (Cyprus); J. M. G. Le Clézio (Nobel Prize), Annick Le Scoëzec Masson (France); Klaus Kropfinger, Helga von Kügelgen, Fred Viebahn (Germany); Stratis Haviaras, Dino Siotis (Greece); Maneka Sanjay Gandhi (Minister for Women and Child Welfare)(India); Giuseppe Bellini, Fabrizio Dall'Aglio, Valerio Grutt, Giuliano Ladolfi, Patrizia Spinato (Italy); Laurens van Krevelen (Netherlands); Francisco de Asís Fernández (Nicaragua); Eugene Schoulgin (Norway); Gloria Guardia (Panama); Breyten Breytenbach (South Africa); ·Frederic Amat, Vicente Cervera, Claudia Comes, Aníbal Salazar Anglada, Fernando Savater (Spain); Kjell Espmark, Lasse Soderberg (Sweden); Josh Appignanesi, Devorah Baum, Ruth Fainlight, Antony Gormley, Philip Hoare, Darian Leader, Neel Mukherjee, Ruth Padel, Cornelia Parker,

Vicken Parsons, Alan Riding, Simon Schama, Ali Smith, Adam Thirlwell, Viktor Wynd, Zinovy Zinik (UK).

Scientists and Environmentalists—USA: Scott Hoffman Black (Xerces Society, chair, IUCN Butterfly Specialist Group), Tierra Curry (Center for Biological Diversity), Serge Dedina (Wildcoast), Jewell James (Lummi Indian Tribe), Sarina Jepson (Xerces Society), Diana Liverman (Institute of the Environment, University of Arizona), Dr. Gary Paul Nabhan (Make Way for Monarchs, University of Arizona), Kurt Russo (Native American Land Conservancy), Scott Slovic (editor, ISLE Interdisciplinary Studies in Literature and Environment), Garrison Sposito (University of California Berkeley), Todd Steiner (Turtle Island Restoration Network), Dr. Steven L. Swartz and Mary Lou Jones (Laguna San Ignacio Ecosystem Science Program). Mexico: Alberto Darszón Israel (UNAM), Eduardo Farah (EspejoRed), Dr. Elideth Fernández, Eduardo Nájera (Costasalvaje), Fernando Ortiz Monasterio (Corpambiental SC), Tiahoga Ruge (Amigos de la Biosfera, AC), Miguel Valencia Mulkay and Adriana Matalonga Rodríguez-Beltrán (Ecocomunidades). UK: Jonathon Porritt (founder director, Forum for the Future), Simon Retallack.

APPENDIX D

Signers of "Open Letter to President Sarney: The Fate of the Amazon," Grupo de los Cien Internacional/Group of 100

Monika van Paemel (Belgium); Margaret Atwood (Canada); Bei Dao (China); Severo Sarduy (Cuba); Miroslav Holub (Czechoslovakia); Paavo Haavikko (Finland); Yves Bonnefoy, Claude Esteban, Eugène Guillevic, Edmond Jabès, Maurice Nadeau, André Pieyre de Mandiargues (France); Seamus Heaney (Ireland); Mario Luzi (Italy); Kazuko Shiraishi (Japan); Tahar Ben Jelloun (Morocco); Corneille, Bert Schierbeek, (Netherlands); Chinua Achebe (Nigeria); Czesław Miłosz (Poland); Norman Manea (Rumania); Breyten Breytenbach (South Africa); Werner Aspenström, Ingmar Bergman, Kjell Espmark, Gunnel Lindblom, Östen Sjöstrand, Lasse Söderberg, Tomas Tranströmer, Per Wästberg, 75 actors from the Swedish Royal Dramatic Theatre (Sweden); Jean Starobinski (Switzerland); Lawrence Ferlinghetti, Allen Ginsberg, John Irving, Philip Lamantia, Denise Levertov, Michael McClure, James Merrill, W. S. Merwin, Arthur M. Schlesinger Jr., Gary Snyder (United States); Michael Hamburger, Hugh Thomas (UK); Andrei Bitov, Anatoly Rybakov (USSR); Günter Grass, Günter Kunert (West Germany).

APPENDIX E

Signers of "Writers and Artists Ask Mexico's President to Cancel Mining Concessions in the Sacred Territory of the Huichol People," Grupo de los Cien Internacional/Group of 100

Homero Aridjis, Gilberto Aceves Navarro, Chloe Aridjis, Eva Aridjis, Lydia Cacho, Miguel Calderón, Elsa Cross, Abraham Cruzvillegas, Ximena Cuevas, Nicolás Echevarría, Manuel Felguérez, Roger von Gunten, Gabriel Kuri, Dr. Lakra, Yoshua Okón, Gabriel Orozco, José Luis Paredes Pacho, Ana Pellicer, Elena Poniatowska, Vicente Rojo, Francisco Toledo, Natalia Toledo, Juan Villoro, Jorge Zepeda Patterson (Mexico); Juan Octavio Prenz (Argentina); Hasna Jasimuddin Moudud (Bangladesh); Ivan Alechine, Pierre Alechinsky, Wim Delvoye (Belgium); Ledo Ivo (Brazil); Margaret Atwood, Gary Geddes, Graeme Gibson, Terence Gower, George McWhirter, Michael Ondaatje, John Ralston Saul, Linda Spalding (Canada); Ariel Dorfman, Alejandro Jodorowsky (Chile); Cecilia Balcazar, Fernando Rendón (Colombia); Zoé Valdés (Cuba); Niki Marangou, Lily Michaelides, Christos Hadjipapas (Cyprus); Yves Bonnefoy, Jean-Clarence Lambert, J. M. G. Le Clézio (France); Tobías Burghardt, Klaus Kropfinger, Helga von Kügelgen, Fred Viebahn (Germany); Yorgos Rouvalis, Dino Siotis, Ersi Sotiropoulos, Vassilis Vassilikos (Greece); Kiran Desai (India); Giuseppe Bellini, Sebastiano Grasso, Patrizia Spinato, Franca Tiberto (Italy); Ananda Devi (Mauritius); Laurens van Krevelen (Netherlands); Francisco de Asís Fernández, Sergio Ramírez (Nicaragua); Chinua Achebe (Nigeria); Eugene Schoulgin (Norway); Gloria Guardia (Panama); Tomaž Šalamun (Slovenia); Breyten Breytenbach (South Africa); Frederic Amat, Carlos García Gual (Spain); Kjell Espmark, Lasse Söderberg, Tomas Tranströmer, Per Wästberg (Sweden); Orhan Pamuk (Turkey); Josh Appignanesi, Lisa Appignanesi, Devorah Baum, Rosie Boycott, Ruth Fainlight, James Lasdun, Darian Leader, Cornelia Parker, Jonathon Porritt, Alan Riding, Anthony Rudolf, Simon Schama, Michael Schmidt, Ali Smith, Anne Stevenson, Simon Winchester (UK); Kwame Anthony Appiah, Paul Auster, Deirdre Bair, Charles Bernstein, Lincoln Brower, Robert Darnton, Serge Dedina, Anthony DePalma, Junot Díaz, Rita Dove, Clayton Eshleman, Janet Brody Esser, Betty Ferber, Elizabeth Ferber, Lawrence Ferlinghetti, Jonathan Safran Foer, Ross Gelbspan, Francisco Goldman, Pete Hamill, Robert Hass, Tom Hayden, Edward Hirsch, Siri Hustvedt, Peter Stephan Jungk, Edmund Keeley, Nicole Krauss, Eric Lax, Amory Lovins, Norman Manea, Peter Matthiessen, Michael McClure, Bill McKibben, Askold Melnyczuk, Molly Moore, Michael Palmer, Francine Prose, Jerome Rothenberg, Dick Russell, Michael Scammell, Grace Schulman, Scott Slovic, A. E. Stallings, Ilan Stavans, Eliot Weinberger, Alan Weisman, Terry Tempest Williams, John Womack Jr. (USA); Carlos Fazio (Uruguay).

APPENDIX F

Signers of "The Morelia Symposium:

Approaching the Year 2000: The Morelia Declaration," Group of 100 advertisement

Miguel Álvarez del Toro, Homero Aridjis, Fernando Césarman, Arturo Gómez-Pompa, Octavio Paz (Mexico); Miguel Grinberg, Roberto Juarroz (Argentina); Monika van Paemel (Belgium); Nélida Piñón (Brazil); Michael Ondaatje (Canada); Margarita Marino de Botero (Colombia); Álvaro Umaña (Costa Rica); Miroslav Holub (Czechoslovakia); J. M. G. Le Clézio (France); Gert Bastian, Petra Kelly (Germany); Gita Mehta, Vikram Seth (India); Yuko Tsushima (Japan); Hans van de Waarsenburg (Netherlands); Augusto Roa Bastos (Paraguay); Evaristo Nugkuag (Peru); Kjell Espmark, Folke Isaksson, Agneta Pleijel (Sweden); Adam Markham (UK); Lester Brown, Sandra Cisneros, Alan Durning, Betty Ferber, Jewell James (Lummi Tribe), Thomas Lovejoy, Amory Lovins, Peter Matthiessen, W. S. Merwin, F. Sherwood Rowland, Kirkpatrick Sale, Jeffrey Wilkerson (United States); Vassily Aksyonov, Vladimir Chernousenko (USSR).

APPENDIX G

Signers of "The Second Morelia Symposium:

Approaching the Year 2000: Overpopulation," Group of 100 advertisement

Homero Aridjis, Fernando Césarman, Luis Manuel Guerra, Octavio Paz, Tiahoga Ruge, Miguel Álvarez del Toro (Mexico); Malika Ladjali (Algeria); Hasna Moudud (Bangladesh); Monika van Paemel (Belgium); Nélida Piñón (Brazil); John Ralston Saul (Canada); Bei Dao (China); Miroslav Holub (Czech Republic); J. M. G. Le Clézio (France); Barbel Bohley (Germany); Yuko Tsushima (Japan); Hans van de Waarsenburg (Netherlands); Breyten Breytenbach (South Africa); Kjell Espmark, Folke Isaksson (Sweden); Adam Markham (UK); Vladimir Chernousenko (Ukraine); Lincoln Brower, Lester Brown, Sandra Cisneros, Victoria Dompka, Rita Dove, Chenoa Egawa (Lummi Nation), Anne Ehrlich, Betty Ferber, Michael Glantz, Sue Halpern, Jewell James (Lummi Nation), Amory Lovins, Peter Matthiessen, Bill McKibben, W. S. Merwin, Peter Raven, Jeffrey Wilkerson, Terry Tempest Williams (USA); Gerardo Budowski (Venezuela).

About the Authors

Homero Aridjis is one of Latin America's greatest living writers and the founding president of Mexico's Group of 100. For his literary and environmental work, he has received many awards, including the United Nations Environmental Program's Global 500 Award, the Orion Society's John Hay Award, the Natural Resources Defense Council's Force for Nature Award, the International Environmental Leadership Award given by Mikhail Gorbachev and Global Green USA, and two Guggenheim Fellowships.

Aridjis is the author of forty-eight books of poetry and prose, and his works have been translated into fifteen languages. He served two terms as president of PEN International. He also served as Mexico's ambassador to Switzerland, The Netherlands, and UNESCO, and most recently was president of the Swedenborg Society. He has been a visiting professor at Indiana, New York, and Columbia Universities and the University of California, Irvine.

Betty Ferber (Aridjis), a graduate of Bryn Mawr College, has served as the international coordinator of the Group of 100 since its founding in 1985. She has been a major force in efforts to protect sea turtles, gray whales, and monarch butterflies, and to prevent the construction of dams on the Usumacinta River and the destruction of tropical forests in Amazonia and Lacandonia. Along with her husband, Homero Aridjis, she was honored by Mikhail Gorbachev and Global Green USA with the Green Cross Millennium Award for International Environmental Leadership. She has translated into English various books by Homero Aridjis, including three novels: *1492: The Life and Times of Juan Cabezon of Castile, The Lord of the Last Days: Visions of the Year 1000,* and *Persephone.*